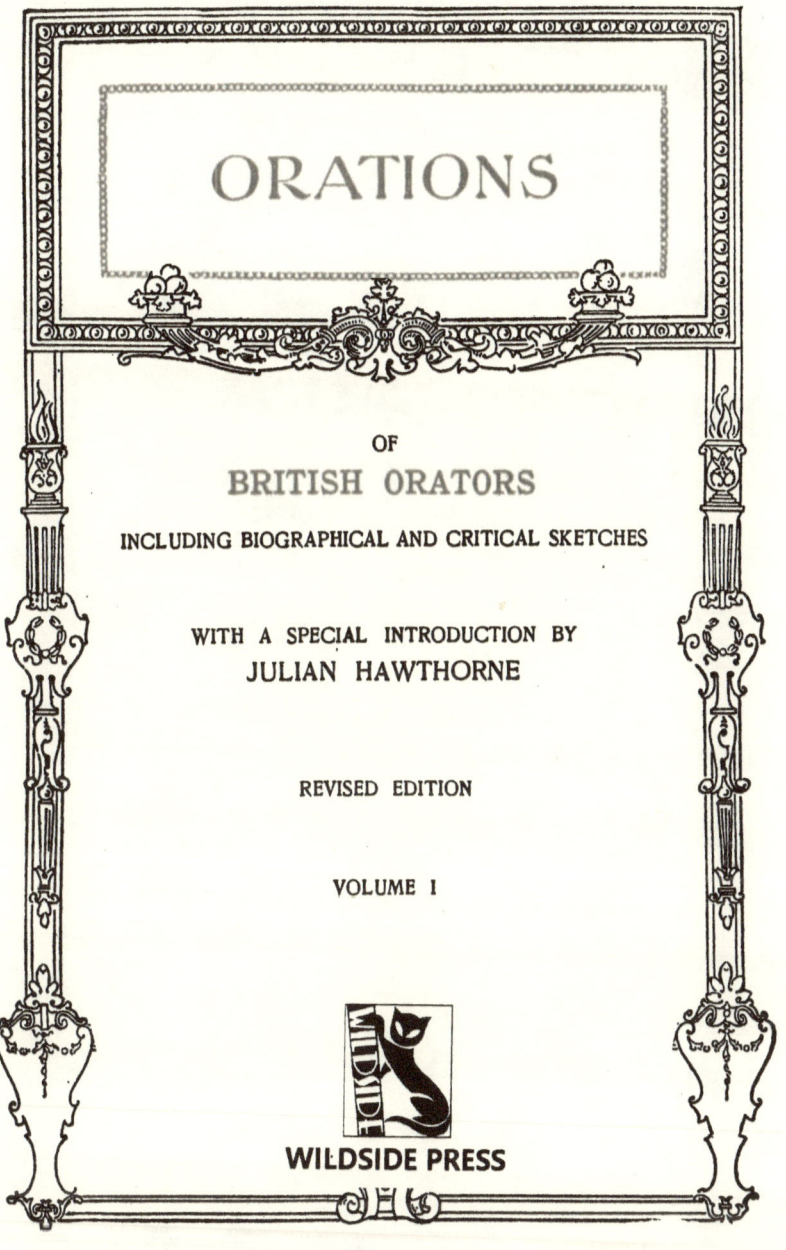

ORATIONS

OF
BRITISH ORATORS

INCLUDING BIOGRAPHICAL AND CRITICAL SKETCHES

WITH A SPECIAL INTRODUCTION BY
JULIAN HAWTHORNE

REVISED EDITION

VOLUME I

WILDSIDE PRESS

SPECIAL INTRODUCTION

I T is a truth of impressive significance that enthusiasm for civil and religious liberty has been, in all ages of history, the leading motive of oratory. Men to whom the gift of eloquence has been vouchsafed seem almost invariably to be inspired to put forth their greatest and most memorable efforts in the cause of God, or of freedom. Demosthenes, in the porticos and Senate chambers of ancient Greece, attained his sublimest height when urging his countrymen to resist the aggressions of Philip of Macedon, who meditated the overthrow of Grecian republicanism. At a later day, Marcus Tullius Cicero thundered forth his denunciations of the conspirator Catiline, because he knew that the success of that conspiracy meant the ruin of Roman institutions. No other cause could so have fired the spirit of these men; and many of the great national tragedies of history have been due to the fact that the people who heard them speak turned aside from their warnings and arguments, and followed the lower paths of material expediency and selfishness.

In early Christian and mediæval times the occasions of oratory were mainly religious; for the doctrines of Christianity were then more absorbing than political ones: mankind, indeed, having fallen under the dominion of temporal tyranny in all civil affairs, and therefore finding their best consolation in aspirations toward spiritual emancipation. Arguments on points of theological controversy also assume a prominent position in the recorded eloquence of those days; because the true interpretation of ambiguous questions of this kind seemed to the contestants to involve matters of pre-eminent import to the welfare of the life beyond the grave.

But when, a thousand years ago, the beginnings of a nation

first assembled in the little island of Britain, and the Saxons and Angles and Danes and Norsemen were becoming welded together into something like a homogeneous people, the instinct for freedom of speech and self-conduct once more took a foremost place in men's minds; and the prayers of John Knox, the dying address of Thomas Cranmer at the stake, the dauntless declaration of John Eliot and of many another, bore witness to the fact that the men of England were destined to be the political orators of the modern world. Here was a nation which must needs be free; and prophets arose among them, able and resolute to give noble and memorable utterance to the vague tendencies of the masses.

Their words became the framework on which the fabric of the future constitution of the empire was to be erected: and each period of their eloquence meant the enfranchisement and felicity of myriads still unborn.

It was not until after Magna Charta had been wrung from John's reluctant pen, however, and Parliament had taken its place as the true court of appeal and forum of the nation, that British eloquence attained any considerable and continuous volume.

The House of Commons became, inevitably and spontaneously, a permanent school of oratory: in which were educated, and where contended, not a few of the greatest masters of human speech that have ever lived. The addresses of Oliver Cromwell, unobservant though many of them seem of the classic canons of public utterance, have within them an iron force and intensity of purpose that give them a controlling influence upon the mind: while Lord Digby's speech against Strafford, and the latter's wonderful reply, show that the art of eloquence was having a new birth after the sleep of ages. The persuasiveness of Taylor and Leighton and the burning conviction of Bunyan and Barrow served to enlarge and deepen the sphere of oratorical activity; the homely ardor of John Wesley recalled the heavenly earnestness of the early Christian epochs; and at length the questions arising upon the disaffection and revolt of the American colonies had the effect of breeding a company of parliamentary giants, whose achievements, when at their best, have seldom been equalled, and perhaps never have been surpassed, in any epoch, ancient or modern. At no time, certainly, were so many sons of thunder gathered together in one place; and in perusing the records of their addresses we shall always find that the worthiest in art, as well as in purpose, are those which speak for human liberty, and against the counsels and machinations of its enemies.

No more patriotic men have lived than were Pitt, Burke and Fox; yet they were the most powerful and persistent champions of their kin across the sea, who were suffering from maladministration of the principles which had made England free, and from betrayal, by members of the government, of trusts and promises whose preservation was vital to any kind of political prosperity. The great attack of Sheridan upon Warren Hastings, again, was a plea against injustice and tyranny in India: and such outbursts as that of Curran for liberty of the press, and of Grattan in behalf of the rights of his down-trodden countrymen, indicate how at all points and in all circumstances the power of oratory was put forth in vindication of the emancipation of man.

From these stirring and heroic days we come through the portals of the nineteenth century to our own epoch. We find William Pitt contending against the ominous power of Napoleon, and the marvellous Irishman, Daniel O'Connell, pleading with matchless power for justice to men of the Catholic faith. The speech of Robert Emmet against the unrighteous sentence passed against his life is one of the most stirring protests ever heard from human lips against the iniquity and the blindness of despotism. Meanwhile, in the field, little cultivated hitherto, of letters and the humanities, men like Brougham and Derby were rivalling the performances of the old Greek Isocrates; Newman, by his exquisite discourses, kept alive the traditions of religious appeal; and Lytton spoke convincingly in the cause of education. But about the middle of the century a handful of men, most prominent among whom were Palmerston, Bright, Disraeli and Gladstone, appeared in the arena, and the echo of their accents is still in our ears to-day. Palmerston was the man of the world in politics, and his addresses are chiefly in the line of expediency, compromise, or what modern *argot* would characterize as bluff. But Bright was a strict political moralist; Disraeli was the statesman of imagination and far-reaching ambition; and Gladstone, whose grand figure, growing constantly greater through the vicissitudes of his long life, is probably second to none of the leading orators of England, and certainly inferior to none in zeal for justice and right. With his name we may fitly close these introductory remarks; and after all none can speak for the orators so well as they speak for themselves.

Julian Hawthorne

CONTENTS

CONTENTS

ILLUSTRATIONS

THE PLOUGHERS

—

BY

HUGH LATIMER

HUGH LATIMER

1485—1555

Latimer was one of the great figures and, with his friend Ridley, among the foremost leaders of the Reformation in England. His father, a sturdy yeoman, cultivated a small farm in Leicestershire, but found the means to send his son to school and later to Cambridge. Dates of events connected with Latimer's early life—even that of his birth—are uncertain. We know, however, that at the time of his conversion to Protestantism Latimer had passed the age of thirty. While a student at Cambridge Latimer was most conscientious in observing the minutest rites of his faith and was a devout Catholic. So severe was he on the innovations of the religious reformers that he made an attack on the opinions of Melanchthon the subject of his oration on taking the degree of bachelor of divinity. In Lent of the year 1530 he preached before the King at Windsor and received distinct marks of royal favor. To the bishops, however, his sermons were distasteful. Wolsey, however, granted him license to preach throughout all England, though the Bishop of Ely had prohibited him from preaching in his diocese. Made chaplain to Henry VIII in 1530, he was incited to put forth still greater energies in the cause that lay nearest to his heart: the freer circulation of the Scriptures, and a wider dissemination of religious truths. He had no liking for mere theological discussions, though his opponents were often disconcerted and confused by his ready wit and his keen satire. His sermons were on the practical duties and issues of every-day life. He desired to point out errors and abuses and to correct them, being fully in sympathy with the besetting hardships and temptations in every station of life. He was imprisoned and excommunicated in 1531, but set at liberty by the direct intervention of the King.

In 1535 Latimer was consecrated Bishop of Worcester. His position had in the mean time changed much in his favor, for when Henry in 1534 repudiated the Pope, Latimer became with Cranmer and Cromwell the chief adviser of the King in ecclesiastical matters. Shortly after the accession of Mary, Latimer, together with Ridley, was led to the stake at Oxford in 1555.

It has been truly said that the preaching of Latimer, more than the edicts of Henry, established the principles of the Reformation in the hearts of the English people. In many of his sermons he gives us a truthful picture of the social and political conditions of his time. They are also curious and valuable as a monument of the language of his time. We may fittingly reproduce here the words of a competent critic and acute observer: "The homely terseness of Latimer's style, his abounding humor, rough, cheery, and playful, but irresistible in its simplicity; his avoidance of dogmatic subtleties and noble advocacy of practical righteousness, his bold and open denunciation of the oppression of the powerful, his scathing diatribes against ecclesiastical hypocrisy, the transparent honesty of his zeal tempered by moderation —these are the qualities which not only rendered his influence so paramount in his lifetime, but have transmitted his memory to posterity." "The Ploughers" is a practical lesson taken from life suitable alike to the daily life of the most humble as well as to the daily life of the most exalted.

THE PLOUGHERS

ALL things which are written are written for our erudition and knowledge.[1] All things that are written in God's book, in the Bible book, in the book of the Holy Scripture, are written to be our doctrine."

I told you in my first sermon, honorable audience, that I purposed to declare unto you two things. The one, what seed should be sown in God's field, in God's plough land; and the other, who should be the sowers. That is to say, what doctrine is to be taught in Christ's church and congregation, and what men should be the teachers and preachers of it. The first part I have told you in the three sermons past, in which I have essayed to set forth my plough, to prove what I could do. And now I shall tell you who be the ploughers; for God's Word is a seed to be sown in God's field—that is, the faithful congregation—and the preacher is the sower. And it is in the Gospel —" *Exivit qui seminat seminare semen suum* " [" A sower went out to sow his seed " (Luke viii. 5)]. He that soweth, the husbandman, the ploughman, went forth to sow his seed; so that the preacher is resembled to a ploughman, as it is in another place—" *Nemo admota arato manu, et a tergo respiciens aptus est regno Dei* " [" No man, having put his hand to the plough, and looking back, is fit for the kingdom of God" (Luke ix. 62)]. No man that putteth his hand to the plough, and looketh back, is apt for the kingdom of God. That is to say, let no preacher be negligent in doing his office. Albeit this is one of the places that hath been racked, as I told you of racking Scriptures. And I have been one of them myself that hath racked it; I cry God mercy for it, and have been one of them that have believed and have expounded it against religious persons that would forsake their order which they had professed, and would go out

[1] Quecumque scripta sunt ad nostram doctrinam scripta sunt ("Whatsoever things were written aforetime, were written for our learning "—Rom. xv. 4). —Preached at the Shrouds, St. Paul's, January 18, 1549.

of their cloister, whereas, indeed, it toucheth not monkery, nor maketh anything at all for any such matter. But it is directly spoken of diligent preaching of the Word of God. For preaching of the Gospel is one of God's plough works, and the preacher is one of God's ploughmen. Ye may not be offended with my similitude, in that I compare preaching to the labor and work of ploughing, and the preacher to a ploughman. Ye may not be offended with this my similitude, for I have been slandered of some persons for such things. It hath been said of me—"O Latimer! nay, as for him, I will never believe him while I live, nor never trust him, for he likened our Blessed Lady to a saffron bag," where, indeed, I never used that similitude. But it was, as I have said unto you before now, according to that which Peter saw before in the spirit of prophecy, and said that there should come afterward men—"*Per quos via veritatis maledictis afficeretur*" [" By reason of whom the way of truth shall be evil spoken of " (2 Peter ii. 2)]. There should come fellows by whom the way of truth should be evil spoken of and slandered. But in case I had used this similitude, it had not been to be reproved, but might have been without reproach. For I might have said thus, as the saffron bag that hath been full of saffron, or hath had saffron in it, doth ever after savour and smell of the sweet saffron that it contained, so our Blessed Lady, who contained and bare Christ in her womb, did ever after resemble the manners and virtues of that precious babe which she bare. And what had our Blessed Lady been the worse for this? or what dishonor was this to our Blessed Lady? But as preachers must be wary and circumspect that they give not any just occasion to be slandered and ill spoken of by the hearers, so must not the auditors be offended without cause. For heaven is in the Gospel likened to a mustard seed. It is compared also to a piece of leaven; and Christ saith that at the last day, He will come like a thief; and what dishonor is this to God? or what derogation is this to heaven? Ye may not then, I say, be offended with my similitude, for because I liken preaching to a ploughman's labor, and a prelate to a ploughman. But now, you will ask me whom I call a prelate. A prelate is that man, whatsoever he be, that hath a flock to be taught of him, whosoever hath any spiritual charge in the faithful congregation, and whosoever he be that hath cure of souls.

And well may the preacher and the ploughman be likened
together. First, for their labor of all seasons of the year; for
there is no time of the year in which the ploughman hath not
some special work to do; as in my country in Leicestershire, the
ploughman hath a time to set forth and to assay his plough, and
other times for other necessary works to be done. And then
they also may be likened together, for the diversity of works and
variety of offices that they have to do. For as the ploughman
first setteth forth his plough, and then tilleth his land, and
breaketh it in furrows, and sometimes ridgeth it up again;
and at another time harroweth it, and clotteth it, and sometimes dungeth it, and hedgeth it, diggeth it, and weedeth it,
purgeth it, and maketh it clean—so the prelate, the preacher,
hath many divers offices to do. He hath first a busy work to
bring his parishioners to a right faith, as Paul calleth it, and
not to a swearing faith, but to a faith that embraceth Christ,
and trusteth to His merits; a lively faith, a justifying faith,
a faith that maketh a man righteous without respect of works,
as ye have it very well declared and set forth in the homily.
He hath then a busy work to bring his flock to a right faith,
and then to confirm them in the same faith; now casting them
down with the law and with threatenings of God for sin; now
ridging them up again with the Gospel, and with the promises
of God's favor; now weeding them by telling them their faults,
and making them forsake sin; now clotting them, by breaking
their stony hearts, and by making them supple-hearted, and
making them to have hearts of flesh—that is, soft hearts—and
apt for doctrine to enter in; now teaching to know God rightly,
and to know their duty to God and their neighbors; now ex-
horting them when they know their duty, that they do it, and
be diligent in it—so that they have a continual work to do.
Great is their business, and therefore great should be their
hire. They have great labors, and therefore they ought to have
good livings, that they may commodiously feed their flock; for
the preaching of the Word of God unto the people is called
meat—Scripture calleth it meat; not strawberries, that come
but once a year, and tarry not long, but are soon gone, but it
is meat. It is no dainties. The people must have meat that
must be familiar and continual, and daily given unto them to
feed upon. Many make a strawberry of it, ministering it but

once a year; but such do not the office of good prelates. For
Christ saith—"*Quis putas est servus prudens et fidelis? qui
dat cibum in tempore*" ["Who then is a faithful and wise
servant, whom his lord hath made ruler over his household, to
give them meat in due season" (Matt. xxiv. 45)]. Who, think
you, is a wise and faithful servant? He that giveth meat in due
time. So that he must at all times convenient preach diligently. "Therefore," saith He, "who trow you is a faithful
servant?" He speaketh it as though it were a rare thing to
find such a one, and as though He should say, there but but
few of them to find in the world. And how few of them there
be throughout this realm that give meat to their flock as they
should do; the visitors can best tell. Too few, too few—the
more is the pity, and never so few as now. By this, then, it
appeareth that a prelate, or any that hath cure of souls, must
diligently and substantially work and labor. Therefore saith
Paul to Timothy—"*Qui episcopatum desiderat, hic bonum
opus desiderat*" ["If a man desire the office of a bishop, he
desireth a good work" (1 Tim. iii. 1)]. He that desireth to
have the office of a bishop, or a prelate, that man desireth a good
work. Then if it be good work, it is work. Ye can make but
a work of it. It is God's work—God's plough, and that plough
God would have still going. Such, then, as loiter and live idly
are not good prelates or ministers. And of such as do not
preach and teach, nor do not their duties, God saith by His
prophet Jeremiah—"*Maledictus qui facit opus Dei fraudulen-
ter*" ["Cursed be he that doeth the work of the Lord deceitfully" (Jer. xlviii. 10)]. Guilefully or deceitfully; some
books have *negligenter*—negligently, or slackly. How many
such prelates, how many such bishops, Lord, for Thy mercy,
are there now in England? And what shall we, in this case,
do? Shall we company with them? O Lord! for Thy mercy,
shall we not company with them? O Lord! whither shall we
fly from them? But cursed be he that doeth the work of God
negligently or guilefully. A sore word for them that are negligent in discharging their office, or have done it fraudulently,
for that is the thing that maketh the people ill. But true it
must be that Christ saith—"*Multi sunt vocati, pauci vero
electi*" ["Many are called, but few are chosen" (Matt. xxii.
14)].

Here have I an occasion, by the way, somewhat to say unto you, yea, for the place that I alleged unto you before, out of Jeremiah the forty-eighth chapter. And it was spoken of a spiritual work of God—a work that was commanded to be done, and it was of shedding blood, and of destroying the cities of Moab. "For," saith he, "cursed be he that keepeth back his sword from shedding of blood" (Jer. xlviii. 10). As Saul, when he kept back the sword from shedding of blood, at what time he was sent against Amalek, was refused of God, for being disobedient to God's commandments, in that he spared Agag the king. So that that place of the prophet was spoken of them that went to the destruction of the cities of Moab, among the which there was one called Nebo, which was much reproved for idolatry, superstition, pride, avarice, cruelty, tyranny, and for hardness of heart, and for these sins was plagued of God, and destroyed. Now, what shall we say of these rich citizens of London? What shall I say of them? Shall I call them proud men of London, malicious men of London, merciless men of London? No, no! I may not say so; they will be offended with me then. Yet must I speak. For is there not reigning in London as much pride, as much covetousness, as much cruelty, as much oppression, as much superstition, as was in Nebo? Yes, I think, and much more too. Therefore, I say, Repent, O London! repent, repent! Thou hearest thy faults told thee; amend them, amend them. I think if Nebo had had the preaching that thou hast, they would have converted. And you, rulers and officers, be wise and circumspect; look to your charge, and see you do your duties, and rather be glad to amend your ill living, than to be angry when you are warned or told of your fault. What ado there was made in London at a certain man, because he said, and indeed, at that time, on a just cause— "Burgesses," quoth he, "nay, butterflies." Lord! what ado there was for that word! And yet, would God they were no worse than butterflies. Butterflies do but their nature; the butterfly is not covetous, is not greedy of other men's goods, is not full of envy and hatred, is not malicious, is not cruel, is not merciless. The butterfly glorieth not in her own deeds, nor preferreth the traditions of men before God's Word; it committeth not idolatry, nor worshippeth false gods. But London cannot abide to be rebuked; such is the nature of man.

If they be pricked, they will kick. If they be rubbed on the gall, they will wince. But yet they will not amend their faults; they will not be evil spoken of. But how shall I speak well of them? If you could be content to receive and follow the Word of God, and favor good preachers—if you could bear to be told of your faults—if you could amend when you hear of them— if you would be glad to reform that is amiss—if I might see any such inclination in you, that leave to be merciless, and begin to be charitable, I would then hope well of you, I would then speak well of you. But London was never so evil as it is now. In times past, men were full of pity and compassion, but now there is no pity, for in London their brother shall die in the streets for cold; he shall lie sick at their door, between stock and stock—I cannot tell what to call it—and perish there for hunger. Was there any more unmercifulness in Nebo? I think not. In times past, when any rich man died in London, they were wont to help the poor scholars of the university with exhibitions. When any man died, they would bequeath great sums of money toward the relief of the poor. When I was a scholar in Cambridge myself, I heard very good report of London, and knew many that had relief of the rich men of London; but now, I can hear no such good report, and yet I inquire of it, and hearken for it, but now charity is waxed cold; none helpeth the scholar, nor yet the poor. And in those days, what did they when they helped the scholars? Many they maintained and gave them languages, that were very papists, and professed the Pope's doctrine; and now that the knowledge of God's Word is brought to light, and many earnestly study and labor to set it forth, now almost no man helpeth to maintain them. O London, London! repent, repent! for I think God is more displeased with London than ever He was with the city of Nebo. Repent, therefore, repent, London! and remember that the same God liveth now that punished Nebo, even the same God, and none other, and He will punish sin as well now as He did then, and He will punish the iniquity of London as well as he did then of Nebo. Amend, therefore, and ye that be prelates, look well to your office; for right prelating is busy laboring, and not lording. Therefore preach and teach, and let your plough be doing; ye lords, I say, that live like loiterers, look well to your office; the plough is your office and charge.

If you live idle and loiter, you do not your duty, you follow not your vocation; let your plough, therefore, be going and not cease, that the ground may bring forth fruit. But now, methinketh I hear one say unto me—" Wot you what you say? Is it a work? Is it a labor? How then hath it happened that we have had so many hundred years so many unpreaching prelates, lording loiterers, and idle ministers?" Ye would have me here to make answer, and to show the cause thereof. Nay, this land is not for me to plough; it is too stony, too thorny, too hard for me to plough. They have so many things that make for them, so many things to lay for themselves, that it is not for my weak team to plough them. They have to lay for themselves long customs, ceremonies, and authority, placing in parliament, and many things more. And I fear me this land is not yet ripe to be ploughed. For, as the saying is, it lacketh weathering, this gear lacketh weathering; at least way, it is not for me to plough. But what shall I look for among thorns but pricking and scratching? What among stones but stumbling? What (I had almost said) among serpents but stinging? But this much I dare say, that since lording and loitering hath come up, preaching hath come down, contrary to the apostles' times. For they preached and lorded not. And now they lord and preach not.

For they that be lords will never go to plough. It is no meet office for them. It is not seeming for their state. Thus come up lording loiterers. Thus crept in unpreaching prelates, and so have they long continued.

For how many unlearned prelates have we now at this day? And no marvel. For if the ploughmen that now be were made lords, they would clean give over ploughing, they would leave off their labor and fall to lording outright, and let the plough stand. And then, both ploughs not walking, nothing should be in the commonweal but hunger. For ever since the prelates were made lords and nobles, the plough standeth. There is no work done; the people starve.

They hawk, they hunt, they card, they dice, they pastime in their prelacies with gallant gentlemen, with their dancing minions, and with their fresh companions, so that ploughing is set aside. And by the lording and loitering, preaching and ploughing is clean gone. And thus, if the ploughmen of the country

were as negligent in their office as prelates be, we should no
longer live, for lack of sustenance.   And as it is necessary for to
have the ploughing for the sustentation of the body, so must
we have also the other for the satisfaction of the soul, or else
we cannot live long ghostly.   For as the body wasteth and
consumeth away for lack of bodily meat, so doth the soul pine
away for default of ghostly meat.   But there be two kinds of
enclosing to let or hinder both these kinds of ploughing.   The
one is an enclosing to let or hinder the bodily ploughing, and
the other to let or hinder the holyday ploughing—the church
ploughing.   The bodily ploughing is taken in and enclosed
through singular commodity.   For what man will let go or
diminish his private commodity for a commonwealth? and who
will sustain any damage for the respect of a public commodity?
The other plough also no man is diligent to set forward, nor
no man will hearken to it; but to hinder and let it, all men's
ears are open, yea, and a great many of this kind of ploughmen
which are very busy, and would seem to be very good work-
men.   I fear me some be rather mock gospellers than faithful
ploughmen.   I know many myself that profess the Gospel, and
live nothing thereafter.   I know them, and have been conversant with some of them.   I know them, and, I speak it with a
heavy heart, there is as little charity and good living in them
as in any other, according to that which Christ said in the Gospel to the great number of people that followed Him as though
they had had an earnest zeal to His doctrine, whereas, indeed,
they had it not—"*Non qui vidistis signa, sed quia comedistis
de panibus*" ["Not because ye saw the miracles, but because
ye did eat of the loaves" (John vi. 26)].   "Ye follow me,"
saith He, "not because ye have seen the signs and miracles that
I have done, but because ye have eaten the bread and refreshed
your bodies."   Therefore you follow me; so that I think many
one nowadays professeth the Gospel for the living's sake, not
for the love they bear to God's Word.   But they that will be
true ploughmen must work faithfully, for God's sake, for the
edifying of their brethren.   And as diligently as the husbandman plougheth for the sustentation of the body, so diligently
must the prelates and ministers labor for the feeding of the
soul; both the ploughs must still be doing, as most necessary
for man.   And wherefore are magistrates ordained, but the

tranquillity of the commonweal may be confirmed, limiting both ploughs?

But now for the default of unpreaching prelates, methinks I could guess what might be said for excusing of them. They are so troubled with lordly living, they be so placed in palaces, couched in courts, ruffling in their rents, dancing in their dominions, burdened with ambassages, pampering of their paunches, like a monk that maketh his jubilee, munching in their mangers, and moiling in their gay manors and mansions, and so troubled with loitering in their lordships, that they cannot attend it. They are otherwise occupied; some in the king's matters; some are ambassadors; some of the Privy Council; some to furnish the court; some are lords of the Parliament; some are presidents; and some are comptrollers of mints. Well, well!

Is this their duty? Is this their office? Is this their calling? Should we have ministers of the Church to be comptrollers of the mint? Is this a meet office for a priest that hath cure of souls? Is this his charge? I would here ask one question. I would fain know who controlleth the devil at home at his parish while he controlleth the mint? If the apostles might not leave the office of preaching to be deacons, shall one leave it for minting?

I cannot tell you, but the saying is, that since priests have been minters, money hath been worse than it was before. And they say that the evilness of money hath made all things dearer. And in this behalf I must speak to England.

Hear, my country England, as Paul said in his First Epistle to the Corinthians, sixth chapter; for Paul was no sitting bishop, but a walking and a preaching bishop. But, when he went from them, he left there behind him the plough going still, for he wrote unto them and rebuked them for going to law and pleading their causes before heathen judges. "Is there," saith he, "utterly among you no wise man to be an arbitrator in matters of judgment? What! not one at all that can judge between brother and brother? But one brother go to law with another, and that under heathen judges." "*Constituite contempts qui sunt in ecclesia,*" etc. ["Set them to judge who are least esteemed in the Church" (1 Cor. vi. 4)]. Appoint them judges that are most abject and vile in the congregation, which he speaketh in rebuking them; for, saith he, " *Ad erubescenciam vestram dico* " [" I speak to your shame " (1 Cor. vi. 5)]. I speak it to your shame. So, England, I speak it to thy shame. Is there never a nobleman to be a lord president, but it must be a prelate? Is there never a wise man in the realm to be a comptroller of the mint? I speak it to your shame, I speak it to your shame. If there be never a wise man, make a water-bearer, a tinker, a cobbler, a slave, a page, comptroller of the mint. Make a mean gentleman, a groom, a yeoman, make a poor beggar lord president—thus I speak, not that I would have it so, but to your shame—if there be never a gentleman meet nor able to be lord president. For why are not the noble-men and young gentlemen of England so brought up in knowl-edge of God and in learning that they may be able to execute offices in the commonwealth? The king hath a great many wards, and I trow there is a court of wards, why is there not a school for the wards, as well as there is a court for their lands? Why are they not set in schools, where they may learn? Or why are they not sent to the universities, that they may be able to serve the king when they come to age? If the wards and young gentlemen were well brought up in learning and in the knowledge of God, they would not when they come of age so much give themselves to other vanities.

And if the nobility be well trained in godly learning, the people would follow the same train. For truly such as the noble-men be, such will the people be. And now the only cause why noblemen be not made lord presidents is because they have not been brought up in learning; therefore, for the love of God, appoint teachers and schoolmasters, you that have charge of youth, and give the teachers stipends worthy their pains, that they may bring them up in grammar, in logic, in rhetoric, in philosophy, in the civil law, and in that which I cannot leave unspoken of, the Word of God. Thanks be unto God, the nobil-ity otherwise is very well brought up in learning and godliness, to the great joy and comfort of England, so that there is now good hope in the youth, that we shall another day have a flour-ishing commonwealth, considering their godly education. Yea, and there be already noblemen enough (though not so as I would wish) able to be lord presidents, and wise men enough for the mint. And as unmeet a thing it is for bishops to be lord presidents, or priests to be minters, as it was for the Corinthians to plead matters of variance before heathen judges. It is also a slander to the noblemen, as though they lacked wisdom and learning to be able for such offices, or else were no men of conscience, or else were not meet to be trusted, and able for such offices; and a prelate hath a charge and cure otherwise, and therefore he cannot discharge his duty and be a lord president too. For a presidentship requireth a whole man, and a bishop cannot be two men. A bishop hath his office, a flock to teach, to look unto, and therefore he cannot meddle with another office, which alone requireth a whole man. He should, therefore, give it over to whom it is meet, and labor in his own business, as Paul writeth to the Thessalonians—" Let every man do his own business, and follow his calling." Let the priest preach, and the nobleman handle the temporal matters. Moses was a marvellous man, a good man. Moses was a wonderful fellow, and did his duty, being a married man. We lack such as Moses was. Well, I would all men would look to their duty, as God hath called them, and then we should have a flourishing Christian commonwealth. And now I would ask a strange question. Who is the most diligent bishop and prelate in all England, that passeth all the rest in doing his office? I can tell, for I know him; who it is, I know him well. But now I think I see you listening and hearkening that I should name him. There is one that passeth all the others, and is the most diligent prelate and preacher in all England. And will ye know who it is? I will tell you. It is the devil. He is the most diligent preacher of all others; he is never out of his diocese; he is never from his cure; ye shall never find him unoccupied; he is ever in his parish; he keepeth residence at all times; ye shall never find him out of the way; call for him when you will, he is ever at home; the diligentest preacher in all the realm, he is ever at his plough; no lording nor loitering can hinder him; he is ever applying his business; ye shall never find him idle, I warrant you. And his office is to hinder religion, to maintain superstition, to set up idolatry, to teach all kinds of papistry; he is ready as can be wished for to set forth his plough, to devise as many ways as can be to deface and obscure God's glory. Where the devil is resident and hath his plough going, there away with books and up with candles, away with Bibles and up with beads,

away with the light of the Gospel and up with the light of
candles, yea, at noonday. Where the devil is resident, that he
may prevail, up with all superstition and idolatry, censing, painting of images, candles, palms, ashes, holy water, and new service of men's inventing, as though man could invent a better
way to honor God with than God himself hath appointed. Down
with Christ's cross, up with purgatory—pick-purse, up with
him—the popish purgatory, I mean. Away with clothing the
naked, the poor, and impotent, up with decking of images and
gay garnishing of stocks and stones; up with man's traditions
and his laws, down with God's traditions and His most holy
Word; down with the old honor due to God, and up with the
new god's honor. Let all things be done in Latin. There must
be nothing but Latin, not as much as "*Memento homo quod
cinis es, et in cinerem reverteris*" (" Remember, man, that thou
art ashes, and into ashes thou shalt return "); which be the
words that the minister speaketh to the ignorant people, when
he giveth them ashes upon Ash-Wednesday, but it must be
spoken in Latin. God's Word may in no wise be translated into
English. Oh, that our prelates would be as diligent to sow the
corn of good doctrine as Satan is to sow cockle and darnel!
And this is the devilish ploughing, the which worketh to have
things in Latin, and letteth the fruitful edification. But here
some man will say to me, " What, sir, are ye so privy of the
devil's counsel that ye know all this to be true?" Truly I know
him too well, and have obeyed him a little too much in conde-
scending to some follies. And I know him as other men do,
yea, that he is ever occupied and ever busy in following his
plough. I know by St. Peter, who saith of him, "*Sicut leo
rugiens circuit querens quem devoret*" ["As a roaring lion,
walketh about, seeking whom he may devour " (1 Peter v. 8)].
He goeth about like a roaring lion, seeking whom he may devour. I would have this text well viewed and examined every
word of it. *Circuit,* he goth about in every corner of his diocese.
He goeth on visitation daily. He leaveth no place of his cure
unvisited. He walketh round about from place to place, and
ceaseth not. *Sicut leo,* as a lion, that is, strongly, boldly, and
proudly, straightly, and fiercely, with high looks, with his proud
countenances, with his stately braggings. *Rugiens,* roaring;
for he letteth not slip any occasion to speak or to roar out when

he seeth his time. *Querens,* he goeth about seeking and not sleeping, as our bishops do, but he seeketh diligently, he search-eth diligently all corners, whereas he may have his prey, he rov-eth abroad in every place of his diocese, he standeth not still, he is never at rest, but ever in hand with his plough, that it may go forward. But there was never such a preacher in England as he is. Who is able to tell his diligent preaching, who every day and every hour laboreth to sow cockle and darnel, that he may bring out of form and out of estimation and room,[2] the institution of the Lord's Supper and Christ's cross, for there he lost his right, for Christ said—" *Nunc judicium est mundi, princeps seculi hujus ejicietur foras*" [" Now is the judgment of this world, now shall the prince of this world be cast out" (John xii. 31)] ; " *Et sicut exultavit Moises serpentem in de-serto, ita exaltari oportet filium hominis*" [" And as Moses lifted up the serpent in the wilderness, even so must the Son of Man be lifted up" (John iii. 14)] ; " *Et cum exaltatus fuero, a terra, omnia traham ad meipsum*" [" And I, if I be lifted up from the earth, will draw all men unto me" (John xii. 32)]. Now is the judgment of this world, and the prince of this world shall be cast out. And as Moses did lift up the serpent in the wilderness, so must the Son of Man be lifted up. And when I shall be lifted up from the earth, I will draw all things unto myself. For the devil was disappointed of his purpose, for he thought all to be his own.

And when he had once brought Christ to the cross, he thought all cocksure. But there lost he all his reigning; for Christ said—" *Omnia traham ad meipsum*" (" I will draw all things to myself"). He meaneth drawing of man's soul to salvation. And that He said He would do *per semetipsum,* by His own self, not by any other body's sacrifice. He meant by His own sacrifice on the cross, where He offered Himself for the redemption of mankind, and not the sacrifice of the mass to be offered by any other. For who can offer Him but Him-self? He was both the offerer and the offering. And this is the prick, this is the mark at the which the devil shooteth, to evacuate the cross of Christ, and to mingle the institution of the Lord's Supper, the which, although he cannot bring to pass, yet he goeth about, by his sleight and subtle means, to frustrate

[2] Place or office.

the same; and these sixteen hundred years he hath been a doer, only purposing to evacuate Christ's death, and to make it of small efficacy and virtue.

For whereas Christ, according as the serpent was lifted up in the wilderness, so would He himself to be exalted, that thereby as many as trusted in Him should have salvation. But the devil would none of that. They would have us saved by a daily oblation propitiatory, by sacrifice expiatory, or remissory.

Now if I should preach in the country among the unlearned, I would tell what propitiatory, expiatory, and remissory is; but here is a learned auditory. Yet for them that be unlearned, I will expound it. Propitiatory, expiatory, remissory, or satisfactory, for they signify all one thing in effect, and is nothing else but a thing whereby to obtain remission of sins, and to have salvation. And this way the devil used to evacuate the death of Christ, that we might have affiance in other things; as in the daily sacrifice of the priest, whereas Christ would have us to trust in His only sacrifice. So He was "*Agnus occisus ab origine mundi*" ["The Lamb slain from the foundation of the world" (Rev. xiii. 8)], the Lamb that hath been slain from the beginning of the world; and therefore He is called, "*Juge sacrificium*" ["A daily sacrifice" (Dan. viii. 11, 12)], a continual sacrifice, and not for the continuance of the mass, as the blanchers have blanched it, and wrested it, and as I myself did once mistake it. But Paul saith—"*Per semetipsum purgatio facta*" ["When He had by Himself purged our sins" (Heb. i. 3)], by Himself, and by none other, Christ made purgation and satisfaction for the whole world. Would Christ this word (by Himself) had been better weighed and looked upon, and *in sanctificationem*, to make them holy; for He is *juge sacrificium*, a continual sacrifice, in effect, fruit, and operation, that like as they who, seeing the serpent hung up in the desert, were put in remembrance of Christ's death, in whom as many as believed were saved; so all men that trusted in the death of Christ shall be saved, as well they that were before as they that came after. For He was a continual sacrifice, as I said, in effect, fruit, operation, and virtue, as though He had from the beginning of the world, and continually should to the world's end, hang still on the cross; and He is as fresh hanging on the cross now, to them that believe and trust in Him, as He was fifteen hundred years ago when He was crucified. Then let us trust upon His only death, and look for none other sacrifice propitiatory, than the same bloody sacrifice, the lively sacrifice, and not a dry sacrifice, but a bloody sacrifice. For Christ himself said—" *Consummatum est* " [" It is finished " (John xix. 30)]. " It is perfectly finished. I have taken at my Father's hand the dispensation of redeeming mankind. I have wrought man's redemption, and have despatched the matter." Why then mingle ye Him? why do ye divide Him? Why make you of Him more sacrifices than one? Paul saith—" *Pascha nostrum immolatus est Christus* " [" Christ our passover is sacrificed for us " (1 Cor. v. 7)], Christ our passover is offered up; so that the thing is done, and Christ hath done it, and He hath done it *semel,* once for all. And it was a bloody sacrifice, not a dry sacrifice.

Why, then, it is not the mass that availeth or profiteth for the quick or the dead! Woe worth thee, O devil! woe worth thee! thou hast prevailed so far and so long that thou hast made England to worship false gods, forsaking Christ their Lord. Woe worth thee, devil. Woe worth thee, devil, and all thine angels; if Christ by His death draweth all things to Himself, and draweth all men to salvation and to heavenly bliss that trust in Him, then the priests at the mass (at the Popish mass, I say), what can they draw when Christ draweth all, but lands and goods from the right heirs? The priests draw goods and riches, benefices and promotions to themselves; and such as believed in their sacrifice they draw to the devil. But Christ it is that draweth souls unto Him by His bloody sacrifice. What have we to do, then, but " *Epulari in Domino* " [" To eat the Lord's Supper " (1 Cor. xi. 20)], to eat in the Lord at His supper. What other service have we to do to Him? and what other sacrifice have we to offer, but the mortification of our flesh? What other oblation have we to make, but of obedience, of good living, of good works, and of helping our neighbors? But as for our redemption, it is done already, it cannot be better. Christ hath done that thing so well that it cannot be amended. It cannot be devised how to make that any better than He hath done it. But the devil, by the help of that Italian bishop yonder, his chaplain, hath labored by all means that he might to frustrate the death of Christ and the merits of His passion. And they have devised for that purpose, to make us believe in other vain things by his pardons, as to have remission of sins for praying on hallowed beads; for drinking of the bakehouse bowl, as a canon of Waltham Abbey once told me, that whensoever they put their loaves of bread into the oven, as many as drank of the pardon bowl should have pardon for drinking of it. A mad thing to give pardon to a bowl. Then to Pope Alexander's holy water, to hallowed bells, palms, candles, ashes, and what not?

And of these things, every one hath taken away some part of Christ's sanctification. Every one hath robbed some part of Christ's passion and cross, and hath mingled Christ's death, and hath been made to be propitiatory and satisfactory, and to put away sin. Yea, and Alexander's holy water yet at this day remaineth in England, and is used as a remedy against spirits, and to chase away devils; yea, and I would this had been the worst. I would this were the worst. But woe worth thee, O devil, that hast prevailed to evacuate Christ's cross, and to mingle the Lord's Supper. These be the Italian bishop's devices, and the devil hath pricked at this mark to frustrate the cross of Christ; he shot at this mark long before Christ came, he shot at this prick four thousand years before Christ hanged on the cross, or suffered His passion.

For the brazen serpent was set up in the wilderness to put men in remembrance of Christ's coming, that like as they who beheld the brazen serpent were healed of their bodily diseases, so they that looked spiritually upon Christ that was to come, in Him should be saved spiritually from the devil. The serpent was set up in memory of Christ to come, but the devil found means to steal away the memory of Christ's coming, and brought the people to worship the serpent's self, and to cense him, to honor him, and to offer to him, to worship him, and to make an idol of him.

And this was done by the market men that I told you of.

And the clerk of the market did it for the lucre and advantage of his master, that thereby his honor might increase, for by Christ's death he could have but small worldly advantage. And even now so hath he certain blanchers belonging to the market, to let and stop the light of the Gospel, and to hinder the king's proceedings in setting forth the Word and glory of God. And when the king's majesty, with the advice of his honorable council, goeth about to promote God's Word, and to set an order in matter of religion, there shall not lack blanchers that will say, " As for images, whereas they have been used to be censed, and to have candles offered unto them, none be so foolish to do it to the stock or stone, or to the image itself, but it is done to God and His honor before the image." And though they should abuse it, these blanchers will be ready to whisper the king in the ear, and to tell him that this abuse is but a small matter. And that the same, with all other like abuses in the Church, may be reformed easily. " It is but a little abuse," say they, " and it may be easily amended. But it should not be taken in hand at the first, for fear of trouble or further inconveniences—the people will not bear sudden alterations: an insurrection may be made after sudden mutation, which may be to the great harm and loss of the realm. Therefore all things shall be well, but not out of hand, for fear of further business." These be the blanchers that hitherto have stopped the Word of God, and hindered the true setting forth of the same. There be so many put-offs, and so many put-byes, so many respects and considerations of worldly wisdom. And I doubt not but there were blanchers in the old time, to whisper in the ear of good King Hezekiah for the maintenance of idolatry done to the brazen serpent, as well as there hath been now of late, and be now, that can blanch the abuse of images and other like things. But good King Hezekiah would not be so blinded; he was like to Apollos, fervent in spirit. He would give no ear to the blanchers; he was not moved with these worldly respects, with these prudent considerations, with these policies; he feared not insurrections of the people. He feared not lest his people would not bear the glory of God; but he (without any of these respects, or policies, or considerations, like a good king, for God's sake, and for conscience sake) by-and-by plucked down the brazen serpent, and destroyed it utterly, and beat it to powder. He out of hand did cast down all images, he destroyed all idolatry, and clearly did extirpate all superstition. He would not hear these blanchers and worldly-wise men, but without delay followed God's cause, and destroyed all idolatry out of hand. Thus did good King Hezekiah; for he was like Apollos, fervent in spirit, and diligent to promote God's glory. And good hope there is that it shall be likewise here in England; for the king's majesty is so brought up in knowledge, virtue, and godliness,

that it is not to be mistrusted but that we shall have all things
well, and that the glory of God shall be spread abroad throughout all parts of the realm, if the prelates will diligently apply
their plough, and be preachers rather than lords; but our
blanchers, who will be lords, and no laborers, when they are
commanded to go and be resident upon their cures, and to
preach in their benefices, they would say, " What! I have set a
deputy there! I have a deputy that looketh well to my flock,
and the which shall discharge my duty." A deputy, quoth he.
I looked for that word all this while. And what a deputy must
he be, trow ye? Even one like himself. It must be a canonist,
that is to say, one that is brought up in the study of the Pope's
laws and decrees. One that will set forth papistry as well as
himself will do, and one that will maintain all superstitious
idolatry.

And one that will nothing at all, or else very weakly, resist
the devil's plough, yea, happy it is if he take not part with the
devil; and when he should be an enemy to him, it is well if he
take not the devil's part against Christ. But in the mean time
the prelates take their pleasures. They are lords, and no laborers; but the devil is diligent at his plough. He is no unpreaching prelate. He is no lordly loiterer from his cure, but
a busy ploughman, so that among all the prelates, and among
all the pack of them that have cure, the devil shall go for my
money. For he still applieth his business. Therefore, ye unpreaching prelates, learn of the devil to be diligent in doing of
your office. Learn of the devil. And if you will not learn of
God nor good men, for shame learn of the devil. " *Ad erubes-
centiam vestram dico* " [" I speak to your shame " (1 Cor. vi.
5)]. I speak it for your shame. If you will not learn of God
nor good men to be diligent in your office, learn of the devil.
Howbeit there is now very good hope that the king's majesty,
being by the help of good governance of his most honorable
councillors, he is trained and brought up in learning and knowledge of God's Word, will shortly provide a remedy, and set an
order herein; which thing that it may so be, let us pray for him.
Pray for him, good people, pray for him; ye have great cause
and need to pray for him.

CHOICE EXAMPLES OF EARLY PRINTING AND ENGRAVING.

Fac-similes from Rare and Curious Books.

PAGE OF THE FIRST ENGLISH PRAYER-BOOK.

The first Prayer-Book of the Reformed Church of England, the precursor of the Book of Common Prayer used at present in England and by the Protestant Episcopal Church of America, was printed in London, at the Grafton press, by Edward Whitchurch, in the year 1549. The title-page is beautiful in its red and black typography, and its border, adorned with the royal arms of England, is remarkable for its daring mixture of grotesque and Renaissance forms. At the lower part of the border we find the little goat-footed satyrs who wear wings, like cherubs, and are a most bizarre and artistic creation.

THE

booke of the common
prayer and admi-
nistracion of
the
Sacramentes, and other
rites and ceremonies of
the Churche: after the
vse of the Churche
of England.

LONDINI IN OFFICINA
Edouardi Whitchurche,

Cum priuilegio ad imprimendum solum

ANNO. DO. 1 5 4 9, Mense
Iunii

SPEECH AT THE STAKE

—

BY

THOMAS CRANMER

THOMAS CRANMER

1489—1556

Thomas Cranmer, Archbishop of Canterbury, an important figure during the Reformation in England, friend and counsellor of Henry VIII, was born on July 2, 1489. He was sent to Cambridge at the age of fourteen, where he entered Jesus College. He was made a fellow of his college in 1510.

It must be considered a mere accident that transferred Cranmer from the quiet seclusion of university life to the din and bustle of the Court of his King. Cranmer's opinion on the validity of Henry's marriage with Catharine of Aragon was reported to the King, and his views being entirely favorable to the King, dispensing, moreover, with the appeal to Rome, Henry sent for Cranmer with the well-authenticated summons: "I will speak to him. Let him be sent for out of hand. This man, I trow, has got the right sow by the ear." Cranmer was now ordered to devote himself entirely to this question of divorce. He was to draw up a treatise defending the position he had taken by arguments from Scripture, the fathers, and decrees from general councils. He then was ordered to plead and defend his arguments before the Universities of Oxford and Cambridge. But he was soon sent to plead before a higher tribunal. The King, still hoping to obtain the consent of Pope Clement VII to his plans of divorce, sent Cranmer to Rome. His visit, however, bore no practical results. He went on a similar mission as ambassador to the Emperor Charles V, achieving no greater success with this monarch than with the Pope. During his stay in Germany Cranmer met the German theologian, Osiander, whose niece he married early in 1532. He was appointed Archbishop of Canterbury in 1533.

During the succeeding years Cranmer invalidated successively the marriages of Anne Boleyn, Anne of Cleves, and Catharine Howard. Cranmer thus became the tool of Henry and involved in the most scandalous transactions of his reign. He renounced his allegiance to Rome in 1535, and in 1548 was at the head of the commission appointed to compose the English prayer-book. He was persuaded by Edward VI to sign the patent which conferred the crown on Lady Jane Grey to the exclusion of Mary and Elizabeth, and on the accession of Mary he was committed to the Tower for treason. He was tried subsequently for heresy, and in spite of many recantations (which he repudiated at the stake) he was burned at the stake, March 21, 1556.

Cranmer used his great influence with the King to the spread of the English Bible among the people, being himself a profound scholar of the Scriptures. In the midst of the many difficulties around him and the controversies that engaged him, Cranmer found time to devote himself to theological speculations. On the subject of his "Defence of Transubstantiation," he became involved in animated discussions with the Bishops of Winchester and the Catholic theologian, Richard Smith. To Cranmer, as one of the eminent prose writers of his time, this tribute has been paid by a distinguished writer and critic on English literature: "His compositions are characterized, if not by any remarkable strength of expression or weight of matter, yet by a full and even flow both of words and thought. On the whole Cranmer was the greatest writer among the founders of the English Reformation." Cranmer's speech at the stake has a peculiar pathos of its own and a sincerity that is at once eloquent and convincing.

SPEECH AT THE STAKE

GOOD people, I had intended indeed to desire you to pray for me; which because Mr. Doctor hath desired, and you have done already, I thank you most heartily for it. And now will I pray for myself, as I could best devise for mine own comfort and say the prayer, word for word, as I have here written it.

[And he read it standing; and afterwards kneeled down and said the Lord's Prayer, and all the people on their knees devoutedly praying with him. His prayer was thus:]

O Father of heaven; O Son of God, redeemer of the word; O Holy Ghost, proceeding from them both, three persons and one God, have mercy upon me, most wretched caitiff and miserable sinner. I, who have offended both heaven and earth, and more grievously than any tongue can express, whither then may I go, or whither should I fly for succor? To heaven I may be ashamed to lift up mine eyes; and in earth I find no refuge. What shall I then do? shall I despair? God forbid. O good God, thou art merciful, and refusest none that come unto thee for succor. To thee, therefore, do I run. To thee do I humble myself saying, O Lord God, my sins be great; but yet have mercy upon me for thy great mercy. O God the Son, thou wast not made man, this great mystery was not wrought for few or small offences. Nor thou didst not give thy Son unto death, O God the Father, for our little and small sins only, but for all the greatest sins of the world, so that the sinner return unto thee with a penitent heart, as I do here at this present. Wherefore have mercy upon me, O Lord, whose property is always to have mercy. For although my sins be great, yet thy mercy is greater. I crave nothing, O Lord, for mine own merits, but for thy Name's sake, that it may be glorified thereby, and for thy dear Son, Jesus Christ's sake.

[Then rising, he said:][1]

All men desire, good people, at the time of their deaths,[2] to give some good exhortation that others may remember after their deaths, and be the better thereby. So I beseech God grant me grace that I may speak something, at this my departing, whereby God may be glorified and you edified.

First, it is an heavy case to see that many folks be so much doted upon the love of this false world, and so careful for it, that for the love of God, or the love of the world to come, they seem to care very little or nothing therefor. This shall be my first exhortation. That you set not overmuch by this false glozing world, but upon God and the world to come; and learn to know what this lesson meaneth, which St. John teacheth, that the love of this world is hatred against God.

The second exhortation is that next unto God you obey your King and Queen willingly and gladly, without murmur and grudging, and not for fear of them only, but much more for the fear of God, knowing that they be God's ministers, appointed by God to rule and govern you. And therefore whoso resisteth them, resisteth God's ordinance.

The third exhortation is, that you love altogether like brethren and sisters. For, alas! pity it is to see what contention and hatred one Christian man hath towards another; not taking each other as sisters and brothers, but rather as strangers and mortal enemies. But I pray you learn and bear well away this one lesson, To do good to all men as much as in you lieth, and to hurt no man, no more than you would hurt your own natural and loving brother or sister. For this you may be sure of, that whosoever hateth any person, and goeth about maliciously to hinder or hurt him, surely, and without all doubt, God is not with that man, although he think himself never so much in God's favor.

The fourth exhortation shall be to them that have great substance and riches of this world, that they will well consider and weigh those sayings of the Scripture. One is of our Saviour, Christ himself, who sayeth, It is hard for a rich man to enter

[1] This speech is recorded in "The Memorials" by John Strype, 1693.
[2] Cranmer was dragged to the stake opposite Baliol College on March 21, 1556, and met his death with the utmost fortitude, exclaiming as he held out his right hand for the flames to consume it, "This unworthy hand! this unworthy hand!"

into heaven; a sore saying, and yet spoken by him that knew the truth. The second is of St. John, whose saying is this, He that hath the substance of this world and seeth his brother in necessity, and shutteth up his mercy from him, how can he say he loveth God? Much more might I speak of every part; but time sufficeth not, I do but put you in remembrance of these things. Let all them that be rich ponder well those sentences; for if ever they had any occasion to show their charity they have now at this present, the poor people being so many, and victuals so dear. For though I have been long in prison, yet I have heard of the great penury of the poor. Consider that which is given to the poor is given to God; whom we have not otherwise present corporally with us, but in the poor.

And now, for so much as I am come to the last end of my life, whereupon hangeth all my life passed and my life to come, either to live with my Saviour Christ in heaven in joy, or else to be in pain ever with wicked devils in hell; and I see before mine eyes presently either heaven ready to receive me, or hell ready to swallow me up; I shall therefore declare unto you my very faith, how I believe, without color or dissimulation; for now is no time to dissemble, whatsoever I have written in times past.

First, I believe in God the Father Almighty, maker of heaven and earth, and every article of the catholic faith, every word and sentence taught by our Saviour Christ, his apostles and prophets, in the Old and New Testaments.

And now I come to the great thing that troubleth my conscience, more than any other thing that ever I said or did in my life; and that is, the setting abroad of writings contrary to the truth. Which here now I renounce and refuse, as things written with my hand, contrary to the truth which I thought in my heart, and writ for fear of death, and to save my life, if it might be; and that is, all such bills, which I have written or signed with mine own hand since my degradation, wherein I have written many things untrue. And forasmuch as my hand offended in writing contrary to my heart, therefore my hand shall be punished; for if I may come to the fire it shall be first burned. And as for the Pope, I refuse him as Christ's enemy and Antichrist, with all his false doctrine.

PRAYER

—

BY

JOHN KNOX

JOHN KNOX

1505—1572

John Knox was born at Haddington, East Lothian, in 1505. He attended school in his native town and in 1522 matriculated at the University of Edinburgh. Little is known of his life before the year 1546, when the martyrdom of Wishart determined him to renounce Catholicism and embrace the new faith. Captured at St. Andrew's Castle by the combined forces of the French and Scotch Catholics, he suffered imprisonment during nearly two years and his health was much impaired by the harsh treatment to which he was **subjected.** On his release in 1548 he went to London and was appointed a preacher in Berwick, later in Newcastle. All his efforts in his polemic discourses were directed to the denunciation of celebrating mass. To escape prosecution, on the accession of Mary, Knox fled to Dieppe in 1553 and after visiting the churches in France and Switzerland he accepted a call from the congregation at Frankfort, then much rent and disturbed by factions. The discourse on "Prayer" shows Knox less in his polemic mood, but rather as one of the great and eloquent preachers of his time. Upon urgent solicitations he became minister to the English congregation at Geneva.

Recalled to Scotland in May, 1559, he entered upon his triumphant course as a reformer. Political necessities had driven the Queen-regent to temporize with the "lords of the congregation," or the reforming nobles. The heads of the party assembling at Dundee, under Erskine of Dun, proceeded to Perth. There the pent-up enthusiasm was roused by a sermon of Knox on the idolatry of the mass and on image-worship. A riot ensued. The "rascal multitude," as Knox himself called them, destroyed the churches and monasteries. Similar disturbances followed at Stirling, Lindores, St. Andrew's, and elsewhere. At length the assistance of Elizabeth and the death of the Queen-regent brought matters to a crisis; a truce was proclaimed, and a free Parliament summoned to settle differences. The result of the Parliament, which met in August, 1560, was the establishment of the reformed Kirk in Scotland. In all this Knox was not only an active agent, but the agent above all others. The arrival of the youthful queen, Mary, in the course of 1561, brought many forebodings to the reformer; he apprehended great dangers to the reformed cause from her well-known devotion to the Church of Rome. The rapid series of events which followed Mary's marriage with Darnley—the revolt of the dissatisfied nobles, with Murray at their head, the murder of Rizzio, and then the murder of Darnley (1567), the Queen's marriage with Bothwell, her defeat and imprisonment, served once more to bring Knox into the field. Further reforms were effected by the Parliament which convened under his sway at the close of 1567. Knox seemed at length to see his great work accomplished. But the bright prospect on which he gazed for a short time was soon overcast—Murray's assassination, and the confusion and discord which sprung out of it, plunged the reformer into profound grief. He retired to St. Andrew's for a while, to escape the danger of assassination with which he had been threatened. At the end of 1572 he returned to Edinburgh; his strength was exhausted; he was "weary of the world," he said; and on November 24th, of that year, he died.

PRAYER

"PRAYER Springeth out of true Faith " (Rom. x.).[1] How necessary is the right invocation of God's name, otherwise called perfect prayer, becometh no Christian to misknow, seeing it is the very branch which springeth forth of true faith, whereof, if any man be destitute, notwithstanding he be endowed with whatsoever other virtues, yet, in the presence of God, he is reputed for no Christian at all. Therefore, a manifest sign it is, that such as in prayer are always negligent do understand nothing of perfect faith. For if the fire be without heat, or the burning lamp without light, then true faith may be without fervent prayer. But because, in times past was, and yet, alas! with no small number is that reckoned to be prayer which in the sight of God was and is nothing less, I intend shortly to touch the circumstances thereof.

What Prayer is.—Who will pray must know and understand that prayer is an earnest and familiar talking with God, to whom we declare our miseries, whose support and help we implore and desire in our adversities, and whom we laud and praise for our benefits received, so that prayer containeth the exposition of our dolors, the desire of God's defence, and the praising of His magnificent name, as the Psalms of David clearly do teach. That this be most reverently done should provoke in us the consideration in whose presence we stand, to whom we speak, and what we desire; standing in the presence of the Omnipotent Creator of heaven and earth, and of all the contents thereof, to whom assist and serve a thousand thousand of angels, giving obedience to His eternal majesty, and speaking unto Him who knoweth the secrets of our hearts, before whom dissimulation and lies are always odious and hateful, and asking that thing which may be most to His glory and to the comfort of our conscience. But diligently should we attend, that such

---

[1] This sermon was first printed at Rome, July, 1554.

29

things as may offend His godly presence to the uttermost of our powers may be removed. And, first, that worldly cares and fleshly cogitations, such as draw us from contemplation of our God, may be expelled from us, that we may freely, without interruption, call upon God. But how difficult and hard is this one thing in prayer to perform, knoweth none better than such as in their prayer are not content to remain within the bonds of their own vanity, but, as it were ravished, do intend to a purity allowed of asking not such things as the foolish reason of man desireth, but which may be pleasant and acceptable in God's presence. Our adversary Satan, at all times compassing us about, is never more ready than when we address and bend ourselves to prayer. Oh, how secretly and subtilely creepeth he into our breasts, and calling us back from God, causeth us to forget what we have to do, as that frequently when we in all reverence should speak of God, we find our hearts talking with the vanities of the world, or with the foolish imaginations of our own conceit.

How the Spirit maketh Intercession for Us.—Without the Spirit of God supporting our infirmities, mightily making intercession for us with unceasable groans, which cannot be expressed with the tongue, there is no hope of anything we can desire according to God's will. I mean not that the Holy Ghost doth mourn and pray, but that He stirreth up our minds, giving unto us a desire or boldness to pray, and causeth us to mourn when we are extracted or pulled therefrom. Which things to conceive no strength of man sufficeth, neither is able of itself; but hereof it is plain, that such as understand not what they pray, or expound not or declare not the desire of their hearts clearly in God's presence, and in time of prayer to their possibility do not expel vain cogitations from their minds, profit nothing in prayer.

Why we should Pray, and also Understand what we do Pray. —Men will object and say, although we understand not what we pray, yet God understandeth, who knoweth the secrets of our hearts; He knoweth also what we need, although we expose not or declare not our necessities unto Him. Such men verily declare themselves never to have understanding what perfect prayer meant, nor to what end Jesus Christ commandeth us to pray; which is, first, that our hearts may be inflamed with continual fear, honor, and love of God, to whom we run for support and help whenever danger or necessity requireth; that we so learning to notify our desires in His presence, He may teach us what is to be desired, and what not; secondly, that we knowing our petitions to be granted by God alone, to Him only must we render and give laud and praise, and that we, ever having His infinite goodness fixed in our minds, may constantly abide to receive that which with fervent prayer we desire.

Why God deferreth our Prayer.—For sometime God deferreth or prolongeth to grant our petitions for the exercise and trial of our faith, and not that He sleepeth, or is absent from us at any time, but that with more gladness we might receive that which with long expectation we have abidden, that thereby we, assured of His eternal providence, so far as the infirmity of our weak, and corrupt, and most weak nature will permit, doubt not but His merciful hand shall relieve us in most urgent necessity and extreme tribulation. Therefore, such men as teach us that necessarily it is not required that we understand what we pray, because God knoweth what we need, would also teach us that neither we honor God, nor yet refer or give unto Him thanks for benefits received; for how shall we honor and praise him whose goodness and liberality we know not? And how shall we know and sometime have experience? And how shall we know that we have received, unless we know verily what we have asked?

The second thing to be observed in perfect prayer is, that standing in the presence of God, we be found such as bear reverence to His Holy law, earnestly repenting our past iniquity, and intending to lead a new life; for otherwise, in vain are all our prayers, as it is written, " Whoso withdraweth his ear, that he may not hear the law, his prayer shall be abominable " (Prov. xv.). Likewise Isaiah and Jeremiah say thus : " Ye shall multiply your prayers, and I shall not hear, because your hands are full of blood; " that is, of all cruelty and mischievous works. Also the Spirit of God appeareth by the mouth of the blind whom Jesus Christ did illuminate, by these words, " We know that God heareth not sinners " (John ix.) ; that is, such as glory and do continue in iniquity.

When Sinners are not heard of God.—So that of necessity true repentance must needs be had, and go before perfect prayer, or sincere invocation of God's name. And unto these two precedents must be annexed the third, which is the direction of ourselves in God's presence, utterly refusing and casting off our own justice with all cogitations and opinion thereof. And let us not think that we shall be heard for anything proceeding of ourselves. For all such as advance, boast, or depend anything upon their own righteousness, repel and hold from the presence of His mercy with the high, proud Pharisee. And, therefore, the most holy men we find in prayers most dejected and humbled. David saith, " O Lord, our Saviour, help us, be merciful unto our sins for Thy own sake. Remember not our old iniquities, but haste Thou, O Lord, and let Thy mercy prevent us " (Psalm lxxix.). Jeremiah saith, " If our iniquities bear testimony against us, do Thou according to Thy own name." And behold Isaiah: " Thou art angry, O Lord, because we have sinned, and are replenished with all wickedness, and our righteousness is like a defiled cloth. But now, O Lord, Thou art our Father; we are clay; Thou art the workman, and we the workmanship of Thy hands. Be not angry, O Lord; remember not our iniquities forever " (Isa. lxiv.). And Daniel, greatly commended of God, maketh in his prayer most humble confession, in these words: " We be sinners, and have offended; we have done ungodly, and fallen from Thy commandment: therefore not in our own righteousness make we our prayers before Thee, but Thy most rich and great mercy bring we forth for us. O Lord, hear; O Lord, be merciful, and spare us, O Lord; attend, help, and cease not, my God, even for Thy own name's sake; do it, for Thy city and Thy people are called after Thy own name " (Dan. ix.). Behold, that in these prayers is no mention of their own righteousness, their own satisfaction, or their own merits; but most humble confession, proceeding from a sorrowful and penitent heart, having nothing whereupon it might depend but the sure mercy of God alone, who had promised to be their God; that is, their help, comfort, defender, and deliverer (as He hath also done to us by Jesus Christ) in time of tribulation. And therefore they despaired not; but after the acknowledging of their sins, called for mercy, and obtained the same. Wherefore, it is plain that such men as in their prayers have respect to any virtue proceeding of themselves, thinking thereby their prayers to be accepted, never prayed aright.

What Fasting and Alms-deeds are with Prayer.—And, albeit, to fervent prayer be joined fasting, watching, and alms-deeds, yet are none of these the cause that God doth accept our prayers. But they are spurs, which suffer us not to vary, but make us more able to continue in prayer, which the mercy of God doth accept.

But here may it be objected that David prayeth, " Keep my life, O Lord, for I am holy: O Lord, save my soul, for I am innocent; and suffer me not to be confounded " (Psalms xxxviii., lxxxvi.). Also Hezekiah: " Remember, Lord, I beseech Thee, that I have walked righteously before Thee, and that I have wrought that which is good in Thy sight " (2 Kings xx.). These words are not spoken of men glorious, neither yet trusting in their own works; but herein they testify themselves to be the sons of God by regeneration, to whom He promiseth always to be merciful, and at all times to hear their prayers.

The Cause of their Boldness was Jesus Christ.—And so their words spring from a wonted, constant, and fervent faith, surely believing that as God, of His infinite mercy, had called them to His knowledge, not suffering them to walk after their own natural wickedness, but partly had taught them to conform themselves to His holy law, and that, for the promised seed's sake, so might He not leave them destitute of comfort, consolation, and defence, in so great and extreme necessity. And so their righteousness allege they not to glory thereof, or to put trust therein, but to strengthen and confirm them in God's promises. And this consolation I would wish to all Christians in their prayers—a testimony of a good conscience to assure them of God's promises; but to obtain what they ask must only depend upon Him, all opinion and thought of our own righteousness laid aside. And, moreover, David, in the words above, compareth himself with King Saul, and with the rest of his enemies who wrongfully did persecute him, desiring of God that they prevail not against him—as he would say, " Unjustly do they persecute me, and therefore, according to my innocency, defend me," for otherwise he confesseth himself most grievously to have offended God, as in the preceding places he clearly testifieth.

Hypocrisy is not Allowed with God.—Thirdly, in prayer is to be observed, that what we ask of God, we must earnestly desire the same, acknowledging ourselves to be indigent and void thereof, and that God alone may grant the petition of our hearts when His good will and pleasure is. For nothing is more odious before God than hypocrisy and dissimulation—that is, when men do ask of God things whereof they have no need, or that they believe to obtain by others than by God alone. As if a man ask of God remission of his sins, thinking, nevertheless, to obtain the same by his own works, or by other men's merits, he doth mock with God, and deceive himself. And, in such cases, do a great number offend, principally the mighty and rich of the earth, who, for a common custom, will pray this part of the Lord's Prayer, " Give us this day our daily bread "—that is, a moderate and reasonable sustentation; and yet their own hearts will testify that they need not so to pray, seeing they abound in all worldly solace and felicity. I mean not that rich men should not pray this part of prayer, but I would they understood what they ought to pray in it (whereof I intend after to speak), and that they ask nothing whereof they felt not themselves marvellously indigent and needful; for unless we call in verity, He will not grant, and except we speak with our whole heart, we shall not find Him.

The fourth rule necessary to be followed in prayer is, a sure hope to obtain what we ask; for nothing more offendeth God than when we ask doubting whether He will grant our petitions, for in so doing we doubt if God be true, if He be mighty and good. Such, saith James, obtain nothing of God (James i.) ; and therefore Jesus Christ commandeth that we firmly believe to obtain whatsoever we ask, for all things are possible unto him that believeth. And therefore, in our prayers, desperation is always to be expelled. I mean not that any man, in extremity of trouble, can be without a present dolor, and without a greater fear of trouble to follow. Trouble and fear are the very spurs to prayer; for when man, compassed about with vehement calamities, and vexed with continual solicitude, having, by help of man, no hope of deliverance, with sore oppressed and punished heart, fearing also greater punishment to follow, from the deep pit of tribulation doth call to God for comfort and support, such prayer ascendeth into God's presence, and returneth not in vain.

As David, in the vehement persecution of Saul, hunted and

chased from every hole, fearing that one day or other he should fall into the hands of his persecutors, after that he had complained that no place of rest was left to him, vehemently prayed, saying, " O Lord, who art my God, in whom alone I trust, save me from them that persecute me, and deliver me from my enemies. Let not this man (meaning Saul) devour my life, as a lion doth his prey, for of none seek I comfort but of Thee alone " (Psalm vii.). In the midst of these anguishes the goodness of God sustained him, so that the present tribulation was tolerable ; and the infallible promises of God so assured him of deliverance, that fear was partly mitigated and gone, as plainly appeareth to such as diligently mark the process of his prayer. For, after long menacing and threatening made to him of his enemy, he concludeth with these words : " The dolor which he intended to me shall fall upon his own pate ; and the violence wherewith he would have oppressed me shall cast down his own head : but I will magnify the Lord according to His righteousness, and shall praise the name of the Most High."

God Delivereth His chosen from their Enemies.—This is not written for David only, but for all such as shall suffer tribulation, to the end of the world. For I, the writer hereof (let this be said to the laud and praise of God alone), in anguish of mind, and vehement tribulation and affliction, called upon the Lord, when not only the ungodly, but even my faithful brethren, yea, and my own self, that is, all natural understanding, judged my case to be irremediable. And yet, in my greatest calamity, and when my pains were most cruel, His eternal wisdom willed that my hands should write, far contrary to the judgment of carnal reason ; which His mercy hath proved true, blessed be His holy name. And therefore dare I be bold in the verity of God's Word to promise that, notwithstanding the vehemency of trouble, the long continuance thereof, the despair of all men, the fearfulness, danger, dolor, and anguish of our own hearts, yet if we call constantly to God, that, beyond expectation of all men, He shall deliver.

Let no man think himself unworthy to call and pray to God, because he hath grievously offended His majesty in times past ; but let him bring to God a sorrowful and repenting heart, saying with David, " Heal my soul, O Lord, for I have offended against Thee. Before I was afflicted, I transgressed; but now let me observe Thy commandments " (Psalms vi., cxix.).

To mitigate or ease the sorrows of our wounded conscience, two plaisters hath our most prudent Physician provided, to give us encouragement to pray, notwithstanding the knowledge of offences committed; that is, a precept and a promise. The precept or commandment to pray is universal, frequently inculcated and repeated in God's Scriptures: " Ask, and it shall be given unto you " (Matt. vii.). " Call upon me in the day of trouble " (Psalm i.). " Watch and pray, that ye fall not into temptation " (Matt. xxvi.). " I command that ye pray ever, without ceasing " (1 Tim. ii.). " Make deprecations incessable, and give thanks in all things " (1 Thess. v.). Which commandments whoso contemneth or despiseth, doth equally sin with him that doth steal. For as this commandment, " Thou shalt not steal," is a precept negative, so " Thou shalt pray," is a commandment affirmative; and God requireth equal obedience of and to all His commandments. Yet more boldly will I say he who, when necessity constraineth, desireth not support and help of God, doth provoke His wrath no less than do such as make false gods, or openly deny God.

He that Prayeth not in Trouble, Denieth God.—For like as it is to know no physician or medicine, or, in knowing them, refuse to use and receive the same, so, not to call upon God in thy tribulation, is like as if thou didst not know God, or else utterly deny Him.

Not to Pray is a Sin most Odious.—Oh! why cease we then to call instantly upon His mercy, having His commandment so to do? Above all our iniquities, we work manifest contempt and despising of Him, when by negligence we delay to call for His gracious support. Whoso calleth on God obeyeth His will, and findeth therein no small consolation, knowing nothing is more acceptable to His majesty than humble obedience.

To this commandment He addeth His most undoubted promise in many places: " Ask, and ye shall receive; seek, and ye shall find " (Matt. vii.). And by the prophet Jeremiah God saith, " Ye shall call upon me, and I shall hear you; ye shall seek, and shall find me " (Jer. xxix.). And by Isaiah He saith, " May the father forget his natural son, or the mother the child of her womb? And although they do, yet shall I not forget such as call upon me." And hereto correspond and agree the words of Jesus Christ, saying, " If ye, being wicked, can give good gifts to your children, much more my heavenly Father shall give the Holy Ghost to them that ask Him " (Matt. vii.). And that we should not think God to be absent, or not to hear us, Moses occurreth, saying, " There is no nation that have their gods so adherent or nigh unto them as our God, who is present at all our prayers " (Deut. iv.). Also the Psalmist, " Near is the Lord to all that call upon Him in verity." And Christ saith, " Wheresoever two or three are gathered together in my name, there am I in the midst of them."

Readiness of God to hear Sinners.—That we may not think that God will not hear us, Isaiah saith, " Before ye cry I shall hear, and while they yet speak I shall answer." And also, " If at even come sorrow or calamity, before the morning spring, I shall reduce [restore], and bring gladness." And these most comfortable words doth the Lord not speak to carnal Israel only, but to all men sore oppressed, abiding God's deliverance : " For a moment and a little season have I turned my face from thee, but in everlasting mercy shall I comfort thee."

The Hope to Obtain our Petitions Should Depend upon the Promises of God.—Oh ! hard are the hearts which so manifold most sweet and sure promises do not mollify, whereupon should depend the hope to obtain our petitions. The indignity or unworthiness of ourselves is not to be regarded; for albeit to the chosen who are departed, in holiness and purity of life we be far inferiors; yet in that part we are equal, in that we have the same commandment to pray, and the same promise to be heard. For His gracious majesty esteemeth not the prayer, neither granteth the petition, for any dignity or worthiness of the person that prayeth, but for His promise' sake only. And therefore, saith David, " Thou hast promised unto Thy servant, O Lord, that Thou wilt build a house for him; wherefore Thy servant hath found in his heart to pray in Thy sight. Now, even so, O Lord, Thou art God, and Thy words are true: Thou hast spoken these good things unto Thy servant. Begin, therefore, to do according to Thy promise: multiply, O Lord, the household of Thy servant." Behold, David altogether dependeth upon God's promise; as also did Jacob, who, after he had confessed himself unworthy of all the benefits received, yet durst he ask greater benefits in time to come, and that because God hath promised. In like manner, let us be encouraged to ask whatsoever the goodness of God hath freely promised. What we should ask principally, we shall hereafter declare.

Of Necessity we must have a Mediator.—The fifth observation which godly prayer requireth is the perfect knowledge of the advocate, intercessor, and mediator; for, seeing no man is of himself worthy to compear or appear in God's presence, by reason that in all men continually resteth sin, which, by itself, doth offend the majesty of God, raising also debate, strife, hatred, and division, betwixt His inviolable justice and us, for the which, unless satisfaction be made by another than by ourselves, so little hope resteth that anything from Him we can attain, that no surety may we have with Him at all. To exeme us from this horrible confusion, our most merciful Father, knowing that our frail minds should hereby have been continually dejected, hath given unto us His only beloved Son, to be unto us righteousness, wisdom, sanctification, and holiness. If in Him we faithfully believe, we are so clad that we may with boldness compear and appear before the throne of God's mercy, doubting nothing, but that whatsoever we ask through our Mediator, that same we shall obtain most assuredly. Here, is most diligently to be observed, that without our Mediator, Fore-speaker, and Peacemaker, we enter not into prayer; for the incallings of such as pray without Jesus Christ are not only vain, but also they are odious and abominable before God. Which thing to us in the Levitical priesthood most evidently was prefigured and declared: for as within the *sanctum sanctorum,* that is, the most holy place, entered no man but the high priest alone, and as all sacrifices offered by any other than by priests only, provoked the wrath of God upon the sacrifice maker; so, whoever doth intend to enter into God's presence, or to make prayers without Jesus Christ, shall find nothing but fearful judgment and horrible damnation. Wherefore it is plain that Turks and Jews, notwithstanding that they do apparently most fervently pray unto God who created heaven and earth, who guideth and ruleth the same, who defendeth the good and punisheth the evil, yet never are their prayers pleasant unto God; neither honor they His holy majesty in anything, because they acknowledge not Jesus Christ. For he who honoreth not the Son, honoreth not the Father. For as the law is a statute that we shall call upon God, and as the promise is made that He shall hear us, so are we commanded only to call through Jesus Christ, by whom alone our petitions we obtain; for in Him alone are all the promises of God confirmed and complete. Whereof, without all controversy, it is plain that such as have called, or call presently unto God by any other means than by Jesus Christ alone, do nothing regard God's will, but obstinately prevaricate, and do against His commandments; and therefore obtain they not their petitions, neither yet have entrance to His mercy; " for no man cometh to the Father," saith Jesus Christ, " but by me." He is the right way: who declineth from Him erreth, and goeth wrong. He is our leader, whom, unless we follow, we shall walk in darkness; and He alone is our captain, without whom, neither praise nor victory ever shall we obtain.

Against such as depend upon the intercession of saints, no otherwise will I contend, but shortly touch the properties of a perfect mediator. First, the words of Paul are most sure, that a mediator is not the mediator of one; that is, wheresoever is required a mediator, there are also two parties; to wit, one party offending, and the other party which is offended; which parties, by themselves may in no ways be reconciled. Secondly, the mediator who taketh upon him the reconciling of these two parties must be such a one as having trust and favor of both parties, yet in some things must differ from both, and must be clean and innocent also of the crime committed against the party offended. Let this be more plain by this subsequent declaration:

Angels may not be Mediators.—The eternal God, standing upon the one part, and all natural men descending of Adam upon the other part; the infinite justice of God is so offended with the transgression of all men, that in no wise can amity be made, except such a one be found as fully may make satisfaction for man's offences. Among the sons of men none was found able; for they were all found criminal in the fault of one; and God, infinite in justice, must abhor the society and sacrifice of sinners. And as to the angels, what might prevail their substitution for man? who, albeit they would have interposed themselves as mediators, yet they had not the infinite righteousness.

Jesus Christ, God and man, is Mediator.—Who, then, shall here be found the peacemaker? Surely the infinite goodness and mercy of God might not suffer the perpetual loss and repudiation of His creatures; and therefore His eternal wisdom provided such a mediator, having wherewith to satisfy the justice of God—differing also from the Godhead—His only Son, clad in the nature of manhood, who interposed Himself a mediator; not as man only; for the pure humanity of Christ of itself might neither make intercession nor satisfaction for us; but God and man. In that He is God He might complete the will of the Father; and in that He is man, pure and clean, without spot or sin, He might offer sacrifice for the purgation of our sins, and satisfaction of God's justice. For unless saints have these two, Godhead equal with the Father, and humanity without sin, the office of mediators saints may not usurp.

But here will be objected, " Who knoweth not Jesus Christ to be the only mediator of our redemption? but that impedeth or hindereth nothing saints and holy men to be mediators, and to make intercession for us." As though that Jesus Christ had been but one hour our mediator, and after, had resigned the office to His servants!

Who maketh other Mediators than Jesus Christ, taketh Honor from Him.—Do not such men gentilly [2] entreat Jesus Christ, detracting from Him such a portion of His honor? Otherwise speak the Scriptures of God, testifying Him to have been made man, and to have proved our infirmities, to have suffered death willingly, to have overcome the same, and all to this end, that He might be our perpetual high sovereign priest, into whose place or dignity none other might enter (Heb. vi., vii., ix., x.). As John saith, " If any man sin, we have an advocate with the Father, even Jesus Christ the righteous " (1 John ii.). Mark well these words John saith, " We have presently a sufficient advocate; whom Paul affirmeth to sit at the right hand of God the Father " (Rom. viii.), and to be the only mediator between God and man; for He alone, saith Ambrose, is our mouth, by whom we speak to God, He is our eyes, by whom we see God, and also our right hand, by whom we offer anything unto the Father, who, unless He make intercession, neither we, neither any of the saints, may have any society or fellowship with God. What creature may say to God the Father, " Let mankind be received into Thy favor; for the pain of his transgression, that

[2] Handsomely.

have I sustained in my own body; for his cause was I encompassed with all infirmities, and so became the most contemned and despised of all men, and yet in my mouth was found no guile nor deceit, but always obedient to Thy will, suffering most grievous death for mankind. And therefore, behold not the sinner, but me, who, by my infinite righteousness, have perfectly satisfied for his offences?" May any other, Jesus Christ except, in these words make intercession for sinners? If they may not, then are they neither mediators, nor yet intercessors. "For albeit," saith Augustine, "Christians do commend one another unto God in their prayers, yet make they not intercession, neither dare they usurp the office of a mediator; no, not Paul, albeit under the Head he was a principal member, because he commendeth himself to the prayers of faithful men." But if any do object, such is not the condition of the saints departed, who now have put off mortality, and bear no longer the fragility of the flesh; although I grant this to be most true, yet are they all compelled to cast their crowns before Him who sitteth on the throne, acknowledging themselves to have been delivered from great affliction, to have been purged by the blood of the Lamb; and therefore none of them do attempt to be a mediator, seeing they neither have being nor righteousness of themselves. But in so great light of the Gospel which now is beginning (praise be to the Omnipotent!), it is not necessary upon such matter long to remain.

Some say, we will use but one mediator, Jesus Christ, to God the Father; but we must have saints, and chiefly the Virgin, the mother of Jesus Christ, to pray for us unto Him.

Against Such as would have Mediators to Jesus Christ.— Alas! whosoever is so minded, showeth himself plainly to know nothing of Jesus Christ rightly. Is He who descended from heaven, and vouchsafed to be conversant with sinners, commanding all sore vexed and sick to come unto Him (Matt. xi.), who, hanging upon the cross, prayed first for His enemies, become now so untractable that He will not hear us without a person to be a mean? O Lord! open the eyes of such, that they may clearly perceive Thy infinite kindness, gentleness, and love towards mankind.

Above all precedents is to be observed, that what we ask of God ought to be profitable to ourselves and to others, and hurtful or dangerous to no man. Secondly, we must consider whether our petitions extend to spiritual or corporal things.

Spiritual things, such as are deliverance from impiety, remission of sins, the gift of the Holy Ghost, and of life everlasting, we should desire absolutely, without any condition, by Jesus Christ, in whom alone all these are promised. And in asking hereof, we should not pray thus, " O Father! forgive our sins if Thou wilt," for His will He hath expressed, saying, " As I live, I desire not the death of a sinner, but rather that he convert, and live," which immutable and solemn oath who calleth in doubt, maketh God a liar, and, as far as in him lieth, would spoil God of His Godhead. For He cannot be God except He be eternal and infallible verity. And John saith, " This is the testimony which God hath testified of His Son, that who believeth in the Son hath eternal life " (1 John v.), to the verity whereof we should steadfastly cleave, although worldly dolor apprehend us; as David, exiled from his kingdom, and deprived of all his glory, secluded not himself from God, but steadfastly believed reconciliation by the promise made, notwithstanding that all creatures on earth had refused, rejected, and rebelled against Him. Happy is the man whom Thou shalt inspire, O Lord!

In asking corporal things, first let us inquire if we be at peace with God in our consciences, by Jesus Christ, firmly believing our sins to be remitted in His blood. Secondly, let us inquire of our own hearts if we know temporal riches or substance not to come to man by accident, fortune, or chance, neither yet by the industry and diligence of man's labor, but to be the liberal gift of God only, whereof we ought to laud and praise His goodness, wisdom, and providence alone.

What Should be Prayed for.—And if this we do truly acknowledge and confess, let us boldly ask of Him whatsoever is necessary for us; as sustentation of the body, health thereof, defence from misery, deliverance from trouble, tranquillity and peace to our commonwealth, prosperous success in our vocations, labors, and affairs, whatsoever they be; which God willeth we ask all of Him, to certify us that all things stand in His government and disposal, and also, by asking and receiving these corporal commodities, we may have taste of His sweetness, and be inflamed with His love, that thereby our faith of reconciliation and remission of our sins may be exercised and take increase.

But, in asking such temporal things, we must observe, first, that if God deferreth or prolongeth to grant our petitions, even so long that He doth apparently reject us, yet let us not cease to call, prescribing Him neither time, neither manner of deliverance, as it is written, " If He prolong time, abide patiently upon Him," and also, " Let not the faithful be too hasty; for God sometimes deferreth, and will not hastily grant, for the probation of our continuance," as the words of Jesus Christ testify; and also that we may receive with greater gladness that which with ardent desire we long have looked for, as Hannah, Sarah, and Elizabeth, after great ignominy of their barrenness and sterility, received fruit of their bosoms with joy.

Secondly, because we know the kirk at all times to be under the cross. In asking temporal commodities, and especially deliverance from trouble, let us offer to God obedience; if it shall please His goodness we be longer exercised, that we may patiently abide it. As David, desirous to be restored to his kingdom, what time he was exiled by his own son, offereth unto God obedience, saying, " If I have found favor in the presence of the Lord, He shall bring me home again. But if He shall say, Thou pleasest me no longer to bear authority, I am obedient; let Him do what seemeth good to Him " (2 Sam. xv.). And the three children unto Nebuchadnezzar did say, " We know that our God whom we worship may deliver us; but if it shall not please Him so to do, let it be known to thee, O king, that thy gods we will not worship " (Dan. iii.).

Better it is to obey God than Man.—Here they [children] gave a true confession of their perfect faith, knowing nothing to be impossible to the omnipotence of God; affirming also themselves to stand in His mercy, for otherwise the nature of man could not willingly give itself to so horrible a torment. But they offer unto God most humble obedience, to be delivered at His good pleasure and will, as we should do in all afflictions; for we know not what to ask or desire as we ought—that is, the frail flesh, oppressed with fear and pain, desireth deliverance, ever abhorring and drawing back from obedience-giving. (O Christian brother, I write by experience!) But the Spirit of God calleth back the mind to obedience, that albeit it desires and abides

for deliverance, yet should it not repine against the good of
God, but incessantly to ask that it may abide with patience.
How hard this battle is no man knoweth but he who in himself
hath suffered trial.

The Petition of the Spirit.—It is to be noted that God sometimes doth grant the petition of the spirit, while He yet deferreth the desire of the flesh. As who doubteth but God did mitigate the heaviness of Joseph, although He sent not hasty
deliverance in his long imprisonment; and that as He gave
him favor in the sight of his jailer, so inwardly also He gave
him consolation in spirit? (Gen. xxxix.) And moreover, God
sometimes granteth the petition of the spirit, while He utterly
repelleth the desire of the flesh. For the petition of the spirit
always is that we may attain to the true felicity, whereunto we
must needs enter by tribulation, and the final death, both of
which the nature of man doth ever abhor. And therefore the
flesh under the cross, and at the sight of death, calleth and
thirsteth for hasty deliverance.

The Flesh striveth against the Spirit.—But God, who alone
knoweth what is expedient for us, sometimes prolongeth the
deliverance of His chosen, and sometimes permitteth them to
drink, before the maturity of age, the bitter cup of corporal
death, that thereby they may receive medicine and cure from all
infirmity. For who doubteth but that John the Baptist desired
to have seen more the days of Jesus Christ, and to have been
longer with Him in conversation? or that Stephen would not
have labored more days in preaching Christ's Gospel, whom,
nevertheless, He suffered hastily to taste of this general sentence? And albeit we see therefore no apparent help to ourselves, not yet to others afflicted, let us not cease to call, thinking
our prayers to be vain; for whatsoever come of our bodies, God
shall give unspeakable comfort to the spirit, and turn all to our
commodities [advantages], beyond our own expectation. The
cause I am so long tedious in this matter is that I know how
hard the battle is between the spirit and the flesh, under the
heavy cross of affliction, where no worldly defence but present
death does appear.

Impediments come of the Weakness of the Flesh.—I know the
grudging and murmuring complaints of the flesh; I know the
anger, wrath, and indignation which it conceiveth against God,

calling all His promises in doubt, and being ready every hour
utterly to fall from God. Against which remains only faith, pro-
voking us to call earnestly, and pray for assistance of God's
Spirit, wherein, if we continue, our most desperate calamities
He shall turn to gladness, and to a prosperous end.

To Thee, O Lord, alone be praise! for with experience I write
this and speak.   .

Where, and for whom, and at what time, we ought to pray, is
not to be passed over with silence.

Private prayer, such as men secretly offer unto God by themselves, requires no special place, although Jesus Christ commandeth, when we pray, to enter into our chamber, and to close
the door, and so to pray secretly unto our Father (Matt. vi.).
Whereby He wills that we should choose for our prayers such
places as might offer least occasion to call us back from prayer,
and also that we should expel forth of our minds in time of our
prayer all vain cogitations; for otherwise, Jesus Christ himself
doth observe no special place of prayer, for we find Him sometimes praying in Mount Olivet, sometimes in the desert, sometimes in the temple, and in the garden. Peter desireth to pray
upon the top of the house (Acts x.). Paul prayed in prison,
and was heard of God, who also commandeth men to pray in all
places, lifting up unto God pure and clean hands, as we find
that the prophets and most holy men did, wheresoever danger or
necessity required.

Appointed Places to Pray in may not be Neglected.—But public and common prayers should be used in the place appointed
for the assembly of the congregation, whence whosoever negligently withdraweth himself is in nowise excusable. I mean
not that to be absent from that place is sin, because that place
is more holy than another; for the whole earth created by God
is equally holy. But the promise made, that " wheresoever two
or three are gathered together in my name, there shall I be in the
midst of them," condemneth all such as despise the congregation gathered in His name. But mark well this word " gathered." I mean not to hear piping, singing, or playing; nor to
patter upon beads or books whereof they have no understanding; nor to commit idolatry, honoring that for God which indeed is no god; for with such will I neither join myself in
common prayer, nor in receiving external sacraments. For in

so doing, I should affirm their superstition and abominable idolatry, which I, by God's grace, never will do, neither counsel others to do, to the end.

What it is to be Gathered in the Name of Christ.—This congregation which I mean should be gathered in the name of Jesus Christ; that is, to laud and magnify God the Father, for the infinite benefits they have received by His only Son, our Lord. In this congregation should be distributed the mystical and last supper of Jesus Christ, without superstition or any more ceremonies than He himself used, and His apostles after Him, in distribution thereof. In this congregation should inquisition be made of the poor among them, and support provided till the time of their next convention; and it should be distributed amongst them. Also in this congregation should be made common prayers, such as all men hearing might understand, that the hearts of all subscribing to the voice of one might with unfeigned and fervent mind say, Amen. Whosoever withdraw themselves from such a congregation (but alas! where shall it be found?) do declare themselves to be no members of Christ's body.

For Whom and at What Time we should Pray.—Now there remaineth for whom and at what time we shall pray. For all men, and at all times, doth Paul command that we shall pray (1 Tim. ii.), and principally for such as are of the household of faith as suffer persecution; and for commonwealths tyrannously oppressed, incessantly should we call, that God of His mercy and power will withstand the violence of such tyrants.

God's Sentence may be Changed.—And when we see the plagues of God, as hunger, pestilence, or war, coming or appearing to reign, then should we with lamentable voices and repenting hearts call unto God, that it would please His infinite mercy to withdraw His hand. Which thing, if we do unfeignedly, He will without doubt revoke His wrath, and, in the midst of His fury, think upon mercy, as we are taught in the Scripture, by His infallible and eternal verity. As in Exodus God saith, " I shall destroy this nation from the face of the earth." And when Moses addresseth himself to pray for them the Lord proceedeth, saying, " Suffer me that I may utterly destroy them." And then Moses falleth down upon his face, and forty days continueth in prayer for the safety of the people, for whom, at the last, he obtained forgiveness. David, in the vehement plague, lamentably called unto God (2 Sam. xxiv.) ; and the King of Nineveh saith, " Who can tell? God may turn and repent, and cease from His fierce wrath, that we perish not " (Jonah iii.). Which examples and scriptures are not written in vain, but to certify us that God of His own native goodness will mitigate His plagues, by our prayers offered by Jesus Christ, although He hath threatened to punish, or is presently punishing : which He testifies by His own words, saying, " If I have prophesied against any nation or people, that they shall be destroyed, if they repent of their iniquity, it shall repent me of the evil which I have spoken against them " (Jer. xviii.). This I write, lamenting the great coldness of men who, under such long scourges of God, are nothing kindled to prayer by repentance, but carelessly sleep in a wicked life, even as though their continuing wars, urgent famine, daily plagues of pestilence, and other contagious, insolent, and strange maladies, were not the present signs of God's wrath provoked by our iniquities.

A Plague threatened to England.—O England, let thy intestine battle and domestic murder provoke thee to purity of life, according to the word which openly hath been proclaimed in thee, otherwise, the cup of the Lord's wrath thou shalt drink. The multitude shall not escape, but shall drink the dregs, and have the cup broken upon their heads; for judgment beginneth in the house of the Lord, and commonly the least offender is first punished, to provoke the more wicked to repentance. But, O Lord, infinite in mercy, if Thou shalt punish, make not consummation; but cut away the proud and luxuriant branches which bear not fruit, and preserve the commonwealths of such as give succor and harbor to Thy contemned messengers, who long have suffered exile in the desert. And let Thy kingdom shortly come, that sin may be ended, death devoured, Thy enemies confounded; that we Thy people, by Thy majesty delivered, may obtain everlasting joy and felicity through Jesus Christ our Savour, to whom be all honor and praise forever. Amen. Hasten, Lord, and tarry not.

Hereafter followeth a confession by John Knox, Minister of Christ's most sacred Evangel, upon the death of that most virtuous and most famous king, Edward VI, King of England, France, and Ireland; in which confession, the said John doth accuse no less his own offences, than the offences of others, to be the cause of the away-taking of that most godly prince, now reigning with Christ, while we abide plagues for our unthankfulness.

Omnipotent and everlasting God, Father of our Lord Jesus Christ, who by Thy eternal providence disposest kingdoms as seemeth best to Thy wisdom: we acknowledge and confess Thy judgments to be righteous, in that Thou hast taken from us, for our ingratitude, and for abusing Thy most holy Word, our native king and earthly comforter. Justly mayest Thou pour forth upon us the uttermost of Thy plagues, for that we have not known the day and time of our merciful visitation. We have contemned Thy Word, and despised Thy mercies: we have transgressed Thy laws, for deceitfully have we wrought every man with our neighbor; oppression and violence we have not abhorred, charity hath not appeared among us, as our profession requireth. We have little regarded the voices of Thy prophets; Thy threatenings we have esteemed vanity and wind. So that in us, as of ourselves, rests nothing worthy of Thy mercies, for all are found fruitless, even the princes with the prophets as withered trees, apt and meet to be burned in the fire of Thy eternal displeasure.

But, O Lord, behold Thy own mercy and kindness, that Thou mayest purge and remove the most filthy burden of our most horrible offences. Let Thy love overcome the severity of Thy judgments, even as it did in giving to the world Thy only Son, Jesus, when all mankind was lost, and no obedience was left in Adam nor in his seed. Regenerate our hearts, O Lord, by the strength of the Holy Ghost: convert Thou us, and we shall be converted: work Thou in us unfeigned repentance, and move Thou our hearts to obey Thy holy laws.

Behold our troubles and apparent destruction, and stay the sword of Thy vengeance before it devour us. Place above us, O Lord, for Thy great mercies' sake, such a head, with such rulers and magistrates as fear Thy name, and will the glory of Christ Jesus to spread. Take not from us the light of Thy Evangel, and suffer no papistry to prevail in this realm. Illuminate the heart of our sovereign lady, Queen Mary, with pregnant gifts of Thy Holy Ghost, and inflame the hearts of her council with Thy true fear and love. Repress Thou the pride of those that would rebel, and remove from all hearts the contempt of Thy Word. Let not our enemies rejoice at our destruction, but look Thou to the honor of Thy own name, O Lord, and let Thy Gospel be preached with boldness in this realm. If Thy justice must punish, then punish our bodies with the rod of Thy mercy. But, O Lord, let us never revolt, nor turn back to idolatry again. Mitigate the hearts of those that persecute us, and let us not faint under the cross of our Saviour; but assist us with the Holy Ghost, even to the end.

VOL. I.—4

SPEECH WHEN IMPEACHED FOR HIGH TREASON

—

BY

THE EARL OF STRAFFORD

(Thomas Wentworth)

THOMAS WENTWORTH, EARL OF STRAFFORD

1593—1641

This man had a romantic and picturesque history; and, as a representative of the royalists of the Stuart epoch, who honestly believed in the divine right of kings, and in the necessity to political prosperity of the dominance of the nobility over the common people, he has received the sympathy of posterity; though it is not likely that he would have survived in men's memories had it not been for the tragedy that attended his end.

Thomas Wentworth was born in London on April 13, 1593, and he entered Parliament at the age of one and twenty, in 1614. He was handsome in person and courtly and winning in manner; and his intellectual ability was far beyond the average. At the outset of his career his generous nature prompted him to array himself against the policy of James; and, during the first years of Charles's reign, he remained in the opposition. Charles recognized his powers, however, and determined to win his support; in 1628 he appointed him to the Council of the North, having first raised him to the peerage; made him of the privy council in 1629, and, in 1632, lord deputy of Ireland. He went to Ireland the following year, and became the chief adviser of his sovereign. The lord-lieutenancy of Ireland followed in 1640, and he was created Earl of Strafford. The war in Scotland had then broken out; and he commanded the King's forces against the Scotch.

It was at this juncture that Parliament began the course of action which terminated in his destruction. A bill of attainder was brought in against the earl, containing twenty-eight counts. These concerned his conduct towards England, Ireland, and Scotland. The main accusation was that he had aroused the hostility of the King against Parliament by leading him to believe that certain members of it " had denied to supply him; and that His Majesty having tried the affections of his people, and been refused, he was absolved from all rules of government, and that he had an army in Ireland which he might employ to reduce this kingdom." Such is the arraignment as it stands in the record of the state trials of England. A paper found by Sir Harry Vane, supporting the evidence given by his father on this charge, was not admitted as evidence by the House of Lords; upon which pretext the bill of attainder was found. The trial excited immense interest; and this was brought to a culmination by the eloquent speech in which Strafford sought to defend himself against his accusers. But the effort was vain; and his royal master was too cowardly and too politic to adopt heroic measures to save him; the earl was convicted, and he was beheaded in London on May 12, 1641. His fate was an omen of that which was to befall Charles himself eight years afterwards.

SPEECH WHEN IMPEACHED FOR HIGH TREASON

Delivered before the House of Lords, April 13, 1641

MY LORDS: This day I stand before you charged with high treason.[1] The burden of the charge is heavy, yet far the more so because it hath borrowed the authority of the House of Commons. If they were not interested, I might expect a no less easy, than I do a safe, issue. But let neither my weakness plead my innocence, nor their power my guilt. If your Lordships will conceive of my defences, as they are in themselves, without reference to either party—and I shall endeavor so to present them—I hope to go hence as clearly justified by you, as I now am in the testimony of a good conscience by myself.

My Lords, I have all along, during this charge, watched to see that poisoned arrow of treason, which some men would fain have feathered in my heart; but, in truth, it hath not been my quickness to discover any such evil yet within my breast, though now, perhaps, by sinister information, sticking to my clothes.

They tell me of a two-fold treason, one against the statute, another by the common law; this direct, that consecutive; this individual, that accumulative; this in itself, that by way of construction.

As to this charge of treason, I must and do acknowledge, that if I had the least suspicion of my own guilt I would save your Lordships the pains. I would cast the first stone. I would pass the first sentence of condemnation against myself. And whether it be so or not, I now refer to your Lordships' judgment and deliberation. You, and you only, under the care and protection

---

[1] There are in the "Parliamentary History" two reports of this speech, one by Whitlocke, and the other by some unknown friend of Strafford. As each has important passages which are not contained in the other, they are here combined by a slight modification of language, in order to give more completeness to this masterly defence.

of my gracious master, are my judges. Under favor, none of the Commons are my peers, nor can they be my judges. I shall ever celebrate the providence and wisdom of your noble ancestors, who have put the keys of life and death, so far as concerns you and your posterity, into your own hands. None but your own selves, my Lords, know the rate of your noble blood: none but yourselves must hold the balance in disposing of the same.[2]

I shall now proceed in repeating my defences as they are reducible to the two main points of treason. And,

I. For treason against the statute, which is the only treason in effect, there is nothing alleged for that but the fifteenth, twenty-second, and twenty-seventh articles.

[Here the earl brought forward the replies which he had previously made to these articles, which contained all the charges of individual acts of treason. The fifteenth article affirmed that he had " inverted the ordinary course of justice in Ireland, and given immediate sentence upon the lands and goods of the king's subjects, under pretence of disobedience; had used a military way for redressing the contempt, and laid soldiers upon the lands and goods of the King's subjects, to their utter ruin." There was a deficiency of proofs as to the facts alleged. The earl declared that " the customs of England differed exceedingly from those of Ireland; and therefore, though *cessing* of men might seem strange here, it was not so there; " and that " nothing was more common there than for the governors to appoint soldiers to put all manner of sentences into execution," as he proved by the testimony of Lord Dillon, Sir Adam Loftus, and Sir Arthur Teringham.

The twenty-seventh article charged him with having, as lieutenant-general, charged on the county of York eightpence a day for supporting the train-bands of said county during one month, when called out; and having issued his warrants without legal authority for the collection of the same. The earl replied that "this money was freely and voluntarily offered by them of Yorkshire, in a petition; and that he had done nothing but on the

[2] Strafford had no chance of acquittal except by inducing the Lords, from a regard to their dignity and safety, to rise above the influence of the Commons as his prosecutors, and of the populace who surrounded Westminster Hall by thousands, demanding his condemnation. In this view, his exordium has admirable dexterity and force. He reverts to the same topic in his peroration, assuring them, with the deepest earnestness and solemnity (and, as the event showed, with perfect truth), that if they gave him up, they must expect to perish with him in the general ruin of the peerage.

THE TRIAL OF THE EARL OF STRAFFORD.

Photogravure from the original painting by W. Fiske.

Thomas Wentworth, Earl of Strafford, a man of undoubted honor and integrity, was one of the most enthusiastic upholders of the royal prerogatives of his master, Charles I. The Commons, under Pym, brought a "Bill of Attainder for High Treason" against him. His trial took place in Westminster Hall, "the hall of William Rufus." Amid all the pomp and circumstance of judicial solemnity, this great man stood up before the eighty peers who were his judges, while Charles I. and Queen Henrietta looked on from a closed gallery, anxious spectators of the scene. The family of Strafford was grouped around him. In his defence he avowed his readiness to suffer every extremity, "were it not for those pledges which a saint in heaven left me." He was abandoned by the King to the fury of his enemies, and on May 12, 1641, was executed by the headsman on Tower Hill, furnishing one more example of loyal ministers who have perished through the selfish ingratitude of princes. The present illustration gives a lively representation of the trial, and has long been one of the most popular of historical pictures.

petition of the county, the King's special command, and the connivance, at least, of the Great Council, and upon a present necessity for the defence and safety of the county, when about to be invaded from Scotland."

The twenty-second and twenty-third articles were the most pressing. Under these he was charged with saying in the Privy Council that " the Parliament had forsaken the King; that the King ought not to suffer himself to be overmastered by the stubbornness of the people; and that, if His Majesty pleased to employ forces, he had some in Ireland that might serve to reduce this kingdom," thus counselling to His Majesty to put down Parliament, and subvert the fundamental laws of the kingdom by force and arms. To this the earl replied, (1.) That there was only one witness adduced to prove these words, viz., Sir Henry Vane, secretary of the Council, but that two or more witnesses are necessary by statute to prove a charge of treason. (2.) That the others who were present, viz., the Duke of Northumberland, the Marquis of Hamilton, Lord Cottington, and Sir Thomas Lucas, did not, as they deposed under oath, remember these words. (3.) That Sir Henry Vane had given his testimony as if he was in doubt on the subject, saying " as I do remember," and " such or such like words," which admitted the words might be " *that* kingdom," meaning Scotland.]

II. As to the other kind, viz., constructive treason, or treason by way of accumulation; to make this out, many articles have been brought against me, as if in a heap of mere felonies or misdemeanors (for they reach no higher) there could lurk some prolific seed to produce what is treasonable! But, my Lords, when a thousand misdemeanors will not make one felony, shall twenty-eight misdemeanors be heightened into treason?

I pass, however, to consider these charges, which affirm that I have designed the overthrow both of religion and of the State.

1. The first charge seemeth to be used rather to make me odious than guilty; for there is not the least proof alleged—nor could there be any—concerning my confederacy with the popish faction. Never was a servant in authority under my lord and master more hated and maligned by these men than myself, and that for an impartial and strict execution of the laws against them; for observe, my Lords, that the greater number of the witnesses against me, whether from Ireland or from Yorkshire,

were of that religion. But for my own resolution, I thank God
I am ready every hour of the day to seal my dissatisfaction to
the Church of Rome with my dearest blood.

Give me leave, my Lords, here to pour forth the grief of my
soul before you. These proceedings against me seem to be exceeding rigorous, and to have more of prejudice than equity—
that upon a supposed charge of hypocrisy or errors in religion,
I should be made so odious to three kingdoms. A great many
thousand eyes have seen my accusations, whose ears will never
hear that when it came to the upshot, those very things were not
alleged against me! Is this fair dealing among Christians?
But I have lost nothing by that. Popular applause was ever
nothing in my conceit. The uprightness and integrity of a good
conscience ever was, and ever shall be, my continual feast; and
if I can be justified in your Lordships' judgments from this
great imputation—as I hope I am, seeing these gentlemen have
thrown down the bucklers—I shall account myself justified by
the whole kingdom, because absolved by you, who are the better
part, the very soul and life of the kingdom.

2. As for my designs against the State, I dare plead as much
innocency as in the matter of religion. I have ever admired the
wisdom of our ancestors, who have so fixed the pillars of this
monarchy that each of them keeps a due proportion and measure
with the others—have so admirably bound together the nerves
and sinews of the State, that the straining of any one may bring
danger and sorrow to the whole economy. The prerogative of
the crown and the propriety of the subject have such natural
relations, that *this* takes nourishment from *that,* and *that* foundation and nourishment from *this.* And so, as in the lute, if
any one string be wound up too high or too low, you have lost
the whole harmony; so here the excess of prerogative is oppression, of pretended liberty in the subject is disorder and anarchy.
The prerogative must be used as God doth his omnipotence,
upon extraordinary occasions; the laws must have place at all
other times. As there must be prerogative because there must
be extraordinary occasions, so the propriety of the subject
is ever to be maintained, if it go in equal pace with the other.
They are fellows and companions that are, and ever must be,
inseparable in a well-ordered kingdom; and no way is so fitting, so natural to nourish and entertain both, as the frequent

use of Parliaments, by which a commerce and acquaintance is kept up between the King and his subjects.[3]

These thoughts have gone along with me these fourteen years of my public employments, and shall, God willing, go with me to the grave! God, His Majesty, and my own conscience, yea, and all of those who have been most accessory to my inward thoughts, can bear me witness that I ever did inculcate this, that the happiness of a kingdom doth consist in a just poise of the King's prerogative and the subject's liberty, and that things could never go well till these went hand in hand together. I thank God for it, by my master's favor, and the providence of my ancestors, I have an estate which so interests me in the commonwealth, that I have no great mind to be a slave, but a subject. Nor could I wish the cards to be shuffled over again, in hopes to fall upon a better set; nor did I ever nourish such base and mercenary thoughts as to become a pander to the tyranny and ambition of the greatest man living. No! I have, and ever shall, aim at a fair but bounded liberty; remembering always that I am a freeman, yet a subject—that I have rights, but under a monarch. It hath been my misfortune, now when I am gray-headed, to be charged by the mistakers of the times, who are so highly bent that all appears to them to be in the extreme for monarchy which is not for themselves. Hence it is that designs, words, yea, intentions, are brought out as demonstrations of my misdemeanors. Such a multiplying-glass is a prejudicate opinion!

The articles against me refer to expressions and actions—my expressions either in Ireland or in England, my actions either before or after these late stirs.

(1.) Some of the expressions referred to were uttered in private, and I do protest against their being drawn to my injury in this place. If, my Lords, words spoken to friends in familiar discourse, spoken at one's table, spoken in one's chamber, spoken in one's sick-bed, spoken, perhaps, to gain better reason, to gain one's self more clear light and judgment by reasoning—if these things shall be brought against a man as treason, this (under favor) takes away the comfort of all human society. By this

[3] Strafford was generally regarded as the secret author of the King's aversion to Parliaments, which had led him to dispense with their use for many years. Hence the above declaration, designed to relieve him from the effects of this prejudice.

means we shall be debarred from speaking—the principal joy
and comfort of life—with wise and good men, to become wiser
and better ourselves. If these things be strained to take away
life, and honor, and all that is desirable, this will be a silent
world! A city will become a hermitage, and sheep will be found
among a crowd and press of people! No man will dare to im-
part his solitary thoughts or opinions to his friend and neighbor!

Other expressions have been urged against me, which were
used in giving counsel to the King. My Lords, these words were
not wantonly or unnecessarily spoken, or whispered in a corner;
they were spoken in full council, when, by the duty of my oath,
I was obliged to speak according to my heart and conscience in
all things concerning the King's service. If I had forborne to
speak what I conceived to be for the benefit of the King and the
people, I had been perjured towards Almighty God. And for
delivering my mind openly and freely, shall I be in danger of
my life as a traitor? If that necessity be put upon me, I thank
God, by his blessing, I have learned not to stand in fear of him
who can only kill the body. If the question be whether I must
be traitor to man or perjured to God, I will be faithful to my
Creator. And whatsoever shall befall me from popular rage
or my own weakness, I must leave it to that almighty Being,
and to the justice and honor of my judges.

My Lords, I conjure you not to make yourselves so unhappy
as to disable your Lordships and your children from undertaking the great charge and trust of this commonwealth. You inherit that trust from your fathers. You are born to great
thoughts. You are nursed for the weighty employments of the
kingdom. But if it be once admitted that a counsellor, for delivering his opinion with others at the council board, *candide
et caste,* with candor and purity of motive, under an oath of
secrecy and faithfulness, shall be brought into question, upon
some misapprehension or ignorance of law—if every word that
he shall speak from sincere and noble intentions shall be drawn
against him for the attainting of him, his children and posterity
—I know not (under favor I speak it) any wise or noble person
of fortune who will, upon such perilous and unsafe terms, adventure to be counsellor to the King. Therefore I beseech your
Lordships so to look on me, that my misfortune may not bring
an inconvenience to yourselves. And though my words were

not so advised and discreet, or so well weighed as they ought to have been, yet I trust your Lordships are too honorable and just to lay them to my charge as high treason. Opinions may make a heretic, but that they make a traitor I have never heard till now.

(2.) I am come next to speak of the actions which have been charged upon me.

[Here the earl went through with the various overt acts alleged, and repeated the sum and heads of what had been spoken by him before. In respect to the twenty-eighth article, which charged him with " a malicious design to engage the kingdoms of England and Scotland in a national and bloody war," but which the managers had not urged in the trial, he added more at large, as follows :]

If that one article had been proved against me, it contained more weighty matter than all the charges besides. It would not only have been treason, but villainy, to have betrayed the trust of His Majesty's army. But as the managers have been sparing, by reason of the times, as to insisting on that article, I have resolved to keep the same method, and not utter the least expression which might disturb the happy agreement intended between the two kingdoms. I only admire how I, being an incendiary against the Scots in the twenty-third article, am become a confederate with them in the twenty-eighth article! how I could be charged for betraying Newcastle, and also for fighting with the Scots at Newburne, since fighting against them was no possible means of betraying the town into their hands, but rather to hinder their passage thither! I never advised war any further than, in my poor judgment, it concerned the very life of the King's authority, and the safety and honor of his kingdom. Nor did I ever see that any advantage could be made by a war in Scotland, where nothing could be gained but hard blows. For my part, I honor that nation, but I wish they may ever be under their own climate. I have no desire that they should be too well acquainted with the better soil of England.

My lords, you see what has been alleged for this constructive, or, rather, destructive treason. For my part, I have not the judgment to conceive that such treason is agreeable to the fundamental grounds either of reason or of law. Not of reason, for how can that be treason in the lump or mass, which is not so in any of its parts? or how can that make a thing treasonable which is not so in itself? Not of law, since neither statute, common law, nor practice hath from the beginning of the government ever mentioned such a thing.

It is hard, my lords, to be questioned upon a law which cannot be shown! Where hath this fire lain hid for so many hundred years, without smoke to discover it, till it thus bursts forth to consume me and my children? My lords, do we not live under laws? and must we be punished by laws before they are made? Far better were it to live by no laws at all; but to be governed by those characters of virtue and discretion, which nature hath stamped upon us, than to put this necessity of divination upon a man, and to accuse him of a breach of law before it is a law at all! If a waterman upon the Thames split his boat by grating upon an anchor, and the same have no buoy appended to it, the owner of the anchor is to pay the loss; but if a buoy be set there, every man passeth upon his own peril. Now where is the mark, where is the token set upon the crime, to declare it to be high treason?

My lords, be pleased to give that regard to the peerage of England as never to expose yourselves to such moot points, such constructive interpretations of law. If there must be a trial of wits, let the subject matter be something else than the lives and honor of peers! It will be wisdom for yourselves and your posterity to cast into the fire these bloody and mysterious volumes of constructive and arbitrary treason, as the primitive Christians did their books of curious arts; and betake yourselves to the plain letter of the law and statute, which telleth what is and what is not treason, without being ambitious to be more learned in the art of killing than our forefathers. These gentlemen tell us that they speak in defence of the Commonwealth against my arbitrary laws. Give me leave to say it, I speak in defence of the Commonwealth against their arbitrary treason!

It is now full two hundred and forty years since any man was touched for this alleged crime to this height before myself. Let us not awaken those sleeping lions to our destruction, by taking up a few musty records that have lain by the walls for so many ages, forgotten or neglected.

My lords, what is my present misfortune may be forever yours! It is not the smallest part of my grief that not the crime of treason, but my other sins, which are exceeding many, have brought me to this bar; and, except your lordships' wisdom provide against it, the shedding of my blood may make way for the tracing out of yours. *You, your estates, your posterity, lie at the stake!*

For my poor self, if it were not for your lordships' interest, and the interest of a saint in heaven, who hath left me here two pledges on earth—[at this his breath stopped, and he shed tears abundantly in mentioning his wife]—I should never take the pains to keep up this ruinous cottage of mine. It is loaded with such infirmities, that in truth I have no great pleasure to carry it about with me any longer. Nor could I ever leave it at a fitter time than this, when I hope that the better part of the world would perhaps think that by my misfortunes I had given a testimony of my integrity to my God, my king, and my country. I thank God, I count not the afflictions of the present life to be compared to that glory which is to be revealed in the time to come!

My lords! my lords! my lords! something more I had intended to say, but my voice and my spirit fail me. Only I do in all humility and submission cast myself down at your lordships' feet, and desire that I may be a beacon to keep you from shipwreck. Do not put such rocks in your own way, which no prudence, no circumspection can eschew or satisfy, but by your utter ruin!

And so, my lords, even so, with all tranquillity of mind, I submit myself to your decision. And whether your judgment in my case—I wish it were not the case of you all—be for life or for death, it shall be righteous in my eyes, and shall be received with a *Te Deum laudamus,* we give God the praise.

SPEECH ON THE DISSOLUTION OF PARLIAMENT

—

BY

OLIVER CROMWELL

OLIVER CROMWELL

1599—1658

Oliver Cromwell was born at Huntingdon on April 25, 1599. He was the grandson of Sir Henry Cromwell, and the son of Robert Cromwell, a man of good property, and a brewer at Huntingdon. Having been educated at the free-school of that city, and at Sidney Sussex College, Cambridge, he became a law student at Lincoln's Inn. Here, however, he did not remain long; as in his twenty-first year he married Elizabeth Bourchier, the daughter of Sir James Bourchier, and settled at Huntingdon.

He was elected member of Parliament for Huntingdon in 1628. His first appearance in Parliament was in February, 1629. In 1640 he represented Cambridge. In his parliamentary career he was remarkable rather for his business-like habits and energy of character, than for elegance of language or gracefulness of delivery. His appearance and dress, too, were plain and unprepossessing. Nevertheless he acquired considerable influence even in Parliament; and in 1642, when it was resolved to levy forces to oppose the king, Cromwell received a commission from the Earl of Essex, and raised a troop of horse at Cambridge, of which he, of course, had the command. He soon distinguished himself by his courage and military skill, especially at the battle of Marston Moor, in 1644; he was excepted from the self-denying ordinance, and soon afterwards won the decisive victory of Naseby. In 1648 he defeated the Scots at Preston, and then invaded Scotland and took Berwick. He was a member of the High Court of Justice for the trial of Charles I, and signed the warrant for his execution. In August 1649, he was named lord-lieutenant and commander-in-chief in Ireland. The great towns submitted without resistance, and Ireland was subdued.

In consequence of the expected return of Prince Charles to Scotland, Cromwell was recalled, leaving Ireton as deputy. He was appointed lord-general, and set out for Scotland. On September 3, 1650, the great battle of Dunbar was fought, and the Scots were totally defeated. Edinburgh surrendered, and Perth was taken some months later. Charles having marched into England, Cromwell followed him, and on September 3, 1651, won the decisive battle of Worcester. In 1663, while the Dutch war was going on, he dissolved the Long Parliament, formed a council of state, and had a new parliament called, which soon resigned its power to Cromwell, and by the "Instrument of Government" he was created "Lord Protector."

He showed himself equal to the hard task he had undertaken, by sharp decisive means keeping down plotting royalists, jealous Presbyterians, and intractable Levellers; and by a magnanimous foreign policy making England greater and more honored than ever. He died on September 3, 1658, the anniversary of his two victories of Dunbar and Worcester.

His "Speech on the Dissolution of Parliament," delivered on January 22, 1655, is a striking specimen of Cromwellian fervor and eloquence, combined with Cromwellian determination to carry things with a high hand.

SPEECH

ON THE DISSOLUTION OF PARLIAMENT

Delivered January 22, 1655

GENTLEMEN: I perceive you are here as the House of Parliament, by your Speaker whom I see here, and by your faces which are in a great measure known to me.

When I first met you in this room it was to my apprehension the hopefulest day that ever mine eyes saw, as to the considerations of this world. For I did look at, as wrapped up in you together with myself, the hopes and the happiness of—though not of the greatest—yet a very great " people "; and the best people in the world. And truly and unfeignedly I thought it so: as a people that have the highest and clearest profession amongst them of the greatest glory, namely, religion: as a people that have been, like other nations, sometimes up and sometimes down in our honor in the world, but yet never so low but we might measure with other nations:—and a people that have had a stamp upon them from God; God having, as it were, summed up all our former honor and glory in the things that are of glory to nations, in an epitome, within these ten or twelve years last past! So that we knew one another at home, and are well known abroad.

And if I be not very much mistaken, we were arrived—as I, and truly I believe as many others, did think—at a very safe port; where we might sit down and contemplate the dispensations of God and our mercies; and might know our mercies not to have been like to those of the ancients—who did make out their peace and prosperity, as they thought, by their own endeavors; who could not say, as we, that all ours were let down to us from God Himself! Whose appearances and providences amongst us are not to be outmatched by any story. Truly this was our condition. And I know nothing else we had to do, save as Israel was commanded in that most excellent Psalm of David: " The things which we have heard and known, and our fathers have told us, we will not hide them from our children; showing to the generation to come the praises of the Lord, and His strength, and His wonderful works that He hath done. For He established a testimony in Jacob, and appointed a law in Israel; which He commanded our fathers that they should make known to their children; that the generation to come might know them, even the children which should be born, who should arise and declare them to their children: that they might set their hope in God, and not forget the works of God, but keep His commandments." [1]

This I thought had been a song and a work worthy of England, whereunto you might happily have invited them—had you had hearts unto it. You had this opportunity fairly delivered unto you. And if a history shall be written of these times and transactions, it will be said, it will not be denied, that these things that I have spoken are true! This talent was put into your hands. And I shall recur to that which I said at the first: I came with very great joy and contentment and comfort, the first time I met you in this place. But we and these nations are, for the present, under some disappointment!—If I had proposed to have played the orator—which I never did affect, nor do, nor I hope shall—I doubt not but upon easy suppositions, which I am persuaded every one among you will grant, we did meet upon such hopes as these.

I met you a second time here: and I confess, at that meeting I had much abatement of my hopes, though not a total frustration. I confess that that which damped my hopes so soon was somewhat that did look like a parricide. It is obvious enough unto you that the then management of affairs did savor of a not owning—too-too much savor, I say, of a not owning of the authority that called you hither. But God left us not without an expedient that gave a second possibility—shall I say possibility? It seemed to me a probability—of recovering out of that dissatisfied condition we were all then in, towards some mutuality of satisfaction. And therefore by that recognition, suiting with the indenture that returned you hither; to which afterwards was also added your own declaration,[2] conformable

[1] Psalm lxxviii. 3–7. [2] " Commons Journals " (vii. 368), September 14, 1654.

to, and in acceptance of, that expedient:—thereby, I say, you had, though with a little check, another opportunity renewed unto you to have made this nation as happy as it could have been if everything had smoothly run on from that first hour of your meeting. And indeed—you will give me liberty of my thoughts and hopes—I did think, as I have formerly found in that way that I have been engaged in as a soldier, that some affronts put upon us, some disasters at the first, have made way for very great and happy successes; and I did not at all despond but the stop put upon you, in like manner, would have made way for a blessing from God. That interruption being, as I thought, necessary to divert you from violent and destructive proceedings; to give time for better deliberations;—whereby leaving the government as you found it, you might have proceeded to have made those good and wholesome laws which the people expected from you, and might have answered the grievances, and settled those other things proper to you as a Parliament: for which you would have had thanks from all that entrusted you.

What hath happened since that time I have not taken public notice of; as declining to intrench on Parliament privileges. For sure I am you will all bear me witness, that from your entering into the House upon the recognition, to this very day, you have had no manner of interruption or hinderance of mine in proceeding to what blessed issue the heart of a good man could propose to himself—to this very day none. You see you have me very much locked up, as to what you have transacted among yourselves, from that time to this. But some things I shall take liberty to speak of to you.

As I may not take notice what you have been doing; so I think I have a very great liberty to tell you that I do not know what you have been doing! I do not know whether you have been alive or dead. I have not once heard from you all this time; I have not: and that you all know. If that be a fault that I have not, surely it hath not been mine!—If I have had any melancholy thoughts, and have sat down by them—why might it not have been very lawful for me to think that I was a person judged unconcerned in all these businesses? I can assure you I have not so reckoned myself! Nor did I reckon myself unconcerned in you. And so long as any just patience

could support my expectation, I would have waited to the uttermost to have received from you the issue of your consultations
and resolutions. I have been careful of your safety, and the
safety of those that you represented, to whom I reckon myself
a servant.

But what messages have I disturbed you withal? What injury or indignity hath been done, or offered, either to your
persons or to any privileges of Parliament, since you sat? I
looked at myself as strictly obliged by my oath, since your
recognizing the government in the authority of which you were
called hither and sat, to give you all possible security, and to
keep you from any unparliamentary interruption. Think you
I could not say more upon this subject, if I listed to expatiate
thereupon? But because my actions plead for me, I shall say
no more of this. I say, I have been caring for you, for your
quiet sitting; caring for your privileges, as I said before, that
they might not be interrupted; have been seeking of God, from
the great God a blessing upon you, and a blessing upon these
nations. I have been consulting if possibly I might, in anything, promote, in my place, the real good of this Parliament,
of the hopefulness of which I have said so much unto you.
And I did think it to be my business rather to see the utmost
issue, and what God would produce by you, than unseasonably
to intermeddle with you.

But, as I said before, I have been caring for you, and for
the peace and quiet of these nations: indeed I have; and that
I shall a little presently manifest unto you. And it leadeth
me to let you know somewhat—which, I fear, I fear, will be,
through some interpretation, a little too justly put upon you;
whilst you have been employed as you have been, and—in all
that time expressed in the government, in that government, I
say in that government—have brought forth nothing that you
yourselves say can be taken notice of without infringement of
your privileges.[3] I will tell you somewhat, which, if it be not
news to you, I wish you had taken very serious consideration

[3]An embarrassed sentence; characteristic
of His Highness. "You have done nothing noticeable upon this 'Somewhat' that
I am about to speak of—nor, indeed, it
seems upon *any* Somewhat,—and *this* was
one you may, without much 'interpretation,' be blamed for doing nothing upon."
"Government" means *instrument of government :* "the time expressed" therein
is *five months*—now, by my way of calcu-
lating it, expired! Which may account
for the embarrassed iteration of the phrase,
on His Highness's part.—[*Carlyle's note.*]

of. If it be news, I wish I had acquainted you with it sooner.
And yet if any man will ask me why I did it not, the reason is
given already: Because I did make it my business to give you
no interruption.

There be some trees that will not grow under the shadow of
other trees: There be some that choose—a man may say so by
way of allusion—to thrive under the shadow of other trees. I
will tell you what hath thriven—I will not say what you have
cherished, under your shadow; that were too hard. Instead
of peace and settlement—instead of mercy and truth being
brought together, and righteousness and peace kissing each
other, by your reconciling the honest people of these nations,
and settling the woful distempers that are amongst us; which
had been glorious things and worthy of Christians to have proposed—weeds and nettles, briers and thorns have thriven under
your shadow! Dissettlement and division, discontent and dissatisfaction; together with real dangers to the whole—have
been more multiplied within these five months of your sitting,
than in some years before! Foundations have also been laid
for the future renewing of the troubles of these nations by all
the enemies of them abroad and at home. Let not these words
seem too sharp: for they are true as any mathematical demonstrations are or can be. I say, the enemies of the peace of these
nations abroad and at home, the discontented humors throughout these nations—which products I think no man will grudge
to call by that name, of briers and thorns—they have nourished
themselves under your shadow!

And that I may clearly be understood: They have taken their
opportunities from your sitting, and from the hopes they had,
which with easy conjecture they might take up and conclude
that there would be no settlement; and they have framed their
designs, preparing for the execution of them accordingly. Now
whether—which appertains not to me to judge of, on their behalf—they had any occasion ministered for this, and from
whence they had it, I list not to make any scrutiny or search.
But I will say this: I think they had it not from me. I am sure
they had not from me. From whence they had, is not my
business now to discourse: but that they had is obvious to every
man's sense. What preparations they have made, to be executed
in such a season as they thought fit to take their opportunity

from: that I know, not as men know things by conjecture, but by certain demonstrable knowledge. That they have been for some time past furnishing themselves with arms; nothing doubting but they should have a day for it; and verily believing that, whatsoever their former disappointments were, they should have more done for them by and from our own divisions, than they were able to do for themselves. I desire to be understood that, in all I have to say of this subject, you will take it that I have no reservation in my mind—as I have not—to mingle things of guess and suspicion with things of fact: but "that" the things I am telling of are fact; things of evident demonstration.

These weeds, briers and thorns—they have been preparing, and have brought their designs to some maturity, by the advantages given to them, as aforesaid, from your sittings and proceedings. But by the waking eye that watched over that cause that God will bless, they have been, and yet are, disappointed. And having mentioned that cause, I say, that slighted cause—let me speak a few words in behalf thereof; though it may seem too long a digression. Whosoever despiseth it, and will say, It is *non causa pro causa*, "a cause without a cause" —the all-searching eye before mentioned will find out that man; and will judge him, as one that regardeth not the works of God nor the operations of His hands! For which God hath threatened that He will cast men down, and not build them up. That man who, because he can dispute, will tell us he knew not when the cause began, nor where it is; but modelleth it according to his own intellect; and submits not to the appearances of God in the world; and therefore lifts up his heel against God, and mocketh at all His providences; laughing at the observations, made up not without reason and the Scriptures, and by the quickening and teaching Spirit which gives life to these other; —calling such observations "enthusiasms": such men, I say, no wonder if they "stumble and fall backwards, and be broken and snared and taken," [4] by the things of which they are so wilfully and maliciously ignorant! The Scriptures say, "The rod has a voice, and He will make Himself known by the judgments which He executeth." And do we not think He will, and does, by the providences of mercy and kindness which He hath for

[4] Isaiah xxviii. 13. A text that had made a great impression upon Cromwell.

His people and their just liberties; " whom He loves as the ap-
ple of His eye "?   Doth He not by them manifest Himself?
And is He not thereby also seen giving kingdoms for them,
" giving men for them, and people for their lives "—as it is in
Isaiah forty-third? [5]   Is not this as fair a lecture and as clear
speaking as anything our dark reason, left to the letter of the
Scriptures, can collect from them?   By this voice has God
spoken very loud on behalf of His people, by judging their enemies in the late war, and restoring them a liberty to worship,
with the freedom of their consciences, and freedom in estates
and persons when they do so.   And thus we have found the
cause of God by the works of God; which are the testimony
of God.   Upon which rock whosoever splits shall suffer shipwreck.   But it is your glory—and it is mine, if I have any in
the world concerning the interest of those that have an interest
in a better world—it is my glory that I know a cause which
yet we have not lost; but do hope we shall take a little pleasure
rather to lose our lives than lose!   But you will excuse this long
digression.

I say unto you, whilst you have been in the midst of these
transactions, that party, that Cavalier party—I could wish some
of them had thrust in here, to have heard what I say—have
been designing and preparing to put this nation in blood again,
with a witness.   But because I am confident there are none of
that sort here, therefore I shall say the less to that.   Only this
I must tell you: They have been making great preparations of
arms; and I do believe it will be made evident to you that they
have raked out many thousands of arms, even all that this city
could afford, for divers months last past.   But it will be said,
" May we not arm ourselves for the defence of our houses?
Will anybody find fault for that? "   Not for that.   But the
reason for their doing so hath been as explicit, and under as
clear proof, as the fact of doing so.   For which I hope, by the
justice of the land, some will, in the face of the nation, answer
it with their lives: and then the business will be pretty well out
of doubt.   Banks of money have been framing, for these and
other such like uses.   Letters have been issued with privy seals
to as great persons as most are in the nation, for the advance of
money—which " letters " have been discovered to us by the

[5] Isaiah xliii. 3, 4.

persons themselves. Commissions for regiments of horse and foot, and command of castles, have been likewise given from Charles Stuart, since your sitting. And what the general insolences of that party have been, the honest people have been sensible of, and can very well testify.

It has not only been thus. But as in a quinsy or pleurisy, where the humor fixeth in one part, give it scope, all " disease " will gather to that place, to the hazarding of the whole : and it is natural to do so till it destroy life in that person on whomsoever this befalls. So likewise will these diseases take accidental causes of aggravation of their distemper. And this was that which I did assert, that they have taken accidental causes for the growing and increasing of those distempers—as much as would have been in the natural body if timely remedy were not applied. And indeed things were come to that pass—in respect of which I shall give you a particular account—that no mortal physician, if the Great Physician had not stepped in, could have cured the distemper. Shall I lay this upon your account, or my own? I am sure I can lay it upon God's account: That if He had not stepped in, the disease had been mortal and destructive !

And what is all this? " What are these new diseases that have gathered to this point? " Truly I must needs still say : " A company of men like briers and thorns ; " and worse, if worse can be. Of another sort than those before mentioned to you. These also have been and yet are endeavoring to put us into blood and into confusion ; more desperate and dangerous confusion than England ever yet saw. And I must say, as when Gideon commanded his son to fall upon Zeba and Zalmunna, and slay them, they thought it more noble to die by the hand of a man than of a stripling—which shows there is some contentment in the hand by which a man falls : so it is some satisfaction if a commonwealth must perish, that it perish by men, and not by the hands of persons differing little from beasts ! That if it must needs suffer, it should rather suffer from rich men than from poor men, who, as Solomon says, " when they oppress, leave nothing behind them, but are as a sweeping rain." Now such as these also are grown up under your shadow. But it will be asked, What have they done? I hope, though they pretend " commonwealth's interest," they have had no encouragement from you; but have, as in the former case, rather taken it than that you have administered any cause unto them for so doing. " Any cause " from delays, from hopes that this Parliament would not settle, from pamphlets mentioning strange votes and resolves of yours; which I hope did abuse you! But thus you see that, whatever the grounds were, these have been the effects. And thus I have laid these things before you; and you and others will be easily able to judge how far you are concerned.

" What these men have done? " They also have labored to pervert, where they could, and as they could, the honest-meaning people of the nation. They have labored to engage some in the army:—and I doubt not that not only they, but some others also, very well known to you, have helped to this work of debauching and dividing the army. They have, they have! I would be loth to say who, where, and how? much more loth to say they were any of your own number. But I can say: Endeavors have been made to put the army into a distemper, and to feed that which is the worst humor in the army. Which, though it was not as mastering humor, yet these took advantage from delay of the settlement, and the practices before mentioned, and the stopping of the pay of the army, to run us into free-quarter, and to bring us into the inconveniences most to be feared and avoided. What if I am able to make it appear, in fact, that some amongst you have run into the city of London, to persuade to petitions and addresses to you for reversing your own votes that you have passed? Whether these practices were in favor of your liberties, or tended to beget hopes of peace and settlement from you; and whether debauching the army in England, as is before expressed, and starving it, and putting it upon free-quarter, and occasioning and necessitating the greatest part thereof in Scotland to march into England, leaving the remainder thereof to have their throats cut there; and kindling by the rest a fire in our own bosoms, were for the advantage of affairs here, let the world judge!

This I tell you also: That the correspondence held with the interest of the Cavaliers, by that party of men called Levellers, who call themselves commonwealth's-men, is in our hands. Whose declarations were framed to that purpose, and ready to be published at the time of their projected common rising;

whereof, " I say," we are possessed; and for which we have
the confession of themselves now in custody; who confess also
they built their hopes upon the assurance they had of the Parliament's not agreeing to a settlement:—whether these humors
have not nourished themselves under your boughs, is the subject
of my present discourse; and I think I shall say not amiss, if I
affirm it to be so. And I must say it again, that that which hath
been their advantage, thus to raise disturbance, hath been by
the loss of those golden opportunities which God had put into
your hands for settlement. Judge you whether these things
were thus, or not, when you first sat down. I am sure things
were not thus! There was a very great peace and sedateness
throughout these nations; and great expectations of a happy
settlement. Which I remembered to you at the beginning in my
speech; and hoped that you would have entered on your business as you found it.

There was a government already in the possession of the
people—I say a government in the possession of the people,
for many months. It hath now been exercised near fifteen
months: and if it were needful that I should tell you how it
came into their possession, and how willingly they received it;
how all law and justice were distributed from it, in every
respect, as to life, liberty and estate; how it was owned by
God, as being the dispensation of His providence after twelve
years' war; and sealed and witnessed unto by the people—I
should but repeat what I said in my last speech unto you in this
place: and therefore I forbear. When you were entered upon
this government; ravelling into it—You know I took no notice
what you were doing—If you had gone upon that foot of account, to have made such good and wholesome provisions for
the good of the people of these nations as were wanted; for the
settling of such matters in things of religion as would have
upheld and given countenance to a godly ministry, and yet as
would have given a just liberty to godly men of different judgments—" to " men of the same faith with them that you call the
orthodox ministry in England, as it is well known the Indepen-
dents are, and many under the form of baptism, who are sound
in the faith, and though they may perhaps be different in judgment in some lesser matters, yet as true Christians both looking for salvation only by faith in the blood of Christ, men pro-

fessing the fear of God, and having recourse to the name of God as to a strong tower—I say you might have had opportunity to have settled peace and quietness amongst all professing godliness; and might have been instrumental, if not to have healed the breaches, yet to have kept the godly of all judgments from running one upon another; and by keeping them from being overrun by a common enemy, " have " rendered them and these nations both secure, happy and well satisfied.

Are these things done; or any things towards them? Is there not yet upon the spirits of men a strange itch? Nothing will satisfy them unless they can press their finger upon their brethren's consciences, to pinch them there. To do this was no part of the contest we had with the common adversary. For " indeed " religion was not the thing at first contested for " at all " : [6] but God brought it to that issue at last; and gave it unto us by way of redundancy; and at last it proved to be that which was most dear to us. And wherein consisted this more than in obtaining that liberty from the tyranny of the bishops to all species of Protestants to worship God according to their own light and consciences? For want of which many of our brethren forsook their native countries to seek their bread from strangers, and to live in howling wildernesses; and for which also many that remained here were imprisoned, and otherwise abused and made the scorn of the nation. Those that were sound in the faith, how proper was it for them to labor for liberty, for a just liberty, that men might not be trampled upon for their consciences! Had not they themselves labored, but lately, under the weight of persecution? And was it fit for them to sit heavy upon others? Is it ingenuous to ask liberty, and not to give it? What greater hypocrisy than for those who were oppressed by the bishops to become the greatest oppressors themselves, so soon as their yoke was removed? I could wish that they who call for liberty now also had not too much of that spirit, if the power were in their hands!—As for profane persons, blasphemers, such as preach sedition; the contentious railers, evil-speakers, who seek by evil words to corrupt good manners; persons of loose conversation—punishment from the civil magistrate ought to meet with these. Because, if they pre-

[6] Power of the militia was the point upon which the actual war began. A statement not false; yet truer in form than it is in essence.—[*Carlyle.*]

tend conscience; yet walking disorderly and not according but contrary to the Gospel, and even to natural lights—they are judged of all. And their sins, being open, make them subjects of the magistrate's sword, who ought not to bear it in vain. The discipline of the army was such, that a man would not be suffered to remain there of whom we could take notice he was guilty of such practices as these.

And therefore how happy would England have been, and you and I, if the Lord had led you on to have settled upon such good accounts as these are, and to have discountenanced such practices as the other, and left men in disputable things free to their own consciences! Which was well provided for by the " instrument of " government; and liberty left to provide against what was apparently evil. Judge you, whether the contesting for things that were provided for by this government hath been profitable expense of time, for the good of these nations! By means whereof you may see you have wholly elapsed your time, and done just nothing!—I will say this to you, in behalf of the Long Parliament: That, had such an expedient as this government been proposed to them; and could they have seen the cause of God thus provided for; and been, by debates, enlightened in the grounds " of it," whereby the difficulties might have been cleared " to them," and the reason of the whole enforced, and the circumstances of time and persons, with the temper and disposition of the people, and affairs both abroad and at home when it was undertaken might have been well weighed " by them ": I think in my conscience— well as they were thought to love their seats—they would have proceeded in another manner than you have done! and not have exposed things to these difficulties and hazards they now are at; nor given occasion to leave the people so dissettled as they now are. Who, I dare say, in the soberest and most judicious part of them, did expect, not a question, but a doing of things in pursuance of the " instrument of " government. And if I be not misinformed, very many of you came up with this satisfaction; having had time enough to weigh and consider the same.

And when I say " such an expedient as this Government "— wherein I dare assert there is a just liberty to the people of God, and the just rights of the people in these nations provided for—I can put the issue thereof upon the clearest reason; whatsoever any go about to suggest to the contrary. But this not being the time and place of such an averment, "I forbear at present." For satisfaction's sake herein, enough is said in a book entitled "A State of the Case of the Commonwealth," published in January, 1653.[7] And for myself, I desire not to keep my place in this government an hour longer than I may preserve England in its just rights, and may protect the people of God in such a just liberty of their consciences as I have already mentioned. And therefore if this Parliament have judged things to be otherwise than as I have stated them—it had been huge friendliness between persons who had such a reciprocation in so great concernments to the public, for them to have convinced me in what particulars therein my error lay! Of which I never yet had a word from you! But if, instead thereof, your time has been spent in setting up somewhat else, upon another bottom than this stands "upon"— it looks as if the laying grounds for a quarrel had rather been designed than to give the people settlement. If it be thus, it's well your labors have not arrived to any maturity at all!

This government called you hither; the constitution thereof being limited so—a single person and a Parliament. And this was thought most agreeable to the general sense of the nation; —having had experience enough, by trial, of other conclusions; judging this most likely to avoid the extremes of monarchy on the one hand, and of democracy on the other;—and yet not to found *dominium in gratia* "either." And if so, then certainly to make the authority more than a mere notion, it was requisite that it should be as it is in this "frame of" government; which puts it upon a true and equal balance. It has been already submitted to the judicious, true and honest people of this nation, whether the balance be not equal? And what their judgment is, is visible—by submission to it; by acting upon it; by restraining their trustees from meddling with it. And it neither asks nor needs any better ratification? But when trustees in Parliament shall, by experience, find any evil in any parts of this "frame of" government, "a question" referred by the government itself to the consideration of the Protector and Parliament

---

[7] "Printed by Thomas Newcomb, London, 1653-4; "—"wrote with great spirit of language and subtilty of argument," says the "Parliamentary History" (xx. 419).

—of which evil or evils time itself will be the best discoverer:
—how can it be reasonably imagined that a person or persons,
coming in by election, and standing under such obligations, and
so limited, and so necessitated by oath to govern for the people's good, and to make their love, under God, the best under-
propping and only safe footing:—how can it, I say, be imagined
that the present or succeeding Protectors will refuse to agree
to alter any such thing in the government as may be found to be
for the good of the people? Or to recede from anything which
he might be convinced casts the balance too much to the single
person? And although, for the present, the keeping up and
having in his power the militia seems the hardest " condition,"
yet if the power of the militia should be yielded up at such a time
as this, when there is as much need of it to keep this cause (now
most evidently impugned by all enemies), as there was to get it
" for the sake of this cause ":—what would become of us all!
Or if it should not be equally placed in him and the Parliament,
but yielded up at any time—it determines his power either for
doing the good he ought, or hindering Parliaments from per-
petuating themselves; from imposing what religion they please
on the consciences of men, or what government they please upon
the nation. Thereby subjecting us to dissettlement in every
Parliament, and to the desperate consequences thereof. And
if the nation shall happen to fall into a blessed peace, how easily
and certainly will their charge be taken off, and their forces
be disbanded! And then where will the danger be to have the
militia thus stated? What if I should say: If there be a dis-
proportion, or disequality as to the power, it is on the other
hand!

And if this be so, wherein have you had cause to quarrel?
What demonstrations have you held forth to settle me to your
opinion? I would you had made me so happy as to have let me
known your grounds! I have made a free and ingenuous confession of my faith to you. And I could have wished it had
been in your hearts to have agreed that some friendly and cordial debates might have been toward mutual conviction. Was
there none amongst you to move such a thing? No fitness to
listen to it? No desire of a right understanding? If it be not
folly in me to listen to town talk, such things have been proposed; and rejected, with stiffness and severity, once and again.

Was it not likely to have been more advantageous to the good of this nation? I will say this to you for myself; and to that I have my conscience as a thousand witnesses, and I have my comfort and contentment in it; and I have the witness too of divers here, who I think truly would scorn to own me in a lie: That I would not have been averse to any alteration, of the good of which I might have been convinced. Although I could not have agreed to the taking it off the foundation on which it stands; namely, the acceptance and consent of the people.

I will not presage what you have been about, or doing, in all this time. Nor do I love to make conjectures. But I must tell you this: That as I undertook this government in the simplicity of my heart and as before God, and to do the part of an honest man, and to be true to the interest—which in my conscience " I think " is dear to many of you; though it is not always understood what God in His wisdom may hide from us, as to peace and settlement :—so I can say that no particular interest, either of myself, estate, honor, or family, are, or have been, prevalent with me to this undertaking. For if you had, upon the old government,[8] offered me this one, this one thing— I speak as thus advised, and before God; as having been to this day of this opinion; and this hath been my constant judgment, well known to many who hear me speak :—if, " I say," this one thing had been inserted, this one thing, that the government should have been placed in my family hereditary, I would have rejected it.[9] And I could have done no other according to my present conscience and light. I will tell you my reason ;— though I cannot tell what God will do with me, nor with you, nor with the nation, for throwing away precious opportunities committed to us.

This hath been my principle; and I liked it, when this government came first to be proposed to me, that it puts us off that hereditary way. Well looking that God hath declared what government He delivered to the Jews; and that He placed it upon such persons as had been instrumental for the conduct and deliverance of His people. And considering that promise in Isaiah, " That God would give rulers as at the first, and

---

[8] Means "the existing instrument of government " without modification of yours.
[9] The matter in debate, running very high at this juncture, in the Parliament, was with regard to the single person's being hereditary. Hence partly the Protector's emphasis here.

judges as at the beginning," I did not know but that God
might " now " begin—and though, at present, with a most unworthy person; yet, as to the future, it might be after this
manner; and I thought this might usher it in! I am speaking
as to my judgment against making government hereditary. To
have men chosen for their love to God, and to truth and justice;
and not to have it hereditary. For as it is in the Ecclesiastes:
" Who knoweth whether he may beget a fool or a wise man? "
Honest or not honest, whatever they be, they must come in,
on that plan; because the Government is made a patrimony!
—And this I perhaps do declare with too much earnestness; as
being my own concernment;—and know not what place it may
have in your hearts, and in those of the good people in the
nation. But however it be, I have comfort in this my truth and
plainness.

I have thus told you my thoughts; which truly I have declared to you in the fear of God, as knowing He will not be
mocked; and in the strength of God, as knowing and rejoicing
that I am supported in my speaking;—especially when I do
not form or frame things without the compass of integrity and
honesty; so that my own conscience gives me not the lie to
what I say. And then in what I say, I can rejoice.

Now to speak a word or two to you. Of that, I must profess
in the name of the same Lord, and wish there had been no
cause that I should have thus spoken to you! I told you that
I came with joy the first time; with some regret the second;
yet now I speak with most regret of all! I look upon you
as having among you many persons that I could lay down
my life individually for. I could, through the grace of God,
desire to lay down my life for you. So far am I from having an
unkind or unchristian heart towards you in your particular
capacities! I have this indeed as a work most incumbent upon
me; this of speaking these things to you. I consulted what
might be my duty in such a day as this; casting up all considerations. I must confess, as I told you, that I did think
occasionally, this nation had suffered extremely in the respects
mentioned; as also in the disappointment of their expectations
of that justice which was due to them by your sitting thus long.
" Sitting thus long; " and what have you brought forth? I
did not nor cannot comprehend what it is. I would be loath to

call it a fate; that were too paganish a word. But there hath been something in it that we had not in our expectations.

I did think also, for myself, that I am like to meet with difficulties; and that this nation will not, as it is fit it should not, be deluded with pretexts of necessity in that great business of raising of money. And were it not that I can make some dilemmas upon which to resolve some things of my conscience, judgment and actions, I should shrink at the very prospect of my encounters. Some of them are general, some are more special. Supposing this cause or this business must be carried on, it is either of God or of man. If it be of man, I would I had never touched it with a finger. If I had not had a hope fixed in me that this cause and this business was of God, I would many years ago have run from it. If it be of God, He will bear it up. If it be of man, it will tumble; as everything that hath been of man since the world began hath done. And what are all our histories, and other traditions of actions in former times, but God manifesting Himself, that He hath shaken, and tumbled down and trampled upon, everything that He had not planted? And as this is, so let the All-wise God deal with it. If this be of human structure and invention, and if it be an old plotting and contriving to bring things to this issue, and that they are not the births of Providence—then they will tumble. But if the Lord take pleasure in England, and if He will do us good—He is very able to bear us up! Let the difficulties be whatsoever they will, we shall in His strength be able to encounter with them. And I bless God I have been inured to difficulties; and I never found God failing when I trusted in Him. I can laugh and sing, in my heart, when I speak of these things to you or elsewhere. And though some may think it is a hard thing to raise money without Parliamentary authority upon this nation; yet I have another argument to the good people of this nation, if they would be safe, and yet have no better principle: Whether they prefer the having of their will though it be their destruction, rather than comply with things of necessity? That will excuse me. But I should wrong my native country to suppose this.

For I look at the people of these nations as the blessing of the Lord: and they are a people blessed by God. They have been so; and they will be so, by reason of that immortal seed

which hath been, and is, among them: those regenerated ones
in the land, of several judgments; who are all the flock of
Christ, and lambs of Christ. " His," though perhaps under
many unruly passions, and troubles of spirit; whereby they
give disquiet to themselves and others: yet they are not so to
God; since to us He is a God of other patience; and He will
own the least of truth in the hearts of His people. And the
people being the blessing of God, they will not be so angry but
they will prefer their safety to their passions, and their real
security to forms, when necessity calls for supplies. Had they
not well been acquainted with this principle, they had never
seen this day of Gospel liberty.

But if any man shall object, " It is an easy thing to talk of
necessities when men create necessities: would not the Lord
Protector make himself great and his family great? Doth not
he make these necessities? And then he will come upon the
people with his argument of necessity ! "—this was something
hard indeed. But I have not yet known what it is to " make
necessities," whatsoever the thoughts or judgments of men are.
And I say this, not only to this assembly, but to the world, That
the man liveth not who can come to me and charge me with
having, in these great revolutions, " made necessities." I challenge even all that fear God. And as God hath said, " My glory
I will not give unto another," let men take heed and be twice
advised how they call His revolutions, the things of God, and
His working of things from one period to another—how, I say,
they call them necessities of men's creation ! For by so doing,
they do vilify and lessen the works of God, and rob Him of His
glory; which He hath said He will not give unto another, nor
suffer to be taken from Him ! We know what God did to Herod,
when he was applauded and did not acknowledge God. And
God knoweth what He will do with men, when they call His
revolutions human designs, and so detract from His glory.
These issues and events have not been forecast; but were sudden Providences in things: whereby carnal and worldly men
are enraged; and under and at which, many, and I fear some
good men, have murmured and repined, because disappointed
of their mistaken fancies. But still all these things have been
the wise disposings of the Almighty; though instruments have
had their passions and frailties. And I think it is an honor to

God to acknowledge the necessities to have been of God's imposing, when truly they have been so, as indeed they have. Let us take our sin in our actions to ourselves; it's much more safe than to judge things so contingent, as if there were not a God that ruled the earth!

We know the Lord hath poured this nation from vessel to vessel till He poured it into your lap, when you came first together. I am confident that it came so into your hands; and was not judged by you to be from counterfeited or feigned necessity, but by Divine providence and dispensation. And this I speak with more earnestness, because I speak for God and not for men. I would have any man to come and tell of the transactions that have been, and of those periods of time wherein God hath made these revolutions; and find where he can fix a feigned necessity! I could recite particulars, if either my strength would serve me to speak, or yours to hear. If you would consider [10] the great hand of God in His great dispensations, you would find that there is scarce a man who fell off, at any period of time when God had any work to do, who can give God or His work at this day a good word.

"It was," say some, "the cunning of the Lord Protector"—I take it to myself—"it was the craft of such a man, and his plot, that hath brought it about!" And, as they say in other countries, "There are five or six cunning men in England that have skill; they do all these things." Oh, what blasphemy is this! Because men that are without God in the world, and walk not with Him, know not what it is to pray or believe, and to receive returns from God, and to be spoken unto by the Spirit of God—who speaks without a Written Word sometimes, yet according to it! God hath spoken heretofore in divers manners. Let Him speak as He pleaseth. Hath He not given us liberty, nay, is it not our duty to go to the law and the testimony? And there we shall find that there have been impressions, in extraordinary cases, as well without the Written Word as with it. And therefore there is no difference in the thing thus asserted from truths generally received—except we will exclude the Spirit; without whose concurrence all other teachings are ineffectual. He doth speak to the hearts and consciences of men; and leadeth them to His law and testimony, and there "also"

[10] "If that you would revolve" in the original.

He speaks to them: and so gives them double teachings. According to that of Job: " God speaketh once, yea twice; " and to that of David: " God hath spoken once, yea twice have I heard this." These men that live upon their *mumpsimus* and *sumpsimus,* their masses and service-books, their dead and carnal worship—no marvel if they be strangers to God, and to the works of God, and to spiritual dispensations. And because they say and believe thus, must we do so too? We, in this land, have been otherwise instructed; even by the Word, and works, and Spirit of God.

To say that men bring forth these things when God doth them—judge you if God will bear this? I wish that every sober heart, though he hath had temptations upon him of deserting this cause of God, yet may take heed how he provokes and falls into the hands of the living God by such blasphemies as these! According to the Tenth of the Hebrews: " If we sin wilfully after that we have received the knowledge of the truth, there remains no more sacrifice for sin." " A terrible word." It was spoken to the Jews who, having professed Christ, apostatized from Him. What then? Nothing but a fearful " falling into the hands of the living God! "—They that shall attribute to this or that person the contrivances and production of those mighty things God hath wrought in the midst of us; and " fancy " that they have not been the revolutions of Christ Himself, " upon whose shoulders the government is laid "—they speak against God, and they fall under His hand without a mediator. That is, if we deny the Spirit of Jesus Christ the glory of all His works in the world; by which He rules kingdoms, and doth administer, and is the rod of His strength—we provoke the mediator: and He may say: I will leave you to God, I will not intercede for you; let Him tear you to pieces! I will leave thee to fall into God's hands; thou deniest me my sovereignty and power committed to me; I will not intercede nor mediate for thee; thou fallest into the hands of the living God!—Therefore whatsoever you may judge men for, howsoever you may say, " This is cunning, and politic, and subtle " —take heed again, I say, how you judge of His revolutions as the product of men's inventions!—I may be thought to press too much upon this theme. But I pray God it may stick upon your hearts and mine. The worldly-minded man knows nothing of this, but is a stranger to it; and thence his atheisms, and mur-murings at instruments, yea, repining at God Himself. And no wonder; considering the Lord hath done such things amongst us as have not been known in the world these thousand years, and yet notwithstanding is not owned by us!

There is another necessity, which you have put upon us, and we have not sought. I appeal to God, angels and men—if I shall " now " raise money according to the article in the gov-ernment, whether I am not compelled to do it! Which " gov-ernment " had power to call you hither; and did;—and instead of seasonably providing for the army, you have labored to overthrow the government, and the army is now upon free-quarter! And you would never so much as let me hear a tittle from you concerning it. Where is the fault? Has it not been as if you had a purpose to put this extremity upon us and the nation? I hope this was not in your minds. I am not willing to judge so:—but such is the state into which we are reduced. By the designs of some in the army who are now in custody it was designed to get as many of them as possible—through discontent for want of money, the army being in a barren coun-try, near thirty weeks behind in pay, and upon other specious pretences—to march for England out of Scotland; and, in dis-content, to seize their General there [General Monk], a faithful and honest man, that so another [Colonel Overton] might head the army. And all this opportunity taken from your delays. Whether will this be a thing of feigned necessity? What could it signify, but " The army are in discontent already; and we will make them live upon stones; we will make them cast off their governors and discipline? " What can be said to this? I list not to unsaddle myself, and put the fault upon your backs. Whether it hath been for the good of England, whilst men have been talking of this thing or the other, and pretending liberty and many good words—whether it has been as it should have been? I am confident you cannot think it has. The nation will not think so. And if the worst should be made of things, I know not what the Cornish men nor the Lincolnshire men may think, or other counties; but I believe they will all think they are not safe A temporary suspension of " caring for the greatest liberties and privileges " (if it were so, which is denied) would not have been of such damage as the not providing against free-

quarter hath run the nation upon. And if it be my " liberty "
to walk abroad in the fields, or to take a journey, yet it is not
my wisdom to do so when my house is on fire!

I have troubled you with a long speech; and I believe it may
not have the same resentment [11] with all that it hath with some.
But because that is unknown to me, I shall leave it to God;—
and conclude with this: That I think myself bound, as in my
duty to God, and to the people of these nations for their safety
and good in every respect—I think it my duty to tell you that
it is not for the profit of these nations, nor for common and public good, for you to continue here any longer. And therefore
I do declare unto you, that I do dissolve this Parliament.[12]

[11] Means " sense excited by it."   [12] Old pamphlet: reprinted in " Parliamentary History," xx. 404-31.

HOW FAR EXAMPLES ARE TO BE FOLLOWED

—

AN ILL MATCH WELL BROKEN OFF

—

BY

THOMAS FULLER

THOMAS FULLER

1608—1661

Thomas Fuller was born at Aldwinkle, Northamptonshire, in the year 1608. At the age of twelve his father, who was rector of that parish, sent him to Cambridge, where he entered Queen's College. He took the degree of bachelor in 1624 and that of master of arts four years later. He was held in such high estimation at his college that, at the age of twenty-three, he was appointed to St. Benet's, Cambridge, where he became very popular as a preacher. Soon afterwards he became prebend of Salisbury and obtained a fellowship in Sidney Sussex College.

Fuller's first publication in 1631 was a poem, entitled "David's Heinous Sin, Hearty Repentance, and Heavy Punishment." His preferment was rapid. He next became rector of Broad Windsor, Dorsetshire, published his "History of the Holy War," in 1639, and removed to London in 1640, where he had been chosen lecturer at the Savoy church in the Strand. The same year he was a member of the convocation at Westminster and one of the select committee appointed to draw up new canons for the better government of the church. During the civil war he became a chaplain to the Royalist army, and while wandering about from place to place collected the material for his "Worthies of England." In 1646 he was successively chosen lecturer at St. Clement's Lane and at St. Bride's, being two years later presented with the living of Waltham, Essex. During the five years following Fuller developed much literary activity, a geographical account of the Holy Land, a collection of lives of modern divines, and a church history of Great Britain appearing during this time. Fuller lived in troublous times, but before his death the tide turned in his favor. In 1658 he received the living at Cromford, Middlesex, was reinstated in his prebend at Salisbury, and appointed chaplain extraordinary to the King. He was made a doctor of divinity at Cambridge by royal decree. He died on August 16, 1661.

His principal work, "The Worthies of England," was published in London in 1662. Valuable for the information on contemporaneous history, it abounds in biographical anecdotes, witty remarks, and acute observations on men and manners of the times. Quaint humor is one of Fuller's characteristics, but his writings are no less remarkable for wisdom, imagination, and when occasion demands, even for pathos. His discourses "How far Examples are to be Followed" and "An Ill Match well Broken Off," are representative of the epigrammatic style that is characteristic of all his writings.

HOW FAR EXAMPLES ARE TO BE FOLLOWED

IN these words [1] Naomi seeks to persuade Ruth to return, alleging the example of Orpah, who, as she saith, was " gone back to her people, and to her gods." Where first we find that all the heathen, and the Moabites amongst the rest, did not acknowledge one true God, but were the worshippers of many gods; for they made every attribute of God to be a distinct deity. Thus, instead of that attribute, the wisdom of God, they feigned Apollo the god of wisdom; instead of the power of God, they made Mars the god of power; instead of that admirable beauty of God, they had Venus the goddess of beauty. But no one attribute was so much abused as God's providence. For the heathen, supposing that the whole world, and all the creatures therein, was too great a diocese to be daily visited by one and the same deity, they therefore assigned sundry gods to several creatures. Thus God's providence in ruling the raging of the seas was counted Neptune; in stilling the roaring wind, Æolus; in commanding the powers of hell, Pluto; yea, sheep had their Pan, and gardens their Pomona; the heathens thus being as fruitful in feigning of gods as the Papists since in making of saints.

Now, because Naomi used the example of Orpah as a motive to work upon Ruth to return, we gather from thence, examples of others set before our eyes are very potent and prevailing arguments to make us follow and imitate them; whether they be good examples, so the forwardness of the Corinthians to relieve the Jews provoked many—or whether they be bad, so the dissembling of Peter at Antioch drew Barnabas and others into the same fault. But those examples, of all others, are most forcible with us which are set by such who are near

[1] " And Naomi said, Behold, thy sister-in-law is gone back unto her people, and unto her gods; return thou after thy sister-in-law " (Ruth i. 15).

to us by kindred, or gracious with us in friendship, or great over us in power.

Let men in eminent places, as magistrates, ministers, fathers, masters (so that others love to dance after their pipe, to sing after their music, to tread after their track), endeavor to propound themselves examples of piety and religion to those that be under them.

When we see any good example propounded unto us, let us strive with all possible speed to imitate it. What a deal of stir is there in the world for civil precedency and priority! Everyone desires to march in the forefront, and thinks it a shame to come lagging in the rearward. O that there were such a holy ambition and heavenly emulation in our hearts, that, as Peter and John ran a race who should come first to the grave of our Saviour, so men would contend who should first attain to true mortification. And when we see a good example set before us, let us imitate it, though it be in one which in outward respects is far our inferior. Shall not our masters be ashamed to see that their men, whose place on earth is to come behind them, in piety towards heaven go before them? Shall not the husband blush to see his wife, who is the weaker vessel in nature, the stronger vessel in grace? Shall not the elder brother dye his cheeks with the color of virtue, to see his younger brother, who was last born, first reborn by faith and the Holy Ghost? Yet let him not therefore envy his brother, as Cain did Abel; let him not be angry with his brother because he is better than himself; but let him be angry with himself, because he is worse than his brother; let him turn all his malice into imitation, all his fretting at him into following of him. Say unto him, as Gehazi did of Naaman, "As the Lord liveth, I will run after him;" and although thou canst not overrun him, nor as yet overlook him; yet give not over to run with him, follow him, though not as Asahel did Abner, hard at the heels; yet as Peter did our Saviour, "afar off;" that though the more slowly, yet as surely thou mayest come to heaven; and though thou wert short of him while he lived, in the race, yet thou shalt be even with him when thou art dead, at the mark.

When any bad example is presented unto us, let us decline and detest it, though the men be never so many or so dear unto us. Imitate Micaiah (1 Kings xxii.), to whom, when the messenger sent to fetch him said, " Behold now, the words of the prophets declare good unto the king with one mouth; let thy word therefore, I pray thee, be like to one of them"; Micaiah answered, " As the Lord liveth, whatsoever the Lord saith unto me, that will I speak." If they be never so dear unto us, we must not follow their bad practice. So must the son please him that begot him, that he doth not displease Him that created him: so must the wife follow him that married her, that she doth not offend Him that made her. Wherefore, as Samson, though bound with new cords, snapped them asunder as tow when it feeleth the fire; so, rather than we should be led by the lewd examples of those that be near and dear unto us, let us break in pieces all their engagements, relations whatsoever.

Now here it will be a labor worthy discourse to consider how far the examples even of good men in the Bible are to be followed. For, as all examples have a great influence on the practice of the beholders, so especially the deeds of good men registered in the Scripture (the calendar of eternity) are most attractive of imitation.

FIRST KIND OF EXAMPLES.—We find in Holy Writ nine several kinds of examples. First, *actions extraordinary;* the doers whereof had peculiar strength and dispensation from God to do them. Thus, Phinehas in a heavenly fury killed Cozbi and Zimri; Samson slew himself and the Philistines in the temple of Dagon; Elias caused fire to descend on the two captains of fifties; Elisha cursed the children, the children of Bethel.

Use of them.—These are written for our instruction, not for our imitation. If, with Elisha, thou canst make a bridge over Jordan with thy cloak, if, with him, thou canst raise dead children, then it is lawful for thee, with Elisha, to curse thy enemies. If thou canst not imitate him in the one, pretend not to follow him in the other.

Abuse of them.—When men propound such examples for their practice, what is said is imputed to Phinehas for righteousness will be imputed to us for iniquity, if, being private men, by a commission of our own penning, we usurp the sword of justice to punish malefactors.

SECOND SORT.—*Actions founded in the ceremonial law;* as,

Abraham's circumcising of Isaac, Hezekiah's eating the passover, Solomon's offering of sacrifices, etc.

Use of them.—We are to be thankful to God that these
shadows in Christ the substance are taken away. Let us not
therefore superstitiously feign that the ghosts of these ceremonies may still walk, which long since were buried in Christ's
grave.

Abuse of them.—By those who still retain them. Excellently Ignatius, *Epist. ad Magnesios,* Οὐ γὰρ Χριστιανισμὸς
οὐκ ἔστιν Ἰουδαϊσμός. Yea, we must forfeit the name of Christians if we still retain such old rites. Let those who are admitted in the college of grace disdain any longer to go to the
school of the ceremonial law, which truly may be called "the
school of Tyrannus."

THIRD SORT.—*Actions which are founded in the judicial law;*
as, punishing theft with fourfold restitution, putting of adul-
terers to death, and raising up seed to the brother, etc.

Use of them.—These oblige men to observe them so far as
they have in them any taste or tincture of a moral law; and as
they bear proportion with those statutes by which every particular country is governed. For the judicial law was by God
calculated alone for the elevation of the Jewish commonwealth.
It suited only with the body of their state; and will not fit any
other commonwealth, except it be equal to Judea in all dimen-
sions—I mean in climate, nature of the soil, disposition of the
people, quality of the bordering neighbors, and many other
particulars, amongst which the very least is considerable.

Abuse of them.—When men, out of an over-imitativeness of
holy precedents, seek to conform all countries to Jewish laws.
That must needs break, which is stretched farther than God
intended it. They may sooner make Saul's armor fit David,
and David's sling and scrip become Saul, than the particular
statutes of one country adequately to comply with another.

FOURTH SORT.—*Actions founded in no law at all, but only
in an ancient custom,* by God winked and connived at; yea,
tolerated, at the leastwise not openly forbidden in precept, or
punished in practice. As polygamy, in the patriarchs having
many wives. Indeed, when God first made the large volume
of the world, and all creatures therein, and set it forth, *cum
regali privilegio,* "Behold, all things therein were very good,"

He made one Eve for one Adam. Polygamy is an *erratum* and needs an *index expurgatorius,* being crept in, being more than what was in the maiden copy; it was the creature of Lamech, no work of God.

Use.—We are herein to wonder at and praise the goodness of God, who was pleased herein to wink at the faults of His dear saints, and to pass by their frailty herein, because they lived in a dark age, wherein His pleasure was not so plainly manifested.

Abuse of them.—If any, in this bright sunshine of the Gospel, pretend, as a plea for their lust, to follow their example.

FIFTH SORT.—*Doubtful examples;* which may be so termed, because it is difficult to decide whether the actors of them therein did offend or no; so that, should a jury of learned writers be empannelled to pass their verdict upon them, they would be puzzled whether to condemn or acquit them, and at last be forced to find it an *ignoramus.* As, whether David did well to dissemble himself frantic, thereby to escape the cruelty of Achish, king of Gath: whether Hushai did well in counterfeiting with Absalom, or whether therein he did not make heaven to bow too much to earth; I mean, policy to intrench upon piety; and so in this act was so good a statesman that he was a bad man.

Use of them.—Let us not meddle with imitation of these actions, that are so full of difficulty and danger that our judgments therein may easily be deceived. The sons of Barzallai (Ezra ii. 63), because their genealogies were doubtful and uncertain, were put by the priesthood, till a priest should rise up " with Urim and Thummim; " by which we may understand some especial man amongst them, who, by God's spirit, might be able to decide the controversies which were questioned in their pedigrees. So let us refrain from following these doubtful examples, till (which in this world is not likely to be) there arise an infallible judge, who can determine in these particulars, whether these actions were well done or no.

Abuse of them.—By such who, though they have room enough besides, yet delight to walk on a narrow bank near the sea, and have an itch to imitate these doubtful examples, wherein there is great danger of miscarrying.

SIXTH SORT.—*Mixed examples,* which contain in them a

double action, the one good, and the other bad, so closely couched together that it is a very hard thing to sever them. Thus, in the unjust steward, there was his wisdom to provide for himself, which God doth commend; and his wickedness, to purloin from his master, which God cannot but condemn. Thus, in the Hebrew midwives (Exod. i.), when they told the lie, there was in them *fides mentis, et fallacia mentientis,* the " faithfulness " of their love to their countrymen, and the " falseness of their lying " to Pharaoh.

Use of them.—Behold, here is wisdom, and let the man that hath understanding discreetly divide betwixt the gold and the dross, the wheat and the chaff; what he is to follow and imitate, and what to shun and avoid. In the first year of the reign of Queen Elizabeth the students of Christ Church, in Oxford, buried the bones of Peter Martyr's wife in the same coffin with the ashes of Fridswick, a popish saint; to this intent, that if Popery (which God forbid) should ever after overspread this land, Papists should be puzzled to part the ashes of a supposed heretic from one of their canonized saints. Thus, in some actions of God's saints in the Bible, which are of a mixed nature; wickedness doth so insensibly unite and incorporate itself with that that is good, that it is very difficult to sever and divide them without a sound and well advised judgment.

Abuse of them.—In such as leave what is good, take what is bad; follow what is to be shunned, shun what is to be followed.

SEVENTH SORT.—*Actions absolutely bad,* so that no charitable comment can be fastened upon them, except we will incur the prophet's curse and woe, to " call good evil, and evil good." Such were the drunkenness of Noah, the incest of Lot, the lying of Abraham, the swearing of Joseph, the adultery of David, the denial of Peter.

Use of them.—Let us read in them, first, a lecture of our own infirmity. Who dare warrant his armor for proof, when David's was shot through? Secondly, let us admire and laud God's mercy, who pardoned and restored these men on their unfeigned repentance. Lastly, let us not despair of pardon ourselves, if through infirmity overtaken, God in like manner is merciful to forgive us.

Abuse of them.—When men either make these their patterns, by which they sin; or after their sinning, allege them for their excuse and defence. Thus Judith did (Judith ix. 2). For whereas that murder which Simeon and Levi did commit upon the Shechemites (Gen. xxxiv. 25), was cursed by Jacob as a most heinous and horrible sin; yet she propounds it as a heroic act, and the unworthy precedent for her imitation: " O Lord God of my father Simeon, to whom thou gavest the sword to take vengeance on the strangers, which opened the womb of a maid, and defiled her," etc.   Well, if the arm of Judith had been as weak as her judgment was herein, I should scarce believe that she ever cut off the head of Holofernes.

EIGHTH SORT.—*Actions which are only good as they are qualified with such a circumstance,* as David's eating the show-bread in a case of absolute necessity, which otherwise was provided for the priests alone.   Such are the doing of servile works on the Lord's Day, when, in case of necessity, they leave off to be *opera servilia,* and become *opera misericordiæ.*

Use of them.—Let us be sure, in imitating of these, to have the same qualifying circumstance, without which otherwise the deed is impious and damnable.

Abuse of them.—In those who imitate the example without any heeding that they are so qualified as the action requires.

NINTH SORT.—The ninth and last sort remains; and such are those which are eminently good; as, the faith of Abraham, the meekness of Moses, the valor of Joshua, the sincerity of Samuel, the plain dealing of Nathanael, etc.   Follow not, then, the infidelity of Thomas, but the faith of Abraham; the testiness of Jonah, but the patience of Job; the adultery of David, but the chastity of Joseph—not the apostasy of Orpah, but the perseverance of Ruth here in my text.

AN ILL MATCH WELL BROKEN OFF*

THE Stoics said to their affections as Abimelech spake to Isaac (Gen. xxvi. 16), "Get you out from amongst us; for you are too strong for us." Because they were too strong for them to master, they therefore would have them totally banished out of their souls, and labor to becalm themselves with an apathy. But far be it from us, after their example, to root out such good herbs (instead of weeds) out of the garden of our nature; whereas affections, if well used, are excellent, if they mistake not their true object, nor exceed in their due measure. Joshua killed not the Gibeonites, but condemned them to be " hewers of wood and drawers of water for the sanctuary." We need not expel passions out of us, if we could conquer them, and make grief draw water-buckets of tears for our sins, and anger kindle fires of zeal and indignation when we see God dishonored. But as that must needs be a deformed face, wherein there is a transposition of the colors—the blueness of the veins being set in the lips; the redness which should be in the cheeks in the nose—so, alas! most misshapen is our soul, since Adam's fall, whereby our affections are so inverted, joy stands where grief should, grief in the place of joy. We are bold where we should fear, fear where we should be bold; love what we should hate, hate what we should love. This gave occasion to the blessed apostle, in my text, to dissuade men from loving that whereon too many dote. " Love not the world."

For the better understanding of which words, know that the devil goes about to make an unfitting match betwixt the soul of a Christian on the one party, and this world on the other. A match too likely to go on, if we consider the simplicity and folly of many Christians (because of the remnants of corruption), easily to be seduced and inveigled, or the bewitching, en-

*" Love not the world " (1 John, ii. 15).

ticing, alluring nature of this world; but God, by St. John, in
my text, forbiddeth the banns—" Love not the world."

In prosecuting whereof, we will first show the worthiness
of a Christian soul; then we will consider the worthlessness of
the world; and from the comparing of these two, this doctrine
will result, that it is utterly unfitting for a Christian to place his
affections on worldly things.

Let us take notice of a Christian's possessions, and of his
possibilities; what he hath in hand, and what he holdeth in hope.
In possession he hath the favor of God, the spirit of adoption
crying in him, " Abba, Father," and many excellent graces of
sanctification in some measure in his heart.   In hope and ex-
pectance he hath the reversion of heaven and happiness (a reversion not to be got after another's death, but his own), and
those happinesses which eye cannot see, nor ear hear, neither it
can enter into the heart of man to conceive.

Now see the worthlessness of the world.   Three loadstones
commonly attract men's affections, and make them to love—
beauty, wit, and wealth.

Beauty the world hath none at all.   I dare boldly say the
world put on her holiday apparel when she was presented by
the devil to our Saviour (Matt. iv. 9).   She never looked so
smug and smooth before or since, and had there been any real
beauty therein, the eagle sight of our Saviour would have seen
it: yet, when all the glory of the world was proffered unto Him
at the price of idolatry, He refused it.   Yet, as old Jezebel,
when she wanted true beauty, stopped up the leaks of age with
adulterated complexion, and painted her face; so the world, in
default of true beauty, decks herself with a false appearing
fairness, which serves to allure amorous fools, and (to give the
world, as well as the devil, her due) she hath for the time a
kind of a pleasing fashionableness.   But what saith St. Paul?
" The fashion of this world passeth away " (1 Cor. vii. 31).
The wit of the world is as little as her beauty, however it may be
cried up by some of her fond admirers; yet as it is (1 Cor. iii.
19), " The wisdom of this world is foolishness with God;" and
cuilibet artifici credandum est in sua arte; what wisdom itself
counts foolishness is folly to purpose.

Her wealth is as small as either: what the world calls " substance " is most subject to accidents, uncertain, unconstant;

even lands themselves in this respect are movables. " Riches make themselves wings, and fly away ;" they may leave us whilst we live, but we must leave them when we die.

Seeing, then, the world hath so little, and the Christian soul so much, let us learn a lesson of holy pride, to practise heavenly ambition. Descend not so far, O Christian, beneath thyself; remember what thou art, and what thou hast; lose not thyself in lavishing thy affections on so disproportioned a mate. There is a double disparity betwixt thy soul and the world.

First, that of age. Perchance the world might make a fit mate for thy old man, thy unregenerate half, thy relics of sin; but to match the old, rotten, withered, worm-eaten world to thy new man, thy new creature, the regenerated and renewed part of thy soul, grey to green, is rather a torture than a marriage—altogether disproportionable.

Secondly, that of quality or condition. Thou art God's freeman. " If I have freed you," saith Christ, " then are you free indeed ;" the world is, or ought to be, thy slave, thy vassal. " For whosoever is born of God overcometh the world: and this is the victory that overcometh the world, even our faith " (1 John v. 4). Be not, then, so base as to make thy vassal thy mate. Alexander denied to marry Darius's daughter, though proffered unto him, scorning to be conquered by her beauty, whose father he had conquered by his valor. Let us not make the world our mistress, whereof we ought to be the master, nor prostitute our affections to a slave we have conquered.

Objection.—Yea, may some say, this is good counsel, if it came in due season. Alas! now it cometh too late, after I have not only long doted, but am even wedded to this world. Infant affection may be easily crushed, but who can tame an old and rooted love? Think you that I have my affection in my hand, as hunters their dogs, to let slip or rate off at pleasure? How, then, shall I unlove the world, which hath been my bosom darling so long?

Answer.—Art thou wedded to the world? then instantly send her a bill of divorce. It need never trouble thy conscience; that match may be lawfully broken off, which was first most unlawfully made. Yea, thou wert long before contracted to God in thy baptism, wherein thou didst solemnly promise thou wouldst " forsake the devil and all his works, the vain pomp and glory of this world." Let the first contract stand; and because it is difficult for those who have long doted on the world to unlove her, we will give some rules how it may be done by degrees. For indeed it is not to be done on a sudden (matters of moment cannot be done in a moment) ; but it is the task of a man's whole life, till the day of his death.

Rules how to unlove the world.—1. Look not with the eyes of covetousness or admiration on the things of the world. The eye is the principal Cinque Port of the soul, wherein love first arrives: *Ut vidi, ut perii!* Now thou mayest look on the things of the world *ut in transitu*—" as in passage " (otherwise we should be forced to shut our eyes) ; and we may behold them with a slighting, neglectful, fastidious look. But take heed to look on them with a covetous eye, as Eve on the forbidden fruit, and Achan on the wedge of gold. Take heed to look on them with the eye of admiration, as the disciples looked on the buildings of the temple (Matt. xxiv. 1), wondering at the eternity of the structure, and conceiving the arch of this world would fall as soon as such stones, riveted to immortality, might be dissolved. Wherefore our Saviour checketh them, " Verily I say unto you, There shall not be left one stone upon another, that shall not be cast down." Excellently Job (xxxi. 1), " I have made a covenant with mine eyes, that I should not behold a woman." A covenant ? But what was the forfeiture Job's eyes were to pay in case he brake it ? It is not expressed on the bond ; but surely the penalty is implied—many brackish tears, which his eyes in repentance must certainly pay, if they observed not the covenant.

2. Silence that spokesman in thy bosom ; I mean, the allurements of the flesh and devil, who improveth his utmost power to advance a match betwixt thy soul and the world. And when any breach happens between thee and the world, so that thou art ready to cast her off, the flesh in thy bosom pleads her cause. " Why wilt thou," saith it, " deprive thyself of those contentments which the world would afford thee ? Why dost thou torment thyself before thy time ? Ruffle thyself in the silks of security ; it will be time enough to put on the sackcloth of repentance when thou liest on thy deathbed." Hearken not to the flesh, her enchantments ; but as Pharaoh charged Moses to get him out of his presence, he should " see his face no more "

(Exod. x. 28), so strive, as much as in thee lieth, to expel these fleshly suggestions from thy presence, to banish them out of thy soul; at leastwise to silence them; though the mischief is, it will be muttering, and though it dare not halloo, it will still be whispering unto thee, in behalf of the world, its old friend, to make a reconciliation betwixt you.

3. Send back again to the world the love-tokens she hath bestowed upon thee; I mean those ill-gotten goods which thou hast gotten by indirect and unwarrantable means. As for those goods which thy parents left thee, friends have given thee, or thou hast procured by Heaven's providence on thy lawful endeavors, these are no love-tokens of the world, but God's gifts; keep them, use them, enjoy them, to His glory. But goods gotten by wrong and robbery, extortion and bribery, force and fraud, these restore and send back: for the world knoweth that she hath a kind of tie and engagement upon thee, so long as thou keepest her tokens; and in a manner thou art obliged in honor, as long as thou detainest the gifts that were hers. Imitate Zaccheus: see how he casts back what the world gave him, "Behold, Lord, the half of my goods I give to the poor; and if I have taken anything from any man by false accusation, I restore him fourfold" (Luke xix. 8).

4. Set thy affections on the God of heaven. The best wedge to drive out an old love is to take in a new.

"*Postquam nos Amaryllis habit, Galatea reliquit.*"

Yea, God deserves our love first, because God "loved us first" (1 John iv. 19). It is enough, indeed, to blunt the sharpest affection, to be returned with scorn and neglect; but it is enough to turn ice into ashes, to be first beloved by One that so well deserves love. Secondly, His is a lasting love: "Having loved His own that were in the world, He loved them to the end" (John xiii. 1). Some men's affection spends itself with its violence, hot at hand, but cold at length; God's is not so—it is continuing. It is recorded in the honor of our King Henry VII, that he never discomposed a favorite, one only excepted, which was William, Lord Stanley; a rare matter, since many princes change their favorites, as well as their clothes, before they are old. But the observation is true of the Lord of heaven without any exception: those who are once estated in His favor, He continues loving unto them to the end.

Hark, then, how He woos us (Isa. lv. 1): "Ho, everyone that thirsteth, come ye to the waters, and he that hath no money; come," etc. How He woos us (Matt. xi. 28): "Come unto me, all ye that labor and are heavy-laden, and I will give you rest. Love His love-letter, His Word, His love-tokens, His sacraments, His spokesmen, His ministers, which labor to favor the match betwixt Him and thy soul. But beware of two things.

1. Take heed of that dangerous conceit, that at the same time thou mayest keep both God and the world, and love these outward delights, as a concubine to thy soul. Nay, God He is "a jealous God;" He will have all, or none at all. There is a city in Germany, pertaining half to the bishop thereof, and half to the Duke of Saxony, who named the city Myndyn, that is, "mine and thine;" because it was theirs *communi jure,* and at this day by corruption it is called Minden. But God will admit of no such divisions; He will hold nothing in coparceny; He will not share or part stakes with any; but He will have all entire to himself alone.

2. Take heed thou dost not only fall out with the world, to fall in with it again, according to that

" Amantium iræ amoris redintegratio est."

For even as some furious gamesters, when they have a bad game, throw their cards out of their hands, and vow to play no more (not so much out of mislike of gaming as of their present game); but when the cards run on their side, they are reconciled to them again; so many men, when the world frowns on them and crosses them, and they miss some preferment they desire, then a qualm of piety comes over their hearts; they are mortified on a sudden, and disavow to have any further dealing with worldly contentments. But when the world smiles on them again, favors and prospers them, they then return to their former love, and doting upon it. Thus Demas (2 Tim. iv. 10) would needs have another farewell embrace of the world, even after his solemn conversion to Christianity: "Demas hath forsaken me, having loved this present world." But when we are once at variance with the world, let us continue at deadly eternal feuds with it; and as it is said of Amnon (2 Sam. xiii. 15), that " the hatred wherewith he hated his sister Tamar was greater than the love wherewith he had loved her;" so (what was cruelty in him will be Christianity in us), once fallen out with the world, let the joint be never set again, that it may be the stronger; but let our hatred be immortal, and so much the stronger by how much our love was before.

SPEECH
ON THE BILL OF ATTAINDER
AGAINST LORD STRAFFORD

—

BY

GEORGE DIGBY

Earl of Bristol

GEORGE DIGBY, EARL OF BRISTOL

1612—1676

George Digby was born in Madrid in the year 1612, when his father resided in that city as English Ambassador to the Court of Spain. He received his education at Magdalen College, Oxford, and entered political life at the age of twenty-eight, being elected member for the county of Dorset in 1640. Lord Digby soon came forward as a determined enemy of the Court. Among the " Speeches on Grievances," his own stands forth as the most bold and impassioned. His argument in favor of triennial Parliament is remarkable for a still higher order of eloquence; in the course of it he made a bitter attack on Strafford, showing the necessity of frequent Parliaments as a control on ministers.

In consequence of the zeal displayed in these matters and as an ardent advocate of the people's rights, Lord Digby was appointed one of the managers of the impeachment of Strafford. In this undertaking he at first displayed great zeal. Clarendon describes Digby as a man of uncommon activity of mind and fertility of invention, bold and impetuous in whatever designs he undertook; but deficient in judgment, inordinately vain and ambitious, of a volatile and unquiet spirit, disposed to separate councils, and governed more by impulse than by fixed principles. Such being the characteristics of the man it is idle to seek for the motives that determined him in his change of attitude during the trial of Strafford.

Much of the celebrity attached to this speech is owing, no doubt, to the circumstances under which it was delivered. The House of Commons must have presented an exciting scene when, at the last moment, one of the managers of the impeachment came forward to abandon his ground; to disclose the proceedings of the Committee in secret session; and to denounce the condemnation of Strafford by a bill of attainder, as an act of murder. But, whatever may be thought of the man, the speech is one of great manliness and force. It is plausible in its statements, just in its distinctions, and weighty in its reasonings. Its diction is worthy to be studied in one respect, at least. It abounds in those direct and pointed forms of speech which sink at once into the heart; and by their very plainness give an air of perfect sincerity to the speaker. These qualities are most important to a speaker who is contending against the force of popular prejudice.

SPEECH ON THE BILL OF ATTAINDER
AGAINST LORD STRAFFORD

Delivered in the House of Commons, April 21, 1641

WE are now upon the point of giving, as much as in us lies, the final sentence unto death or life, on a great minister of state and peer of this kingdom, Thomas, Earl of Strafford, a name of hatred in the present age for his practices, and fit to be made a terror to future ages by his punishment. I have had the honor to be employed by the House in this great business, from the first hour it was taken into consideration. It was a matter of great trust; and I will say with confidence that I have served the House in it, not only with industry, according to my ability, but with most exact faithfulness and justice.

And as I have hitherto discharged my duty to this House and to my country in the progress of this great cause, so I trust I shall do now, in the last period of it, to God and to a good conscience. I do wish the peace of that to myself, and the blessing of Almighty God to me and my posterity, according as my judgment on the life of this man shall be consonant with my heart, and the best of my understanding in all integrity.

I know well that by some things I have said of late, while this bill was in agitation, I have raised some prejudices against me in the cause. Yea, some (I thank them for their plain dealing) have been so free to tell me, that I have suffered much by the backwardness I have shown in the bill of attainder of the Earl of Strafford, against whom I have formerly been so keen, so active.

I beg of you, Mr. Speaker, and the rest, but a suspension of judgment concerning me, till I have opened my heart to you, clearly and freely, in this business. Truly, sir, I am still the same in my opinion and affections as to the Earl of Strafford. I confidently believe him to be the most dangerous minister, the most insupportable to free subjects, that can be charactered. I believe his practices in themselves to have been as high and tyrannical as any subject ever ventured on; and the malignity of them greatly aggravated by those rare abilities of his, whereof God hath given him the use, but the devil the application. In a word, I believe him to be still that grand apostate to the Commonwealth, who must not expect to be pardoned in this world till he be despatched to the other.

And yet let me tell you, Mr. Speaker, my hand must not be to that despatch. I protest, as my conscience stands informed, I had rather it were off.

Let me unfold to you the mystery, Mr. Speaker: I will not dwell much upon justifying to you my seeming variance at this time from what I was formerly, by putting you in mind of the difference between prosecutors and judges—how misbecoming that fervor would be in a judge which, perhaps, was commendable in a prosecutor. Judges we are now, and must, therefore, put on another personage. It is honest and noble to be earnest in order to the discovery of truth; but when that hath been brought so far as it can be to light, our judgment thereupon ought to be calm and cautious. In prosecution upon probable grounds, we are accountable only for our industry or remissness; but in judgment, we are deeply responsible to Almighty God for its rectitude or obliquity. In cases of life, the judge is God's steward of the party's blood, and must give a strict account for every drop.

But, as I told you, Mr. Speaker, I will not insist long upon this ground of difference in me now from what I was formerly. The truth of it is, sir, the same ground whereupon I with the rest of the few to whom you first committed the consideration of my Lord Strafford, brought down our opinion that it was fit he should be accused of treason—upon the same ground, I was engaged with earnestness in his prosecution; and had the same ground remained in that force of belief in me, which till very lately it did, I should not have been tender in his condemnation. But truly, sir, to deal plainly with you, that ground of our accusation—that which should be the basis of our judgment of the Earl of Strafford as to treason—is, to my understanding, quite vanished away.

This it was, Mr. Speaker—his advising the King to employ the army in Ireland to reduce England. This I was assured would be proved, before I gave my consent to his accusation. I was confirmed in the same belief during the prosecution, and fortified most of all in it, after Sir Henry Vane's preparatory examination, by assurances which that worthy member, Mr. Pym, gave me, that his testimony would be made convincing by some notes of what passed in the Junto (Privy Council) concurrent with it. This I ever understood would be of some other counsellor; but you see now, it proves only to be a copy of the same secretary's notes, discovered and produced in the manner you have heard; and those such disjointed fragments of the venomous part of discourses—no results, no conclusions of councils, which are the only things that secretaries should register, there being no use of the other but to accuse and bring men into danger.

But, sir, this is not that which overthrows the evidence with me concerning the army in Ireland, nor yet that all the rest of the Junto remember nothing of it; but this, sir, which I shall tell you, is that which works with me, under favor, to an utter overthrow of his evidence as touching the army of Ireland. Before, while I was prosecutor, and under tie of secrecy, I might not discover (disclose) any weakness of the cause, which now, as judge, I must.

Mr. Secretary Vane was examined thrice upon oath at the preparatory committee. The first time he was questioned as to all the interrogatories; and to that part of the seventh which concerns the army in Ireland, he said positively these words: " I cannot charge him with that; " but for the rest, he desired time to recollect himself, which was granted him. Some days after, he was examined a second time, and then deposed these words concerning the King's being absolved from rules of government, and so forth, very clearly. But being pressed as to that part of the Irish army, again he said he could say " nothing to that." Here we thought we had done with him, till divers weeks after, my Lord of Northumberland, and all others of the Junto, denying to have heard anything concerning those words of reducing England by the Irish army, it was thought fit to examine the secretary once more; and then he deposed these words to have been spoken by the Earl of Strafford to

His Majesty: "You have an army in Ireland, which you may employ here to reduce [or some word to that sense] this kingdom." Mr. Speaker, these are the circumstances which, I confess with my conscience, thrust quite out of doors that grand article of our charge concerning his desperate advice to the King of employing the Irish army here.

Let not this, I beseech you, be driven to an aspersion upon Mr. Secretary, as if he should have sworn otherwise than he knew or believed. He is too worthy to do that. Only let this much be inferred from it, that he, who twice upon oath, with time of recollection, could not remember anything of such a business, might well, a third time, misremember somewhat; and in this business the difference of one word " here " for " there," or " that " for " this," quite alters the case; the latter also being the more probable, since it is confessed on all hands that the debate then was concerning a war with Scotland and, you may remember, that at the bar he once said " employ there." And thus, Mr. Speaker, have I faithfully given you an account what it is that hath blunted the edge of the hatchet, or bill, with me, towards my Lord Strafford.

This was that whereupon I accused him with a free heart; prosecuted him with earnestness; and had it to my understanding been proved, should have condemned him with innocence; whereas now I cannot satisfy my conscience to do it. I profess I can have no notion of anybody's intent to subvert the laws treasonably, but by force; and this design of force not appearing, all his other wicked practices cannot amount so high with me. I can find a more easy and natural spring from whence to derive all his other crimes, than from an intent to bring in tyranny, and make his own posterity, as well as us, slaves; viz., from revenge, from pride, from passion, and from insolence of nature. But had this of the Irish army been proved, it would have diffused a complexion of treason over all. It would have been a withe indeed, to bind all those other scattered and lesser branches, as it were, into a fagot of treason.

I do not say but the rest of the things charged may represent him a man as worthy to die, and perhaps worthier than many a traitor. I do not say but they may justly direct us to enact that they shall be treason for the future. But God keep me from giving judgment of death on any man, and of ruin to his innocent posterity, upon a law made *à posteriori*. Let the mark be set on the door where the plague is, and then let him that will enter, die.

I know, Mr. Speaker, there is in Parliament a double power of life and death by bill; a judicial power, and a legislative. The measure of the one is, what is legally just; of the other, what is prudentially and politically fit for the good and preservation of the whole. But these two, under favor, are not to be confounded in judgment. We must not piece out want of legality with matter of convenience, nor the defailance of prudential fitness with a pretence of legal justice.

To condemn my Lord of Strafford judicially, as for treason, my conscience is not assured that the matter will bear it; and to do it by the legislative power, my reason consultively cannot agree to that, since I am persuaded that neither the lords nor the King will pass this bill; and, consequently that our passing it will be a cause of great divisions and contentions in the state. Therefore my humble advice is, that, laying aside this bill of attainder, we may think of another, saving only life; such as may secure the state from my Lord of Strafford, without endangering it as much by division concerning his punishment, as he hath endangered it by his practices.

If this may not be hearkened unto, let me conclude in saying that to you all, which I have thoroughly inculcated upon mine own conscience, on this occasion. Let every man lay his hand upon his own heart, and seriously consider what we are going to do with a breath: either justice or murder—justice on the one side, or murder, heightened and aggravated to its supremest extent, on the other! For, as the casuists say, He who lies with his sister commits incest; but he that marries his sister, sins higher, by applying God's ordinance to his crime; so, doubtless, he that commits murder with the sword of justice, heightens that crime to the utmost.

The danger being so great, and the case so doubtful, that I see the best lawyers in diametrical opposition concerning it; let every man wipe his heart as he does his eyes, when he would judge of a nice and subtle object. The eye, if it be pre-tinctured with any color, is vitiated in its discerning. Let us take heed of a blood-shotten eye in judgment. Let every man purge his heart clear of all passions. I know this great and wise body politic can have none; but I speak to individuals from the weakness which I find in myself. Away with personal animosities! Away with all flatteries to the people, in being the sharper against him because he is odious to them! Away with all fears, lest by sparing his blood they may be incensed! Away with all such considerations, as that it is not fit for a Parliament that one accused by it of treason, should escape with life! Let not former vehemence of any against him, nor fear from thence that he cannot be safe while that man lives, be an ingredient in the sentence of any one of us.

Of all these corruptives of judgment, Mr. Speaker, I do, before God, discharge myself to the utmost of my power; and do now, with a clear conscience, wash my hands of this man's blood by this solemn protestation, that my vote goes not to the taking of the Earl of Strafford's life.

THE HEAVENLY FOOTMAN

—

BY

JOHN BUNYAN

JOHN BUNYAN

1628—1688

John Bunyan was born at Elstow, near Bedford, in 1628. His father was a tinker, but gave his son such education as could be had at the village school, and brought him up to his own trade. The force of his imagination and the influence of the religious excitement of the age early appeared in fits of agitation and religious terror. He had a propensity to profane swearing, but lived a decent and moral life. In 1645 he served a short time in the parliamentary army, and soon afterwards he became subject to most painful mental conflicts, agonizing doubts and fears. In consequence of the friendly counsels and help of religious neighbors he joined the Baptists at Bedford, and soon began preaching. In 1660 he shared the persecution then carried on against Dissenters, and was thrown into Bedford Gaol. All attempts to coax or terrify him into promising to preach no more failed, and there he remained for twelve years. He preached to the prisoners, made tagged laces for sale, read the Bible and the Book of Martyrs, and at last began to write. He wrote various controversial tracts, and had even to dispute with his own party in defence of " open communion." He was liberated in 1672. His name was then widely known, his influence was great: and he was called " Bishop of the Baptists." He took cold on a benevolent excursion, fever followed, and he died at London in August, 1688, and was buried in Bunhill Fields.

The " Pilgrim's Progress," which has given Bunyan's name world-wide fame, was partly written in Bedford Gaol. It circulated at first among the poor, was soon widely known, and eagerly read. The tenth edition appeared in 1685. No religious book but the Bible and the " Imitation of Jesus Christ " has been translated into so many languages. It has long been no less the delight of the educated and refined than it was at first of the poor and ignorant. Bunyan's " Holy War," as an allegory, is only surpassed by the " Pilgrim's Progress." His other works are very numerous, the best known being the " Grace Abounding " and " Jerusalem Sinner Saved." " The Heavenly Footman," the sermon given here, partakes in many respects of the peculiar style he displayed in his sermons as well as in his prose writings.

THE HEAVENLY FOOTMAN

So run that ye may obtain.—1 Cor. ix. 24

HEAVEN and happiness is that which everyone desireth, insomuch that wicked Balaam would say: " Let me die the death of the righteous, and let my last end be like his." Yet, for all this, there are but very few that do obtain that ever-to-be-desired glory, insomuch that many eminent professors drop short of a welcome from God into this pleasant place. The Apostle, therefore, because he did desire the salvation of the souls of the Corinthians, to whom he writes this epistle, layeth them down in these words such counsel which, if taken, would be for their help and advantage.

Firstly, not to be wicked, and sit still, and wish for heaven, but to run for it.

Secondly, not to content themselves with every kind of running, but, saith he, " So run that ye may obtain." As if he should say, some, because they would not lose their souls, they begin to run betimes, they run apace, they run with patience, they run the right way. Do you so run. Some run from both father and mother, friends and companions, and thus, that they may have the crown. Do you so run. Some run through temptations, afflictions, good report, evil report, that they may win the pearl. Do you so run. " So run that ye may obtain."

These words, they are taken from men's running for a wager —a very apt similitude to set before the eyes of the saints of the Lord. " Know you not that they which run in a race run all, but one obtains the prize? So run that ye may obtain." That is, do not only run, but be sure you win as well as run. " So run that ye may obtain."

I shall not need to make any great ado in opening the words at this time, but shall rather lay down one doctrine that I do find in them ; and in prosecuting that, I shall show you, in some measure, the scope of the words.

The doctrine is this: They that will have heaven must run for it; I say, they that will have heaven, they must run for it. I beseech you to heed it well. "Know ye not that they which run in a race run all, but one obtaineth the prize? So run ye." The prize is heaven, and if you will have it you must run for it. You have another Scripture for this in the twelfth of the Hebrews, the first, second, and third verses: "Wherefore seeing also," saith the Apostle, "that we are compassed about with so great a cloud of witnesses, let us lay aside every weight, and the sin which doth so easily beset us, and let us run with patience the race that is set before us." And let us run, saith he.

Again, saith Paul, "I so run, not as uncertainly: so fight I," etc.

But before I go any further:

1. Fleeing. Observe, that this running is not an ordinary, or any sort of running, but it is to be understood of the swiftest sort of running; and, therefore, in the sixth of the Hebrews, it is called a fleeing: "That we might have strong consolation, who have fled for refuge, to lay hold on the hope set before us." Mark, who have fled. It is taken from that twentieth of Joshua, concerning the man that was to flee to the city of refuge, when the avenger of blood was hard at his heels, to take vengeance on him for the offence he had committed; therefore it is a running or fleeing for one's life: A running with all might and main, as we used to say. So run.

2. Pressing. Secondly, this running in another place is called a pressing. "I press towards the mark"; which signifieth that they that will have heaven, they must not stick at any difficulties they meet with; but press, crowd, and thrust through all that may stand between heaven and their souls. So run.

3. Continuing. Thirdly, this running is called in another place, a continuing in the way of life. "If you continue in the faith grounded, and settled, and be not moved away from the hope of the Gospel of Christ." Not to run a little now and then, by fits and starts, or halfway, or almost thither, but to run for my life, to run through all difficulties, and to continue therein to the end of the race, which must be to the end of my life. "So run that ye may obtain." And the reasons for this point are these:

1. Because all or everyone that runneth doth not obtain the

prize; there may be many that do run, yea, and run far too, who yet miss of the crown that standeth at the end of the race. You know that all that run in a race do not obtain the victory; they all run, but one wins. And so it is here; it is not every-one that runneth, nor everyone that seeketh, nor everyone that striveth, for the mastery, that hath it. " Though a man do strive for the mastery," saith Paul, " yet he is not crowned, unless he strive lawfully ; " that is, unless he so run, and so strive, as to have God's approbation. What, do ye think that every heavy-heeled professor will have heaven? What, every lazy one? every wanton and foolish professor, that will be stopped by anything, kept back by anything, that scarce run-neth so fast heavenward as a snail creepeth on the ground? Nay, there are some professors that do not go on so fast in the way of God as a snail doth go on the wall, and yet these think that heaven and happiness are for them. But stay, there are many more that run than there be that obtain; therefore he that will have heaven must run for it.

2. Because you know that though a man do run, yet if he do not overcome, or win, as well as run, what will they be the better for their running? They will get nothing. You know the man that runneth, he doth do it that he may win the prize: but if he doth not obtain it, he doth lose his labor, spend his pains and time, and that to no purpose; I say, he getteth nothing. And ah! how many such runners will there be found in the day of judgment? Even multitudes, multitudes that have run, yea, run so far as to come to heaven-gates, and not able to get any further, but there stand knocking, when it is too late, crying, Lord, Lord, when they have nothing but rebukes for their pains. Depart from me, you come not here, you come too late, you run too lazily; the door is shut. " When once the master of the house is risen up," saith Christ, " and hath shut to the door, and ye begin to stand without, and to knock, saying, Lord, Lord, open to us, I will say, I know you not, depart !" O sad will the state of those be that run and miss; therefore, if you will have heaven, you must run for it; and " so run that ye may obtain."

3. Because the way is long (I speak metaphorically), and there is many a dirty step, many a high hill, much work to do, a wicked heart, world, and devil to overcome; I say, there are many steps to be taken by those that intend to be saved, by

running or walking in the steps of that faith of our father Abraham. Out of Egypt thou must go through the Red Sea; thou must run a long and tedious journey, through the vast howling wilderness, before thou come to the land of promise.

4. They that will go to heaven they must run for it; because, as the way is long, so the time in which they are to get to the end of it is very uncertain; the time present is the only time; thou hast no more time allotted thee than that thou now enjoyest: "Boast not thyself of to-morrow, for thou knowest not what a day may bring forth." Do not say, I have time enough to get to heaven seven years hence, for, I tell thee, the bell may toll for thee before seven days more be ended; and when death comes, away thou must go, whether thou art provided or not; and therefore look to it; make no delays; it is not good dallying with things of so great concernment as the salvation or damnation of thy soul. You know he that hath a great way to go in a little time, and less by half than he thinks of, he had need to run for it.

5. They that will have heaven, they must run for it; because the devil, the law, sin, death, and hell follow them. There is never a poor soul that is going to heaven, but the devil, the law, sin, death, and hell make after that soul. "The devil, your adversary, as a roaring lion goeth about, seeking whom he may devour." And I will assure you, the devil is nimble, he can run apace, he is light of foot, he hath overtaken many, he hath turned up their heels, and hath given them an everlasting fall. Also, the law that can shoot a great way; have a care thou keep out of the reach of those great guns, the Ten Commandments. Hell also hath a wide mouth; it can stretch itself further than you are aware of. And as the angel said to Lot: "Take heed, look not behind thee, neither tarry thou in all the plain" (that is, anywhere between this and heaven), "lest thou be consumed;" so say I to thee, Take heed, tarry not, lest either the devil, hell, death, or the fearful curses of the law of God, do overtake thee, and throw thee down in the midst of thy sins, so as never to rise and recover again. If this were well considered, then, thou, as well as I, wouldst say, They that will have heaven must run for it.

6. They that will go to heaven must run for it; because perchance the gates of heaven may be shut shortly. Sometimes

sinners have not heaven-gates open to them so long as they suppose; and if they be once shut against a man, they are so heavy, that all the men in the world, nor all the angels in heaven, are not able to open them. " I shut, and no man can open," saith Christ. And how if thou shouldst come but one quarter of an hour too late? I tell thee, it will cost thee an eternity to bewail thy misery in. Francis Spira can tell thee what it is to stay till the gates of mercy be quite shut; or to run so lazily, that they be shut before thou get within them. What, to be shut out! what, out of heaven! Sinner, rather than lose it run for it; yea, and " so run that thou mayest obtain."

7. Lastly, because if thou lose, thou losest all, thou losest soul, God, Christ, heaven, ease, peace! Besides, thou layest thyself open to all the shame, contempt, and reproach, that either God, Christ, saints, the world, sin, the devil, and all, can lay upon thee. As Christ saith of the foolish builder, so will I say of thee, if thou be such a one who runs and misses; I say, even all that go by will begin to mock at thee, saying, This man began to run well, but was not able to finish. . . .

In the next place, be not daunted though thou meetest with never so many discouragements in thy journey thither. That man that is resolved for heaven, if Satan cannot win him by flatteries, he will endeavor to weaken him by discouragements, saying: " Thou art a sinner, thou hast broken God's law, thou art not elected, thou comest too late, the day of grace is passed; God doth not care for thee, thy heart is naught, thou art lazy," with a hundred other discouraging suggestions. And thus it was with David, where he saith: " I had fainted, unless I had believed to see the loving-kindness of the Lord in the land of the living." As if he should say, the devil did so rage, and my heart was so base, that had I judged according to my own sense and feeling, I had been absolutely distracted; but I trusted to Christ in the promise, and looked that God would be as good as his promise, in having mercy upon me, an unworthy sinner; and this is that which encouraged me and kept me from fainting. And thus must thou do when Satan, or the law, or thy own conscience, do go about to dishearten thee, either by the greatness of thy sins, the wickedness of thy heart, the tediousness of the way, the loss of outward enjoyments, the hatred that thou wilt procure from the world, or the like; then thou must

encourage thyself with the freeness of the promises, the tender-
heartedness of Christ, the merits of his blood, the freeness of his
invitations to come in, the greatness of the sin of others that
have been pardoned, and that the same God, through the same
Christ, holdeth forth the same grace as free as ever. If these
be not thy meditations, thou wilt draw very heavily in the way
to heaven, if thou do not give up all for lost, and so knock off
from following any further; therefore, I say, take heart in
thy journey, and say to them that seek thy destruction. " Rejoice not against me, O my enemy, for when I fall I shall arise,
when I sit in darkness the Lord shall be a light unto me." So
run.

Take heed of being offended at the cross that thou must go
by before thou come to heaven. You must understand (as I
have already touched) that there is no man that goeth to heaven
but he must go by the cross. The cross is the standing way-
mark by which all they that go to glory must pass.

" We must through much tribulation enter into the kingdom
of heaven." " Yea, and all that will live godly in Christ Jesus
shall suffer persecution." If thou art in thy way to the kingdom, my life for thine thou wilt come at the cross shortly (the
Lord grant thou dost not shrink at it, so as to turn thee back
again). " If any man will come after me," saith Christ, " let
him deny himself, and take up his cross daily, and follow me."
The cross, it stands, and hath stood, from the beginning, as a
way-mark to the kingdom of heaven. You know, if one ask
you the way to such and such a place, you, for the better direction, do not only say, " This is the way," but then also say, " You
must go by such a gate, by such a stile, such a bush, tree, bridge,"
or such like; why, so it is here; art thou inquiring the way
to heaven? Why, I tell thee, Christ is the way; into him thou
must get—into his righteousness—to be justified; and if thou
art in him, thou wilt presently see the cross; thou must go
close by it, thou must touch it—nay, thou must take it up, or else
thou wilt quickly go out of the way that leads to heaven, and
turn up some of those crooked lanes that lead down to the
chambers of death.

Now thou mayest know the cross by these six things:

1. It is known in the doctrine of justification.

2. In the doctrine of mortification.

3. In the doctrine of perseverance.
4. In self-denial.
5. Patience.
6. Communion with poor saints.

1. In the doctrine of justification, there is a great deal of the cross in that a man is forced to suffer the destruction of his own righteousness for the righteousness of another. This is no easy matter for a man to do; I assure to you it stretcheth every vein in his heart, before he will be brought to yield to it. What, for a man to deny, reject, abhor, and throw away all his prayers, tears, alms, keeping of Sabbaths, hearing, reading, with the rest, in the point of justification, and to count them accursed; and to be willing, in the very midst of the sense of his sins, to throw himself wholly upon the righteousness and obedience of another man, abhorring his own, counting it as deadly sin, as the open breach of the law—I say, to do this in deed and in truth is the biggest piece of the cross; and, therefore, Paul calleth this very thing a suffering, where he saith: " And I have suffered the loss of all things (which principally was his righteousness) that I might win Christ, and be found in him, not having (but rejecting) my own righteousness." That is the first.

2. In the doctrine of mortification is also much of the cross. Is it nothing for a man to lay hands on his vile opinions, on his vile sins, on his bosom sins, on his beloved, pleasant, darling sins, that stick as close to him as the flesh sticks to the bones? What, to lose all these brave things that my eyes behold, for that which I never saw with my eyes? What, to lose my pride, my covetousness, my vain company, sports, and pleasures, and the rest? I tell you, this is no easy matter; if it were, what need all those prayers, sighs, watchings? What need we be so backward to it? Nay, do you not see that some men, before they will set about this work, they will even venture the loss of their souls, heaven, God, Christ, and all? What means else all those delays and put-offs, saying, " Stay a little longer, I am loth to leave my sins while I am so young, and in health "? Again, what is the reason else that others do it so by the halves, coldly and seldom, notwithstanding they are convinced over and over; nay, and also promise to amend, and yet all's in vain? I will assure you, to cut off right hands, and to pluck out right eyes, is no pleasure to the flesh.

3. The doctrine of perseverance is also cross to the flesh; which is not only to begin but to hold out, not only to bid fair, and to say: " Would I had heaven," but so to know Christ, put on Christ, and walk with Christ, so as to come to heaven. Indeed, it is no great matter to begin to look for heaven, to begin to seek the Lord, to begin to shun sin; O but it is a very great matter to continue with God's approbation: " My servant Caleb," saith God, " is a man of another spirit, he hath followed me (followed me always, he hath continually followed me) fully, he shall possess the land." Almost all the many thousands of the children of Israel in their generation fell short of perseverance when they walked from Egypt towards the land of Canaan. Indeed, they went to work at first pretty willingly, but they were very short-winded, they were quickly out of breath, and in their hearts they turned back again into Egypt.

It is an easy matter for a man to run hard for a spurt, for a furlong, for a mile or two: Oh, but to hold out for a hundred, for a thousand, for ten thousand miles, that man that doth this, he must look to meet with cross, pain, and wearisomeness to the flesh, especially if, as he goeth, he meeteth with briars and quagmires, and other incumbrances, that make his journey so much the more painful.

Nay, do you not see with your eyes daily that perseverance is a very great part of the cross? Why else do men so soon grow weary? I could point out a many, that after they have followed the ways of God about a twelvemonth, others it may be two, three, or four (some more, and some less) years, they have been beat out of wind, have taken up their lodging and rest before they have gotten half-way to heaven, some in this, some in that sin, and have secretly, nay, sometimes openly, said that the way is too straight, the race too long, the religion too holy—I cannot hold out; I can go no further.

And so likewise of the other three, to wit: patience, self-denial, communion, and communication with and to the poor saints: How hard are these things? It is an easy matter to deny another man, but it is not so easy a matter to deny one's self; to deny myself out of love to God, to his Gospel, to his saints, of this advantage, and of that gain; nay, of that which otherwise I might lawfully do, were it not for offending them. That Scripture is but seldom read, and seldomer put in practice, which saith, " I will eat no flesh while the world standeth, if it make my brother to offend " ; again, " We that are strong ought to bear the infirmities of the weak, and not to please ourselves." But how froward, how hasty, how peevish, and self-resolved, are the generality of professors at this day! Also how little considering the poor, unless it be to say, " Be thou warmed and filled ! " But to give is a seldom work ; also especially to give to any poor. I tell you all things are cross to flesh and blood ; and that man that hath but a watchful eye over the flesh, and also some considerable measure of strength against it, he shall find his heart in these things like unto a starting horse, that is rode without a curbing bridle, ready to start at everything that is offensive to him—yea, and ready to run away, too, do what the rider can.

It is the cross which keepeth those that are kept from heaven. I am persuaded, were it not for the cross, where we have one professor we should have twenty ; but this cross, that is it which spoileth all.

Some men, as I said before, when they come at the cross they can go no further, but back again to their sins they must go. Others they stumble at it, and break their necks ; others again, when they see the cross is approaching, they turn aside to the left hand, or to the right hand, and so think to get to heaven another way ; but they will be deceived. " For all that will live godly in Christ Jesus shall," mark, " shall be sure to suffer persecution." There are but few when they come at the cross, cry, " Welcome cross ! " as some of the martyrs did to the stake they were burned at. Therefore, if you meet with the cross in thy journey, in what manner soever it be, be not daunted, and say, " Alas, what shall I do now ! " But rather take courage, knowing that by the cross is the way to the kingdom. Can a man believe in Christ, and not be hated by the devil ? Can he make a profession of this Christ, and that sweetly and convincingly, and the children of Satan hold their tongues ? Can darkness agree with light, or the devil endure that Christ Jesus should be honored both by faith and a heavenly conversation, and let that soul alone at quiet ? Did you never read that " the dragon persecuted the woman " ? And that Christ saith, " In the world you shall have tribulations " ?

Beg of God that he would do these two things for thee :

First, enlighten thine understanding; and, second, inflame thy will. If these two be but effectually done there is no fear but thou wilt go safe to heaven.

One of the great reasons why men and women do so little regard the other world is because they see so little of it; and the reason why they see so little of it is because they have their understanding darkened. And, therefore, saith Paul, "Do not you believers walk as do other Gentiles, even in the vanity of their minds having their understanding darkened, being alienated from the life of God through the ignorance (or foolishness) that is in them, because of the blindness of their heart." Walk not as those, run not with them: alas, poor souls, they have their understandings darkened, their hearts blinded, and that is the reason they have such undervaluing thoughts of the Lord Jesus Christ and the salvation of their souls. For when men do come to see the things of another world, what a God, what a Christ, what a heaven, and what an eternal glory there is to be enjoyed; also, when they see that it is possible for them to have a share in it, I tell you it will make them run through thick and thin to enjoy it. Moses, having a sight of this, because his understanding was enlightened, "He feared not the wrath of the king, but chose rather to suffer afflictions with the people of God than to enjoy the pleasures of sin for a season. He refused to be called the son of the king's daughter," accounting it wonderful riches to be accounted worthy of so much as to suffer for Christ, with the poor despised saints; and that was because he saw him who was invisible, and had respect unto the recompense of reward. And this is that which the Apostle usually prayeth for in his epistles for the saints, namely, "That they might know what is the hope of God's calling, and the riches of the glory of his inheritance in the saints; and that they might be able to comprehend with all saints what is the breadth, and length, and depth, and height, and know the love of Christ, which passeth knowledge." Pray, therefore, that God would enlighten thy understanding; that will be a very great help unto thee. It will make thee endure many a hard brunt for Christ; as Paul saith, "After you were illuminated ye endured a great sight of afflictions; you took joyfully the spoiling of your goods, knowing in yourselves that ye have in heaven a better and an enduring substance." If there be never such a rare jewel lie just in a man's way, yet if he sees it not he will rather trample upon it than stoop for it, and it is because he sees it not. Why, so it is here, though heaven be worth never so much, and thou hast never so much need of it, yet if thou see it not—that is, have not thy understanding opened or enlightened to see—thou wilt not regard at all: therefore cry to the Lord for enlightening grace and say, " Lord, open my blind eyes; Lord, take the veil off my dark heart," show me the things of the other world, and let me see the sweetness, the glory, and excellency of them for Christ's sake. This is the first.

Cry to God that he would inflame thy will also with the things of the other world. For when a man's will is fully set to do such or such a thing, then it must be a very hard matter that shall hinder that man from bringing about his end. When Paul's will was set resolvedly to go up to Jerusalem, though it was signified to him before what he should there suffer, he was not daunted at all; nay, saith he, " I am ready [or willing] not only to be bound, but also to die at Jerusalem for the name of the Lord Jesus." His will was inflamed with love to Christ; and therefore all the persuasions that could be used wrought nothing at all.

Your self-willed people, nobody knows what to do with them: we used to say, " He will have his own will, do all what you can." Indeed, to have such a will for heaven is an admirable advantage to a man that undertaketh a race thither; a man that is resolved, and hath his will fixed; saith he: " I will do my best to advantage myself; I will do my worst to hinder my enemies; I will not give out as long as I can stand; I will have it or I will lose my life; though he slay me, yet will I trust in him. I will not let thee go except thou bless me." I will, I will, I will, O this blessed inflamed will for heaven! What is it like? If a man be willing, then any argument shall be matter of encouragement; but if unwilling, then any argument shall give discouragement. This is seen both in saints and sinners; in them that are the children of God, and also those that are the children of the devil. As,

1. The saints of old, they being willing and resolved for heaven, what could stop them? Could fire and faggot, sword or halter, stinking dungeons, whips, bears, bulls, lions, cruel rackings, stoning, starving, nakedness? " And in all these

things they were more than conquerors, through him that loved them," who had also made them " willing in the day of his power."

2. See again, on the other side, the children of the devil, because they are not willing; how many shifts and starting-holes they will have. I have married a wife; I have a farm; I shall offend my landlord; I shall offend my master; I shall lose my trading; I shall lose my pride, my pleasures; I shall be mocked and scoffed: therefore I dare not come. I, saith another, will stay till I am older, till my children are out, till I am got a little aforehand in the world, till I have done this and that, and the other business: but, alas! the thing is, they are not willing; for, were they but soundly willing, these, and a thousand such as these, would hold them no faster than the cords held Samson, when he broke them like burnt flax. I tell you the will is all: that is one of the chief things which turns the wheel either backwards or forwards; and God knoweth that full well, and so likewise doth the devil, and therefore they both endeavor very much to strengthen the will of their servants. God, he is for making of his a willing people to serve him; and the devil, he doth what he can to possess the will and affection of those that are his with love to sin; and therefore when Christ comes close to the matter, indeed, saith he, " You will not come to me. How often would I have gathered you as a hen doth her chickens, but you would not." The devil had possessed their wills, and so long he was sure enough of them. Oh, therefore, cry hard to God to inflame thy will for heaven and Christ: thy will, I say, if that be rightly set for heaven, thou wilt not be beat off with discouragements; and this was the reason that when Jacob wrestled with the angel, though he lost a limb, as it were, and the hollow of his thigh was put out of joint as he wrestled with him, yet, saith he, " I will not," mark, " I will not let thee go except thou bless me." Get thy will tipped with the heavenly grace, and resolution against all discouragements, and then thou goest full speed for heaven; but if thou falter in thy will, and be not found there, thou wilt run hobbling and halting all the way thou runnest, and also to be sure thou wilt fall short at last. The Lord give thee a will and courage.

UNION OF ENGLAND AND SCOTLAND

—

BY

LORD BELHAVEN

(John Hamilton)

JOHN HAMILTON, LORD BELHAVEN

1656—1708

Lord Belhaven belonged to the Hamilton family. He was one of the old Presbyterian lords, highly educated, especially in classical literature; lofty in his demeanor; dauntless in spirit; and wholly devoted to the peculiar interests of his country. He was born in 1656, and died in 1708.

A century had elapsed since the union of the English and Scottish crowns in the person of James I, and Scotland still remained a distinct kingdom. Scotland was governed by alternate corruption and force. Her nobility and gentry were drawn to England in great numbers, and her merchants and tradesmen were led to transfer their capital to the sister kingdom, in consequence of the superior facilities for trade which were there enjoyed. There was one point where England was vulnerable. It was the succession to the crown. This had been settled by the English Parliament on the Protestant line in the House of Hanover, and it was fully expected that the Parliament of Scotland would readily unite in the same measure. Instead of this, the Scotch, in 1704, enacted that "the same person should be incapable of succeeding in both kingdoms, unless a free communication of trade, the benefits of the Navigation Act, and liberty of the Plantations was first obtained."

It was now obvious that concessions must be made on both sides. The ministry of Queen Anne, therefore, proposed that commissioners from the two kingdoms should meet at London, to devise a plan of Union. This was accordingly done, in the month of April, 1706; and, after long negotiations, it was agreed, that the two kingdoms should be united into one under the British Parliament, with the addition of sixteen Scottish peers to the House of Lords, and of forty-five Scottish members to the House of Commons; that the Scotch should be entitled to all the privileges of the English in respect to trade, and be subject to the same excise and duties; that Scotland should receive £398,000 as a compensation or " equivalent " for the share of liability she assumed in the English debt of £20,000,000; and that the churches of England and Scotland respectively should be confirmed in all their rights and privileges, as a fundamental condition of the Union.

These arrangements were kept secret until October, 1706, when the Scottish Parliament met. The moment the articles were read in that body, they were met with a burst of indignant reprobation from every quarter. A federal union which should confer equal advantages for trade, was all that the Scotch in general had ever contemplated: an incorporating union, which should abolish their Parliament and extinguish their national existence, was what most Scotchmen had never dreamed of. It was with sentiments like these that, when the first article of the treaty was read, Lord Belhaven arose, and addressed the Parliament of Scotland in the following speech. It was designed merely to open the discussion which was expected to follow. It was a simple burst of feeling, in which the great leader of the country party poured out his emotions in view of that act of parricide, as he considered it, to which the Parliament was now called. He felt that no regard to consequences, no loss or advancement of trade, manufactures, or national wealth, ought to have the weight of a feather, when the honor and existence of his country were at stake.

UNION OF ENGLAND AND SCOTLAND

M Y LORD CHANCELLOR: When I consider the affair of a union betwixt the two nations, as expressed in the several articles thereof, and now the subject of our deliberation at this time,[1] I find my mind crowded with a variety of melancholy thoughts; and I think it my duty to disburden myself of some of them by laying them before, and exposing them to, the serious consideration of this honorable House.

I think I see a free and independent kingdom delivering up that which all the world hath been fighting for since the days of Nimrod; yea, that for which most of all the empires, kingdoms, states, principalities, and the dukedoms of Europe are at this time engaged in the most bloody and cruel wars; to wit, a power to manage their own affairs by themselves, without the assistance and counsel of any other.

I think I see a national Church, founded upon a rock, secured by a claim of right, hedged and fenced about by the strictest and most pointed legal sanctions that sovereignty could contrive, voluntarily descending into a plain, upon an equal level with Jews, Papists, Socinians, Arminians, Anabaptists, and other sectaries.

I think I see the noble and honorable peerage of Scotland, whose valiant predecessors led armies against their enemies upon their own proper charges and expense, now divested of their followers and vassalages; and put upon such an equal foot with their vassals, that I think I see a petty English exciseman receive more homage and respect than what was paid formerly to their quondam MacCallammores.

I think I see the present peers of Scotland, whose noble ancestors conquered provinces, overran countries, reduced and subjected towns and fortified places, exacted tribute through the greatest part of England, now walking in the Court of Requests, like so many English attorneys; laying aside their walking swords when in company with the English peers, lest their self-defence should be found murder.

I think I see the honorable estate of barons, the bold assertors of the nation's rights and liberties in the worst of times, now setting a watch upon their lips, and a guard upon their tongues, lest they may be found guilty of *scandalum magnatum,* a speaking evil of dignities.

I think I see the royal state of burghers walking their desolate streets, hanging down their heads under disappointments wormed out of all the branches of their old trade, uncertain what hand to turn to, necessitated to become 'prentices to their unkind neighbors; and yet, after all, finding their trade so fortified by companies, and secured by prescriptions, that they despair of any success therein.

I think I see our learned judges laying aside their pratiques and decisions, studying the common law of England, gravelled with *certioraris, nisi priuses,* writs of error, verdicts, injunctions, demurs, etc., and frightened with appeals and avocations, because of the new regulations and rectifications they may meet with.

I think I see the valiant and gallant soldiery either sent to learn the plantation trade abroad, or at home petitioning for a small subsistence, as a reward of their honorable exploits; while their old corps are broken, the common soldiers left to beg, and the youngest English corps kept standing.

I think I see the honest industrious tradesman loaded with new taxes and impositions, disappointed of the equivalents,[2] drinking water in place of ale, eating his saltless pottage, petitioning for encouragement to his manufactures, and answered by counter-petitions.

In short, I think I see the laborious ploughman, with his corn spoiling upon his hands for want of sale, cursing the day of his birth, dreading the expense of his burial, and uncertain whether to marry or do worse.

[2] [The "equivalent," or compensation, of £398,000 spoken of above, was to be distributed, a great portion of it, to the shareholders of the African and India Company, who had suffered so severely by the breaking up of the Darien Settlement. As the shares must, in many instances, have changed hands, great inequality and disappointment were to be expected in the distribution of this money, which was likely, in most cases, to go into the hands of the friends of Government, as a bribe or recompense for services on this occasion.]

I think I see the incurable difficulties of the landed men, fettered under the golden chain of "equivalents," their pretty daughters petitioning for want of husbands, and their sons for want of employment.

I think I see our mariners delivering up their ships to their Dutch partners; and what through presses and necessity, earning their bread as underlings in the Royal English Navy!

But above all, my lord, I think I see our ancient mother, Caledonia, like Cæsar, sitting in the midst of our senate, ruefully looking round about her, covering herself with her royal garment, attending the fatal blow, and breathing out her last with an *et tu quoque mi fili!*

Are not these, my lord, very afflicting thoughts? And yet they are but the least part suggested to me by these dishonorable articles. Should not the consideration of these things vivify these dry bones of ours! Should not the memory of our noble predecessors' valor and constancy rouse up our drooping spirits? Are our noble predecessors' souls got so far into the English cabbage-stalk and cauliflowers, that we should show the least inclination that way? Are our eyes so blinded, are our ears so deafened, are our hearts so hardened, are our tongues so faltered, are our hands so fettered, that in this our day—I say, my lords, in this our day—we should not mind the things that concern the very being and well-being of our ancient kingdom, before the day be hid from our eyes?

No, my lord, God forbid! Man's extremity is God's opportunity: He is a present help in time of need—a deliverer, and that right early! Some unforeseen providence will fall out, that may cast the balance; some Joseph or other will say, "Why do ye strive together, since ye are brethren?" None can destroy Scotland save Scotland's self. Hold your hands from the pen, and you are secure! There will be a Jehovah-Jireh; and some ram will be caught in the thicket, when the bloody knife is at our mother's throat. Let us, then, my lord, and let our noble patriots behave themselves like men, and we know not how soon a blessing may come.

I design not at this time to enter into the merits of any one particular article. I intend this discourse as an introduction to what I may afterwards say upon the whole debate, as it falls in before this honorable House; and therefore, in the further prosecution of what I have to say, I shall insist upon a few particulars, very necessary to be understood before we enter into the detail of so important a matter.

I shall therefore, in the first place, endeavor to encourage a free and full deliberation, without animosities and heats. In the next place, I shall endeavor to make an inquiry into the nature and source of the unnatural and dangerous divisions that are now on foot within this isle, with some motives showing that it is our interest to lay them aside at this time. And all this with all deference, and under the correction of this honorable House.

My Lord Chancellor, the greatest honor that was done unto a Roman was to allow him the glory of a triumph; the greatest and most dishonorable punishment was that of a parricide. He that was guilty of parricide was beaten with rods upon his naked body till the blood gushed out of all the veins of his body; then he was sewed up in a leathern sack called a *culeus*, with a cock, a viper, and an ape, and thrown headlong into the sea.

My lord, patricide is a greater crime than parricide, all the world over.

In a triumph, my lord, when the conqueror was riding in his triumphal chariot, crowned with laurels, adorned with trophies, and applauded with huzzas, there was a monitor appointed to stand behind him to warn him not to be high-minded nor puffed up with overweening thoughts of himself; and to his chariot were tied a whip and a bell, to remind him that, notwithstanding all his glory and grandeur, he was accountable to the people for his administration, and would be punished as other men if found guilty.

The greatest honor among us, my lord, is to represent the sovereign's sacred person [as High Commissioner] in Parliament; and in one particular it appears to be greater than that of a triumph, because the whole legislative power seems to be entrusted with him. If he give the royal assent to an act of the estates, it becomes a law obligatory upon the subject, though contrary to or without any instructions from the sovereign. If he refuse the royal assent to a vote in Parliament, it cannot be a law, though he has the sovereign's particular and positive instructions for it.

His Grace the Duke of Queensberry, who now represents Her Majesty in this session of Parliament, hath had the honor of that great trust as often, if not more, than any Scotchman ever had. He hath been the favorite of two successive sovereigns; and I cannot but commend his constancy and perseverance, that, notwithstanding his former difficulties and unsuccessful attempts, and maugre some other specialties not yet determined, his grace has yet had the resolution to undertake the most unpopular measure last. If his grace succeed in this affair of a union, and that it prove for the happiness and welfare of the nation, then he justly merits to have a statue of gold erected for himself; but if it shall tend to the entire destruction and abolition of our nation, and that we, the nation's trustees, shall go into it, then I must say that a whip and a bell, a cock, a viper, and an ape, are but too-small punishments for any such bold unnatural undertaking and complaisance.

1. That I may pave the way, my lord, to a full, calm, and free reasoning upon this affair, which is of the last consequence unto this nation, I shall mind this honorable House that we are the successors of those noble ancestors who founded our monarchy, framed our laws, amended, altered, and corrected them from time to time, as the affairs and circumstances of the nation did require, without the assistance or advice of any foreign power or potentate, and who, during the time of two thousand years, have handed them down to us, a free independent nation, with the hazard of their lives and fortunes. Shall not we, then, argue for that which our progenitors have purchased for us at so dear a rate, and with so much immortal honor and glory? God forbid! Shall the hazard of a father unbind the ligaments of a dumb son's tongue? and shall we hold our peace when our *patria*, our country, is in danger?[3] I say this, my lord, that I may encourage every individual member of this House to speak his mind freely. There are many wise and prudent men among us who think it not worth their while to open their mouths; there are others who can speak very well, and to good purpose, who shelter themselves under the shameful cloak of silence, from a fear of the frowns of great men and parties. I have observed, my lord, by my experience, the greatest number of speakers in the most trivial affairs; and it will always prove

[3] In allusion to the story of Crœsus and his dumb child, as related by Herodotus.

so while we come not to the right understanding of the oath *de fideli,* whereby we are bound not only to give our vote but our faithful advice in Parliament, as we should answer to God. And in our ancient laws the representatives of the honorable barons and the royal boroughs are termed " spokesmen." It lies upon your lordships, therefore, particularly to take notice of such whose modesty makes them bashful to speak. Therefore I shall leave it upon you, and conclude this point with a very memorable saying of an honest private gentleman to a great queen, upon occasion of a state project, contrived by an able statesman, and the favorite to a great king, against a peaceful obedient people, because of the diversity of their laws and constitutions: " If at this time thou hold thy peace, salvation shall come to the people from another place, but thou and thy house shall perish." I leave the application to each particular member of this House.

2. My lord, I come now to consider our divisions. We are under the happy reign, blessed be God, of the best of queens, who has no evil design against the meanest of her subjects; who loves all her people, and is equally beloved by them again; and yet, that under the happy influence of our most excellent Queen, there should be such divisions and factions, more dangerous and threatening to her dominions than if we were under an arbitrary government, is most strange and unaccountable. Under an arbitrary prince all are willing to serve, because all are under a necessity to obey, whether they will or not. He chooses, therefore, whom he will, without respect to either parties or factions; and if he think fit to take the advice of his councils or parliaments, every man speaks his mind freely, and the prince receives the faithful advice of his people, without the mixture of self-designs. If he prove a good prince, the government is easy; if bad, either death or a revolution brings a deliverance, whereas here, my lord, there appears no end of our misery, if not prevented in time. Factions are now become independent, and have got footing in councils, in parliaments, in treaties, in armies, in incorporations, in families, among kindred; yea, man and wife are not free from their political jars.

It remains, therefore, my lord, that I inquire into the nature of these things; and since the names give us not the right idea of the thing, I am afraid I shall have difficulty to make myself well understood.

The names generally used to denote the factions are Whig and Tory; as obscure as that of Guelfs and Ghibellines; yea, my lord, they have different significations, as they are applied to factions in each kingdom. A Whig in England is a heterogeneous creature: in Scotland he is all of a piece. A Tory in England is all of a piece, and a statesman: in Scotland he is quite otherwise—an anti-courtier and anti-statesman.

A Whig in England appears to be somewhat like Nebuchadnezzar's image, of different metals, different classes, different principles, and different designs; yet take them altogether, they are like a piece of some mixed drugget of different threads; some finer, some coarser, which, after all, make a comely appearance and an agreeable suit. Tory is like a piece of loyal home-made English cloth, the true staple of the nation, all of a thread; yet if we look narrowly into it, we shall perceive a diversity of colors, which, according to the various situations and positions, make various appearances. Sometimes Tory is like the moon in its full; as appeared in the affair of the Bill of Occasional Conformity. Upon other occasions, it appears to be under a cloud, and as if it were eclipsed by a greater body; as it did in the design of calling over the illustrious Princess Sophia. However, by this we may see their designs are to outshoot Whig in his own bow.

Whig, in Scotland, is a true blue Presbyterian, who, without considering time or power, will venture his all for the Kirk, but something less for the State. The greatest difficulty is how to describe a Scotch Tory. Of old, when I knew them first, Tory was an honest-hearted, comradeish fellow, who, provided he was maintained and protected in his benefices, titles, and dignities, by the State, was the less anxious who had the government of the Church. But now, what he is since *jure divino* came in fashion, and that Christianity, and by consequence salvation, comes to depend upon Episcopal ordination, I profess I know not what to make of him; only this I must say for him, that he endeavors to do by opposition that which his brother in England endeavors by a more prudent and less scrupulous method.

Now, my lord, from these divisions there has got up a kind

of aristocracy, something like the famous triumvirate at Rome. They are a kind of undertakers and pragmatic statesmen, who, finding their power and strength great, and answerable to their designs, will make bargains with our gracious sovereign; they will serve her faithfully, but upon their own terms; they must have their own instruments, their own measures. This man must be turned out, and that man put in, and then they will make her the most glorious queen in Europe.

Where will this end, my lord? Is not Her Majesty in danger by such a method? Is not the monarchy in danger? Is not the nation's peace and tranquillity in danger? Will a change of parties make the nation more happy? No, my lord. The seed is sown that is like to afford us a perpetual increase. It is not an annual herb, it takes deep root; it seeds and breeds; and if not timely prevented by Her Majesty's royal endeavors, will split the whole island in two.

3. My lord, I think, considering our present circumstances at this time, the Almighty God has reserved this great work for us. We may bruise this hydra of division and crush this cockatrice's egg. Our neighbors in England are not yet fitted for any such thing; they are not under the afflicting hand of Providence, as we are. Their circumstances are great and glorious; their treaties are prudently managed, both at home and abroad; their generals brave and valorous, their armies successful and victorious; their trophies and laurels memorable and surprising; their enemies subdued and routed, their strongholds besieged and taken. Sieges relieved, marshals killed and taken prisoners, provinces and kingdoms are the results of their victories. Their royal navy is the terror of Europe; their trade and commerce extended through the universe, encircling the whole habitable world, and rendering their own capital city the emporium for the whole inhabitants of the earth.[4] And which is yet more than all these things, the subjects freely bestowing their treasure upon their sovereign; and above all, these vast riches, the sinews of war, and without which all the glorious success had proved abortive, these treasures are managed with such faithfulness and nicety, that they answer seasonably all their demands, though at never so great a distance.

[4] [Perhaps in allusion to the battle of Blenheim and other victories of Marlborough which had recently taken place.]

Upon these considerations, my lord, how hard and difficult a thing will it prove to persuade our neighbors to a self-denying bill.

'Tis quite otherwise with us, my lord, as we are an obscure, poor people, though formerly of better account, removed to a distant corner of the world, without name, and without alliances; our posts mean and precarious; so that I profess I don't think any one post in the kingdom worth the briguing [seeking] after, save that of being commissioner to a long session of a factious Scotch Parliament, with an antedated commission, and that yet renders the rest of the ministers more miserable. What hinders us then, my lord, to lay aside our divisions, to unite cordially and heartily together in our present circumstances, when our all is at stake? Hannibal, my lord, is at our gates— Hannibal is come within our gates—Hannibal is come the length of this table—he is at the foot of the throne. He will demolish the throne if we take not notice. He will seize upon these regalia. He will take them as our *spolia opima,* and whip us out of this House, never to return again.

For the love of God, then, my lord, for the safety and welfare of our ancient kingdom, whose sad circumstances I hope we shall yet convert into prosperity and happiness! We want no means if we unite. God blessed the peacemakers. We want neither men nor sufficiency of all manner of things necessary to make a nation happy. All depends upon management. *Concordiâ res parvæ crescunt*—small means increase by concord. I fear not these articles, though they were ten times worse than they are, if we once cordially forgive one another, and that according to our proverb, " Bygones be bygones," and fair play for time to come. For my part, in the sight of God, and in the presence of this honorable House, I heartily forgive every man, and beg that they may do the same to me. And I do most humbly propose that his grace my lord commissioner may appoint an *Agape,* may order a love-feast for this honorable House, that we may lay aside all self-designs, and after our fasts and humiliations, may have a day of rejoicing and thankfulness; may eat our meat with gladness, and our bread with a merry heart. Then shall we sit each man under his own fig-tree, and the voice of the turtle shall be heard in our land, a bird famous for constancy and fidelity.

My lord, I shall pause here, and proceed no further in my discourse, till I see if his grace my lord commissioner [Queensberry] will receive any humble proposals for removing misunderstandings among us, and putting an end to our fatal divisions. Upon my honor, I have no other design; and I am content to beg the favor upon my bended knees.

[No answer.]

My Lord Chancellor, I am sorry that I must pursue the thread of my sad and melancholy story. What remains is more afflictive than what I have already said. Allow me then to make this meditation—that if our posterity, after we are all dead and gone, shall find themselves under an ill-made bargain, and shall have recourse of our records for the names of the managers who made that treaty by which they have suffered so much, they will certainly exclaim: " Our nation must have been reduced to the last extremity at the time of this treaty! All our great chieftains, all our noble peers, who once defended the rights and liberties of the nation, must have been killed, and lying dead on the bed of honor, before the nation could ever condescend to such mean and contemptible terms! Where were the great men of the noble families—the Stewarts, Hamiltons, Grahams, Campbells, Johnstons, Murrays, Homes, Kers? Where were the two great officers of the Crown, the Constable and the Marischal of Scotland? Certainly all were extinguished, and now we are slaves forever! "

But the English records; how will they make their posterity reverence the names of those illustrious men who made that treaty and forever brought under those fierce, warlike, and troublesome neighbors, who had struggled so long for independency, shed the best blood of their nation, and reduced a considerable part of their country to become waste and desolate!

I see the English constitution remaining firm—the same two Houses of Parliament; the same taxes, customs, and excise; the same trade in companies, the same municipal laws, while all ours are either subjected to new regulations, or annihilated forever! And for what? Only that we may have the honor to pay their old debts; and may have some few persons present [in Parliament] as witnesses to the validity of the deed, when they are pleased to contract more!

Good God! What? Is this an entire surrender?

My lord, I find my heart so full of grief and indignation, that I must beg pardon not to finish the last part of my discourse: but pause that I may drop a tear as the prelude to so sad a story![5]

[5] [This fervent appeal had no effect. The Treaty of Union was ratified by a majority of thirty-three out of two hundred and one members. That it was carried by bribery is now matter of history. Documents have been brought to light showing that the sum of £20,000 was sent to Queensberry for this purpose by the English Ministers; and the names of those to whom the money was paid are given in full.—EDITOR.]

ON A MOTION FOR HIS REMOVAL

—

BY

SIR ROBERT WALPOLE

Earl of Orford

SIR ROBERT WALPOLE, EARL OF ORFORD

1676—1745

Walpole was in some respects the most modern of eighteenth century statesmen; it was he who first adopted, in his speeches before Parliament, that easy, colloquial style which now prevails there, and which Englishmen like, because it makes no pretence of addressing anything but the plainest common-sense. He was, as a politician, entirely unprincipled, and yet he had neither the ambition nor the cynicism which are usually associated with such a character; he was constitutionally an indolent man, and a weak one; but he loved the surroundings of public life; he enjoyed the ascendancy which high place and his own exceptional talent gave him over men; and he could not resist the will of his King, who supplied by persistence and obstinacy what was lacking in him in the way of brains and magnanimity. Walpole would more than once have acted a nobler and more far-seeing part than he actually did, had it not been for the sinister influence of George II; but in the end he always yielded to the latter, and thereby rendered his own lot an unhappy one; for his conscience, refusing to be utterly smothered, stirred reproachfully in his breast, and his pride was hurt by the servility and baseness of the rôle which he was too often forced to play. More than once in his career did this outwardly gay and indifferent man of the world confess himself to be the most miserable of men.

He received his early education at Eton School, and at the University of Cambridge; and afterwards " completed " it—as the phrase was—by a tour on the Continent, visiting France and Germany. He entered Parliament in 1701, and a few years later was made member of the council for Prince George; he embraced Whig principles, and was appointed Secretary at War in 1708. He was also treasurer of the navy; and when in 1710, Henry Sacheverell, a clergyman and Tory, who had been an associate of Addison, and was noted for his eloquence as a preacher, criticised the Whig ministry in two sermons preached at Southwark, he was prosecuted at the instance of Godolphin, the aged statesman and financier, assisted by Walpole, and sentenced to three years' suspension. But the Marlboroughs fell that year, and Godolphin with them, and the clergyman was reinstated by a Tory ministry. Before his reinstatement, Walpole had been accused and convicted of bribery, expelled from Parliament, and committed to the Tower; but he was too useful a man to stay there, and in the following year (1713) we find him once more in the House; and his career thenceforth was outwardly a blaze of success; he was twice prime minister, and was created Earl of Orford in 1742. He died three years afterwards.

CHOICE EXAMPLES OF CLASSIC ARCHITECTURE.

THE PARTHENON AT ATHENS.

Photogravure from a photograph.

The Parthenon, the temple of Minerva, at Athens, is usually regarded as the most perfect specimen of Greek architecture. Many of the sculptures have been transported to England, and are now in the British Museum, where they form, with some other relics of antiquity, the collection known as the *Elgin Marbles*.

ON A MOTION FOR HIS REMOVAL

IT has been observed by several gentlemen, in vindication of this motion, that if it should be carried, neither my life, liberty, nor estate will be affected. But do the honorable gentlemen consider my character and reputation as of no moment? Is it no imputation to be arraigned before this House, in which I have sat forty years, and to have my name transmitted to posterity with disgrace and infamy? I will not conceal my sentiments, that to be named in Parliament as a subject of inquiry is to me a matter of great concern. But I have the satisfaction, at the same time, to reflect, that the impression to be made depends upon the consistency of the charge and the motives of the prosecutors.[1]

Had the charge been reduced to specific allegations, I should have felt myself called upon for a specific defence. Had I served a weak or wicked master, and implicitly obeyed his dictates, obedience to his commands must have been my only justification. But as it has been my good fortune to serve a master who wants no bad ministers, and would have hearkened to none, my defence must rest on my own conduct. The consciousness of innocence is also a sufficient support against my present prosecutors. A further justification is derived from a consideration of the views and abilities of the prosecutors. Had I been guilty of great enormities, they want neither zeal and inclination to bring them forward, nor ability to place them in the most prominent point of view. But as I am con-

[1] [A speech delivered in the House of Commons, February, 1741. Sandys, the leader of the opposition against Walpole, made a long speech to the effect that Walpole had been at the head of affairs for twenty years, and that the people were tired of him as a minister, and hated him as a man; he concluded by moving " that an humble address be presented to His Majesty, that he would be graciously pleased to remove the Right Honorable Sir Robert Walpole, Knight of the Most Noble Order of the Garter, First Commissioner for executing the office of Treasurer of the Exchequer, Chancellor and Under Treasurer of the Exchequer, and one of His Majesty's Most Honorable Privy Council, from His Majesty's presence and councils forever."]

scious of no crime, my own experience convinces me that none can be justly imputed.

I must therefore ask the gentlemen from whence does this attack proceed? From the passions and prejudices of the parties combined against me, who may be divided into three classes, the Boys,[2] the riper Patriots, and the Tories. The Tories I can easily forgive. They have unwillingly come into the measure; and they do me honor in thinking it necessary to remove me, as their only obstacle. What, then, is the inference to be drawn from these premises? That demerit with my opponents ought to be considered as merit with others. But my great and principal crime is my long continuance in office; or, in other words, the long exclusion of those who now complain against me. This is the heinous offence which exceeds all others. I keep from them the possession of that power, those honors, and those emoluments, to which they so ardently and pertinaciously aspire. I will not attempt to deny the reasonableness and necessity of a party war; but, in carrying on that war, all principles and rules of justice should not be departed from. The Tories must confess that the most obnoxious persons have felt few instances of extra-judicial power. Wherever they have been arraigned, a plain charge has been exhibited against them. They have had an impartial trial, and have been permitted to make their defence. And will they, who have experienced this fair and equitable mode of proceeding, act in direct opposition to every principle of justice, and establish this fatal precedent of parliamentary inquisition? Whom would they conciliate by a conduct so contrary to principle and precedent?

Can it be fitting in them [the Tories] who have divided the public opinion of the nation, to share it with those who now appear as their competitors? With the men of yesterday, the boys in politics, who would be absolutely contemptible did not their audacity render them detestable? With the mock patriots, whose practice and professions prove their selfishness and malignity; who threatened to pursue me to destruction, and who have never for a moment lost sight of their object? These men, under the name of Separatists, presume

---

[2] [The "Boys" was the familiar name of a band of the younger Whigs.—EDITOR.]

to call themselves exclusively the nation and the people, and under that character assume all power. In their estimation, the King, Lords, and Commons are a faction, and they are the Government. Upon these principles they threaten the destruction of all authority, and think they have a right to judge, direct, and resist all legal magistrates. They withdraw from Parliament because they succeed in nothing; and then attribute their want of success, not to its true cause, their own want of integrity and importance, but to the effect of places, pensions, and corruption. May it not be asked on this point, Are the people on the Court side more united than on the other? Are not the Tories, Jacobites, and Patriots equally determined? What makes this strict union? What cements this heterogeneous mass? Party engagements and personal attachments. However different their views and principles, they all agree in opposition. The Jacobites distress the government they would subvert; the Tories contend for party prevalence and power. The Patriots, from discontent and disappointment, would change the ministry, that themselves may exclusively succeed. They have labored this point twenty years unsuccessfully. They are impatient of longer delay. They clamor for change of measures, but mean only change of ministers.

In party contests, why should not both sides be equally steady? Does not a Whig administration as well deserve the support of the Whigs as the contrary? Why is not principle the cement in one as well as the other; especially when my opponents confess that all is levelled against one man? Why this one man? Because they think, vainly, nobody else could withstand them. All others are treated as tools and vassals. The one is the corrupter; the numbers corrupted. But whence this cry of corruption, and exclusive claim of honorable distinction? Compare the estates, characters, and fortunes of the Commons on one side with those on the other. Let the matter be fairly investigated. Survey and examine the individuals who usually support the measures of government, and those who are in opposition. Let us see to whose side the balance preponderates. Look round both Houses, and see to which side the balance of virtue and talents preponderates! Are all these on one side, and not on the other?

Or are all these to be counterbalanced by an affected claim to the exclusive title of patriotism? Gentlemen have talked a great deal of patriotism. A venerable word, when duly practised. But I am sorry to say that of late it has been so much hackneyed about, that it is in danger of falling into disgrace. The very idea of true patriotism is lost, and the term has been prostituted to the very worst of purposes. A patriot, sir! Why, patriots spring up like mushrooms! I could raise fifty of them within the four-and-twenty hours. I have raised many of them in one night. It is but refusing to gratify an unreasonable or an insolent demand, and up starts a patriot. I have never been afraid of making patriots; but I disdain and despise all their efforts. This pretended virtue proceeds from personal malice and disappointed ambition. There is not a man among them whose particular aim I am not able to ascertain, and from what motive they have entered into the lists of opposition.

I shall now consider the articles of accusation which they have brought against me, and which they have not thought fit to reduce to specific charges; and I shall consider these in the same order as that in which they were placed by the honorable member who made the motion. First, in regard to foreign affairs; secondly, to domestic affairs; and, thirdly, to the conduct of the war.

1. As to foreign affairs, I must take notice of the uncandid manner in which the gentlemen on the other side have managed the question, by blending numerous treaties and complicated negotiations into one general mass.

To form a fair and candid judgment of the subject, it becomes necessary not to consider the treaties merely insulated, but to advert to the time in which they were made, to the circumstances and situation of Europe when they were made, to the peculiar situation in which I stand, and to the power which I possessed. I am called repeatedly and insidiously prime and sole minister. Admitting, however, for the sake of argument, that I am prime and sole minister in this country, am I, therefore, prime and sole minister of all Europe? Am I answerable for the conduct of other countries as well as for that of my own? Many words are not wanting to show that the particular view of each court occasioned the dangers which affected the public tranquillity; yet the whole is charged to my account. Nor is this sufficient. Whatever was the conduct of England, I am equally arraigned. If we maintained ourselves in peace, and took no share in foreign transactions, we are reproached for tameness and pusillanimity. If, on the contrary, we interfered in these disputes, we are called Don Quixotes, and dupes to all the world. If we contracted guarantees it was asked, Why is the nation wantonly burdened? If guarantees were declined, we were reproached with having no allies.

I have, however, sir, this advantage, that all the objections now alleged against the conduct of the administration to which I have the honor to belong, have already been answered to the satisfaction of a majority of both Houses of Parliament, and I believe to the satisfaction of a majority of the better sort of people in the nation. I need, therefore, only repeat a few of these answers that have been made already, which I shall do in the order of time in which the several transactions happened; and consequently must begin with our refusing to accept of the sole mediation offered us by Spain, on the breach between that Court and the Court of France, occasioned by the dismission of the Infanta of Spain.

I hope it will not be said we had any reason to quarrel with France upon that account; and therefore, if our accepting of that mediation might have produced a rupture with France, it was not our duty to interfere unless we had something very beneficial to expect from the acceptance. A reconciliation between the courts of Vienna and Madrid, it is true, was desirable to all Europe as well as to us, provided it had been brought about without any design to disturb our tranquillity or the tranquillity of Europe. But both parties were then so high in their demands that we could hope for no success; and if the negotiation had ended without effect, we might have expected the common fate of arbitrators, the disobliging of both. Therefore, as it was our interest to keep well with both, I must still think it was the most prudent part we could act to refuse the offered mediation.

The next step of our foreign conduct, exposed to reprehension, is the Treaty of Hanover.[3] Sir, if I were to give the true history of that treaty, which no gentleman can desire I should, I am sure I could fully justify my own conduct. But as I do not desire to justify my own conduct without justifying his late Majesty's conduct, I must observe that his late Majesty had such information as convinced not only him, but those of his council, both at home and abroad, that some dangerous designs had been formed between the Emperor and Spain at the time of their concluding the treaty of Vienna, in May, 1725; designs, sir, which were dangerous not only to the liberties of this nation, but to the liberties of Europe. They were not only to wrest Gibraltar and Port Mahon from this nation, and force the Pretender upon us; but they were to have Don Carlos married to the Emperor's eldest daughter, who would thereby have had a probability of uniting in his person, or in the person of some of his successors, the crowns of France and Spain, with the imperial dignity and the Austrian dominions. It was therefore highly reasonable, both in France and us, to take the alarm at such designs, and to think betimes of preventing their being carried into execution. But with regard to us, it was more particularly our business to take the alarm, because we were to have been immediately attacked. I shall grant, sir, it would have been very difficult, if not impossible, for Spain and the Emperor joined together, to have invaded or made themselves masters of any of the British dominions. But will it be said they might not have invaded the King's dominions in Germany, in order to force him to a compliance with what they desired of him as King of Great Britain? And if those dominions had been invaded on account of a quarrel with this nation, should we not have been obliged, both in honor and interest, to defend them? When we were thus threatened, it was therefore absolutely necessary for us to make an alliance with France; and that we might not trust too much to their assistance, it was likewise necessary to form

[3] [Spain and Germany had formed a secret compact (at first suspected, and afterward confirmed by secret intelligence) for conjointly attacking the dominions of England. To counteract this, England, in 1725, united with France, Prussia, Denmark, and Holland, in an opposing league, by a compact called the Treaty of Hanover, from the place where it was made. The evidence of these facts could not then be brought forward to defend the ministry; and hence the Treaty of Hanover, and the consequent expenditures on the Continent, were extremely unpopular in England. But subsequent disclosures have made it nearly or quite certain, that everything here alleged by Walpole was strictly true.]

alliances with the northern powers, and with some of the princes in Germany, which we never did, nor ever could do, without granting them immediate subsidies. These measures were, therefore, I still think, not only prudent, but necessary; and by these measures we made it much more dangerous for the Emperor and Spain to attack us than it would otherwise have been.

But still, sir, though by these alliances we put ourselves upon an equal footing with our enemies in case of an attack, yet, in order to preserve the tranquillity of Europe as well as our own, there was something else to be done. We knew that war could not be begun and carried on without money; we knew that the Emperor had no money for that purpose without receiving large remittances from Spain; and we knew that Spain could make no such remittances without receiving large returns of treasure from the West Indies. The only way, therefore, to render these two powers incapable of disturbing the tranquillity of Europe, was by sending a squadron to the West Indies to stop the return of the Spanish galleons; and this made it necessary, at the same time, to send a squadron to the Mediterranean for the security of our valuable possessions in that part of the world. By these measures the Emperor saw the impossibility of attacking us in any part of the world, because Spain could give him no assistance either in money or troops; and the attack made by the Spaniards upon Gibraltar was so feeble that we had no occasion to call upon our allies for assistance. A small squadron of our own prevented their attacking it by sea, and from their attack by land we had nothing to fear. They might have knocked their brains out against inaccessible rocks to this very day without bringing that fortress into any danger.

I do not pretend, sir, to be a great master of foreign affairs. In that post in which I have the honor to serve His Majesty it is not my business to interfere; and as one of His Majesty's council, I have but one voice. But if I had been the sole adviser of the Treaty of Hanover, and of all the measures which were taken in pursuance of it, from what I have said I hope it will appear that I do not deserve to be censured either as a weak or a wicked minister on that account.

The next measures which incurred censure were the guar-

antee of the Pragmatic Sanction by the second Treaty of
Vienna, and the refusal of the Cabinet to assist the House of
Austria, in conformity with the articles of that guarantee.[4]

As to the guarantee of the Pragmatic Sanction I am really
surprised to find that measure objected to. It was so universally approved of, both within doors and without, that till this
very day I think no fault was ever found with it, unless it was
that of being too long delayed. If it was so necessary for
supporting the balance of power in Europe, as has been insisted on in this debate, to preserve entire the dominions of
the House of Austria, surely it was not our business to insist
upon a partition of them in favor of any of the princes of the
empire. But if we had, could we have expected that the House
of Austria would have agreed to any such partition, even for
the acquisition of our guarantee? The King of Prussia had,
it is true, a claim upon some lordships in Silesia; but that
claim was absolutely denied by the Court of Vienna, and was
not at that time so much insisted on by the late King of Prussia. Nay, if he had lived till this time, I believe it would not
now have been insisted on; for he acceded to that guarantee
without any reservation of that claim; therefore I must look
upon this as an objection which has since arisen from an accident that could not then be foreseen or provided against.

I must therefore think, sir, that our guarantee of the Pragmatic Sanction, or our manner of doing it, cannot now be
objected to, nor any person censured by Parliament for advising that measure. In regard to the refusal of the Cabinet
to assist the House of Austria, though it was prudent and right
in us to enter into that guarantee, we were not therefore
obliged to enter into every broil the House of Austria might
afterward lead themselves into. And therefore we were not
in honor obliged to take any share in the war which the Emperor brought upon himself in the year 1733; nor were we
in interest obliged to take a share in that war as long as neither
side attempted to push their conquests further than was consistent with the balance of power in Europe, which was a case
that did not happen. For the power of the House of Austria
was not diminished by the event of that war, because they got
Tuscany, Parma, and Placentia in lieu of Naples and Sicily;

[4] [In allusion to the instrument drawn up by Charles VI, of Germany, called a Pragmatic Sanction, by which all his hereditary estates were to go to his female descendants.]

nor was the power of France much increased, because Lorraine was a province she had taken and kept possession of during every war in which she had been engaged.

As to the disputes with Spain, they had not then reached such a height as to make it necessary for us to come to an open rupture. We had then reason to hope that all differences would be accommodated in an amicable manner; and while we have any such hopes, it can never be prudent for us to engage ourselves in war, especially with Spain, where we have always had a very beneficial commerce. These hopes, it is true, sir, at last proved abortive; but I never heard it was a crime to hope for the best. This sort of hope was the cause of the late convention. If Spain had performed her part of that preliminary treaty, I am sure it would not have been wrong in us to have hoped for a friendly accommodation; and for that end to have waited nine or ten months longer, in which time the plenipotentiaries were, by the treaty, to have adjusted all the differences subsisting between the two nations. But the failure of Spain in performing what had been agreed to by this preliminary put an end to all our hopes, and then, and not till then, it became prudent to enter into hostilities, which were commenced as soon as possible after the expiration of the term limited for the payment of the £95,000.

Strong and virulent censures have been cast on me for having commenced the war without a single ally; and this deficiency has been ascribed to the multifarious treaties in which I have bewildered myself. But although the authors of this imputation are well apprised that all these treaties have been submitted to and approved by Parliament, yet they are now brought forward as crimes, without appealing to the judgment of Parliament, and without proving or declaring that all or any of them were advised by me. A supposed sole minister is to be condemned and punished as the author of all; and what adds to the enormity is, that an attempt was made to convict him uncharged and unheard, without taking into consideration the most arduous crisis which ever occurred in the annals of Europe. Sweden corrupted by France; Denmark tempted and wavering; the Landgrave of Hesse-Cassel almost gained; the King of Prussia, the Emperor, and the Czarina, with whom alliances had been negotiating, dead; the Austrian dominions claimed by Spain and Bavaria; the Elector of Saxony hesitating whether he should accede to the general confederacy planned by France; the Court of Vienna irresolute and indecisive. In this critical juncture, if France enters into engagements with Prussia, and if the Queen of Hungary hesitates and listens to France, are all or any of those events to be imputed to English counsels? And if to English counsels, why are they to be attributed to one man?

2. I now come, sir, to the second head, the conduct of domestic affairs. And here a most heinous charge is made, that the nation has been burdened with unnecessary expenses, for the sole purpose of preventing the discharge of our debts and the abolition of taxes. But this attack is more to the dishonor of the whole Cabinet council than to me. If there is any ground for this imputation, it is a charge upon King, Lords, and Commons, as corrupted or imposed upon. And they have no proof of these allegations, but affect to substantiate them by common fame and public notoriety!

No expense has been incurred but what has been approved of, and provided for, by Parliament. The public treasure has been duly applied to the uses to which it was appropriated by Parliament, and regular accounts have been annually laid before Parliament of every article of expense. If by foreign accidents, by the disputes of foreign states among themselves, or by their designs against us, the nation has often been put to an extraordinary expense, that expense cannot be said to have been unnecessary; because, if by saving it we had exposed the balance of power to danger, or ourselves to an attack, it would have cost, perhaps, a hundred times that sum before we could recover from that danger, or repel that attack.

In all such cases there will be a variety of opinions. I happened to be one of those who thought all these expenses necessary, and I had the good fortune to have the majority of both Houses of Parliament on my side. But this, it seems, proceeded from bribery and corruption. Sir, if any one instance had been mentioned, if it had been shown that I ever offered a reward to any member of either House, or ever threatened to deprive any member of his office or employment, in order to influence his vote in Parliament, there might have been some ground for this charge. But when it is so generally laid, I do not know what I can say to it, unless it be to deny it as generally and as positively as it has been asserted. And, thank God! till some proof be offered, I have the laws of the land, as well as the laws of charity, in my favor.

Some members of both Houses have, it is true, been removed from their employments under the Crown; but were they ever told, either by me, or by any other of His Majesty's servants, that it was for opposing the measures of the administration in Parliament? They were removed because His Majesty did not think fit to continue them longer in his service. His Majesty had a right so to do; and I know no one that has a right to ask him, "What doest thou?" If His Majesty had a mind that the favors of the Crown should circulate, would not this of itself be a good reason for removing any of his servants? Would not this reason be approved of by the whole nation, except those who happen to be the present possessors? I cannot, therefore, see how this can be imputed as a crime, or how any of the King's ministers can be blamed for his doing what the public has no concern in; for if the public be well and faithfully served, it has no business to ask by whom.

As to the particular charge urged against me, I mean that of the army debentures, I am surprised, sir, to hear anything relating to this affair charged upon me. Whatever blame may attach to this affair, it must be placed to the account of those that were in power when I was, as they call it, the country gentleman.[5] It was by them this affair was introduced and conducted, and I came in only to pay off those public securities, which their management had reduced to a great discount; and consequently to redeem our public credit from that reproach which they had brought upon it. The discount at which these army debentures were negotiated was a strong and prevalent reason with Parliament to apply the sinking fund first to the payment of those debentures; but the sinking fund could not be applied to that purpose till it began to produce something considerable, which was not till the year 1727. That the sinking fund was then to receive a great addition, was a fact publicly known in 1726; and if some people were sufficiently quick-sighted to foresee that the Parliament would

[5] One who held himself bound to neither party.

probably make this use of it, and cunning enough to make the most of their own foresight, could I help it, or could they be blamed for doing so? But I defy my most inveterate enemy to prove that I had any hand in bringing these debentures to a discount, or that I had any share in the profits by buying them up.

In reply to those who confidently assert that the national debt is not decreased since 1727, and that the sinking fund has not been applied to the discharge of the public burdens, I can with truth declare, that a part of the debt has been paid off; and the landed interest has been very much eased with respect to that most unequal and grievous burden, the land tax. I say so, sir, because upon examination it will appear, that within these sixteen or seventeen years no less than £8,000,000 of our debt has been actually discharged by the due application of the sinking fund; and at least £7,000,000 has been taken from that fund, and applied to the ease of the land tax. For if it had not been applied to the current service, we must have supplied that service by increasing the land tax; and as the sinking fund was originally designed for paying off our debts, and easing us of our taxes, the application of it in ease of the land tax was certainly as proper and necessary a use as could be made. And I little thought that giving relief to landed gentlemen would have been brought against me as a crime.

3. I shall now advert to the third topic of accusation—the conduct of the war. I have already stated in what manner, and under what circumstances, hostilities commenced; and as I am neither general nor admiral—as I have nothing to do either with our navy or army—I am sure I am not answerable for the prosecution of it. But were I to answer for everything, no fault could, I think, be found with my conduct in the prosecution of the war. It has from the beginning been carried on with as much vigor, and as great care of our trade, as was consistent with our safety at home, and with the circumstances we were in at the beginning of the war. If our attacks upon the enemy were too long delayed, or if they have not been so vigorous or so frequent as they ought to have been, those only are to blame who have for many years been haranguing against standing armies; for, without a sufficient number of

regular troops in proportion to the numbers kept up by our neighbors, I am sure we can neither defend ourselves nor offend our enemies. On the supposed miscarriages of the war, so unfairly stated, and so unjustly imputed to me, I could, with great ease, frame an incontrovertible defence. But as I have trespassed so long on the time of the House, I shall not weaken the effect of that forcible exculpation so generously and disinterestedly advanced by the right honorable gentleman who so meritoriously presides at the Admiralty.

If my whole administration is to be scrutinized and arraigned, why are the most favorable parts to be omitted? If facts are to be accumulated on one side, why not on the other? And why may not I be permitted to speak in my own favor? Was I not called by the voice of the King and the nation to remedy the fatal effects of the South Sea project, and to support declining credit? Was I not placed at the head of the treasury when the revenues were in the greatest confusion? Is credit revived, and does it now flourish? Is it not at an incredible height? and if so, to whom must that circumstance be attributed? Has not tranquillity been preserved both at home and abroad, notwithstanding a most unreasonable and violent opposition? Has the true interest of the nation been pursued, or has trade flourished? Have gentlemen produced one instance of this exorbitant power; of the influence which I extend to all parts of the nation; of the tyranny with which I oppress those who oppose, and the liberality with which I reward those who support me? But having first invested me with a kind of mock dignity, and styled me a prime minister, they impute to me an unpardonable abuse of that chimerical authority which they only have created and conferred. If they are really persuaded that the army is annually established by me, that I will have the sole disposal of posts and honors, that I employ this power in the destruction of liberty and the diminution of commerce, let me awaken them from their delusion. Let me expose to their view the real condition of the public weal. Let me show them that the Crown has made no encroachments, that all supplies have been granted by Parliament, that all questions have been debated with the same freedom as before the fatal period in which my counsels are said to have gained the ascendancy—an ascendancy from which they deduce the loss of trade, the approach of slavery, the preponderance of prerogative, and the extension of influence. But I am far from believing that they feel those apprehensions which they so earnestly labor to communicate to others; and I have too high an opinion of their sagacity not to conclude that, even in their own judgment, they are complaining of grievances that they do not suffer, and promoting rather their private interest than that of the public.

What is this unbounded sole power which is imputed to me? How has it discovered itself, or how has it been proved?

What have been the effects of the corruption, ambition, and avarice with which I am so abundantly charged?

Have I ever been suspected of being corrupted? A strange phenomenon, a corrupter himself not corrupt! Is ambition imputed to me? Why then do I still continue a commoner? I, who refused a white staff and a peerage? I had, indeed, like to have forgotten the little ornament about my shoulders [the garter], which gentlemen have so repeatedly mentioned in terms of sarcastic obloquy. But surely, though this may be regarded with envy or indignation in another place, it cannot be supposed to raise any resentment in this House, where many may be pleased to see those honors which their ancestors have worn, restored again to the Commons.

Have I given any symptoms of an avaricious disposition? Have I obtained any grants from the Crown since I have been placed at the head of the treasury? Has my conduct been different from that which others in the same station would have followed? Have I acted wrong in giving the place of auditor to my son, and in providing for my own family? I trust that their advancement will not be imputed to me as a crime, unless it shall be proved that I placed them in offices of trust and responsibility for which they were unfit.

But while I unequivocally deny that I am sole and prime minister, and that to my influence and direction all the measures of the Government must be attributed, yet I will not shrink from the responsibility which attaches to the post I have the honor to hold; and should, during the long period in which I have sat upon this bench, any one step taken by Government be proved to be either disgraceful or disadvantageous to the nation, I am ready to hold myself accountable.

To conclude, sir, though I shall always be proud of the honor of any trust or confidence from His Majesty, yet I shall always be ready to remove from his councils and presence when he thinks fit; and therefore I should think myself very little concerned in the event of the present question, if it were not for the encroachment that will thereby be made upon the prerogatives of the Crown. But I must think that an address to His Majesty to remove one of his servants, without so much as alleging any particular crime against him, is one of the greatest encroachments that was ever made upon the prerogatives of the Crown. And therefore, for the sake of my master, without any regard for my own, I hope all those who have a due regard for our constitution, and for the rights and prerogatives of the Crown, without which our constitution cannot be preserved, will be against this motion.

THE GIN ACT

—

BY

LORD CHESTERFIELD
(Philip Dormer Stanhope)

PHILIP DORMER STANHOPE, LORD CHESTERFIELD

1694—1773

Philip Dormer Stanhope, the fourth Earl of Chesterfield, was something more than the mere cynical authority on deportment that history describes him. He came of a noble line of statesmen, soldiers, and men of letters, and was himself a person of strong abilities and wide accomplishments. His cultivation of society polish, and the more deliberate and elaborate arts whereby a man insinuates himself into the favor of those above him, and wins the approval of women, for good purposes or evil ones—these were but the finish that he put upon the inner structure of qualities and education which nature and opportunity had furnished him with, and which were designed to give the nobler elements their best effect. He was a man who, in a less artificial and corrupt environment, might have been a good and lovable as well as a clever and successful man; but he lived at a period when to be an intriguer in society and politics, a courtier and a man of fashion, was the height of social ambition, and the way to substantial power and rewards; and Chesterfield thus became the leader in a direction which he might otherwise not have pursued at all. He elevated politeness into a science, and manners into philosophy; or we might put it that he degraded philosophy into behavior. At all events, he is not unjustly renowned for this rather than for other achievements, inasmuch as he therein opened a new field, but one which has been since then widely cultivated. He and La Rochefoucauld, the author of the " Maxims," together supplied the accoutrements with which the man of the world of the eighteenth century could equip himself. His letters to his son, which were not written for publication (though they were published immediately upon their author's death), have had a much more visible effect upon later ages than they had upon the stupid and clumsy individual for whom they were intended.

Lord Chesterfield took a course at Cambridge University, and then entered the diplomatic service, and when he was about fifty years of age, was appointed to the considerable office of Lord Lieutenant of Ireland. He was always well disposed towards literature, and was one of the eminent persons whose names are associated with Samuel Johnson's famous dictionary; though not in a manner reflecting credit upon himself. But he gave Johnson the opportunity to write him a letter which has served as a model of manly independence for literary men ever since; Johnson's irony turning upon the point that Chesterfield had neglected him when his favor might have advanced the cause of learning, and noticed him only when it had become evident that learning no longer needed a patron, but on the contrary was in a position to reflect honor upon himself.

The oratory of Chesterfield was such as might be looked for in a man of his varied talents and knowledge of the world; it lacks the higher qualities, perhaps because it was not exerted in high causes; but it has merit enough to deserve preservation.

THE GIN ACT

THE bill[1] now under our consideration appears to me to deserve a much closer regard than seems to have been paid to it in the other House, through which it was hurried with the utmost precipitation, and where it passed almost without the formality of a debate. Nor can I think that earnestness with which some lords seem inclined to press it forward here consistent with the importance of the consequences which may with great reason be expected from it.

To desire, my lords, that this bill may be considered in a committee, is only to desire that it may gain one step without opposition, that it may proceed through the forms of the House by stealth, and that the consideration of it may be delayed till the exigencies of the Government shall be so great as not to allow time for raising the supplies by any other method.

By this artifice, gross as it is, the patrons of this wonderful bill hope to obstruct a plain and open detection of its tendency. They hope, my lords, that the bill shall operate in the same manner with the liquor which it is intended to bring into more general use; and that, as those who drink spirits are drunk before they are well aware that they are drinking, the effects of this law shall be perceived before we know that we have made it. Their intent is to give us a dram of policy, which is to be swallowed before it is tasted, and which, when once it is swallowed, will turn our heads.

But, my lords, I hope we shall be so cautious as to examine the draught which these state empirics have thought proper to offer us; and I am confident that a very little examination will convince us of the pernicious qualities of their new preparation, and show that it can have no other effect than that of poisoning the public.

The law before us, my lords, seems to be the effect of that

---

[1] This speech was delivered in the House of Lords, February 21, 1743, on a bill for granting licenses to ginshops. By the revenue thus gained it was proposed to carry on the German war of George II.

practice of which it is intended likewise to be the cause, and to be dictated by the liquor of which it so effectually promotes the use; for surely it never before was conceived, by any man intrusted with the administration of public affairs, to raise taxes by the destruction of the people.

Nothing, my lords, but the destruction of all the most laborious and useful part of the nation can be expected from the license which is now proposed to be given, not only to drunkenness, but to drunkenness of the most detestable and dangerous kind; to the abuse not only of intoxicating, but of poisonous liquors.

Nothing, my lords, is more absurd than to assert that the use of spirits will be hindered by the bill now before us, or indeed that it will not be in a very great degree promoted by it. For what produces all kind of wickedness but the prospect of impunity on one part, or the solicitation of opportunity on the other? Either of these have too frequently been sufficient to overpower the sense of morality, and even of religion; and what is not to be feared from them when they shall unite their force and operate together, when temptations shall be increased, and terror taken away?

It is allowed by those who have hitherto disputed on either side of this question, that the people appear obstinately enamored of this new liquor. It is allowed on both parts that this liquor corrupts the mind and enervates the body, and destroys vigor and virtue, at the same time that it makes those who drink it too idle and feeble for work; and, while it impoverishes them by the present expense, disables them from retrieving its ill consequences by subsequent industry.

It might be imagined, my lords, that those who had thus far agreed would not easily find any occasions of dispute. Nor would any man, unacquainted with the motives by which parliamentary debates are too often influenced, suspect that after the pernicious qualities of this liquor, and the general inclination among the people to the immoderate use of it, had been thus fully admitted, it could be afterward inquired whether it ought to be made more common; whether this universal thirst for poison ought to be encouraged by the legislature, and whether a new statute ought to be made to secure drunkards in the gratification of their appetites.

To pretend, my lords, that the design of this bill is to prevent or diminish the use of spirits, is to trample upon common-sense, and to violate the rules of decency as well as of reason. For when did any man hear that a commodity was prohibited by licensing its sale, or that to offer and refuse is the same action?

It is indeed pleaded that it will be made dearer by the tax which is proposed, and that the increase of the price will diminish the number of the purchasers; but it is at the same time expected that this tax shall supply the expense of a war on the Continent. It is asserted, therefore, that the consumption of spirits will be hindered, and yet that it will be such as may be expected to furnish, from a very small tax, a revenue sufficient for the support of armies, for the re-establishment of the Austrian family, and the repressing of the attempts of France.

Surely, my lords, these expectations are not very consistent; nor can it be imagined that they are both formed in the same head, though they may be expressed by the same mouth. It is, however, some recommendation of a statesman when, of his assertions, one can be found reasonable or true, and in this, praise cannot be denied to our present ministers. For though it is undoubtedly false that this tax will lessen the consumption of spirits, it is certainly true that it will produce a very large revenue—a revenue that will not fail but with the people from whose debaucheries it arises.

Our ministers will therefore have the same honor with their predecessors, of having given rise to a new fund; not indeed for the payment of our debts, but for much more valuable purposes; for the cheering of our hearts under oppression, and for the ready support of those debts which we have lost all hopes of paying. They are resolved, my lords, that the nation which no endeavors can make wise, shall, while they are at its head, at least be very merry; and, since public happiness is the end of government, they seem to imagine that they shall deserve applause by an expedient which will enable every man to lay his cares asleep, to drown sorrow, and lose in the delights of drunkenness both the public miseries and his own.

Luxury, my lords, is to be taxed, but vice prohibited, let the difficulties in executing the law be what they will. Would you lay a tax on the breach of the ten commandments? Would not such a tax be wicked and scandalous; because it would imply an indulgence to all those who could pay the tax? Is not this a reproach most justly thrown by Protestants upon the Church of Rome? Was it not the chief cause of the Reformation? And will you follow a precedent which brought reproach and ruin upon those that introduced it? This is the very case now before us. You are going to lay a tax, and consequently to indulge a sort of drunkenness, which almost necessarily produces a breach of every one of the ten commandments? Can you expect the reverend bench will approve of this? I am convinced they will not; and therefore I wish I had seen it full upon this occasion. I am sure I have seen it much fuller upon other occasions, in which religion had no such deep concern.

We have already, my lords, several sorts of funds in this nation, so many that a man must have a good deal of learning to be master of them. Thanks to His Majesty, we have now among us the most learned man of the nation in this way. I wish he would rise up and tell us what name we are to give this new fund. We have already the Civil List Fund, the Sinking Fund, the Aggregate Fund, the South Sea Fund, and God knows how many others. What name we are to give this new fund I know not, unless we are to call it the Drinking Fund. It may perhaps enable the people of a certain foreign territory [Hanover] to drink claret, but it will disable the people of this kingdom from drinking anything else but gin; for when a man has, by gin drinking, rendered himself unfit for labor or business, he can purchase nothing else; and then the best thing he can do is to drink on till he dies.

Surely, my lords, men of such unbounded benevolence as our present ministers deserve such honors as were never paid before; they deserve to bestride a butt upon every sign-post in the city, or to have their figures exhibited as tokens where this liquor is to be sold by the license which they have procured. They must be at least remembered to future ages as the " happy politicians " who, after all expedients for raising taxes had been employed, discovered a new method of draining the last relics of the public wealth, and added a new revenue to the Government. Nor will those who shall hereafter enumerate the several funds now established among us, forget, among the benefactors to their country, the illustrious authors of the Drinking Fund.

May I be allowed, my lords, to congratulate my countrymen and fellow-subjects upon the happy times which are now approaching, in which no man will be disqualified from the privilege of being drunk; when all discontent and disloyalty will be forgotten, and the people, though now considered by the ministry as enemies, shall acknowledge the leniency of that government under which all restraints are taken away?

But, to a bill for such desirable purposes, it would be proper, my lords, to prefix a preamble, in which the kindness of our intentions should be more fully explained, that the nation may not mistake our indulgence for cruelty, nor consider their benefactors as their persecutors. If, therefore, this bill be considered and amended (for why else should it be considered?) in a committee, I shall humbly propose that it shall be introduced in this manner: " Whereas, the designs of the present ministry, whatever they are, cannot be executed without a great number of mercenaries, which mercenaries cannot be hired without money; and whereas the present disposition of this nation to drunkenness inclines us to believe that they will pay more cheerfully for the undisturbed enjoyment of distilled liquors than for any other concession that can be made by the Government; be it enacted, by the King's most excellent Majesty, that no man shall hereafter be denied the right of being drunk on the following conditions."

This, my lords, to trifle no longer, is the proper preamble to this bill, which contains only the conditions on which the people of this kingdom are to be allowed henceforward to riot in debauchery, in debauchery licensed by law and countenanced by the magistrates. For there is no doubt but those on whom the inventors of this tax shall confer authority will be directed to assist their masters in their design to encourage the consumption of that liquor from which such large revenues are expected, and to multiply without end those licenses which are to pay a yearly tribute to the Crown.

By this unbounded license, my lords, that price will be lessened, from the increase of which the expectations of the efficacy of this law are pretended; for the number of retailers will lessen the value, as in all other cases, and lessen it more than this tax will increase it. Besides, it is to be considered that at present the retailer expects to be paid for the danger which he incurs by an unlawful trade, and will not trust his reputation or his purse to the mercy of his customer without a profit proportioned to the hazard; but, when once the restraint shall be taken away, he will sell for common gain, and it can hardly be imagined that, at present, he subjects himself to informations and penalties for less than sixpence a gallon.

The specious pretence on which this bill is founded, and, indeed, the only pretence that deserves to be termed specious, is the propriety of taxing vice; but this maxim of government has, on this occasion, been either mistaken or perverted. Vice, my lords, is not properly to be taxed, but suppressed; and heavy taxes are sometimes the only means by which that suppression can be attained. Luxury, my lords, or the excess of that which is pernicious only by its excess, may very properly be taxed, that such excess, though not strictly unlawful, may be made more difficult. But the use of those things which are simply hurtful, hurtful in their own nature, and in every degree, is to be prohibited. None, my lords, ever heard, in any nation, of a tax upon theft or adultery, because a tax implies a license granted for the use of that which is taxed to all who shall be willing to pay it.

During the course of this long debate I have endeavored to recapitulate and digest the arguments which have been advanced, and have considered them both separately and conjointly; but find myself at the same distance from conviction as when I first entered the House.

In vindication of this bill, my lords, we have been told that the present law is ineffectual; that our manufacture is not to be destroyed, or not this year; that the security offered by the present bill has induced great numbers to subscribe to the new fund; that it has been approved by the Commons; and that if it be found ineffectual, it may be amended another session.

All these arguments, my lords, I shall endeavor to examine, because I am always desirous of gratifying those great men to whom the administration of affairs is intrusted, and have always very cautiously avoided the odium of disaffection, which they will undoubtedly throw, in imitation of their predecessors, upon all those whose wayward consciences shall oblige them to hinder the execution of their schemes.

With a very strong desire, therefore, though with no great

hopes, of finding them in the right, I venture to begin my inquiry, and engage in the examination of their first assertion, that the present law against the abuse of strong liquors is without effect.

I hope, my lords, it portends well to my inquiry that the first position which I have to examine is true; nor can I forbear to congratulate your lordships upon having heard from the new ministry one assertion not to be contradicted.

It is evident, my lords, from daily observation, and demonstrable from the papers upon the table, that every year, since the enacting of the last law, that vice has increased which it was intended to repress, and that no time has been so favorable to the retailers of spirits as that which has passed since they were prohibited.

It may therefore be expected, my lords, that having agreed with the ministers in their fundamental proposition, I shall concur with them in the consequence which they draw from it; and having allowed that the present law is ineffectual, should admit that another is necessary.

But, my lords, in order to discover whether this consequence be necessary, it must first be inquired why the present law is of no force. For, my lords, it will be found, upon reflection, that there are certain degrees of corruption that may hinder the effect of the best laws. The magistrates may be vicious, and forbear to enforce that law by which themselves are condemned; they may be indolent, and inclined rather to connive at wickedness, by which they are not injured themselves, than to repress it by a laborious exertion of their authority; or they may be timorous, and, instead of awing the vicious, may be awed by them.

In any of these cases, my lords, the law is not to be condemned for its inefficacy, since it only fails by the defect of those who are to direct its operations. The best and most important laws will contribute very little to the security or happiness of a people, if no judges of integrity and spirit can be found among them. Even the most beneficial and useful bill that ministers can possibly imagine, a bill for laying on our estates a tax of the fifth part of their yearly value, would be wholly without effect if collectors could not be obtained.

I am therefore, my lords, yet doubtful whether the inefficacy of the law now subsisting necessarily obliges us to provide another; for those that declared it to be useless owned, at the same time, that no man endeavored to enforce it, so that perhaps its only defect may be that it will not execute itself.

Nor, though I should allow that the law is at present impeded by difficulties which cannot be broken through, but by men of more spirit and dignity than the ministers may be inclined to trust with commissions of the peace, yet it can only be collected that another law is necessary, not that the law now proposed will be of any advantage.

Great use has been made of the inefficacy of the present law to decry the proposal made by the noble lord [a member of the Opposition] for laying a high duty upon these pernicious liquors. High duties have already, as we are informed, been tried without advantage. High duties are at this hour imposed upon those spirits which are retailed, yet we see them every day sold in the streets, without the payment of the tax required, and therefore it will be folly to make a second essay of means, which have been found, by the essay of many years, unsuccessful.

It has been granted on all sides in this debate, nor was it ever denied on any other occasion, that the consumption of any commodity is most easily hindered by raising its price, and its price is to be raised by the imposition of a duty. This, my lords, which is, I suppose, the opinion of every man, of whatever degree of experience or understanding, appears likewise to have been thought of by the authors of the present law, and therefore they imagined that they had effectually provided against the increase of drunkenness by laying upon that liquor which should be retailed in small quantities a duty which none of the inferior classes of drunkards would be able to pay.

Thus, my lords, they conceived that they had reformed the common people without infringing the pleasures of others, and applauded the happy contrivance by which spirits were to be made dear only to the poor, while every man who could afford to purchase two gallons was at liberty to riot at his ease, and, over a full, flowing bumper, look down with contempt upon his former companions, now ruthlessly condemned to disconsolate sobriety.

But, my lords, this intention was frustrated, and the project, ingenious as it was, fell to the ground; for, though they had laid a tax, they unhappily forgot this tax would make no addition to the price unless it was paid, and that it would not be paid unless some were empowered to collect it.

Here, my lords, was the difficulty; those who made the law were inclined to lay a tax from which themselves should be exempt, and therefore would not charge the liquor as it issued from the still; and when once it was dispersed in the hands of petty dealers, it was no longer to be found without the assistance of informers, and informers could not carry on the business of prosecution without the consent of the people.

It is not necessary to dwell any longer upon the law, the repeal of which is proposed, since it appears already that it failed only from a partiality not easily defended, and from the omission of what we now propose, the collecting the duty from the still-head.

If this method be followed, there will be no longer any need of informations or of any rigorous or new measures; the same officers that collect a smaller duty may levy a greater; nor can they be easily deceived with regard to the quantities that are made—the deceits, at least, that can be used are in use already; they are frequently detected and suppressed; nor will a larger duty enable the distillers to elude the vigilance of the officers with more success.

Against this proposal, therefore, the inefficacy of the present law can be no objection. But it is urged that such duties would destroy the trade of distilling, and a noble lord has been pleased to express great tenderness for a manufacture so beneficial and extensive.

That a large duty, levied at the still, would destroy, or very much impair, the trade of distilling, is certainly supposed by those who defend it, for they proposed it only for that end: and what better method can they propose, when they are called to deliberate upon a bill for the prevention of the excessive use of distilled liquors?

The noble lord has been pleased kindly to inform us that the trade of distilling is very extensive; that it employs great numbers; and that they have arrived at an exquisite skill, and therefore—note well the consequence—the trade of distilling is not to be discouraged.

Once more, my lords, allow me to wonder at the different conceptions of different understandings. It appears to me that since the spirits which the distillers produce are allowed to enfeeble the limbs and vitiate the blood, to pervert the heart and obscure the intellects, that the number of distillers should be no argument in their favor; for I never heard that a law against theft was repealed or delayed because thieves were numerous. It appears to me, my lords, that if so formidable a body are confederated against the virtue or the lives of their fellow-citizens, it is time to put an end to the havoc, and to interpose, while it is yet in our power, to stop the destruction.

So little, my lords, am I affected with the merit of the wonderful skill which the distillers are said to have attained, that it is, in my opinion, no faculty of great use to mankind to prepare palatable poison; nor shall I ever contribute my interest for the reprieve of a murderer, because he has, by long practice, obtained great dexterity in his trade.

If their liquors are so delicious that the people are tempted to their own destruction, let us at length, my lords, secure them from these fatal draughts, by bursting the vials that contain them. Let us crush at once these artists in slaughter, who have reconciled their countrymen to sickness and to ruin, and spread over the pitfalls of debauchery such baits as cannot be resisted.

The noble lord has, indeed, admitted that this bill may not be found sufficiently coercive, but gives us hopes that it may be improved and enforced another year, and persuades us to endeavor a reformation of drunkenness by degrees, and, above all, to beware at present of hurting the manufacture.

I am very far, my lords, from thinking that there are, this year, any peculiar reasons for tolerating murder; nor can I conceive why the manufacture should be held sacred now, if it be to be destroyed hereafter. We are, indeed, desired to try how far this law will operate, that we may be more able to proceed with due regard to this valuable manufacture.

With regard to the operations of the law, it appears to me that it will only enrich the Government without reforming the people; and I believe there are not many of a different opinion. If any diminution of the sale of spirits be expected from it, it is to be considered that this diminution will, or will not, be such as is desired for the reformation of the people. If it be sufficient, the manufacture is at an end, and all the reasons against a higher duty are of equal force against this; but if it is not sufficient, we have, at least, omitted part of our duty, and have neglected the health and virtue of the people.

I cannot, my lords, yet discover why a reprieve is desired for this manufacture—why the present year is not equally propitious to the reformation of mankind as any will be that may succeed it. It is true we are at war with two nations, and perhaps with more; but war may be better prosecuted without money than without men. And we but little consult the military glory of our country if we raise supplies for paying our armies by the destruction of those armies that we are contriving to pay.

We have heard the necessity of reforming the nation by degrees urged as an argument for imposing first a lighter duty, and afterward a heavier. This complacence for wickedness, my lords, is not so defensible as that it should be battered by arguments in form, and therefore I shall only relate a reply made by Webb, the noted walker, upon a parallel occasion.

This man, who must be remembered by many of your lordships, was remarkable for vigor, both of mind and body, and lived wholly upon water for his drink, and chiefly upon vegetables for his other sustenance. He was one day recommending his regimen to one of his friends who loved wine, and who perhaps might somewhat contribute to the prosperity of this spirituous manufacture, and urged him, with great earnestness, to quit a course of luxury by which his health and his intellects would equally be destroyed. The gentleman appeared convinced, and told him "that he would conform to his counsel, and thought he could not change his course of life at once, but would leave off strong liquors by degrees." "By degrees!" says the other, with indignation. "If you should unhappily fall into the fire, would you caution your servants not to pull you out but by degrees?"

This answer, my lords, is applicable to the present case. The nation is sunk into the lowest state of corruption; the people are not only vicious, but insolent beyond example. They not only break the laws, but defy them; and yet some of your lordships are for reforming them by degrees!

I am not so easily persuaded, my lords, that our ministers

really intend to supply the defects that may hereafter be discovered in this bill. It will doubtless produce money, perhaps much more than they appear to expect from it. I doubt not but the licensed retailers will be more than fifty thousand, and the quantity retailed must increase with the number of retailers. As the bill will, therefore, answer all the ends intended by it, I do not expect to see it altered; for I have never observed ministers desirous of amending their own errors, unless they are such as have caused a deficiency in the revenue.

Besides, my lords, it is not certain that when this fund is mortgaged to the public creditors, they can prevail upon the Commons to change the security. They may continue the bill in force for the reasons, whatever they are, for which they have passed it, and the good intentions of our ministers, however sincere, may be defeated, and drunkenness, legal drunkenness, established in the nation.

This, my lords, is very reasonable, and therefore we ought to exert ourselves for the safety of the nation while the power is yet in our own hands, and, without regard to the opinion or proceedings of the other House show that we are yet the chief guardians of the people.

The ready compliance of the Commons with the measures proposed in this bill has been mentioned here, with a view, I suppose, of influencing us, but surely by those who had forgotten our independence, or resigned their own. It is not only the right but the duty of either House to deliberate, without regard to the determinations of the other; for how should the nation receive any benefit from the distinct powers that compose the legislature unless the determinations are without influence upon each other? If either the example or authority of the Commons can divert us from following our own convictions, we are no longer part of the legislature; we have given up our honors and our privileges, and what then is our concurrence but slavery, or our suffrage but an echo?

The only argument, therefore, that now remains is the expediency of gratifying those by whose ready subscription the exigencies our new statesmen have brought upon us have been supported, and of continuing the security by which they have been encouraged to such liberal contributions.

Public credit, my lords, is indeed of very great importance, but public credit can never be long supported without public virtue; nor, indeed, if the Government could mortgage the morals and health of the people would it be just and rational to confirm the bargain. If the ministry can raise money only by the destruction of their fellow-subjects, they ought to abandon those schemes for which the money is necessary; for what calamity can be equal to unbounded wickedness?

But, my lords, there is no necessity for a choice which may cost our ministers so much regret, for the same subscriptions may be procured by an offer of the same advantages to a fund of any other kind, and the sinking fund will easily supply any deficiency that might be suspected in another scheme.

To confess the truth, I should feel very little pain from an account that the nation was for some time determined to be less liberal of their contributions, and that money was withheld till it was known in what expeditions it was to be employed, to what princes subsidies were to be paid, and what advantages were to be purchased by it for our country. I should rejoice, my lords, to hear that the lottery by which the deficiencies of this duty are to be supplied was not filled, and that the people were grown at last wise enough to discern the fraud and to prefer honest commerce, by which all may be gainers, to a game by which the greatest number must certainly be losers.

The lotteries, my lords, which former ministers have proposed have always been censured by those who saw their nature and their tendency. They have been considered as legal cheats, by which the ignorant and the rash are defrauded, and the subtle and avaricious often enriched; they have been allowed to divert the people from trade, and to alienate them from useful industry. A man who is uneasy in his circumstances and idle in his disposition, collects the remains of his fortune and buys tickets in a lottery, retires from business, indulges himself in laziness, and waits, in some obscure place, the event of his adventure. Another, instead of employing his stock in trade, rents a garret, and makes it his business, by false intelligence and chimerical alarms, to raise and sink the price of tickets alternately, and takes advantage of the lies which he has himself invented.

Such, my lords, is the traffic that is produced by this scheme of getting money; nor were these inconveniences unknown to the present ministers in the time of their predecessors, whom they never ceased to pursue with the loudest clamors whenever the exigencies of the Government reduced them to a lottery.

If I, my lords, might presume to recommend to our ministers the most probable method of raising a large sum for the payment of the troops of the Electorate, I should, instead of the tax and lottery now proposed, advise them to establish a certain number of licensed wheel-barrows, on which the laudable trade of thimble and button might be carried on for the support of the war, and shoe-boys might contribute to the defence of the House of Austria by raffling for apples.

Having now, my lords, examined, with the utmost candor, all the reasons which have been offered in defence of the bill, I cannot conceal the result of my inquiry. The arguments have had so little effect upon my understanding that, as every man judges of others by himself, I cannot believe that they have any influence even upon those that offer them, and therefore I am convinced that this bill must be the result of considerations which have been hitherto concealed, and is intended to promote designs which are never to be discovered by the authors before their execution.

With regard to these motives and designs, however artfully concealed, every lord in this House is at liberty to offer his conjectures.

When I consider, my lords, the tendency of this bill, I find it calculated only for the propagation of diseases, the suppression of industry, and the destruction of mankind. I find it the most fatal engine that ever was pointed at a people—an engine by which those who are not killed will be disabled, and those who preserve their limbs will be deprived of their senses.

This bill, therefore, appears to be designed only to thin the ranks of mankind, and to disburden the world of the multitudes that inhabit it; and is perhaps the strongest proof of political sagacity that our new ministers have yet exhibited. They well know, my lords, that they are universally detested, and that whenever a Briton is destroyed, they are freed from an enemy; they have therefore opened the flood-gates of gin upon the nation, that, when it is less numerous, it may be more easily governed.

Other ministers, my lords, who had not attained to so great a knowledge in the art of making war upon their country, when they found their enemies clamorous and bold, used to awe them with prosecutions and penalties, or destroy them like burglars, with prisons and with gibbets. But every age, my lords, produces some improvement; and every nation, however degenerate, gives birth, at some happy period of time, to men of great and enterprising genius. It is our fortune to be witnesses of a new discovery in politics. We may congratulate ourselves upon being contemporaries with those men who have shown that hangmen and halters are unnecessary in a state; and that ministers may escape the reproach of destroying their enemies by inciting them to destroy themselves.

This new method may, indeed, have upon different constitutions a different operation; it may destroy the lives of some and the senses of others; but either of these effects will answer the purposes of the ministry, to whom it is indifferent, provided the nation becomes insensible whether pestilence or lunacy prevails among them. Either mad or dead the greatest part of the people must quickly be, or there is no hope of the continuance of the present ministry.

For this purpose, my lords, what could have been invented more efficacious than an establishment of a certain number of shops at which poison may be vended—poison so prepared as to please the palate, while it wastes the strength, and only kills by intoxication? From the first instant that any of the enemies of the ministry shall grow clamorous and turbulent, a crafty hireling may lead him to the ministerial slaughter-house, and ply him with their wonder-working liquor till he is no longer able to speak or think; and, my lords, no man can be more agreeable to our ministers than he that can neither speak nor think, except those who speak without thinking.

But, my lords, the ministers ought to reflect that though all the people of the present age are their enemies, yet they have made no trial of the temper and inclinations of posterity. Our successors may be of opinions very different from ours. They may perhaps approve of wars on the Continent, while our plantations are insulted and our trade obstructed; they may think the support of the House of Austria of more importance to us than our own defence; and may perhaps so far differ from their fathers, as to imagine the treasures of Britain very properly employed in supporting the troops, and increasing the splendor, of a foreign Electorate.

FREE GRACE

—

BY

JOHN WESLEY

JOHN WESLEY

1703—1791

A vast force had its abiding-place in this son of an English clergyman of the Established Church; though it was not till he had passed his first youth that he himself comprehended the extent of his powers and influence. His mental and religious development was gradual, as is often the case with men of strong character; he was to live eighty-eight years, and there was time for him to arrive at an understanding with himself; and he had the steadfastness and courage to do the work which he believed the Lord laid upon him, when he understood what it was, and what it involved. There was at all times a calmness, and perhaps a coldness, in Wesley; a deliberation and persistence, which produced their effect in the long run; so that to the end of his long life he continually increased in sway over the minds of his followers. Many preachers were more impassioned in the pulpit than he, and effected more striking immediate results; but they lacked his sustained and relentless power. His love of order and method in all things was one of his leading traits, and led to the name which was bestowed by outsiders upon his sect, and which he accepted as a suitable one. He perceived the value of discipline and regularity, and the church which he founded gained immense strength from this source. There was none of the military parade and nomenclature which characterize the present Salvation Army; no uniforms, and war-cries, and sensational campaigns; but the organization was none the less rigid and effective. He impressed his own personality upon it; and it has retained the stamp ever since.

Wesley was born in 1703; and if he ever had a boyhood, nothing is known of it; so far as we know, he was always sedate and disposed to seriousness; there is no symptom of a passionate nature subdued by a vigorous will; none of those terrific spiritual experiences which toss a soul between heaven and hell. Wesley went to Charterhouse School, and thence to Christ Church, Oxford, afterwards being elected fellow of Lincoln College, and graduating master of arts in 1726. At this time he had not contemplated taking any advanced part in religious or theological matters; but the reading of Law's " Serious Call "—a devotional work of the period—prompted him to assume stricter devotional observances; and having associated some young men of his own grave complexion with himself, they adopted the habit of meeting together for systematic religious study. Everything was methodical with these pious and solemn youths, and it was at this time that their frivolous fellows dubbed them " Methodists." Wesley now imagined himself converted as thoroughly as a man could be; though in this idea he afterwards declared himself to have been egregiously mistaken. But his assurance of grace at this juncture was such that when an opportunity offered to go out to the newly founded colony of Georgia, in America, to convert the Indians, he felt himself to be just the person for the emergency. Thither, therefore, brimming over with sanctified self-complacency, he went; but his success was by no means equal to his anticipations. In the first place, the Indians could not be approached; they had not yet satisfied themselves that white men had any business in their hunting-grounds; and they would in the meanwhile have none of his religion. The settlers were at first amenable enough; but ere long Wesley's strict High Church notions, and what seemed the grotesque fanaticism of his life, offended the people; and their hostility was confirmed by his refusing the sacrament of the Lord's Supper to a young lady whom he had designed to marry, but who preferred a more human husband. He returned to England in consequence of this affair; and it was then that he realized that he, who was so ready to convert others, had never been really converted himself. After a period of self-examination, he experienced, at a quarter before nine o'clock on the evening of May 24, 1738, the mystic change of heart which called him to a true divine life and ministry. His memorandum of the precise hour of the occurrence is characteristic of him. From that time, at all events, his entire attitude, and the direction of his energies, were altered. He began to travel from place to place, preaching often several times a day, visiting prisons and country villages, and gaining followers at every step. His exhortations, in spite of their rigid calmness, produced effects upon his audiences such as have become familiar under the efforts of revivalists in our day; swoonings, outcries, sudden receptions of grace, and public confessions of sin. Whitefield, the Calvinistic Methodist, had already taken up open-air preaching, and for a time he and Wesley joined forces; but differences afterwards arose, and they separated.

The Wesleyan Methodists grew stronger, as an organization, every day, and gained a great number of followers; but they also excited a good deal of popular odium, as has uniformly been the lot of new sects. In 1749 Wesley married a rich widow, but could not agree with her, and they soon separated. When the war of the American Revolution began, he wrote " A Calm Address to the American Colonies," which had some temporary influence on his own followers at least. After the end of the struggle, Wesley ordained preachers for America by imposition of hands, and consecrated a bishop for the Methodist Episcopal Church; thus openly renouncing the principles of orthodox Episcopalianism. This step alienated many, among them Wesley's own brother, Charles.

" He had," says a contemporary, " a countenance wherein mildness and gravity were very pleasingly blended, and which, in old age, appeared extremely venerable. In manners he was social, polite, and conversable, without any gloom or austerity. In the pulpit he was fluent, clear and argumentative, often amusing, but never reaching the eloquence of passion." His labors continued unremittingly up to the last week of his life; he died on March 2, 1791.

FREE GRACE

HOW freely does God love the world! While we were yet sinners, "Christ died for the ungodly." While we were "dead in sin," God "spared not his own Son, but delivered Him up for us all."[1] And how freely with Him does He "give us all things!" Verily, free grace is all in all.

The grace or love of God, whence cometh our salvation, is free in all, and free for all.

First, It is free in all to whom it is given. It does not depend on any power or merit in man; no, not in any degree, neither in whole, nor in part. It does not in any wise depend either on the good works or righteousness of the receiver; not on anything he has done, or anything he is. It does not depend on his endeavors. It does not depend on his good tempers, or good desires, or good purposes and intentions; for all these flow from the free grace of God; they are the streams only, not the fountain. They are the fruits of free grace, and not the root. They are not the cause, but the effects of it. Whatsoever good is in man, or is done by man, God is the author and doer of it. Thus is His grace free in all; that is, no way depending on any power or merit in man, but on God alone, who freely gave us His own Son, and "with Him freely giveth us all things."

But is it free for all, as well as in all? To this some have answered, "No; it is free only for those whom God hath ordained to life; and they are but a little flock. The greater part of mankind God hath ordained to death; and it is not free for them. Them God hateth; and, therefore, before they were born, decreed they should die eternally. And this He absolutely

---

[1] " He that spared not His own Son, but delivered Him up for us all, how shall He not with Him also freely give us all things?" (Rom. viii. 32.) This sermon was preached at Bristol, in the year 1740.

181

decreed, because so was His good pleasure—because it was
His sovereign will. Accordingly, they are born for this—to
be destroyed body and soul in hell. And they grow up under
the irrevocable curse of God, without any possibility of redemption; for what grace God gives, He gives only for this,
to increase, not prevent, their damnation."

This is that decree of predestination. But methinks I hear
one say, " This is not the predestination which I hold: I hold
only the election of grace. What I believe is no more than this
—that God, before the foundation of the world, did elect a certain number of men to be justified, sanctified, and glorified.
Now, all these will be saved, and none else; for the rest of mankind God leaves to themselves. So they follow the imaginations
of their own hearts, which are only evil continually, and, wax-
ing worse and worse, are at length justly punished with everlasting destruction."

Is this all the predestination which you hold? Consider; perhaps this is not all. Do not you believe God ordained them to
this very thing? If so, you believe the whole decree; you hold
predestination in the full sense which has been above described.
But it may be you think you do not. Do not you then believe
God hardens the hearts of them that perish? Do not you believe He (literally) hardened Pharaoh's heart; and that for this
end He raised him up, or created him? Why, this amounts to
just the same thing. If you believe Pharaoh, or any one man
upon earth, was created for this end—to be damned—you hold
all that has been said of predestination. And there is no need
you should add that God seconds His decree, which is supposed
unchangeable and irresistible, by hardening the hearts of those
vessels of wrath whom that decree had before fitted for destruction.

Well, but it may be you do not believe even this; you do not
hold any decree of reprobation; you do not think God decrees
any man to be damned, nor hardens, irresistibly fits him, for
damnation; you only say, " God eternally decreed that all being
dead in sin He would say to some of the dry bones, Live, and to
others He would not; that, consequently, these should be made
alive, and those abide in death—these should glorify God by
their salvation, and those by their destruction."

Is not this what you mean by the election of grace? If it be,

I would ask one or two questions: Are any who are not thus elected saved? or were any, from the foundation of the world? Is it possible any man should be saved unless he be thus elected? If you say, " No," you are but where you was; you are not got one hair's breadth further; you still believe that, in consequence of an unchangeable, irresistible decree of God, the greater part of mankind abide in death, without any possibility of redemption; inasmuch as none can save them but God, and He will not save them. You believe He hath absolutely decreed not to save them; and what is this but decreeing to damn them? It is, in effect, neither more nor less; it comes to the same thing; for if you are dead, and altogether unable to make yourself alive, then, if God has absolutely decreed He will make only others alive, and not you, He hath absolutely decreed your everlasting death; you are absolutely consigned to damnation. So then, though you use softer words than some, you mean the self-same thing; and God's decree concerning the election of grace according to your account of it, amounts to neither more less than what others call God's decree of reprobation.

Call it, therefore, by whatever name you please, election, preterition, predestination, or reprobation, it comes in the end to the same thing. The sense of all is plainly this—by virtue of an eternal, unchangeable, irresistible decree of God, one part of mankind are infallibly saved, and the rest infallibly damned; it being impossible that any of the former should be damned, or that any of the latter should be saved.

But if this be so, then is all preaching vain. It is needless to them that are elected; for they, whether with preaching or without, will infallibly be saved. Therefore, the end of preaching —to save souls—is void with regard to them; and it is useless to them that are not elected, for they cannot possibly be saved. They, whether with preaching or without, will infallibly be damned. The end of preaching is, therefore, void with regard to them likewise; so that in either case our preaching is vain, as your hearing is also vain.

This, then, is a plain proof that the doctrine of predestination is not a doctrine of God, because it makes void the ordinance of God; and God is not divided against Himself. A second is that it directly tends to destroy that holiness which is the end of all the ordinances of God. I do not say none who hold it are holy (for God is of tender mercy to those who are unavoidably entangled in errors of any kind) ; but that the doctrine itself— that every man is either elected or not elected from eternity, and that the one must inevitably be saved, and the other inevitably damned—has a manifest tendency to destroy holiness in general ; for it wholly takes away those first motives to follow after it, so frequently proposed in Scripture, the hope of future reward and fear of punishment, the hope of heaven and fear of hell. That these shall go away into everlasting punishment, and those into life eternal, is no motive to him to struggle for life who believes his lot is cast already ; it is not reasonable for him so to do, if he thinks he is unalterably adjudged either to life or death. You will say, " But he knows not whether it is life or death." What then ?—this helps not the matter ; for if a sick man knows that he must unavoidably die, or unavoidably recover, though he knows not which, it is unreasonable for him to take any physic at all. He might justly say (and so I have heard some speak, both in bodily sickness and in spiritual), " If I am ordained to life, I shall live ; if to death, I shall die ; so I need not trouble myself about it." So directly does this doctrine tend to shut the very gate of holiness in general—to hinder unholy men from ever approaching thereto, or striving to enter in thereat.

As directly does this doctrine tend to destroy several particular branches of holiness. Such are meekness and love—love, I mean, of our enemies—of the evil and unthankful. I say not, that none who hold it have meekness and love (for as is the power of God, so is His mercy) ; but that it naturally tends to inspire or increase a sharpness or eagerness of temper, which is quite contrary to the meekness of Christ ; as then specially appears, when they are opposed on this head. And it as naturally inspires contempt or coldness towards those whom we suppose outcasts from God. " O but," you say, " I suppose no particular man a reprobate." You mean you would not if you could help it ; but you cannot help sometimes applying your general doctrine to particular persons ; the enemy of souls will apply it for you. You know how often he has done so. But you rejected the thought with abhorrence. True ; as soon as you could ; but how did it sour and sharpen your spirit in the mean time ? You well know it was not the spirit of love which you then felt towards that poor sinner, whom you supposed or suspected, whether you would or no, to have been hated of God from eternity.

Thirdly, this doctrine tends to destroy the comfort of religion, the happiness of Christianity. This is evident as to all those who believe themselves to be reprobated, or who only suspect or fear it. All the great and precious promises are lost to them; they afford them no ray of comfort, for they are not the elect of God; therefore they have neither lot nor portion in them. This is an effectual bar to their finding any comfort or happiness, even in that religion whose ways are designed to be " ways of pleasantness, and all her paths peace."

And as to you who believe yourselves the elect of God, what is your happiness? I hope, not a notion, a speculative belief, a bare opinion of any kind, but a feeling possession of God in your heart, wrought in you by the Holy Ghost, or the witness of God's Spirit with your spirit that you are a child of God. This, otherwise termed " the full assurance of faith," is the true ground of a Christian's happiness. And it does indeed imply a full assurance that all your past sins are forgiven, and that you are now a child of God. But it does not necessarily imply a full assurance of our future perseverance. I do not say this is never joined to it, but that it is not necessarily implied therein; for many have the one who have not the other.

Now, this witness of the Spirit experience shows to be much obstructed by this doctrine; and not only in those who, believing themselves reprobated, by this belief thrust it far from them, but even in them that have tasted of that good gift, who yet have soon lost it again, and fallen back into doubts, and fears, and darkness—horrible darkness that might be felt. And I appeal to any of you who hold this doctrine, to say, between God and your own hearts, whether you have not often a return of doubts and fears concerning your election or perseverance. If you ask, " Who has not? " I answer, very few of those that hold this doctrine; but many, very many of those that hold it not, in all parts of the earth—many of those who know and feel that they are in Christ to-day, and " take no thought for the morrow "; who " abide in Him " by faith from hour to hour, or, rather, from moment to moment; many of these have enjoyed the uninterrupted witness of His Spirit, the continual light of His countenance, from the moment wherein they first believed, for many months or years, to this day.

That assurance of faith which these enjoy excludes all doubt and fear. It excludes all kinds of doubt and fear concerning their future perseverance; though it is not properly, as was said before, an assurance of what is future, but only of what now is. And this needs not for its support a speculative belief, that whoever is once ordained to life must live; for it is wrought, from hour to hour, by the mighty power of God, " by the Holy Ghost which is given unto them." And therefore that doctrine is not of God, because it tends to obstruct, if not destroy, this great work of the Holy Ghost, whence flows the chief comfort of religion, the happiness of Christianity.

Again, how uncomfortable a thought is this, that thousands and millions of men, without any preceding offence or fault of theirs, were unchangeably doomed to everlasting burnings. How peculiarly uncomfortable must it be to those who have put on Christ, to those who, being filled with bowels of mercy, tenderness, and compassion, could even " wish themselves accursed for their brethren's sake."

Fourthly, this uncomfortable doctrine directly tends to destroy our zeal for good works. And this it does, first, as it naturally tends (according to what was observed before) to destroy our love to the greater part of mankind, namely, the evil and unthankful. For whatever lessens our love, must so far lessen our desire to do them good. This it does, secondly, as it cuts off one of the strongest motives to all acts of bodily mercy, such as feeding the hungry, clothing the naked, and the like— viz., the hope of saving their souls from death. For what avails it to relieve their temporal wants, who are just dropping into eternal fire? " Well, but run and snatch them as brands out of the fire." Nay, this you suppose impossible. They were appointed thereunto, you say, from eternity, before they had done either good or evil. You believe it is the will of God they should die. And " who hath resisted His will?" But you say you do not know whether these are elected or not. What then? If you know they are the one or the other—that they are either elected, or not elected—all your labor is void and vain. In either case, your advice, reproof, or exhortation is as needless and useless as our preaching. It is needless to them that are elected, for they will infallibly be saved without it. It is useless to them that are not elected, for with or without it they will infallibly be damned; therefore you cannot, consistently with your principles, take any pains about their salvation. Consequently, those principles directly tend to destroy your zeal for good works; for all good works; but particularly for the greatest of all, the saving of souls from death.

But, fifthly, this doctrine not only tends to destroy Christian holiness, happiness, and good works, but hath also a direct and manifest tendency to overthrow the whole Christian revelation. The point which the wisest of the modern unbelievers must industriously labor to prove, is, that the Christian revelation is not necessary. They well know, could they once show this, the conclusion would be too plain to be denied, " if it be not necessary, it is not true." Now, this fundamental point you give up. For supposing that eternal, unchangeable decree, one part of mankind must be saved, though the Christian revelation were not in being, and the other part of mankind must be damned, notwithstanding that revelation. And what would on infidel desire more? You allow him all he asks. In making the Gospel thus unnecessary to all sorts of men you give up the whole Christian cause. " O tell it not in Gath. Publish it not in the streets of Askelon, lest the daughters of the uncircumcised rejoice; " lest the sons of unbelief triumph.

And as this doctrine manifestly and directly tends to overthrow the whole Christian revelation, so it does the same thing, by plain consequence, in making that revelation contradict itself. For it is grounded on such an interpretation of some texts (more or fewer it matters not) as flatly contradicts all the other texts, and indeed the whole scope and tenor of Scripture. For instance, the assertors of this doctrine interpret that text of Scripture, " Jacob have I loved, but Esau have I hated," as implying that God in a literal sense hated Esau, and all the reprobated, from eternity. Now, what can possibly be a more flat contradiction than this, not only to the whole scope and tenor of Scripture, but also to all those particular texts which expressly declare, " God is love?" Again, they infer from that text, " I will have mercy on whom I will have mercy " (Rom. ix. 15), that God is love only to some men, viz., the elect, and that He hath mercy for those only; flatly contrary to which is the whole tenor of Scripture, as is that express declaration in particular, " The Lord is loving unto every man; and His mercy is over

all His works " (Psalm cxlv. 9). Again, they infer from that
and the like texts, " It is not of him that willeth, nor of him that
runneth, but of God that showeth mercy," that He showeth
mercy only to those to whom He had respect from all eternity.
Nay, but who replieth against God now? You now contradict
the whole oracles of God, which declare throughout, " God is no
respector of persons " (Acts x. 34) : " There is no respect of
persons with Him " (Rom. ii. 11). Again, from that text,
" The children being not yet born, neither having done any good
or evil, that the purpose of God according to election might
stand, not of works, but of Him that calleth; it was said unto
her," unto Rebecca, " The elder shall serve the younger; " you
infer, that our being predestinated, or elect, no way depends on
the foreknowledge of God. Flatly contrary to this are all the
Scripture, and those in particular, " Elect according to the foreknowledge of God " (1 Peter, i. 2) ; " Whom He did foreknow,
He also did predestinate " (Rom. viii. 29).

And " the same Lord over all is rich " in mercy " to all that
call upon Him " (Rom. x. 12). But you say, " No, He is such
only to those for whom Christ died. And those are not all, but
only a few, whom God hath chosen out of the world; for He
died not for all, but only for those who were ' chosen in Him
before the foundation of the world ' (Eph. i. 4)." Flatly contrary to your interpretation of these Scriptures, also, is the
whole tenor of the New Testament; as are in particular those
texts: " Destroy not him with thy meat, for whom Christ died "
(Rom. xiv. 15)—a clear proof that Christ died, not only for
those that are saved, but also for them that perish; He is " the
Saviour of the world " (John iv. 42) ; He is " the Lamb of God
that taketh away the sins of the world " (i. 29) ; " He is the propitiation, not for our sins only, but also for the sins of the whole
world " (1 John, ii. 2). " He," the living God, " is the Saviour
of all men " (1 Tim., iv. 10) ; " He gave Himself a ransom for
all " (ii. 6) ; " He tasted death for every man " (Heb. ii. 9).

If you ask, " Why then are not all men saved? " the whole
law and the testimony answer, First, Not because of any decree
of God; not because it is His pleasure they should die; for,
" As I live, saith the Lord God," " I have no pleasure in the
death of him that dieth " (Ezek. xviii. 3, 32). Whatever be the
cause of their perishing, it cannot be His will, if the oracles of

God are true; for they declare, " He is not willing that any should perish, but that all should come to repentance " (2 Peter iii. 9) ; " He willeth that all men should be saved." And they, secondly, declare what is the cause why all men are not saved, namely, that they will not be saved. So our Lord expressly, " Ye will not come unto me that ye may have life " (John v. 40). " The power of the Lord is present to heal " them, but they will not be healed. " They reject the counsel," the merciful counsel of God, " against themselves," as did their stiff-necked fore-fathers. And therefore are they without excuse; because God would save them, but they will not be saved. This is the con-demnation, " How often would I have gathered you together, and ye would not " (Matt. xxiii. 37).

Thus manifestly does this doctrine tend to overthrow the whole Christian revelation, by making it contradict itself; by giving such an interpretation of some texts, as flatly contra-dicts all the other texts, and indeed the whole scope and tenor of Scripture—an abundant proof that it is not of God. But neither is this all, for, seventhly, it is a doctrine full of blas-phemy, of such blasphemy as I should dread to mention, but that the honor of our gracious God, and the cause of His truth, will not suffer me to be silent. In the cause of God, then, and from a sincere concern for the glory of His great name, I will mention a few of the horrible blasphemies contained in this hor-rible doctrine. But first, I must warn every one of you that hears, as ye will answer it at the great day, not to charge me (as some have done) with blaspheming, because I mention the blas-phemy of others. And the more you are grieved with them that do thus blaspheme, see that ye " confirm your love towards them " the more, and that your heart's desire, and continual prayer to God, be, " Father, forgive them, for they know not what they do ! "

This premised, let it be observed that this doctrine represents our blessed Lord " Jesus Christ the righteous, the only begotten Son of the Father, full of grace and truth," as a hypocrite, a deceiver of the people, a man void of common sincerity. For it cannot be denied that He everywhere speaks as if He were will-ing that all men should be saved; therefore, to say that He was not willing that all men should be saved, is to represent Him as a mere hypocrite and dissembler. It cannot be denied that the gracious words which come out of His mouth are full of invitations to all sinners: to say, then, that He did not intend to save all sinners is to represent Him as a gross deceiver of the people. You cannot deny that He says, "Come unto me, all ye that are weary and heavy laden!" If, then, you say He calls those that cannot come, those whom He can make able to come, but will not, how is it possible to describe greater insincerity? You represent Him as mocking His helpless creatures, by offering what He never intends to give. You describe Him as saying one thing and meaning another; as pretending the love which He had not. Him, in whose mouth was no guile, you make full of deceit, void of common sincerity; then especially, when drawing nigh the city, He wept over it, and said, "O Jerusalem! Jerusalem! thou that killest the prophets and stonest them that are sent unto thee, how often would I have gathered thy children together, and ye would not!" Now, if you say they would, but He would not, you represent Him (which who could bear?) as weeping crocodile tears over the prey which He had doomed to destruction!

Such blasphemy this, as one would think, might make the ears of a Christian tingle! But there is yet more behind; for just as it honors the Son, so doth this doctrine honor the Father. It destroys all His attributes at once; it overturns both His justice, mercy, and truth. Yes, it represents the most holy God as worse than the devil; as more false, more cruel, and more unjust! More false, because the devil, liar as he is, hath never said he willeth all mankind to be saved; more unjust, because the devil cannot, if he would, be guilty of such injustice as you ascribe to God, when you say that God condemned millions of souls to everlasting fire, prepared for the devil and his angels, for continuing in sin, which, for want of that grace He will not give them, they cannot avoid; and more cruel, because that unhappy spirit seeketh rest and findeth none. So that his own restless misery is a kind of temptation to him to tempt others; but God resteth in His high and holy place, so that to suppose Him, out of His mere motion, of His pure will and pleasure, happy as He is, to doom His creatures, whether they will or not, to endless misery, is to impute such cruelty to Him as we cannot impute to the great enemy of God and men. It is to represent the most high God (he that hath ears to hear, let him hear!) as more cruel, false, and unjust than the devil.

This is the blasphemy clearly contained in the horrible doctrine of predestination. And here I fix my foot. On this I
join issue with every assertor of it. You represent God as worse
than the devil; more false, more cruel, more unjust. But you
say you will prove it by Scripture. Hold! What will you prove
by Scripture? that God is worse than the devil? It cannot be.
Whatever that Scripture proves, it never proves this; whatever
be its true meaning, it cannot mean this. Do you ask what is
its true meaning, then? If I say I know not, you have gained
nothing; for there are many Scriptures, the true sense whereof
neither you nor I shall know till death is swallowed up in victory. But this I know, better it were to say it had no sense at
all than it had such a sense as this. It cannot mean, whatever
it mean beside, that the God of truth is a liar. Let it mean what
it will, it cannot mean that the judge of all the world is unjust.
No Scripture can mean that God is not love, or that His mercy
is not over all His works; that is, whatever it prove beside, no
Scripture can prove predestination.

This is the blasphemy for which I abhor the doctrine of predestination; a doctrine, upon the supposition of which, if one
could possibly suppose it for a moment—call it election, reprobation, or what you please (for all comes to the same thing)—
one might say to our adversary the devil, " Thou fool, why dost
thou prowl about any longer? Thy lying in wait for souls is
as needless and as useless as our preaching. Hearest thou not
that God hath taken thy work out of thy hands, and that He doth
it more effectually? Thou, with all thy principalities and powers, canst only so assault that we may resist thee; but He can
irresistibly destroy both body and soul in hell! Thou canst only
entice; but His unchangeable decree, to leave thousands of
souls in death, compels them to continue in sin till they drop into
everlasting burnings. Thou temptest, He forces us to be
damned, for we cannot resist His will. Thou fool! why goest
thou about any longer, seeking whom thou mayst devour?
Hearest thou not that God is the devouring lion, the destroyer
of souls, the murderer of men? Moloch caused only children
to pass through the fire, and that fire was soon quenched; or the
corruptible body being consumed, its torments were at an end;
but God, thou art told, by His eternal decree, fixed before they
had done good or evil, causes not only children of a span long,

but the parents also, to pass through the fire of hell; that fire which never shall be quenched; and the body which is cast thereinto, being now incorruptible and immortal, will be ever consuming and never consumed; but the smoke of their torment, because it is God's good pleasure, ascendeth up forever."

Oh, how would the enemy of God and men rejoice to hear these things were so! How would he cry aloud and spare not. How would he lift up his voice and say, To your tents, O Israel! Flee from the face of this God or ye shall utterly perish. But whither will ye flee? Into heaven? He is there. Down to hell? He is there also. Ye cannot flee from an omnipresent almighty tyrant. And whether ye flee or stay I call heaven, His throne, and earth, His footstool, to witness against you; ye shall perish, shall perish eternally! Sing, O hell, and rejoice ye that are under the earth! for God, even the mighty God, hath spoken and devoted to death thousands of souls, from the rising of the sun unto the going down thereof. Here, O death, is thy sting! Here, O grave, is thy victory! Nations yet unborn, or ever they have done good or evil, are doomed never to see the light of life, but thou shalt gnaw upon them forever and ever. Let all those morning stars sing together, who fell with Lucifer, son of the morning. Let all the sons of hell shout for joy, for the decree is past, and who shall annul it?

Yes, the decree is past; and so it was before the foundation of the world. But what decree? Even this: " I will set before the sons of men life and death, blessing and cursing; " and " the soul that chooseth life shall live, as the soul that chooseth death shall die." This decree, whereby whom God " did foreknow, He did predestinate," was indeed from everlasting; this, whereby all who suffer Christ to make them alive, are " elect according to the foreknowledge of God," now standeth fast, even as the moon, and the faithful witness in heaven; and when heaven and earth shall pass away, yet this shall not pass away, for it is as unchangeable and eternal as the being of God that gave it. This decree yields the strongest encouragement to abound in all good works, and in all holiness, and it is a well-spring of joy, of happiness also, to our great and endless comfort. This is worthy of God. It is every way consistent with the perfection of His nature. It gives us the noblest view, both of His justice, mercy, and truth. To this agrees the whole scope of the Christian revelation, as well as all the parts thereof. To this Moses and all the prophets bear witness, and our blessed Lord and all His apostles. Thus Moses, in the name of his Lord, " I call heaven and earth to record against you this day, that I have set before you life and death, blessing and cursing; therefore choose life, that thou and thy seed may live." Thus Ezekiel (to cite one prophet for all), " The soul that sinneth, it shall die. The son shall not bear (eternally) the iniquity of the father. The righteousness of the righteous shall be upon him, and the wickedness of the wicked shall be upon him." Thus our blessed Lord, " If any man thirst, let him come to me and drink." Thus His great apostle, St. Paul, " God commandeth all men, every-where, to repent." All men, everywhere; every person, in every place, without any exception either of place or person. Thus St. James, " If any of you lack wisdom, let him ask of God, who giveth to all men liberally, and upbraideth not, and it shall be given him." Thus St. Peter, " The Lord is not willing that any should perish, but that all should come to repentance." And thus St. John, " If any man sin, we have an advocate with the Father, and He is the propitiation for our sins; and not for ours only, but for the sins of the whole world."

Oh, hear ye this, ye that forget God! Ye cannot charge your death upon Him. " Have I any pleasure at all that the wicked should die? saith the Lord God. Repent and turn from your transgressions, so iniquity shall not be your ruin. Cast away from you all your transgressions whereby you have trans-gressed; for why will ye die, O house of Israel? For I have no pleasure in the death of him that dieth, saith the Lord God. Wherefore turn yourselves, and live ye." " As I live, saith the Lord God, I have no pleasure in the death of the wicked. Turn ye, turn ye from your evil ways; for why will ye die, O house of Israel?"

ON THE RIGHT OF ENGLAND TO TAX AMERICA

—

BY

LORD MANSFIELD

(William Murray)

WILLIAM MURRAY, LORD MANSFIELD

1705—1793

William Murray, whose genius elevated him to the peerage under the title of Lord Mansfield, and who was the greatest jurist of the eighteenth century, if not the greatest who ever sat upon the English bench, was a Scotchman, born at Scone in 1705. As he died in 1793, his life just covered the eighteenth century, whose greatest legal luminary he became. His talents were apparent from the first; he was not a flower that bloomed late, but he was a born scholar, and seemed to suck in learning with his mother's milk. His progress in the line of public preferment was rapid and steady, and there were no reverses in his career; he made no mistakes, and his services were so invaluable that there was no danger of his being superseded by any rival. He had become familiar with Greek and Latin long before most boys are out of the dame-school; and we are told that he was wont to amuse himself, in his boyish days, by setting over the Greek and Roman orators into English and back again; he had classic poetry by heart, and conversed in the tongue of Cicero as readily as in his own. He must have foreseen his career from the first; for he early began a systematic study of eloquence, and never pretermitted it, so that when he was called to the bar he was already a past master of all those arts and refinements which other men learn laboriously by practice in the courts, and before juries and assemblies. There was no man of his time who had such a thorough and available familiarity with history as he; he knew whatever man had done or thought in the past, and was therefore the more easily master of what was most expedient to be done in the present. Such breadth and command of knowledge bred a calmness and judicial temper in him which peculiarly fitted him for the great functions he was destined to perform; and would naturally be discouraging to an opponent who must take his information from Mansfield in regard to whatever subject might come up for argument. He was appointed solicitor-general in 1742, and his duties in this office brought him in contact with William Pitt, who was his only worthy antagonist. In debate he was almost invincible, as might be expected from his ready and accurate erudition; but all his accomplishments did not betray him into any neglect in the matter of specially preparing himself for whatever matter might be under discussion; he worked with just as much assiduity as if he had been a novice. The fruits of this application were magnificent; while in the court of the King's Bench he was called upon to decide many thousands of cases; and of them all there were but two in which his associate justices failed to support his opinions. The best panegyric upon him was pronounced by an American, Joseph Story; and inasmuch as Mansfield, by his official position, was necessarily opposed to the American colonies in their struggles for independence, the praise of this great American gains added weight. "England and America," declares Story, "and the civilized world lie under the deepest obligations to him. Wherever commerce shall extend its social influences; wherever contracts shall be expounded upon the eternal principles of right and wrong; wherever moral delicacy and judicial refinement shall be infused into the municipal code to persuade men to be honest and to keep them so; wherever the intercourse of mankind shall aim at something more elevated than the grovelling spirit of barter, in which meanness and avarice and fraud strive for mastery over ignorance, credulity, and folly: the name of Lord Mansfield will be held in reverence by the good and the wise, by the honest merchant, the enlightened lawyer, the just statesman, and the conscientious judge. His judgments should not be referred to on the spur of particular occasions, but should be studied as models of judicial reasoning and eloquence." Since the time of Lord Bacon, there has been no man of whom such a eulogy could be truthfully spoken; and Bacon, though supreme in intellect even over Mansfield, was his inferior in the moral qualities which make a man's memory honored after he is gone.

His style of oratory was different in principle from that of Chatham; it was tranquil and unemotional, and sought no sensational effects or victories of surprise. He saw his subject from beginning to end at a single view; he noted its various features, and selected those which it was most expedient to enforce. He then proceeded by calm reasonings, not appearing to force the assent, but rendering it inevitable by appeal to man's recognition of unquestionable facts and inevitable deductions. It seemed to his hearers as if they were judges passing upon evidence, and that there could be but one verdict; but it was the verdict which Mansfield desired. He carefully avoided all oratorical flights, as prone to alarm his auditors into fancying that their judgment was to be won over by artifice; he adopted a tone of dispassionate conversation, dignified, limpid, and cogent. He was the most formidable and the fairest foe with which the colonies had to contend; if there were anything irrational or unjust in their attitude or claims, Mansfield was certain to put his finger quietly and immovably upon the very spot.

At the time of his appointment to the King's Bench, in 1756, he entered the Cabinet, and was one of its most effective members, whose word few cared to dispute. Apart from his relation to the War of the Revolution, he applied himself chiefly to expounding the principles of equity with regard to commerce; and his work in this direction won him the title of " Founder of English Commercial Law." He died in 1793 at the ripe age of eighty-eight; an almost perfect type of all that a great judge should be, and seldom is.

ON THE RIGHT OF ENGLAND TO TAX AMERICA

Delivered in the House of Lords, February 3, 1766

M Y LORDS: I shall speak to the question strictly as a matter of right; for it is a proposition in its nature so perfectly distinct from the expediency of the tax that it must necessarily be taken separate, if there is any true logic in the world; but of the expediency or inexpediency I will say nothing. It will be time enough to speak upon that subject when it comes to be a question.

I shall also speak to the distinctions which have been taken, without any real difference, as to the nature of the tax; and I shall point out, lastly, the necessity there will be of exerting the force of the superior authority of government, if opposed by the subordinate part of it.

I am extremely sorry that the question has ever become necessary to be agitated, and that there should be a decision upon it. No one in this House will live long enough to see an end put to the mischief which will be the result of the doctrine which has been inculcated; but the arrow is shot and the wound already given. I shall certainly avoid personal reflections. No one has had more cast upon him than myself; but I never was biased by any consideration of applause from without, in the discharge of my public duty; and, in giving my sentiments according to what I thought law, I have relied upon my own consciousness. It is with great pleasure I have heard the noble lord who moved the resolution express himself in so manly and sensible a way, when he recommended a dispassionate debate, while, at the same time, he urged the necessity of the House coming to such a resolution, with great dignity and propriety of argument.

I shall endeavor to clear away from the question all that mass
of dissertation and learning displayed in arguments which have
been fetched from speculative men who have written upon
the subject of government, or from ancient records, as being
little to the purpose. I shall insist that these records are no
proofs of our present constitution. A noble lord has taken up
his argument from the settlement of the constitution at the
revolution; I shall take up my argument from the constitution
as it now is. The constitution of this country has been always
in a moving state, either gaining or losing something; and with
respect to the modes of taxation, when we get beyond the reign
of Edward I, or of King John, we are all in doubt and obscurity.
The history of those times is full of uncertainties. In regard
to the writs upon record, they were issued some of them according to law, and some not according to law; and such [i.e., of the
latter kind] were those concerning ship-money, to call assemblies to tax themselves, or to compel benevolences. Other taxes
were raised from escuage, fees for knights' service and by other
means arising out of the feudal system. Benevolences are contrary to law; and it is well known how people resisted the
demands of the Crown in the case of ship-money, and were
persecuted by the Court; and if any set of men were to meet
now to lend the King money, it would be contrary to law, and
a breach of the rights of Parliament.

I shall now answer the noble lord particularly upon the cases
he has quoted. With respect to the Marches of Wales, who
were the borderers, privileged for assisting the King in his
war against the Welsh in the mountains, their enjoying this
privilege of taxing themselves was but of a short duration,
and during the life of Edward I, till the Prince of Wales came
to be the King; and then they were annexed to the Crown,
and became subject to taxes like the rest of the dominions of
England; and from thence came the custom, though unnecessary, of naming Wales and the town of Monmouth in all proclamations and in acts of Parliament. Henry VIII was the
first who issued writs for it to return two members to Parliament. The Crown exercised this right ad libitum, from whence
arises the inequality of representation in our constitution at
this day. Henry VIII issued a writ to Calais to send one
burgess to Parliament. One of the counties palatine [I think

he said Durham] was taxed fifty years to subsidies, before it sent members to Parliament. The clergy were at no time unrepresented in Parliament. When they taxed themselves, it was done with the concurrence and consent of Parliament, who permitted them to tax themselves upon their petition, the Convocation sitting at the same time with the Parliament. They had, too, their representatives always sitting in this House, bishops and abbots; and, in the other House, they were at no time without a right of voting singly for the election of members; so that the argument fetched from the case of the clergy is not an argument of any force, because they were at no time unrepresented here.

The reasoning about the colonies of Great Britain, drawn from the colonies of antiquity, is a mere useless display of learning; for the colonies of the Tyrians in Africa, and of the Greeks in Asia, were totally different from our system. No nation before ourselves formed any regular system of colonization, but the Romans; and their system was a military one, and of garrisons placed in the principal towns of the conquered provinces. The States of Holland were not colonies of Spain; they were States dependent upon the House of Austria in a feudal dependence. Nothing could be more different from our colonies than that flock of men, as they have been called, who came from the North and poured into Europe. Those emigrants renounced all laws, all protection, all connection with their mother countries. They chose their leaders, and marched under their banners to seek their fortunes and establish new kingdoms upon the ruins of the Roman empire.

But our colonies, on the contrary, emigrated under the sanction of the Crown and Parliament. They were modelled gradually into their present forms, respectively, by charters, grants, and statutes; but they were never separated from the mother country, or so emancipated as to become *sui juris*. There are several sorts of colonies in British America. The charter colonies, the proprietary governments, and the King's colonies. The first colonies were the charter colonies, such as the Virginia Company; and these companies had among their directors members of the privy council and of both Houses of Parliament; they were under the authority of the privy council, and had agents resident here, responsible for their proceedings. So much were they considered as belonging to the Crown, and not to the King personally (for there is a great difference, though few people attend to it), that when the two Houses, in the time of Charles I, were going to pass a bill concerning the colonies, a message was sent to them by the King that they were the King's colonies, and that the bill was unnecessary, for that the privy council would take order about them; and the bill never had the royal assent. The Commonwealth Parliament, as soon as it was settled, were very early jealous of the colonies separating themselves from them; and passed a resolution or act (and it is a question whether it is not in force now) to declare and establish the authority of England over its colonies.

But if there was no express law, or reason founded upon any necessary inference from an express law, yet the usage alone would be sufficient to support that authority; for, have not the colonies submitted ever since their first establishment to the jurisdiction of the mother country? In all questions of property, the appeals from the colonies have been to the privy council here; and such causes have been determined, not by the law of the colonies, but by the law of England. A very little while ago there was an appeal on a question of limitation in a devise of land with remainders; and, notwithstanding the intention of the testator appeared very clear, yet the case was determined contrary to it, and that the land should pass according to the law of England. The colonies have been obliged to recur very frequently to the jurisdiction here, to settle the disputes among their own governments. I well remember several references on this head, when the late Lord Hardwicke was attorney-general, and Sir Clement Wearg solicitor-general. New Hampshire and Connecticut were in blood about their differences; Virginia and Maryland were in arms against each other. This shows the necessity of one superior decisive jurisdiction, to which all subordinate jurisdictions may recur. Nothing, my lords, could be more fatal to the peace of the colonies at any time than the Parliament giving up its authority over them; for, in such a case, there must be an entire dissolution of government. Considering how the colonies are composed, it is easy to foresee there would be no end of feuds and factions among the several separate governments, when once there shall be no one government here or there of sufficient force or authority to decide their mutual differences; and, government being dissolved, nothing remains but that the colonies must either change their constitution, and take some new form of government, or fall under some foreign power. At present the several forms of their constitution are very various, having been produced, as all governments have been originally, by accident and circumstances. The forms of government in every colony were adopted, from time to time, according to the size of the colony; and so have been extended again, from time to time, as the numbers of their inhabitants and their commercial connections outgrew the first model. In some colonies, at first there was only a governor assisted by two or three counsel; then more were added; afterward courts of justice were erected; then assemblies were created. Some things were done by instructions from the secretaries of state; other things were done by order of the King and council; and other things by commissions under the great seal. It is observable, that in consequence of these establishments from time to time, and of the dependency of these governments upon the supreme legislature at home, the lenity of each government in the colonies has been extreme toward the subject; and a great inducement has been created for people to come and settle in them. But, if all those governments which are now independent of each other, should become independent of the mother country, I am afraid that the inhabitants of the colonies are very little aware of the consequences. They would feel in that case very soon the hand of power more heavy upon them in their own governments, than they have yet done, or have ever imagined.

The constitutions of the different colonies are thus made up of different principles. They must remain dependent, from the necessity of things, and their relations to the jurisdiction of the mother country; or they must be totally dismembered from it, and form a league of union among themselves against it, which could not be effected without great violences. No one ever thought the contrary till the trumpet of sedition was blown. Acts of Parliament have been made, not only without a doubt of their legality, but with universal applause, the great object of which has been ultimately to fix the trade of the colonies, so as to centre in the bosom of that country from whence they took their original. The Navigation Act shut up their intercourse with foreign countries. Their ports have been made subject to customs and regulations which have cramped and diminished their trade. And duties have been laid, affecting the very inmost parts of their commerce, and, among others, that of the post; yet all these have been submitted to peaceably, and no one ever thought till now of this doctrine, that the colonies are not to be taxed, regulated, or bound by Parliament. A few particular merchants were then, as now, displeased at restrictions which did not permit them to make the greatest possible advantages of their commerce in their own private and peculiar branches. But, though these few merchants might think themselves losers in articles which they had no right to gain, as being prejudicial to the general and national system, yet I must observe that the colonies, upon the whole, were benefited by these laws. For these restrictive laws, founded upon principles of the most solid policy, flung a great weight of naval force into the hands of the mother country, which was to protect its colonies. Without a union with her, the colonies must have been entirely weak and defenceless, but they thus became relatively great, subordinately, and in proportion as the mother country advanced in superiority over the rest of the maritime powers in Europe, to which both mutually contributed, and of which both have reaped a benefit, equal to the natural and just relation in which they both stand reciprocally, of dependency on one side, and protection on the other.

There can be no doubt, my lords, but that the inhabitants of the colonies are as much represented in Parliament as the greatest part of the people of England are represented; among nine millions of whom there are eight which have no votes in electing members of Parliament. Every objection, therefore, to the dependency of the colonies upon Parliament, which arises to it upon the ground of representation, goes to the whole present constitution of Great Britain; and I suppose it is not meant to new-model that too. People may form speculative ideas of perfection, and indulge their own fancies or those of other men. Every man in this country has his particular notion of liberty; but perfection never did, and never can exist in any human institution. To what purpose, then, are arguments drawn from a distinction, in which there is no real difference—of a virtual and actual representation? A member of

Parliament, chosen for any borough, represents not only the constituents and inhabitants of that particular place, but he represents the inhabitants of every other borough in Great Britain. He represents the city of London, and all the other commons of this land, and the inhabitants of all the colonies and dominions of Great Britain; and is, in duty and conscience, bound to take care of their interests.

I have mentioned the customs and the post tax. This leads me to answer another distinction, as false as the above; the distinction of internal and external taxes. The noble lord who quoted so much law, and denied upon those grounds the right of the Parliament of Great Britain to lay internal taxes upon the colonies, allowed at the same time that restrictions upon trade, and duties upon the ports, were legal. But I cannot see a real difference in this distinction; for I hold it to be true, that a tax laid in any place is like a pebble falling into and making a circle in a lake, till one circle produces and gives motion to another, and the whole circumference is agitated from the centre. For nothing can be more clear than that a tax of ten or twenty per cent. laid upon tobacco, either in the ports of Virginia or London, is a duty laid upon the inland plantations of Virginia, a hundred miles from the sea, wheresoever the tobacco grows.

I do not deny but that a tax may be laid injudiciously and injuriously, and that people in such a case may have a right to complain. But the nature of the tax is not now the question; whenever it comes to be one, I am for lenity. I would have no blood drawn. There is, I am satisfied, no occasion for any to be drawn. A little time and experience of the inconveniences and miseries of anarchy, may bring people to their senses.

With respect to what has been said or written upon this subject, I differ from the noble lord, who spoke of Mr. Otis and his book with contempt, though he maintained the same doctrine in some points, while in others he carried it farther than Otis himself, who allows everywhere the supremacy of the Crown over the colonies. No man, on such a subject, is contemptible. Otis is a man of consequence among the people there. They have chosen him for one of their deputies at the Congress and general meeting from the respective governments. It was said, the man is mad. What then? One madman often makes many. Masaniello was mad. Nobody doubts it; yet, for all that, he overturned the government of Naples. Madness is catching in all popular assemblies and upon all popular matters. The book is full of wildness. I never read it till a few days ago, for I seldom look into such things. I never was actually acquainted with the contents of the Stamp Act till I sent for it on purpose to read it before the debate was expected. With respect to authorities in another House, I know nothing of them. I believe that I have not been in that House more than once since I had the honor to be called up to this; and, if I did know anything that passed in the other House, I could not, and would not, mention it as an authority here. I ought not to mention any such authority. I should think it beneath my own and your lordship's dignity to speak of it.

I am far from bearing any ill will to the Americans; they are a very good people, and I have long known them. I began life with them, and owe much to them, having been much concerned in the Plantation causes before the privy council; and so I became a good deal acquainted with American affairs and people. I dare say their heat will soon be over, when they come to feel a little the consequences of their opposition to the legislature. Anarchy always cures itself; but the ferment will continue so much the longer, while hot-headed men there find that there are persons of weight and character to support and justify them here.

Indeed, if the disturbances should continue for a great length of time, force must be the consequence, an application adequate to the mischief, and arising out of the necessity of the case; for force is only the difference between a superior and subordinate jurisdiction. In the former, the whole force of the legislature resides collectively, and when it ceases to reside, the whole connection is dissolved. It will, indeed, be to very little purpose that we sit here enacting laws, and making resolutions, if the inferior will not obey them, or if we neither can nor dare enforce them; for then, and then, I say, of necessity, the matter comes to the sword. If the offspring are grown too big and too resolute to obey the parent, you must try which is the strongest, and exert all the powers of the mother country to decide the contest.

I am satisfied, notwithstanding, that time and a wise and

steady conduct may prevent those extremities which would be fatal to both. I remember well when it was the violent humor of the times to decry standing armies and garrisons as dangerous, and incompatible with the liberty of the subject. Nothing would do but a regular militia. The militia are embodied; they march; and no sooner was the militia law thus put into execution, but it was then said to be an intolerable burden upon the subject, and that it would fall, sooner or later, into the hands of the Crown. That was the language, and many counties petitioned against it. This may be the case with the colonies. In many places they begin already to feel the effects of their resistance to government. Interest very soon divides mercantile people; and, although there may be some mad, enthusiastic, or ill-designing people in the colonies, yet I am convinced that the greatest bulk, who have understanding and property, are still well affected to the mother country. You have, my lords, many friends still in the colonies; and take care that you do not, by abdicating your own authority, desert them and yourselves, and lose them forever.

In all popular tumults, the worst men bear the sway at first. Moderate and good men are often silent for fear or modesty, who, in good time, may declare themselves. Those who have any property to lose are sufficiently alarmed already at the progress of these public violences and violations, to which every man's dwelling, person, and property are hourly exposed. Numbers of such valuable men and good subjects are ready and willing to declare themselves for the support of government in due time, if government does not fling away its own authority.

My lords, the Parliament of Great Britain has its rights over the colonies; but it may abdicate its rights.

There was a thing which I forgot to mention. I mean, the manuscript quoted by the noble lord. He tells you that it is there said, that if the act concerning Ireland had passed, the Parliament might have abdicated its rights as to Ireland. In the first place, I heartily wish, my lords, that Ireland had not been named, at a time when that country is of a temper and in a situation so difficult to be governed; and when we have already here so much weight upon our hands, encumbered wite the extensiveness, variety, and importance of so many objects in a vast and too busy empire, and the national system shattered and exhausted by a long, bloody, and expensive war, but more so by our divisions at home, and a fluctuation of counsels. I wish Ireland, therefore, had never been named.

I pay as much respect as any man to the memory of Lord Chief Justice Hale; but I did not know that he had ever written upon the subject; and I differ very much from thinking with the noble lord, that this manuscript ought to be published. So far am I from it, that I wish the manuscript had never been named; for Ireland is too tender a subject to be touched. The case of Ireland is as different as possible from that of our colonies. Ireland was a conquered country; it had its *pacta conventa* and its *regalia*. But to what purpose is it to mention the manuscript? It is but the opinion of one man. When it was written, or for what particular object it was written, does not appear. It might possibly be only a work of youth, or an exercise of the understanding, in sounding and trying a question problematically. All people, when they first enter professions, make their collections pretty early in life; and the manuscript may be of that sort. However, be it what it may, the opinion is but problematical; for the act to which the writer refers never passed, and Lord Hale only said, that if it had passed, the Parliament might have abdicated their right.

But, my lords, I shall make this application of it. You may abdicate your right over the colonies. Take care, my lords, how you do so, for such an act will be irrevocable. Proceed, then, my lords, with spirit and firmness; and, when you shall have established your authority, it will then be a time to show your lenity. The Americans, as I said before, are a very good people, and I wish them exceedingly well; but they are heated and inflamed. The noble lord who spoke before ended with a prayer. I cannot end better than by saying to it Amen; and in the words of Maurice, Prince of Orange, concerning the Hollanders: "God bless this industrious, frugal, and well-meaning, but easily-deluded people."

ON THE RIGHT OF TAXING AMERICA

—

BY

WILLIAM PITT

Lord Chatham

WILLIAM PITT, EARL OF CHATHAM

1708—1778

The seventy years which cover this man's life include an important epoch in the history of England; but there can be no doubt that had this man not lived at that time, the course of events would have been seriously modified. He flourished at a moment when English public men had fallen to low ideals and corrupt practices; the reigns of the two first Georges had marked a decadence in morality from the brief reform begun by William of Orange; and the third George, though a man of conscientious purpose and honest life, was afflicted not only with grave defects of character and temperament; but he was also intermittently insane, and never sound in political judgment. He selected to act for him in government men whose opinions either coincided with his own, or could be bent to accord with them; with the inevitable consequence that he was served by such as were either lacking in principle, or deficient in brains. Had there been no exceptions to this rule, England must have suffered severely in reputation and power.

But William Pitt was a man of an altogether superior stamp. While he had that profound reverence and even awe for the representative of royalty on the throne that was natural to the age in which he lived, he combined with it a still higher regard for political integrity and the rights of mankind. "Upon his brow shame was ashamed to sit;" and he opened the path and encouraged the development of other statesmen who cared for something better than mere place and favor. During the years of his connection with Parliament some of the most brilliant names in the annals of the remarkable body were inscribed upon its roll; and such oratory was heard in those halls as has perhaps never been equalled in modern times.

Pitt was a Cornishman, born in 1708; he graduated at Oxford, and after leaving Trinity, got a cornetcy in the dragoons. Fancy vainly conjectures what his career might have been as a soldier; there were wars enough, and such a man must have won distinction in any line of effort; but Pitt entered Parliament in 1735, in his twenty-eighth year, and from that time his function in life was determined. He was a Whig in politics; and after serving in various capacities, he was driven from office in 1755, after leading a severe attack upon the government. But he was back again almost immediately, and forming a coalition with the Duke of Newcastle, dominated the government as Secretary of State. The glory which England gained from the Seven Years' War was largely due to him, and when he resigned office in 1761 he was already the most eminent statesman in England. In 1766 he entered the House of Lords as Lord Chatham; and his immortality, for Americans at any rate, dates from the period when he began his support of the cause of the colonies against the policy of the King. His last speech, and one of his greatest, was delivered but a month before his death, urging that an end be put to the War of the American Revolution.

Chatham was the idol of the people, and the bugbear of the aristocracy, though personally no aristocrat was prouder and haughtier than he. But he had a great heart and a well-balanced and capacious brain; he had passion and imagination; and an eloquence which, if we may take the verdict of all his contemporaries, friendly and hostile, was almost irresistible. Political liberty was born in the world, and he was among its foremost and most puissant champions. His enthusiasm for the national honor of his country was an undying and consuming fire in his breast; but precisely because his ideal of that honor was so lofty, he would countenance no acts in the rulers of England which tended to prefer a temporary advantage, or a mercenary gain, to a lasting and therefore invincible glory. To talents naturally splendid he added the careful and unremitting training of the public speaker; he was, in a high sense, a consummate actor; every gesture, every intonation of his wonderful voice, had its due effect. In some of his flights he fairly appalled his hearers; at other times he won them by the most persuasive and contagious methods. He never uttered what he did not believe, and the conviction of his honesty which was thus established was one of the surest elements in his wonderful power. The wisdom of his counsel was proved by the outcome of the events to which it referred; and this made it practically impossible, in a constitutional monarchy, to successfully oppose his recommendations.

His speeches have the sweep and momentum of some great planetary body; for while he comprehended all minor details of his subject, he never lingered in them, but moved to his aim with a swiftness and passion which carried all with him, while never seeking to surprise their logical judgment. Behind him always loomed that incorruptible and sublime ethical conviction which is after all the strongest element in success of a lasting kind. He believed in himself, because he felt himself to be the instrument of purposes higher than any selfhood; and even his arrogance aided his influence, because it was felt to be animated by devotion to truth and good. He did not, indeed, always prevail, at the moment, against the stupidity or infatuation of his opponents; but the ends he advocated, and the views he inculcated, uniformly prevailed sooner or later. Had George III listened to Chatham's advice, the United States might still have been British colonies; but the political freedom which he urged became their portion in fuller measure than if their independence (which he deprecated) had not been incidentally achieved.

ON THE RIGHT OF TAXING AMERICA

Delivered in the House of Commons, January 14, 1766

M R. SPEAKER: I came to town but to-day. I was a stranger to the tenor of His Majesty's speech, and the proposed address, till I heard them read in ·this House. Unconnected and unconsulted, I have not the means of information. I am fearful of offending through mistake, and therefore beg to be indulged with a second reading of the proposed address. [The address being read, Mr. Pitt went on:] I commend the King's speech, and approve of the address in answer, as it decides nothing, every gentleman being left at perfect liberty to take such a part concerning America as he may afterwards see fit. One word only I cannot approve of: an " early," is a word that does not belong to the notice the ministry have given to Parliament of the troubles in America. In a matter of such importance, the communication ought to have been immediate!

I speak not now with respect to parties. I stand up in this place single and independent. As to the late ministry [turning himself to Mr. Grenville, who sat within one of him], every capital measure they have taken has been entirely wrong! As to the present gentlemen, to those at least whom I have in my eye [looking at the bench where General Conway sat with the lords of the treasury], I have no objection. I have never been made a sacrifice by any of them. Their characters are fair; and I am always glad when men of fair character engage in His Majesty's service. Some of them did me the honor to ask my opinion before they would engage. These will now do me the justice to own, I advised them to do it—but, notwithstanding (for I love to be explicit), I cannot give them my confidence. Pardon me, gentlemen [bowing to the ministry], confidence is a plant of slow growth in an aged bosom. Youth is the season of credulity.

213

By comparing events with each other, reasoning from effects to causes, methinks I plainly discover the traces of an overruling influence.

There is a clause in the Act of Settlement obliging every minister to sign his name to the advice which he gives to his sovereign. Would it were observed! I have had the honor to serve the Crown, and if I could have submitted to influence, I might have still continued to serve: but I would not be responsible for others. I have no local attachments. It is indifferent to me whether a man was rocked in his cradle on this side or that side of the Tweed. I sought for merit wherever it was to be found. It is my boast, that I was the first minister who looked for it, and found it, in the mountains of the North. I called it forth, and drew into your service a hardy and intrepid race of men— men, who, when left by your jealousy, became a prey to the artifices of your enemies, and had gone nigh to have overturned the state in the war before the last. These men, in the last war, were brought to combat on your side. They served with fidelity, as they fought with valor, and conquered for you in every part of the world. Detested be the national reflections against them! They are unjust, groundless, illiberal, unmanly! When I ceased to serve His Majesty as a minister, it was not the country of the man by which I was moved—but the man of that country wanted wisdom, and held principles incompatible with freedom.

It is a long time, Mr. Speaker, since I have attended in Parliament. When the resolution was taken in this House to tax America, I was ill in bed. If I could have endured to be carried in my bed—so great was the agitation of my mind for the consequences—I would have solicited some kind hand to have laid me down on this floor, to have borne my testimony against it! It is now an act that has passed. I would speak with decency of every act of this House; but I must beg the indulgence of the House to speak of it with freedom.

I hope a day may soon be appointed to consider the state of the nation with respect to America. I hope gentlemen will come to this debate with all the temper and impartiality that His Majesty recommends, and the importance of the subject requires; a subject of greater importance than ever engaged the attention of this House, that subject only excepted, when, near a century ago, it was the question whether you yourselves were to be bond or free. In the mean time, as I cannot depend upon my health for any future day (such is the nature of my infirmities), I will beg to say a few words at present, leaving the justice, the equity, the policy, the expediency of the act to another time.

I will only speak to one point—a point which seems not to have been generally understood; I mean to the right. Some gentlemen [alluding to Mr. Nugent] seem to have considered it as a point of honor. If gentlemen consider it in that light, they leave all measures of right and wrong, to follow a delusion that may lead to destruction. It is my opinion that this kingdom has no right to lay a tax upon the colonies. At the same time, I assert the authority of this kingdom over the colonies to be sovereign and supreme, in every circumstance of government and legislation whatsoever. They are the subjects of this kingdom; equally entitled with yourselves to all the natural rights of mankind and the peculiar privileges of Englishmen; equally bound by its laws, and equally participating in the constitution of this free country. The Americans are the sons, not the bastards of England! Taxation is no part of the governing or legislative power. The taxes are a voluntary gift and grant of the Commons alone. In legislation the three estates of the realm are alike concerned; but the concurrence of the peers and the Crown to a tax is only necessary to clothe it with the form of a law. The gift and grant is of the Commons alone. In ancient days, the Crown, the barons, and the clergy possessed the lands. In those days, the barons and the clergy gave and granted to the Crown. They gave and granted what was their own! At present, since the discovery of America, and other circumstances permitting, the Commons are become the proprietors of the land. The Church (God bless it!) has but a pittance. The property of the lords, compared with that of the commons, is as a drop of water in the ocean; and this House represents those commons, the proprietors of the lands; and those proprietors virtually represent the rest of the inhabitants. When, therefore, in this House, we give and grant, we give and grant what is our own. But in an American tax, what do we do? "We, your Majesty's Commons for Great Britain, give and grant to your Majesty"—what? Our own property! No! "We give and grant to your Majesty " the property of your Majesty's commons of America! It is an absurdity in terms.

The distinction between legislation and taxation is essentially necessary to liberty. The Crown and the peers are equally legislative powers with the Commons. If taxation be a part of simple legislation, the Crown and the peers have rights in taxation as well as yourselves; rights which they will claim, which they will exercise, whenever the principle can be supported by power.

There is an idea in some that the colonies are virtually represented in the House. I would fain know by whom an American is represented here. Is he represented by any knight of the shire, in any county in this kingdom? Would to God that respectable representation was augmented to a greater number! Or will you tell him that he is represented by any representative of a borough? a borough which, perhaps, its own representatives never saw! This is what is called the rotten part of the constitution. It cannot continue a century. If it does not drop, it must be amputated. The idea of a virtual representation of America in this House is the most contemptible idea that ever entered into the head of a man. It does not deserve a serious refutation.

The commons of America, represented in their several assemblies, have ever been in possession of the exercise of this, their constitutional right, of giving and granting their own money. They would have been slaves if they had not enjoyed it! At the same time, this kingdom, as the supreme governing and legislative power, has always bound the colonies by her laws, by her regulations, and restrictions in trade, in navigation, in manufactures, in everything, except that of taking their money out of their pockets without their consent.

Here I would draw the line:

" Quam ultra citraque neque consistere rectum."

[When Lord Chatham had concluded, General Conway rose, and avowed his complete approval of that part of the previous speech which related to American affairs, but denied altogether that " secret overruling influence which had been hinted at." Mr. George Grenville also spoke on the tumults and riots which had taken place in the colonies, and declared that they bordered on rebellion.]

"I cannot," said Mr. Grenville, "understand the difference between external and internal taxes. They are the same in effect, and differ only in name. That this kingdom has the sovereign, the supreme legislative power over America, is granted; it cannot be denied; and taxation is a part of that sovereign power. It is one branch of the legislation. It is, it has been, exercised over those who are not, who were never represented. It is exercised over the India Company, the merchants of London, the proprietors of the stocks, and over many great manufacturing towns. It was exercised over the county palatine of Chester, and the bishopric of Durham before they sent any representatives to Parliament. I appeal for proof to the preambles of the acts which gave them representatives; one in the reign of Henry VIII, the other in that of Charles II." [Mr. Grenville then quoted the acts, and desired that they might be read; which being done, he said:] "When I proposed to tax America I asked the House if any gentleman would object to the right; I repeatedly asked it, and no man would attempt to deny it. Protection and obedience are reciprocal. Great Britain protects America; America is bound to yield obedience. If not, tell me when the Americans were emancipated? When they want the protection of this kingdom, they are always very ready to ask it. That protection has always been afforded them in the most full and ample manner. The nation has run herself into an immense debt to give them their protection; and now, when they are called upon to contribute a small share towards the public expense — an expense arising from themselves—they renounce your authority, insult your officers, and break out, I might almost say, into open rebellion. The seditious spirit of the colonies owes its birth to the factions in this House. Gentlemen are careless of the consequences of what they say, provided it answers the purposes of opposition. We were told we trod on tender ground. We were bid to expect disobedience. What is this but telling the Americans to stand out against the law, to encourage their obstinacy with the expectation of support from hence? 'Let us only hold out a little,' they would say, 'our friends will soon be in power.' Ungrateful people of America! Bounties have been extended to them. When I had the honor of serving the Crown, while you yourselves were loaded with an enormous debt, you gave bounties on their lumber, on their iron, their hemp, and many other articles. You have relaxed in their favor the Act of Navigation, that palladium of the British commerce; and yet I have been abused in all the public papers as an enemy to the trade of America. I have been particularly charged with giving orders and instructions to prevent the Spanish trade, and thereby stopping the channel by which alone North America used to be supplied with cash for remittances to this country. I defy any man to produce any such orders or instructions. I discouraged no trade but what was illicit, what was prohibited by an act of Parliament. I desire a West India merchant [Mr. Long], well known in the city, a gentleman of character, may be examined. He will tell you that I offered to do everything in my power to advance the trade of America. I was above giving an answer to anonymous calumnies; but in this place it becomes one to wipe off the aspersion."

[Here Grenville stopped and Pitt was clamorously called upon to speak.]

Mr. Pitt said: I do not apprehend I am speaking twice. I did expressly reserve a part of my subject, in order to save the time of this House; but I am compelled to proceed in it. I do not speak twice; I only finish what I designedly left imperfect. But if the House is of a different opinion, far be it from me to indulge a wish of transgression against order. I am content, if it be your pleasure, to be silent. [Here he paused. The House resounding with *Go on! go on!* he proceeded:]

Gentlemen, sir, have been charged with giving birth to sedition in America. They have spoken their sentiments with freedom against this unhappy act, and that freedom has become their crime. Sorry I am to hear the liberty of speech in this House imputed as a crime. But the imputation shall not discourage me. It is a liberty I mean to exercise. No gentleman ought to be afraid to exercise it. It is a liberty by which the gentleman who calumniates it might have profited. He ought to have desisted from his project. The gentleman tells us America is obstinate; America is almost in open rebellion. I rejoice that America has resisted. Three millions of people, so dead to all the feelings of liberty as voluntarily to submit to be slaves, would have been fit instruments to make slaves of the rest. I come not here armed at all points, with law cases and acts of Parliament, with the statute book doubled down in dog's ears, to defend the cause of liberty. If I had, I myself would have cited the two cases of Chester and Durham. I would have cited them to show that, even under former arbitrary reigns, Parliaments were ashamed of taxing a people without their consent, and allowed them representatives. Why did the gentleman confine himself to Chester and Durham? He might have taken a higher example in Wales—Wales, that never was taxed by Parliament till it was incorporated. I would not debate a particular point of law with the gentleman. I know his abilities. I have been obliged to his diligent researches. But, for the defence of liberty, upon a general principle, upon a constitutional principle, it is a ground on which I stand firm—on which I dare meet any man. The gentleman tells us of many who are taxed, and are not represented—the India Company, merchants, stockholders, manufacturers. Surely many of these are represented in other capacities, as owners of land, or as freemen of boroughs. It is a misfortune that more are not equally represented. But they are all inhabitants, and as such, are they not virtually represented? Many have it in their option to be actually represented. They have connections with those that elect, and they have influence over them. The gentleman mentioned the stockholders. I hope he does not reckon the debts of the nation as a part of the national estate.

Since the accession of King William many ministers, some of great, others of more moderate abilities, have taken the lead of government. [Here Mr. Pitt went through the list of them, bringing it down till he came to himself, giving a short sketch of the characters of each, and then proceeded:] None of these thought, or even dreamed, of robbing the colonies of their constitutional rights. That was reserved to mark the era of the late administration. Not that there were wanting some, when I had the honor to serve His Majesty, to propose to me to burn my fingers with an American stamp act. With the enemy at their back, with our bayonets at their breasts, in the day of their distress, perhaps the Americans would have submitted to the imposition; but it would have been taking an ungenerous, an unjust advantage. The gentleman boasts of his bounties to America! Are not these bounties intended finally for the benefit of this kingdom? If they are not, he has misapplied the national treasures!

I am no courtier of America. I stand up for this kingdom. I maintain that the Parliament has a right to bind, to restrain America. Our legislative power over the colonies is sovereign and supreme. When it ceases to be sovereign and supreme, I would advise every gentleman to sell his lands, if he can, and embark for that country. When two countries are connected together like England and her colonies, without being incorporated, the one must necessarily govern. The greater must rule the less. But she must so rule it as not to contradict the fundamental principles that are common to both.

If the gentleman does not understand the difference between external and internal taxes, I cannot help it. There is a plain distinction between taxes levied for the purposes of raising a revenue, and duties imposed for the regulation of trade, for the accommodation of the subject; although, in the consequences, some revenue may incidentally arise from the latter.

The gentleman asks, "When were the colonies emancipated?" I desire to know, when were they made slaves? But I dwell not upon words. When I had the honor of serving His Majesty I availed myself of the means of information which I derived from my office. I speak, therefore, from knowledge. My materials were good. I was at pains to collect, to digest, to consider them; and I will be bold to affirm that the profits to Great Britain from the trade of the colonies, through all its branches, is two millions a year. This is the fund that carried you triumphantly through the last war. The estates that were rented at £2,000 a year, threescore years ago, are at three thousand at present. Those estates sold then from fifteen to eighteen years' purchase; the same may now be sold for thirty. You owe this to America. This is the price America pays you for her protection. And shall a miserable financier come with a boast, that he can bring " a pepper-corn " into the exchequer by the loss of millions to the nation? I dare not say how much higher these profits may be augmented.

Omitting the immense increase of people, by natural population, in the northern colonies, and the emigration from every part of Europe, I am convinced on other grounds that the commercial system of America may be altered to advantage. You have prohibited where you ought to have encouraged. You have encouraged where you ought to have prohibited. Improper restraints have been laid on the continent in favor of the islands. You have but two nations to trade with in America. Would you had twenty! Let acts of Parliament in consequence of treaties remain; but let not an English minister become a custom-house officer for Spain, or for any foreign power. Much is wrong! Much may be amended for the general good of the whole!

Does the gentleman complain he has been misrepresented in the public prints? It is a common misfortune. In the Spanish affair of the last war, I was abused in all the newspapers for having advised His Majesty to violate the laws of nations with regard to Spain. The abuse was industriously circulated even in hand-bills. If administration did not propagate the abuse, administration never contradicted it. I will not say what advice I did give the King. My advice is in writing, signed by myself, in the possession of the Crown. But I will say what advice I did not give to the King. I did not advise him to violate any of the laws of nations.

As to the report of the gentleman's preventing in some way the trade for bullion with the Spaniards, it was spoken of so confidently that I own I am one of those who did believe it to be true.

The gentleman must not wonder he was not contradicted when, as minister, he asserted the right of Parliament to tax America. I know not how it is, but there is a modesty in this House which does not choose to contradict a minister. Even your chair, sir, looks too often towards St. James's. I wish gentlemen would get the better of this modesty. If they do not, perhaps the collective body may begin to abate of its respect for the representative. Lord Bacon has told me that a great question would not fail of being agitated at one time or another. I was willing to agitate such a question at the proper season, viz., that of the German war—*my* German war, they called it! Every session I called out, Has anybody any objection to the German war? Nobody would object to it, one gentleman only excepted, since removed to the Upper House by succession to an ancient barony [Lord Le Despencer, formerly Sir Francis Dashwood]. He told me he did not like a German war. I honored the man for it, and was sorry when he was turned out of his post.

A great deal has been said without doors of the power, of the strength of America. It is a topic that ought to be cautiously meddled with. In a good cause, on a sound bottom, the force of this country can crush America to atoms. I know the valor of your troops. I know the skill of your officers. There is not a company of foot that has served in America, out of which you may not pick a man of sufficient knowledge and experience to make a governor of a colony there. But on this ground, on the Stamp Act, which so many here will think a crying injustice, I am one who will lift up my hands against it.

In such a cause, your success would be hazardous. America, if she fell, would fall like the strong man; she would embrace the pillars of the State, and pull down the constitution along with her: Is this your boasted peace—not to sheathe the sword in its scabbard, but to sheathe it in the bowels of your countrymen? Will you quarrel with yourselves, now the whole House of Bourbon is united against you; while France disturbs your fisheries in Newfoundland, embarrasses your slave trade to Africa, and withholds from your subjects in Canada their property stipulated by treaty; while the ransom for the Manillas is denied by Spain, and its gallant conqueror basely traduced into a mean plunderer; a gentleman [Colonel Draper] whose noble and generous spirit would do honor to the proudest grandee of the country? The Americans have not acted in all things with prudence and temper: they have been wronged: they have been driven to madness by injustice. Will you punish them for the madness you have occasioned? Rather let prudence and temper come first from this side. I will undertake for America that she will follow the example. There are two lines in a ballad of Prior's, of a man's behavior to his wife, so applicable to you and your colonies, that I cannot help repeating them:

> " Be to her faults a little blind;
> Be to her virtues very kind."

Upon the whole, I will beg leave to tell the House what is my opinion. It is, that the Stamp Act be repealed absolutely, totally, and immediately. That the reason for the repeal be assigned, viz., because it was founded on an erroneous principle. At the same time, let the sovereign authority of this country over the colonies be asserted in as strong terms as can be devised, and be made to extend to every point of legislation whatsoever; that we may bind their trade, confine their manufactures, and exercise every power whatsoever, except that of taking their money out of their pockets without their consent.

ON CONCILIATION WITH AMERICA

—

BY

EDMUND BURKE

EDMUND BURKE

1729—1797

Burke was born in Dublin in 1729, and died in 1797 at Beaconsfield in England. He took his degree at Dublin University in 1748, entered Parliament in 1766, spoke on American taxation in 1774; received in 1782-3 the appointments of Paymaster-General and Privy Councillor, and managed the impeachment of Warren Hastings from 1786 to 1794. He wrote his essays on "Natural Society" and on the "Sublime and Beautiful" in 1756, and one on the "Revolution in France" in 1790. During this lifetime of sixty-eight years he made a mark in the world which will make him remembered and loved as long as the language in which he wrote and spoke exists.

For consistent sublimity and magnanimity of character there was no man in England during Burke's time that could rival him. He had naturally a mind of the finest quality; and the education by which it was developed was perfectly suited to bring out its best powers. In childhood he began his studies with the Bible, much of which, from repeated readings, he knew by heart; and the splendid language of the Hebrew prophets lived in his memory, and imparted grandeur and color to his own speeches afterwards. From the Bible he turned to Shakespeare and Milton; and he tempered the imaginative splendor of these writers with the intellectual light and substantial wisdom of Bacon. He studied these writers, not with a view to furnishing himself with material for future triumphs; but simply from the predisposition of his nature, which spontaneously inclined him to whatever was best and highest in human thought and literature. He passed his life on the mountain-tops; in a mental region far above all common and selfish concerns; breathing habitually an atmosphere which few can inhale even temporarily without exhaustion. Nevertheless, recognizing that he was a citizen of the world, he did not fail to qualify himself for usefulness to society by acquainting himself with worldly matters, and with the cast of thought of men of practical affairs. But thanks to the elevation of his standpoint, and the transcendent faculties with which he was endowed, he did easily, and as it were by condescension, what others labored to accomplish less masterfully; and the consummate power which he constantly evinced in treating of matters of current politics and every-day philosophy awakened the wonder and reverence of the most eminent of his contemporaries. He could not, however, express himself upon any given subject without so illuminating it, and relating it to all subjects of its class, that his comments and expositions are to-day as valuable as they were a century ago; and men of our time who wish to qualify themselves for the handling of public affairs cannot do so more effectively than by giving diligent study to the orations and essays of Burke. In spite of his heroic stature and sublime look he was personally the most modest and unassuming of men; he could not help being loftier than others, but he assumed no arrogance on that account; and though, as Johnson remarked of him, no man could stand for half an hour under a gateway

227

beside him, listening to his chance talk while waiting for a shower to pass by, without feeling convinced that whoever he might be, he was the first man in England—yet no one would ever be able to assert that Burke himself rated himself above the level of his fellow-creatures.

Burke was the unfailing champion of the American colonies from first to last; and he spoke from the outset with authority; for before he was thirty, and ten years previous to his appearance in Parliament, he had written a book on the history of the colonies, the preparation of which required accurate knowledge of the conditions prevailing there, and of the future possibilities of the nation which was mewing its mighty youth across the Atlantic. For four years, moreover, from 1771, he had acted as the agent of the New York colony in England; and the consequence of the intimate knowledge thus acquired was that, when he made his first speech on American taxation, Chatham, who next to him had made a study of America, declared that Burke had left him little or nothing to say.

As was inevitable, Burke, by dint of the eminence of his own genius, was almost from the first brought in contact with all the first minds in England, in every walk of life; and he did not fail to derive from them the best that each had to offer him. Doubtless he gave more than he took; yet he thus received substantial accessions to his culture, which had the effect of making him better able to deal practically with practical affairs. Imaginative and poetical genius is not often allied with talent for political affairs; but this union existed in Burke, and was largely due to his determination to round out his abilities, instead of giving them the one-sided development which we commonly find in men. He kept his feet on the firm earth while his head reached towards the stars.

It is not possible to point to any one speech of Burke's and affirm that it was his best. But the address on "Conciliation with America" is probably the most significant and edifying for Americans. It was spoken March 22, 1775. In it will be found the best and most characteristic elements of his oratory: breadth of thought, fertility and aptness of illustration, the faculty of exhibiting all sides of a topic, so that it may be comprehended in the round instead of merely in outline; command of the entirety of his theme, so that he is able to treat its various parts in their just proportions; and that remarkable ease and spontaneity of diction which gets out of words the best that is in them, and puts meaning into the lightest phrase. Over all there is a glamour and a grace which lifts the speech into the higher regions of creative imagination, while never abandoning the loyalty to truth and fact which gives imagination its soundest warrant.

ON CONCILIATION WITH AMERICA

M R. SPEAKER: I hope, sir, that, notwithstanding the austerity of the chair, your good nature will incline you to some degree of indulgence towards human frailty. You will not think it unnatural that those who have an object depending, which strongly engages their hopes and fears, should be somewhat inclined to superstition. As I came into the House full of anxiety about the event of my emotion, I found, to my infinite surprise, that the grand penal bill, by which we had passed sentence on the trade and sustenance of America, is to be returned to us from the other House. I do confess, I could not help looking on this event as a fortunate omen. I look upon it as a sort of providential favor, by which we are put once more in possession of our deliberative capacity, upon a business so very questionable in its nature, so very uncertain in its issue. By the return of this bill, which seemed to have taken its flight forever, we are, at this very instant, nearly as free to choose a plan for our American government, as we were on the first day of the session. If, sir, we incline to the side of conciliation, we are not at all embarrassed (unless we please to make ourselves so) by any incongruous mixture of coercion and restraint. We are therefore called upon, as it were by a superior warning voice, again to attend to America; to attend to the whole of it together; and to review the subject with an unusual degree of care and calmness.

Surely it is an awful subject, or there is none so on this side of the grave. When I first had the honor of a seat in this House the affairs of that continent pressed themselves upon us as the most important and most delicate object of parliamentary attention. My little share in this great deliberation oppressed me. I found myself a partaker in a very high trust; and having no sort of reason to rely on the strength of my natural abilities for the proper execution of that trust, I was obliged to take more

than common pains to instruct myself in everything which relates to our colonies. I was not less under the necessity of
forming some fixed ideas concerning the general policy of the
British Empire. Something of this sort seemed to be indispen-
sable, in order, amid so vast a fluctuation of passions and opinions, to concentre my thoughts; to ballast my conduct; to preserve me from being blown about by every wind of fashionable
doctrine. I really did not think it safe or manly to have fresh
principles to seek upon every fresh mail which should arrive
from America.

At that period I had the fortune to find myself in perfect
concurrence with a large majority in this House. Bowing under
that high authority, and penetrated with the sharpness and
strength of that early impression, I have continued ever since
in my original sentiments without the least deviation. Whether
this be owing to an obstinate perseverance in error, or to a religious adherence to what appears to me truth and reason, it is
in your equity to judge.

Sir, Parliament having an enlarged view of objects, made,
during this interval, more frequent changes in their sentiment
and their conduct than could be justified in a particular person
upon the contracted scale of private information. But though I
do not hazard anything approaching to a censure on the motives of former Parliaments to all those alterations, one fact is
undoubted—that under them the state of America has been
kept in continual agitation. Everything administered as remedy
to the public complaint, if it did not produce, was at least followed by, a heightening of the distemper; until, by a variety of
experiments, that important country has been brought into her
present situation—a situation which I will not miscall, which
I dare not name, which I scarcely know how to comprehend in
the terms of any description.

In this posture, sir, things stood at the beginning of the
session. About that time a worthy member of great parliamentary experience, who, in the year 1766, filled the chair of the
American committee with much ability, took me aside, and,
lamenting the present aspect of our politics, told me things were
come to such a pass that our former methods of proceeding in
the House would be no longer tolerated. That the public tribunal (never too indulgent to a long and unsuccessful opposi-

tion) would now scrutinize our conduct with unusual severity. That the very vicissitudes and shiftings of ministerial measures, instead of convicting their authors of inconstancy and want of system, would be taken as an occasion of charging us with a predetermined discontent, which nothing could satisfy; while we accused every measure of vigor as cruel, and every proposal of lenity as weak and irresolute. The public, he said, would not have patience to see us play the game out with our adversaries: we must produce our hand. It would be expected that those who, for many years, had been active in such affairs should show that they had formed some clear and decided idea of the principles of colony government, and were capable of the ground which might be laid for future and permanent tranquillity.

I felt the truth of what my honorable friend represented, but I felt my situation too. His application might have been made with far greater propriety to many other gentlemen. No man was, indeed, ever better disposed or worse qualified for such an undertaking than myself. Though I gave so far into his opinion that I immediately threw my thoughts into a sort of parliamentary form, I was by no means equally ready to produce them. It generally argues some degree of natural impotence of mind or some want of knowledge of the world, to hazard plans of government, except from a seat of authority. Propositions are made, not only ineffectually, but somewhat disreputably, when the minds of men are not properly disposed for their reception; and, for my part, I am not ambitious of ridicule—not absolutely a candidate for disgrace.

Besides, sir, to speak the plain truth, I have in general no very exalted opinion of the virtue of paper government, nor of any politics in which the plan is to be wholly separated from the execution. But when I saw that anger and violence prevailed every day more and more, and that things were hastening towards an incurable alienation of our colonies, I confess my caution gave way. I felt this as one of those few moments in which decorum yields to a higher duty. Public calamity is a mighty leveller, and there are occasions when any, even the slightest, chance of doing good, must be laid hold on, even by the most inconsiderable person.

To restore order and repose to an empire so great and so

distracted as ours is merely in the attempt an undertaking that would ennoble the flights of the highest genius, and obtain pardon for the efforts of the meanest understanding. Struggling a good while with these thoughts, by degrees I felt myself more firm. I derived, at length, some confidence from what in other circumstances usually produces timidity. I grew less anxious, even from the idea of my own insignificance. For, judging of what you are by what you ought to be, I persuaded myself that you would not reject a reasonable proposition because it had nothing but its reason to recommend it. On the other hand, being totally destitute of all shadow of influence, natural or adventitious, I was very sure that if my proposition were futile or dangerous—if it were weakly conceived or improperly timed, there was nothing exterior to it of power to awe, dazzle, or delude you. You will see it just as it is, and you will treat it just as it deserves.

The proposition is peace. Not peace through the medium of war; not peace to be hunted through the labyrinth of intricate and endless negotiations; not peace to arise out of universal discord, fomented from principle, in all parts of the empire; not peace to depend on the juridical determination of perplexing questions, or the precise marking the shadowy boundaries of a complex government. It is simple peace, sought in its natural course and its ordinary haunts. It is peace sought in the spirit of peace, and laid in principles purely pacific. I propose, by removing the ground of the difference, and by restoring the former unsuspecting confidence of the colonies in the mother country, to give permanent satisfaction to your people; and, far from a scheme of ruling by discord, to reconcile them to each other in the same act, and by the bond of the very same interest, which reconciles them to British government.

My idea is nothing more. Refined policy ever has been the parent of confusion, and ever will be so as long as the world endures. Plain good intention, which is as easily discovered at the first view as fraud is surely detected at last, is (let me say) of no mean force in the government of mankind. Genuine simplicity of heart is a healing and cementing principle. My plan, therefore, being formed upon the most simple grounds imaginable, may disappoint some people when they hear it. It has nothing to recommend it to the pruriency of curious ears. There is nothing at all new and captivating in it. It has nothing of the splendor of the project which has been lately laid upon your table by the noble lord in the blue ribbon. It does not propose to fill your lobby with squabbling colony agents, who will require the interposition of your mace at every instant to keep the peace among them. It does not institute a magnificent auction of finance, where captivated provinces come to general ransom by bidding against each other, until you knock down the hammer, and determine a proportion of payments beyond all the powers of algebra to equalize and settle.

The plan which I shall presume to suggest derives, however, one great advantage from the proposition and registry of that noble lord's project. The idea of conciliation is admissible. First, the House, in accepting the resolution moved by the noble lord, has admitted, notwithstanding the menacing front of our address, notwithstanding our heavy bill of pains and penalties, that we do not think ourselves precluded from all ideas of free grace and bounty.

The House has gone farther; it has declared conciliation admissible, previous to any submission on the part of America. It has even shot a good deal beyond that mark, and has admitted that the complaints of our former mode of exerting the right of taxation were not wholly unfounded. That right, thus exerted, is allowed to have had something reprehensible in it, something unwise, or something grievous; since, in the midst of our heat and resentment, we, of ourselves, have proposed a capital alteration, and, in order to get rid of what seemed so very exceptionable, have instituted a mode that is altogether new; one that is, indeed, wholly alien from all the ancient methods and forms of Parliament.

The principle of this proceeding is large enough for my purpose. The means proposed by the noble lord for carrying his ideas into execution, I think, indeed, are very indifferently suited to the end; and this I shall endeavor to show you before I sit down. But, for the present, I take my ground on the admitted principle. I mean to give peace. Peace implies reconciliation; and, where there has been a material dispute, reconciliation does in a manner always imply concession on the one part or on the other. In this state of things I make no difficulty in affirming that the proposal ought to originate from us. Great and acknowledged force is not impaired, either in effect or in opinion, by an unwillingness to exert itself. The superior power may offer peace with honor and with safety. Such an offer from such a power will be attributed to magnanimity. But the concessions of the weak are the concessions of fear. When such a one is disarmed, he is wholly at the mercy of his superior, and he loses forever that time and those chances which, as they happen to all men, are the strength and resources of all inferior power.

The capital leading questions on which you must this day decide, are these two: First, whether you ought to concede; and, secondly, what your concession ought to be.

On the first of these questions we have gained, as I have just taken the liberty of observing to you, some ground. But I am sensible that a good deal more is still to be done. Indeed, sir, to enable us to determine both on the one and the other of these great questions with a firm and precise judgment, I think it may be necessary to consider distinctly:

The true nature and the peculiar circumstances of the object which we have before us; because, after all our struggle, whether we will or not, we must govern America according to that nature and to those circumstances, and not according to our imaginations; not according to abstract ideas of right; by no means according to mere general theories of government, the resort to which appears to me, in our present situation, no better than arrant trifling. I shall therefore endeavor, with your leave, to lay before you some of the most material of these circumstances in as full and as clear a manner as I am able to state them.

The first thing that we have to consider with regard to the nature of the object is the number of people in the colonies. I have taken for some years a good deal of pains on that point. I can by no calculation justify myself in placing the number below two millions of inhabitants of our own European blood and color, besides at least five hundred thousand others, who form no inconsiderable part of the strength and opulence of the whole. This, sir, is, I believe, about the true number. There is no occasion to exaggerate, where plain truth is of so much weight and importance. But whether I put the present numbers too high or too low is a matter of little moment. Such is the strength with which population shoots in that part of the world, that, state the numbers as high as we will, while the dispute continues, the exaggeration ends. While we are discussing any given magnitude, they are grown to it. While we spend our time in deliberating on the mode of governing two millions, we shall find we have two millions more to manage. Your children do not grow faster from infancy to manhood, than they spread from families to communities, and from villages to nations.

I put this consideration of the present and the growing numbers in the front of our deliberation; because, sir, this consideration will make it evident to a blunter discernment than yours that no partial, narrow, contracted, pinched, occasional system will be at all suitable to such an object. It will show you that it is not to be considered as one of those *minima* which are out of the eye and consideration of the law; not a paltry excrescence of the state; not a mean dependent, who may be neglected with little damage, and provoked with little danger. It will prove that some degree of care and caution is required in the handling such an object; it will show that you ought not, in reason, to trifle with so large a mass of the interests and feelings of the human race. You could at no time do so without guilt; and, be assured, you will not be able to do it long with impunity.

But the population of this country, the great and growing population, though a very important consideration, will lose much of its weight, if not combined with other circumstances. The commerce of your colonies is out of all proportion beyond the numbers of the people. This ground of their commerce, indeed, has been trod some days ago, and with great ability, by a distinguished person at your bar. This gentleman, after thirty-five years—it is so long since he appeared at the same place to plead for the commerce of Great Britain—has come again before you to plead the same cause, without any other effect of time, than that, to the fire of imagination and extent of erudition which even then marked him as one of the first literary characters of his age, he has added a consummate knowledge in the commercial interest of his country, formed by a long course of enlightened and discriminating experience.

Sir, I should be inexcusable in coming after such a person with any detail, if a great part of the members who now fill the House had not the misfortune to be absent when he appeared at your bar. Besides, sir, I propose to take the matter at periods of time somewhat different from his. There is, if I mistake not, a point of view, from whence, if you will look at this subject, it is impossible that it should not make an impression upon you.

I have in my hand two accounts: one a comparative state of the export trade of England to its colonies as it stood in the year 1704, and as it stood in the year 1772; the other a state of the export trade of this country to its colonies alone, as it stood in 1772, compared with the whole trade of England to all parts of the world, the colonies included, in the year 1704. They are from good vouchers; the latter period from the accounts on your table, the earlier from an original manuscript of Davenant, who first established the inspector-general's office, which has been ever since his time so abundant a source of parliamentary information.

The export trade to the colonies consists of three great branches: the African, which, terminating almost wholly in the colonies, must be put to the account of their commerce; the West Indian, and the North American. All these are so interwoven that the attempt to separate them would tear to pieces the contexture of the whole, and, if not entirely destroy, would very much depreciate the value of all the parts. I therefore consider these three denominations to be, what in effect they are, one trade.

The trade to the colonies, taken on the export side, at the beginning of this century, that is, in the year 1704, stood thus:

Exports to North America and the West Indies..... £483,265
To Africa 86,665

£569,930

In the year 1772, which I take as a middle year between the highest and lowest of those lately laid on your table, the account was as follows:

To North America and the West Indies........... £4,791,734
To Africa 866,398
To which, if you add the export trade from Scotland,
   which had in 1704 no existence................ 364,000

£6,022,132

From five hundred and odd thousand, it has grown to six millions. It has increased no less than twelve-fold. This is the state of the colony trade, as compared with itself at these two periods, within this century; and this is matter for meditation. But this is not all. Examine my second account. See how the export trade to the colonies alone in 1772 stood in the other point of view, that is, as compared to the whole trade of England in 1704.

The whole export trade of England, including that
    to the colonies, in 1704...................... £6,509,000
Exported to the colonies alone, in 1772............ 6,024,000
                                                  Difference.. £485,000

The trade with America alone is now within less than £500,-000 of being equal to what this great commercial nation, England, carried on at the beginning of this century with the whole world! If I had taken the largest year of those on your table, it would rather have exceeded. But, it will be said, is not this American trade an unnatural protuberance, that has drawn the juices from the rest of the body? The reverse. It is the very food that has nourished every other part into its present magnitude. Our general trade has been greatly augmented, and augmented more or less in almost every part to which it ever extended, but with this material difference, that of the six millions which in the beginning of the century constituted the whole mass of our export commerce, the colony trade was but one twelfth part; it is now (as a part of sixteen millions) considerably more than a third of the whole. This is the relative proportion of the importance of the colonies of these two periods; and all reasoning concerning our mode of treating them must have this proportion as its basis, or it is a reasoning weak, rotten, and sophistical.

Mr. Speaker, I cannot prevail on myself to hurry over this great consideration. It is good for us to be here. We stand where we have an immense view of what is, and what is past. Clouds, indeed, and darkness, rest upon the future. Let us, however, before we descend from this noble eminence, reflect that this growth of our national prosperity has happened within the short period of the life of man. It has happened within sixty-eight years. There are those alive whose memory might touch the two extremities. For instance, my Lord Bathurst might remember all the stages of the progress. He was in 1704 of an age at least to be made to comprehend such things. He was then old enough *"acta parentum jam legere et quæ sit poterit cognoscere virtus."* Suppose, sir, that the angel of this auspicious youth, foreseeing the many virtues which made him one of the most amiable, as he is one of the most fortunate men of his age, had opened to him in vision, that when, in the fourth generation, the third prince of the House of Brunswick had sat twelve years on the throne of that nation, which, by the happy issue of moderate and healing councils, was to be made Great Britain, he should see his son, Lord Chancellor of England, turn back the current of hereditary dignity to its fountain, and raise him to a higher rank of peerage, while he enriched the family with a new one. If, amid these bright and happy scenes of domestic honor and prosperity, that angel should have drawn up the curtain, and unfolded the rising glories of his country, and while he was gazing with admiration on the then commercial grandeur of England, the genius should point out to him a little speck, scarce visible in the mass of the national interest, a small seminal principle rather than a formed body, and should tell him: "Young man, there is America—which at this day serves for little more than to amuse you with stories of savage men and uncouth manners; yet shall, before you taste death, show itself equal to the whole of that commerce which now attracts the envy of the world. Whatever England has been growing to by a progressive increase of improvement, brought in by varieties of people, by succession of civilizing conquests and civilizing settlements in a series of seventeen hundred years, you shall see as much added to her by America in the course of a single life!" If this state of his country had been foretold to him, would it not require all the sanguine credulity of youth, and all the fervid glow of enthusiasm, to make him believe it? Fortunate man, he has lived to see it! Fortunate indeed, if he lived to see nothing to vary the prospect and cloud the setting of his day!

Excuse me, sir, if, turning from such thoughts, I resume this comparative view once more. You have seen it on a large scale; look at it on a small one. I will point out to your attention a particular instance of it in the single province of Pennsylvania. In the year 1704 that province called for £11,459 in value of your commodities, native and foreign. This was the whole. What did it demand in 1772? Why nearly fifty times as much; for in that year the export to Pennsylvania was £507,909, nearly equal to the export to all the colonies together in the first period.

I choose, sir, to enter into these minute and particular details, because generalities, which, in all other cases are apt to heighten and raise the subject, have here a tendency to sink it. When we speak of the commerce with our colonies, fiction lags after truth; invention is unfruitful, and imagination cold and barren.

So far, sir, as to the importance of the object in the view of its commerce, as concerned in the exports from England. If I were to detail the imports, I could show how many enjoyments they procure, which deceive the burden of life; how many materials which invigorate the springs of national industry, and extend and animate every part of our foreign and domestic commerce. This would be a curious subject indeed; but I must prescribe bounds to myself in a matter so vast and various.

I pass, therefore, to the colonies in another point of view —their agriculture. This they have prosecuted with such a spirit, that, besides feeding plentifully their own growing multitude, their annual export of grain, comprehending rice, has, some years ago, exceeded a million in value. Of their last harvest I am persuaded they will export much more. At the beginning of the century some of these colonies imported corn from the mother country. For some time past the Old World has been fed from the New. The scarcity which you have felt would have been a desolating famine, if this child of your old age, with a true filial piety, with a Roman charity, had not put the full breast of its youthful exuberance to the mouth of its exhausted parent.

As to the wealth which the colonies have drawn from the sea by their fisheries, you had all that matter fully opened at your bar. You surely thought those acquisitions of value, for they seemed even to excite your envy; and yet, the spirit by which that enterprising employment has been exercised, ought rather, in my opinion, to have raised your esteem and admiration. And pray, sir, what in the world is equal to it? Pass by the other parts, and look at the manner in which the people of New England have of late carried on the whale fishery. While we follow them among the tumbling mountains of ice, and behold them penetrating into the deepest frozen recesses of Hudson's Bay and Davis's Straits—while we are looking for them beneath the Arctic Circle, we hear that they have pierced into the opposite region of polar cold—that they are at the antipodes, and engaged under the frozen Serpent of the south. Falkland Island, which seemed too remote and romantic an object for the grasp of national ambition, is but a stage and resting-place in the progress of their victorious industry. Nor is the equinoctial heat more discouraging to them than the accumulated winter of both the poles. We know that while some of them draw the line, and strike the harpoon on the coast of Africa, others run the longitude, and pursue their gigantic game along the coast of Brazil. No sea but what is vexed by their fisheries. No climate that is not witness to their toils. Neither the perseverance of Holland, nor the activity of France, nor the dexterous and firm sagacity of English enterprise, ever carried this most perilous mode of hardy industry to the extent to which it has been pushed by this recent people—a people who are still, as it were, but in the gristle, and not yet hardened into the bone of manhood. When I contemplate these things—when I know that the colonies in general owe little or nothing to any care of ours, and that they are not squeezed into this happy form by the constraints of watchful and suspicious government, but that, through a wise and salutary neglect, a generous nature has been suffered to take her own way to perfection—when I reflect upon these effects—when I see how profitable they have been to us, I feel all the pride of power sink, and all presumption in the wisdom of human contrivances melt, and die away within me. My rigor relents. I pardon something to the spirit of liberty.

I am sensible, sir, that all which I have asserted in my detail is admitted in the gross; but that quite a different conclusion is drawn from it. America, gentlemen say, is a noble object. It is an object well worth fighting for. Certainly it is, if fighting a people be the best way of gaining them. Gentlemen in this respect will be led to their choice of means by their complexions and their habits. Those who understand the military art will, of course, have some predilection for it. Those who wield the thunder of the State may have more confidence in the efficacy of arms. But I confess, possibly for want of this knowledge, my opinion is much more in favor of prudent management than of force; considering force not as an odious, but a feeble, instrument for preserving a people so numerous, so active, so growing, so spirited as this, in a profitable and subordinate connection with us.

First, sir, permit me to observe, that the use of force alone is but temporary. It may subdue for a moment, but it does not remove the necessity of subduing again; and a nation is not governed which is perpetually to be conquered.

My next objection is its uncertainty. Terror is not always the effect of force; and an armament is not a victory. If you do not succeed, you are without resource; for, conciliation failing, force remains; but, force failing, no farther hope of reconciliation is left. Power and authority are sometimes bought by kindness, but they can never be begged as alms by an impoverished and defeated violence.

A farther objection to force is, that you impair the object by your very endeavors to preserve it. The thing you fought for is not the thing which you recover; but depreciated, sunk, wasted, and consumed in the contest. Nothing less will content me than whole America. I do not choose to consume its strength along with our own, because in all parts it is the British strength that I consume. I do not choose to be caught by a foreign enemy at the end of this exhausting conflict, and still less in the midst of it. I may escape; but I can make no insurance against such an event. Let me add that I do not choose wholly to break the American spirit, because it is the spirit that has made the country.

Lastly, we have no sort of experience in favor of force as an instrument in the rule of our colonies. Their growth and their utility have been owing to methods altogether different. Our ancient indulgence has been said to be pursued to a fault. It may be so; but we know, if feeling is evidence, that our fault was more tolerable than our attempt to mend it; and our sin far more salutary than our penitence.

These, sir, are my reasons for not entertaining that high opinion of untried force, by which many gentlemen, for whose sentiments in other particulars I have great respect, seem to be so greatly captivated.

But there is still behind a third consideration concerning this object, which serves to determine my opinion on the sort of policy which ought to be pursued in the management of America, even more than its population and its commerce—I mean its temper and character. In this character of the Americans a love of freedom is the predominating feature, which marks and distinguishes the whole; and, as an ardent is always a jealous affection, your colonies become suspicious, restive, and untractable, whenever they see the least attempt to wrest from them by force, or shuffle from them by chicane, what they think the only advantage worth living for. This fierce spirit of liberty is stronger in the English colonies, probably, than in any other people of the earth, and this from a variety of powerful causes, which, to understand the true temper of their minds, and the direction which this spirit takes, it will not be amiss to lay open somewhat more largely.

First, the people of the colonies are descendants of Englishmen. England, sir, is a nation which still, I hope, respects, and formerly adored her freedom. The colonists emigrated from you when this part of your character was most predominant; and they took this bias and direction the moment they parted from your hands. They are, therefore, not only devoted to liberty, but to liberty according to English ideas and on English principles. Abstract liberty, like other mere abstractions, is not to be found. Liberty inheres in some sensible object; and every nation has formed to itself some favorite point which, by way of eminence, becomes the criterion of their happiness. It happened you know, sir, that the great contests for freedom in this country were, from the earliest times chiefly upon the question of taxing. Most of the contests in the ancient commonwealths turned primarily on the right of election of magistrates, or on the balance among the several orders of the State. The question of money was not with them so immediate. But in England it was otherwise. On this point of taxes the ablest pens and most eloquent tongues have been exercised; the greatest spirits have acted and suffered. In order to give the fullest satisfaction concerning the importance of this point, it was not only necessary for those who in argument defended the excellence of the English constitution, to insist on this privilege of granting money as a dry point of fact, and to prove that the right had been acknowledged in ancient parchments and blind usages to reside in a certain body called the House of Commons. They went much farther: they attempted to prove (and they succeeded) that in theory it ought to be so, from the particular nature of a House of Commons, as an immediate representative of the people, whether the old records had delivered this oracle or not. They took infinite pains to inculcate, as a fundamental principle, that, in all monarchies, the people must, in effect, themselves, mediately or immediately, possess the power of granting their own money, or no shadow of liberty could subsist. The colonies draw from you, as with their life-blood, those ideas and principles. Their love of liberty, as with you, fixed and attached on this specific point of taxing. Liberty might be safe or might be endangered in twenty other particulars, without their being much pleased or alarmed. Here they felt its pulse; and, as they found that beat, they thought themselves sick or sound. I do not say whether they were right or wrong in applying your general arguments to their own case. It is not easy, indeed, to make a monopoly of theorems and corollaries. The fact is that they did thus apply those general arguments; and your mode of governing them, whether through lenity or indolence, through wisdom or mistake, confirmed them in the imagination that they, as well as you, had an interest in these common principles.

They were further confirmed in these pleasing errors by the form of their provincial legislative assemblies. Their governments are popular in a high degree; some are merely popular; in all, the popular representative is the most weighty; and this share of the people in their ordinary government never fails to inspire them with lofty sentiments, and with a strong aversion from whatever tends to deprive them of their chief importance.

If anything were wanting to this necessary operation of the form of government, religion would have given it a complete effect. Religion, always a principle of energy, in this new people is no way worn out or impaired; and their mode of professing it is also one main cause of this free spirit. The people are Protestants; and of that kind which is the most averse to all implicit submission of mind and opinion. This is a persuasion not only favorable to liberty, but built upon it. I do not think, sir, that the reason of this averseness in the dissenting churches from all that looks like absolute government, is so much to be sought in their religious tenets as in their history. Everyone knows that the Roman Catholic religion is at least coeval with most of the governments where it prevails; that it has generally gone hand in hand with them; and received great favor and every kind of support from authority. The Church of England, too, was formed from her cradle under the nursing care of regular government. But the dissenting interests have sprung up in direct opposition to all the ordinary powers of the world, and could justify that opposition only on a strong claim to natural liberty. Their very existence depended on the powerful and unremitted assertion of that claim. All Protestantism, even the most cold and passive, is a kind of dissent. But the religion most prevalent in our northern colonies is a refinement on the principle of resistance; it is the dissidence of dissent; and the Protestantism of the Protestant religion. This religion, under a variety of denominations, agreeing in nothing but in the communion of the spirit of liberty, is predominant in most of the northern provinces; where the Church of England, notwithstanding its legal rights, is in reality no more than a sort of private sect, not composing, most probably, the tenth of the people. The colonists left England when this spirit was high, and in the emigrants was the highest of all; and even that stream of foreigners, which has been constantly flowing into these colonies, has, for the greatest part, been composed of dissenters from the establishments of their several countries, and have brought with them a temper and character far from alien to that of the people with whom they mixed.

Sir, I can perceive by their manner that some gentlemen object to the latitude of this description, because in the southern colonies the Church of England forms a large body, and has a regular establishment. It is certainly true. There is, however, a circumstance attending these colonies, which, in my opinion, fully counterbalances this difference, and makes the spirit of liberty still more high and haughty than in those to the northward. It is that in Virginia and the Carolinas they have a vast multitude of slaves. Where this is the case in any part of the world, those who are free are by far the most proud and jealous of their freedom. Freedom is to them not only an enjoyment, but a kind of rank and privilege. Not seeing

there that freedom, as in countries where it is a common blessing, and as broad and general as the air, may be united with
much abject toil, with great misery, with all the exterior of servitude, liberty looks, among them, like something that is more
noble and liberal. I do not mean, sir, to commend the superior
morality of this sentiment, which has at least as much pride as
virtue in it; but I cannot alter the nature of man. The fact is
so; and these people of the southern colonies are much more
strongly, and with a higher and more stubborn spirit, attached
to liberty than those to the northward. Such were all the ancient
commonwealths; such were our Gothic ancestors; such, in our
days, were the Poles, and such will be all masters of slaves who
are not slaves themselves. In such a people the haughtiness
of domination combines with the spirit of freedom, fortifies
it, and renders it invincible.

Permit me, sir, to add another circumstance in our colonies,
which contributes no mean part towards the growth and effect
of this untractable spirit—I mean their education. In no country perhaps in the world is the law so general a study. The
profession itself is numerous and powerful; and in most provinces it takes the lead. The greater number of the deputies sent
to Congress were lawyers. But all who read, and most do read,
endeavor to obtain some smattering in that science. I have been
told by an eminent bookseller that in no branch of his business,
after tracts of popular devotion, were so many books as those
on the law exported to the Plantations. The colonists have
now fallen into the way of printing them for their own use. I
hear that they have sold nearly as many of Blackstone's " Com-
mentaries " in America as in England. General Gage marks
out this disposition very particularly in a letter on your table.
He states that all the people in his government are lawyers, or
smatterers in law; and that in Boston they have been enabled,
by successful chicane, wholly to evade many parts of one of
your capital penal constitutions. The smartness of debate will
say that this knowledge ought to teach them more clearly the
rights of legislature, their obligations to obedience, and the
penalties of rebellion. All this is mighty well. But my honorable and learned friend [the Attorney-General, afterwards Lord
Thurlow] on the floor, who condescends to mark what I say
for animadversion, will disdain that ground. He has heard,

as well as I, that when great honors and great emoluments do not win over this knowledge to the service of the State it is a formidable adversary to government. If the spirit be not tamed and broken by these happy methods, it is stubborn and litigious. *Abeunt studia in mores.* This study renders men acute, inquisitive, dexterous, prompt in attack, ready in defence, full of resources. In other countries, the people, more simple and of a less mercurial cast, judge of an ill principle in government only by an actual grievance. Here they anticipate the evil, and judge of the pressure of the grievance by the badness of the principle. They augur misgovernment at a distance; and snuff the approach of tyranny in every tainted breeze.

The last cause of this disobedient spirit in the colonies is hardly less powerful than the rest, as it is not merely moral, but laid deep in the natural constitution of things. Three thousand miles of ocean lie between you and them. No contrivance can prevent the effect of this distance in weakening government. Seas roll and months pass between the order and the execution; and the want of a speedy explanation of a single point is enough to defeat the whole system. You have, indeed, " winged ministers " of vengeance, who carry your bolts in their pouches to the remotest verge of the sea. But there a power steps in that limits the arrogance of raging passion and furious elements, and says: " So far shalt thou go, and no farther." Who are you, that should fret and rage, and bite the chains of nature? Nothing worse happens to you than does to all nations who have extensive empire; and it happens in all the forms into which empire can be thrown. In large bodies the circulation of power must be less vigorous at the extremities. Nature has said it. The Turk cannot govern Egypt, and Arabia, and Koordistan as he governs Thrace; nor has he the same dominion in Crimea and Algiers which he has at Broosa and Smyrna. Despotism itself is obliged to truck and huckster. The Sultan gets such obedience as he can. He governs with a loose rein, that he may govern at all; and the whole of the force and vigor of his authority in his centre is derived from a prudent relaxation in all his borders. Spain, in her provinces, is, perhaps, not so well obeyed as you are in yours. She complies too; she submits; she watches times. This is the immutable condition, the eternal law, of extensive and detached empire.

Then, sir, from these six capital sources of descent, of form of government, of religion in the northern provinces, of manners in the southern, of education, of the remoteness of situation from the first mover of government—from all these causes a fierce spirit of liberty has grown up. It has grown with the growth of the people in your colonies, and increased with the increase of their wealth; a spirit that, unhappily meeting with an exercise of power in England, which, however lawful, is not reconcilable to any ideas of liberty, much less with theirs, has kindled this flame, that is ready to consume us.

I do not mean to commend either the spirit in this excess, or the moral causes which produce it. Perhaps a more smooth and accommodating spirit of freedom in them would be more acceptable to us. Perhaps ideas of liberty might be desired, more reconcilable with an arbitrary and boundless authority. Perhaps we might wish the colonists to be persuaded that their liberty is more secure when held in trust for them by us, as guardians during a perpetual minority, than with any part of it in their own hands. But the question is not whether their spirit deserves praise or blame. What, in the name of God, shall we do with it? You have before you the object, such as it is, with all its glories, with all its imperfections on its head. You see the magnitude, the importance, the temper, the habits, the disorders. By all these considerations we are strongly urged to determine something concerning it. We are called upon to fix some rule and line for our future conduct, which may give a little stability to our politics, and prevent the return of such unhappy deliberations as the present. Every such return will bring the matter before us in a still more untractable form. For, what astonishing and incredible things have we not seen already? What monsters have not been generated from this unnatural contention? While every principle of authority and resistance has been pushed upon both sides, as far as it would go, there is nothing so solid and certain, either in reasoning or in practice, that it has not been shaken. Until very lately, all authority in America seemed to be nothing but an emanation from yours. Even the popular part of the colony constitution derived all its activity, and its first vital movement, from the pleasure of the Crown. We thought, sir, that the utmost which the discontented colonists could do, was to disturb authority,

We never dreamed they could of themselves supply it, knowing
in general what an operose business it is to establish a government absolutely new. But having, for our purposes in this
contention, resolved that none but an obedient assembly should
sit, the humors of the people there, finding all passage through
the legal channel stopped, with great violence broke out another
way. Some provinces have tried their experiment, as we have
tried ours; and theirs has succeeded. They have formed a government sufficient for its purposes, without the bustle of a revolution, or the troublesome formality of an election. Evident
necessity and tacit consent have done the business in an instant.
So well they have done it, that Lord Dunmore (the account is
among the fragments on your table) tells you, that the new institution is infinitely better obeyed than the ancient government
ever was in its most fortunate periods. Obedience is what
makes government, and not the names by which it is called; not
the name of governor, as formerly, or committee, as at present.
This new government has originated directly from the people,
and was not transmitted through any of the ordinary artificial
media of a positive constitution. It was not a manufacture
ready formed, and transmitted to them in that condition from
England. The evil arising from hence is this: that the colonists having once found the possibility of enjoying the advantages of order in the midst of a struggle for liberty, such
struggles will not henceforward seem so terrible to the settled
and sober part of mankind as they had appeared before the trial.

Pursuing the same plan of punishing by the denial of the
exercise of government to still greater lengths, we wholly ab-
rogated the ancient government of Massachusetts. We were
confident that the first feeling, if not the very prospect of
anarchy, would instantly enforce a complete submission. The
experiment was tried. A new, strange, unexpected face of
things appeared. Anarchy is found tolerable. A vast province
has now subsisted, and subsisted in a considerable degree of
health and vigor, for near a twelvemonth, without governor,
without public council, without judges, without executive magistrates. How long it will continue in this state, or what may
arise out of this unheard-of situation, how can the wisest of
us conjecture? Our late experience has taught us, that many
of those fundamental principles, formerly believed infallible,

are either not of the importance they were imagined to be, or that we have not at all adverted to some other far more important and far more powerful principles, which entirely overrule those we had considered as omnipotent. I am much against any farther experiments, which tend to put to the proof any more of these allowed opinions, which contribute so much to the public tranquillity. In effect, we suffer as much at home by this loosening of all ties, and this concussion of all established opinions, as we do abroad. For, in order to prove that the Americans have no right to their liberties, we are every day endeavoring to subvert the maxims which preserve the whole spirit of our own. To prove that the Americans ought not to be free, we are obliged to depreciate the value of freedom itself; and we never seem to gain a paltry advantage over them in debate, without attacking some of those principles, or deriding some of those feelings, for which our ancestors have shed their blood.

But, sir, in wishing to put an end to pernicious experiments, I do not mean to preclude the fullest inquiry. Far from it. Far from deciding on a sudden or partial view, I would patiently go round and round the subject, and survey it minutely in every possible aspect. Sir, if I were capable of engaging you to an equal attention, I would state that, as far as I am capable of discerning, there are but three ways of proceeding relative to this stubborn spirit which prevails in your colonies and disturbs your government. These are, to change that spirit, as inconvenient, by removing the causes; to prosecute it as criminal; or to comply with it as necessary. I would not be guilty of an imperfect enumeration. I can think of but these three. Another has, indeed, been started—that of giving up the colonies; but it met so slight a reception that I do not think myself obliged to dwell a great while upon it. It is nothing but a little sally of anger, like the frowardness of peevish children, who, when they cannot get all they would have, are resolved to take nothing.

The first of these plans, to change the spirit, as inconvenient, by removing the causes, I think is the most like a systematic proceeding. It is radical in its principle, but it is attended with great difficulties, some of them little short, as I conceive, of impossibilities. This will appear by examining into the plans which have been proposed.

As the growing population of the colonies is evidently one

cause of their resistance, it was last session mentioned in both
Houses by men of weight, and received, not without applause,
that, in order to check this evil, it would be proper for the
Crown to make no farther grants of land. But to this scheme
there are two objections. The first, that there is already so
much unsettled land in private hands as to afford room for
an immense future population, although the Crown not only
withheld its grants, but annihilated its soil. If this be the case,
then the only effect of this avarice of desolation, this hoarding
of a royal wilderness, would be to raise the value of the possessions in the hands of the great private monopolists without any
adequate check to the growing and alarming mischief of population.

But if you stopped your grants, what would be the consequence? The people would occupy without grants. They have
already so occupied in many places. You cannot station garrisons in every part of these deserts. If you drive the people
from one place, they will carry on their annual tillage, and remove with their flocks and herds to another. Many of the people in the back settlements are already little attached to particular situations. Already they have topped the Appalachian
Mountains. From thence they behold before them an immense
plain, one vast, rich, level meadow—a square of five hundred
miles. Over this they would wander without a possibility of restraint. They would change their manners with the habits of
their life; would soon forget a government by which they were
disowned; would become hordes of English Tartars; and,
pouring down upon your unfortified frontiers a fierce and irresistible cavalry, become masters of your governors and your
counsellors, your collectors and controllers, and of all the slaves
that adhered to them. Such would, and, in no long time, must
be the effect of attempting to forbid as a crime, and to suppress
as an evil, the command and blessing of Providence, " Increase
and multiply." Such would be the happy result of an endeavor
to keep as a lair of wild beasts that earth which God by an
express charter has given to the children of men. Far different, and surely much wiser, has been our policy hitherto.
Hitherto we have invited our people, by every kind of bounty, to
fixed establishments. We have invited the husbandman to look
to authority for his title. We have taught him piously to be-

lieve in the mysterious virtue of wax and parchment. We have thrown each tract of land, as it was peopled, into districts, that the ruling power should never be wholly out of sight. We have settled all we could, and we have carefully attended every settlement with government.

Adhering, sir, as I do, to this policy, as well as for the reasons I have just given, I think this new project of hedging in population to be neither prudent nor practicable.

To impoverish the colonies in general, and in particular to arrest the noble course of their marine enterprises, would be a more easy task. I freely confess it. We have shown a disposition to a system of this kind; a disposition even to continue the restraint after the offence, looking on ourselves as rivals to our colonies, and persuaded that of course we must gain all that they shall lose. Much mischief we may certainly do. The power inadequate to all other things is often more than sufficient for this. I do not look on the direct and immediate power of the colonies to resist our violence as very formidable. In this, however, I may be mistaken. But when I consider that we have colonies for no purpose but to be serviceable to us, it seems to my poor understanding a little preposterous to make them unserviceable in order to keep them obedient. It is, in truth, nothing more than the old, and, as I thought, exploded problem of tyranny, which proposes to beggar its subject into submission. But, remember, when you have completed your system of impoverishment, that nature still proceeds in her ordinary course; that discontent will increase with misery; and that there are critical moments in the fortunes of all states, when they who are too weak to contribute to your prosperity may be strong enough to complete your ruin. "*Spoliatis arma supersunt.*"

The temper and character which prevail in our colonies are, I am afraid, unalterable by any human art. We cannot, I fear, falsify the pedigree of this fierce people, and persuade them that they are not sprung from a nation in whose veins the blood of freedom circulates. The language in which they would hear you tell them this tale would detect the imposition. Your speech would betray you. An Englishman is the unfittest person on earth to argue another Englishman into slavery.

I think it is nearly as little in our power to change their repub lican religion as their free descent; or to substitute the Roman Catholic as a penalty, or the Church of England as an improvement. The mode of inquisition and dragooning is going out of fashion in the Old World, and I should not confide much to their efficacy in the New. The education of the Americans is also on the same unalterable bottom with their religion. You cannot persuade them to burn their books of curious science; to banish their lawyers from their courts of law; or to quench the lights of their assemblies, by refusing to choose those persons who are best read in their privileges. It would be no less impracticable to think of wholly annihilating the popular assemblies in which these lawyers sit. The army, by which we must govern in their place, would be far more chargeable to us; not quite so effectual; and perhaps, in the end, full as difficult to be kept in obedience.

With regard to the high aristocratic spirit of Virginia and the southern colonies, it has been proposed, I know, to reduce it, by declaring a general enfranchisement of their slaves. This project has had its advocates and panegyrists, yet I never could argue myself into an opinion of it. Slaves are often much attached to their masters. A general wild offer of liberty would not always be accepted. History furnishes few instances of it. It is sometimes as hard to persuade slaves to be free as it is to compel freemen to be slaves; and in this auspicious scheme we should have both these pleasing tasks on our hands at once. But when we talk of enfranchisement, do we not perceive that the American master may enfranchise too, and arm servile hands in defence of freedom? A measure to which other people have had recourse more than once, and not without success, in a desperate situation of their affairs.

Slaves as these unfortunate black people are, and dull as all men are from slavery, must they not a little suspect the offer of freedom from that very nation which has sold them to their present masters? From that nation, one of whose causes of quarrel with those masters is their refusal to deal any more in that inhuman traffic? An offer of freedom from England would come rather oddly, shipped to them in an African vessel, which is refused an entry into the ports of Virginia or Carolina, with a cargo of three hundred Angola negroes. It would be curious to see the Guinea captain attempt at the same instant to publish his proclamation of liberty and to advertise the sale of slaves.

But let us suppose all these moral difficulties got over. The ocean remains. You cannot pump this dry; and as long as it continues in its present bed, so long all the causes which weaken authority by distance will continue.

> " Ye gods! annihilate but space and time,
>   And make two lovers happy! "

was a pious and passionate prayer, but just as reasonable as many of these serious wishes of very grave and solemn politicians.

If, then, sir, it seems almost desperate to think of any alterative course for changing the moral causes (and not quite easy to remove the natural) which produce the prejudices irreconcilable to the late exercise of our authority, but that the spirit infallibly will continue, and, continuing, will produce such effects as now embarrass us, the second mode under consideration is to prosecute that spirit in its overt acts as criminal.

At this proposition I must pause a moment. The thing seems a great deal too big for my ideas of jurisprudence. It should seem, to my way of conceiving such matters, that there is a very wide difference in reason and policy between the mode of proceeding on the irregular conduct of scattered individuals, or even of bands of men, who disturb order within the state, and the civil dissensions which may, from time to time, on great questions, agitate the several communities which compose a great empire. It looks to me to be narrow and pedantic to apply the ordinary ideas of criminal justice so this great public contest. I do not know the method of drawing up an indictment against a whole people. I cannot insult and ridicule the feelings of millions of my fellow-creatures, as Sir Edward Coke insulted one excellent individual at the bar. I am not ripe to pass sentence on the gravest public bodies, intrusted with magistracies of great authority and dignity, and charged with the safety of their fellow-citizens, upon the very same title that I am. I really think that, for wise men, this is not judicious; for sober men, not decent; for minds tinctured with humanity, not mild and merciful.

Perhaps, sir, I am mistaken in my idea of an empire, as distinguished from a single state or kingdom. But my idea of it is this; that an empire is the aggregate of many states, under one common head, whether this head be a monarch or a presiding republic. It does, in such constitutions, frequently happen (and nothing but the dismal, cold, dead uniformity of servitude can prevent its happening) that the subordinate parts have many local privileges and immunities. Between these privileges and the supreme common authority the line may be extremely nice. Of course, disputes—often, too, very bitter disputes, and much ill blood, will arise. But, though every privilege is an exemption, in the case, from the ordinary exercise of the supreme authority, it is no denial of it. The claim of a privilege seems rather, *ex vi termini,* to imply a superior power; for to talk of the privileges of a state or of a person who has no superior is hardly any better than speaking nonsense. Now, in such unfortunate quarrels among the component parts of a great political union of communities, I can scarcely conceive anything more completely imprudent than for the head of the empire to insist that, if any privilege is pleaded against his will or his acts, his whole authority is denied; instantly to proclaim rebellion, to beat to arms, and to put the offending provinces under the ban. Will not this, sir, very soon teach the provinces to make no distinctions on their part? Will it not teach them that the government against which a claim of liberty is tantamount to high treason, is a government to which submission is equivalent to slavery? It may not always be quite convenient to impress dependent communities with such an idea.

We are, indeed, in all disputes with the colonies, by the necessity of things, the judge. It is true, sir; but I confess that the character of judge in my own cause is a thing that frightens me. Instead of filling me with pride, I am exceedingly humbled by it. I cannot proceed with a stern, assured, judicial confidence, until I find myself in something more like a judicial character. I must have these hesitations as long as I am compelled to recollect that, in my little reading upon such contests as these, the sense of mankind has at least as often decided against the superior as the subordinate power. Sir, let me add, too, that the opinion of my having some abstract right in my favor would not put me much at my ease in passing sentence, unless I could be sure that there were no rights which in their exercise under certain circumstancs, were not the most odious of all wrongs, and the most vexatious of all injustice. Sir, these considerations have great weight with me, when I find things so circumstanced that I see the same party at once a civil litigant against me in point of right and a culprit before me; while I sit as criminal judge on acts of his whose moral quality is to be decided on upon the merits of that very litigation. Men are every now and then put, by the complexity of human affairs, into strange situations; but justice is the same, let the judge be in what situation he will.

There is, sir, also a circumstance which convinces me that this mode of criminal proceeding is not, at least in the present stage of our contest, altogether expedient, which is nothing less than the conduct of those very persons who have seemed to adopt that mode, by lately declaring a rebellion in Massachusetts Bay, as they had formerly addressed to have traitors brought hither, under an act of Henry VIII, for trial. For, though rebellion is declared, it is not proceeded against as such; nor have any steps been taken toward the apprehension or conviction of any individual offender, either on our late or our former address; but modes of public coercion have been adopted, and such as have much more resemblance to a sort of qualified hostility towards an independent power than the punishment of rebellious subjects. All this seems rather inconsistent; but it shows how difficult it is to apply these juridical ideas to our present case.

In this situation let us seriously and coolly ponder. What is it we have got by all our menaces, which have been many and ferocious? What advantage have we derived from the penal laws we have passed, and which, for the time, have been severe and numerous? What advances have we made towards our object by the sending of a force which, by land and sea, is no contemptible strength? Has the disorder abated? Nothing less. When I see things in this situation, after such confident hopes, bold promises, and active exertions, I cannot, for my life, avoid a suspicion that the plan itself is not correctly right.

If then, the removal of the causes of this spirit of American liberty be, for the greater part, or rather entirely, impracticable; if the ideas of criminal process be inapplicable, or, if applicable, are in the highest degree inexpedient, what way yet remains? No way is open but the third and last—to comply with the American spirit as necessary, or, if you please, to submit to it as a necessary evil.

If we adopt this mode, if we mean to conciliate and concede, let us see, of what nature the concessions ought to be. To ascertain the nature of our concession, we must look at their complaint. The colonies complain that they have not the characteristic mark and seal of British freedom. They complain that they are taxed in Parliament in which they are not represented. If you mean to satisfy them at all, you must satisfy them with regard to this complaint. If you mean to please any people, you must give them the boon which they ask; not what you may think better for them, but of a kind totally different. Such an act may be a wise regulation, but it is no concession, whereas our present theme is the mode of giving satisfaction.

Sir, I think you must perceive that I am resolved this day to have nothing at all to do with the question of the right of taxation. Some gentlemen startle, but it is true. I put it totally out of the question. It is less than nothing in my consideration. I do not, indeed, wonder, nor will you, sir, that gentlemen of profound learning are fond of displaying it on this profound subject. But my consideration is narrow, confined, and wholly limited to the policy of the question. I do not examine whether the giving away a man's money be a power excepted and reserved out of the general trust of government, and how far all mankind, in all forms of polity, are entitled to an exercise of that right by the charter of nature; or whether, on the contrary, a right of taxation is necessarily involved in the general principle of legislation, and inseparable from the ordinary supreme power. These are deep questions, where great names militate against each other; where reason is perplexed; and an appeal to authorities only thickens the confusion; for high and reverend authorities lift up their heads on both sides, and there is no sure footing in the middle. The point is

> " That Serbonian bog
> Betwixt Damieta and Mount Cassius old,
> Where armies whole have sunk."

I do not intend to be overwhelmed in this bog, though in such respectable company. The question with me is, not whether you have a right to render your people miserable, but whether it is not your interest to make them happy. It is not what a lawyer tells me I may do, but what humanity, reason, and justice tell me

I ought to do. Is a politic act the worse for being a generous one? Is no concession proper but that which is made from your want of right to keep what you grant? Or does it lessen the grace or dignity of relaxing in the exercise of an odious claim, because you have your evidence-room full of titles, and your magazines stuffed with arms to enforce them? What signify all those titles and all those arms? Of what avail are they, when the reason of the thing tells me that the assertion of my title is the loss of my suit, and that I could do nothing but wound myself by the use of my own weapons?

Such is steadfastly my opinion of the absolute necessity of keeping up the concord of this empire by a unity of spirit, though in a diversity of operations, that, if I were sure the colonists had, at their leaving this country, sealed a regular compact of servitude; that they had solemnly abjured all the rights of citizens; that they had made a vow to renounce all ideas of liberty for them and their posterity to all generations, yet I should hold myself obliged to conform to the temper I found universally prevalent in my own day, and to govern two millions of men, impatient of servitude, on the principles of freedom. I am not determining a point of law. I am restoring tranquillity, and the general character and situation of a people must determine what sort of government is fitted for them. That point nothing else can or ought to determine.

My idea, therefore, without considering whether we yield as matter of right, or grant as matter of favor, is to admit the people of our colonies into an interest in the constitution, and, by recording that admission in the journals of Parliament, to give them as strong an assurance as the nature of the thing will admit, that we mean forever to adhere to that solemn declaration of systematic indulgence.

Some years ago the repeal of a revenue act, upon its understood principle, might have served to show that we intended an unconditional abatement of the exercise of a taxing power. Such a measure was then sufficient to remove all suspicion, and to give perfect content. But unfortunate events, since that time, may make something farther necessary, and not more necessary for the satisfaction of the colonies, than for the dignity and consistency of our own future proceedings.

I have taken a very incorrect measure of the disposition of the

House, if this proposal in itself would be received with dislike. I think, sir, we have few American financiers. But our misfortune is, we are too acute; we are too exquisite in our conjectures of the future, for men oppressed with such great and present evils. The more moderate among the opposers of parliamentary concessions freely confess that they hope no good from taxation, but they apprehend the colonists have farther views, and, if this point were conceded, they would instantly attack the trade laws. These gentlemen are convinced that this was the intention from the beginning, and the quarrel of the Americans with taxation was no more than a cloak and cover to this design. Such has been the language even of a gentleman [Mr. Rice] of real moderation, and of a natural temper well adjusted to fair and equal government. I am, however, sir, not a little surprised at this kind of discourse, whenever I hear it; and I am the more surprised, on account of the arguments which I constantly find in company with it, and which are often urged from the same mouths and on the same day.

For instance, when we allege that it is against reason to tax a people under so many restraints in trade as the Americans, the noble lord in the blue ribbon shall tell you that the restraints on trade are futile and useless; of no advantage to us, and of no burden to those on whom they are imposed; that the trade of America is not secured by the acts of navigation, but by the natural and irresistible advantage of a commercial preference.

Such is the merit of the trade laws in this posture of the debate. But when strong internal circumstances are urged against the taxes; when the scheme is dissected; when experience and the nature of things are brought to prove, and do prove, the utter impossibility of obtaining an effective revenue from the colonies; when these things are pressed, or rather press themselves, so as to drive the advocates of colony taxes to a clear admission of the futility of the scheme; then, sir, the sleeping trade laws revive from their trance, and this useless taxation is to be kept sacred, not for its own sake, but as a counterguard and security of the laws of trade.

Then, sir, you keep up revenue laws which are mischievous, in order to preserve trade laws that are useless. Such is the wisdom of our plan in both its members. They are separately given up as of no value, and yet one is always to be defended for the sake of the other. But I cannot agree with the noble lord, nor with the pamphlet from whence he seems to have borrowed these ideas, concerning the inutility of the trade laws; for, without idolizing them, I am sure they are still, in many ways, of great use to us; and in former times, they have been of the greatest. They do confine, and they do greatly narrow the market for the Americans; but my perfect conviction of this does not help me in the least to discern how the revenue laws form any security whatsoever to the commercial regulations, or that these commercial regulations are the true ground of the quarrel, or that the giving way in any one instance of authority is to lose all that may remain unconceded.

One fact is clear and indisputable. The public and avowed origin of this quarrel was on taxation. This quarrel has, indeed, brought on new disputes on new questions, but certainly the least bitter, and the fewest of all, on the trade laws. To judge which of the two be the real radical cause of quarrel, we have to see whether the commercial dispute did, in order of time, precede the dispute on taxation. There is not a shadow of evidence for it. Next, to enable us to judge whether at this moment a dislike to the trade laws be the real cause of quarrel, it is absolutely necessary to put the taxes out of the question by a repeal. See how the Americans act in this position, and then you will be able to discern correctly what is the true object of the controversy, or whether any controversy at all will remain. Unless you consent to remove this cause of difference, it is impossible, with decency, to assert that the dispute is not upon what it is avowed to be. And I would, sir, recommend to your serious consideration, whether it be prudent to form a rule for punishing people, not on their own acts, but on your conjectures. Surely it is preposterous at the very best. It is not justifying your anger by their misconduct, but it is converting your ill will into their delinquency.

But the colonies will go farther. Alas! alas! when will this speculating against fact and reason end? What will quiet these panic fears which we entertain of the hostile effect of a conciliatory conduct? Is it true that no case can exist in which it is proper for the sovereign to accede to the desires of his discontented subjects? Is there anything peculiar in this case to make a rule for itself? Is all authority of course lost, when it is not pushed to the extreme? Is it a certain maxim that the fewer causes of dissatisfaction are left by government the more the subject will be inclined to resist and rebel?

All these objections being, in fact, no more than suspicions, conjectures, divinations, formed in defiance of fact and experience, they did not, sir, discourage me from entertaining the idea of a conciliatory concession, founded on the principles which I have just stated.

In forming a plan for this purpose I endeavored to put myself in that frame of mind which was the most natural and the most reasonable, and which was certainly the most probable means of securing me from all error. I set out with a perfect distrust of my own abilities; a total renunciation of every speculation of my own; and with a profound reverence for the wisdom of our ancestors, who have left us the inheritance of so happy a constitution and so flourishing an empire, and, what is a thousand times more valuable, the treasury of the maxims and principles which formed the one and obtained the other.

During the reigns of the kings of Spain of the Austrian family, whenever they were at a loss in the Spanish councils, it was common for their statesmen to say, that they ought to consult the genius of Philip II. The genius of Philip II might mislead them; and the issue of their affairs showed that they had not chosen the most perfect standard. But, sir, I am sure that I shall not be misled, when, in a case of constitutional difficulty, I consult the genius of the English constitution. Consulting at that oracle (it was with all due humility and piety), I found four capital examples in a similar case before me: those of Ireland, Wales, Chester, and Durham.

Ireland, before the English conquest, though never governed by a despotic power, had no Parliament. How far the English Parliament itself was at that time modelled according to the present form, is disputed among antiquarians. But we have all the reason in the world to be assured that a form of Parliament, such as England then enjoyed, she instantly communicated to Ireland; and we are equally sure that almost every successive improvement in constitutional liberty, as fast as it was made here, was transmitted thither. The feudal baronage and the feudal knighthood, the roots of our primitive constitution, were early transplanted into that soil, and grew and flourished there.

Magna Charta, if it did not give us originally the House of Commons, gave us, at least a House of Commons of weight and consequence. But your ancestors did not churlishly sit down alone to the feast of Magna Charta. Ireland was made immediately a partaker. This benefit of English laws and liberties, I confess, was not at first extended to all Ireland. Mark the consequence. English authority and English liberty had exactly the same boundaries. Your standard could never be advanced an inch before your privileges. Sir John Davis shows beyond a doubt that the refusal of a general communication of these rights was the true cause why Ireland was five hundred years in subduing; and after the vain projects of a military government, attempted in the reign of Queen Elizabeth, it was soon discovered that nothing could make that country English, in civility and allegiance, but your laws and your forms of legislature. It was not English arms, but the English constitution, that conquered Ireland. From that time Ireland has ever had a general Parliament, as she had before a partial Parliament. You changed the people; you altered the religion; but you never touched the form or the vital substance of free government in that kingdom. You deposed kings; you restored them; you altered the succession to theirs, as well as to your own crown; but you never altered their constitution; the principle of which was respected by usurpation; restored with the restoration of monarchy, and established, I trust, forever, by the glorious revolution. This has made Ireland the great and flourishing kingdom that it is; and from a disgrace and a burden intolerable to this nation, has rendered her a principal part of our strength and ornament. This country cannot be said to have ever formally taxed her. The irregular things done in the confusion of mighty troubles, and on the hinge of great revolutions, even if all were done that is said to have been done, form no example. If they have any effect in argument, they make an exception to prove the rule. None of your own liberties could stand a moment if the casual deviations from them, at such times, were suffered to be used as proofs of their nullity. By the lucrative amount of such casual breaches in the constitution, judge what the stated and fixed rule of supply has been in that kingdom. Your Irish pensioners would starve if they had no other fund to live on than taxes granted by English authority.

Turn your eyes to those popular grants from whence all your great supplies are come, and learn to respect that only source of public wealth in the British Empire.

My next example is Wales. This country was said to be reduced by Henry III. It was said more truly to be so by Edward I. But though then conquered, it was not looked upon as any part of the realm of England. Its old constitution, whatever that might have been, was destroyed, and no good one was substituted in its place. The care of that tract was put into the hands of Lords Marchers—a form of government of a very singular kind; a strange heterogeneous monster, something between hostility and government; perhaps it has a sort of resemblance, according to the modes of those times, to that of commander-in-chief at present, to whom all civil power is granted as secondary. The manners of the Welsh nation followed the genius of the government. The people were ferocious, restive, savage, and uncultivated; sometimes composed, never pacified. Wales, within itself, was in perpetual disorder; and it kept the frontier of England in perpetual alarm. Benefits from it to the State there were none. Wales was only known to England by incursion and invasion.

Sir, during that state of things, Parliament was not idle. They attempted to subdue the fierce spirit of the Welsh by all sorts of rigorous laws. They prohibited by statute the sending all sorts of arms into Wales, as you prohibit by proclamation (with something more of doubt on the legality) the sending arms to America. They disarmed the Welsh by statute, as you attempted (but still with more question on the legality) to disarm New England by an instruction. They made an act to drag offenders from Wales into England for trial, as you have done (but with more hardship) with regard to America. By another act, where one of the parties was an Englishman, they ordained that his trial should be always by English. They made acts to restrain trade, as you do; and they prevented the Welsh from the use of fairs and markets, as you do the Americans from fisheries and foreign ports. In short, when the statute-book was not quite so much swelled as it is now, you find no less than fifteen acts of penal regulation on the subject of Wales.

Here we rub our hands—a fine body of precedents for the authority of Parliament and the use of it—I admit it fully; and pray add likewise to these precedents, that all the while Wales rid this kingdom like an incubus; that it was an unprofitable and oppressive burden; and that an Englishman travelling in that country could not go six yards from the highroad without being murdered.

The march of the human mind is slow. Sir, it was not until after two hundred years discovered that, by an eternal law, Providence had decreed vexation to violence, and poverty to rapine. Your ancestors did, however, at length open their eyes to the ill husbandry of injustice. They found that the tyranny of a free people could of all tyrannies the least be endured, and that laws made against a whole nation were not the most effectual methods for securing its obedience. Accordingly, in the twenty-seventh year of Henry VIII, the course was entirely altered. With a preamble stating the entire and perfect rights of the Crown of England, it gave to the Welsh all the rights and privileges of English subjects. A political order was established; the military power gave way to the civil; the marches were turned into counties. But that a nation should have a right to English liberties, and yet no share at all in the fundamental security of these liberties, the grant of their own property, seemed a thing so incongruous, that, eight years after, that is, in the thirty-fifth of that reign, a complete and not ill-proportioned representation by counties and boroughs was bestowed upon Wales by act of Parliament. From that moment, as by a charm, the tumults subsided; obedience was restored; peace, order, and civilization followed in the train of liberty. When the day-star of the English constitution had arisen in their hearts, all was harmony within and without.

> " *Simul alba nautis*
> *Stella refulsit,*
> *Defluit saxis agatatus humor :*
> *Concidunt venti, fugiuntque nubes ;*
> *Et minax (quod sic voluere) ponto*
> *Unda recumbit.*"

The very same year the county palatine of Chester received the same relief from its oppressions and the same remedy to its disorders. Before this time Chester was little less distempered than Wales. The inhabitants, without rights themselves, were the fittest to destroy the rights of others; and from thence Richard II drew the standing army of archers with which for a time he oppressed England. The people of Chester applied to Parliament in a petition penned as I shall read to you:

" To the King our sovereign lord, in most humble wise shown unto your excellent Majesty, the inhabitants of your Grace's county palatine of Chester; that where the said county palatine of Chester is and hath been always hitherto exempt, excluded, and separated out and from your high court of Parliament, to have any knights and burgesses within the said court; by reason whereof the said inhabitants have hitherto sustained manifold disherisons, losses, and damages, as well in their lands, goods, and bodies, as in the good, civil, and politic governance and maintenance of the Commonwealth of their said country. (2) And, forasmuch as the said inhabitants have always hitherto been bound by the acts and statutes made and ordained by your said highness and your most noble progenitors, by authority of the said court, as far forth as other counties, cities, and boroughs have been, that have had their knights and burgesses within your said court of Parliament, and yet have had neither knight nor burgess there for the said county palatine; the said inhabitants, for lack thereof, have been oftentimes touched and grieved with acts and statutes made within the said court, as well derogatory unto the most ancient jurisdictions, liberties, and privileges of your said county palatine, as prejudicial unto the Commonwealth, quietness, rest, and peace of your Grace's most bounden subjects inhabiting within the same."

What did Parliament with this audacious address? Reject it as a libel? Treat it as an affront to government? Spurn it as a derogation from the rights of legislature? Did they toss it over the table? Did they burn it by the hands of the common hangman? They took the petition of grievance, all rugged as it was, without softening or temperament, unpurged of the original bitterness and indignation of complaint; they made it the very preamble to their act of redress, and consecrated its principle to all ages in the sanctuary of legislation.

Here is my third example. It was attended with the success of the two former. Chester, civilized as well as Wales, has demonstrated that freedom, and not servitude, is the cure of anarchy, as religion, and not atheism, is the true remedy for superstition. Sir, this pattern of Chester was followed in the reign of Charles II with regard to the county palatine of Durham, which is my fourth example. This county had long lain out of the pale of free legislation. So scrupulously was the example of Chester followed that the style of the preamble is nearly the same with that of the Chester act; and without affecting the abstract extent of the authority of Parliament, it recognizes the equity of not suffering any considerable district in which the British subjects may act as a body to be taxed without their own voice in the grant.

Now, if the doctrines of policy contained in these preambles, and the force of these examples in the acts of Parliament, avail anything, what can be said against applying them with regard to America? Are not the people of America as much Englishmen as the Welsh? The preamble of the act of Henry VIII says the Welsh speak a language no way resembling that of His Majesty's English subjects. Are the Americans not as numerous? If we may trust the learned and accurate Judge Barrington's account of North Wales, and take that as a standard to measure the rest, there is no comparison. The people cannot amount to above 200,000; not a tenth part of the number in the colonies. Is America in rebellion? Wales was hardly ever free from it. Have you attempted to govern America by penal statutes? You made fifteen for Wales. But your legislative authority is perfect with regard to America. Was it less perfect in Wales, Chester, and Durham! But America is virtually represented. What! does the electric force of virtual representation more easily pass over the Atlantic than pervade Wales, which lies in your neighborhood; or than Chester and Durham, surrounded by abundance of representation that is actual and palpable? But, sir, your ancestors thought this sort of virtual representation, however ample, to be totally insufficient for the freedom of the inhabitants of territories that are so near, and comparatively so inconsiderable. How, then, can I think is sufficient for those which are infinitely greater and infinitely more remote?

You will now, sir, perhaps imagine that I am on the point of proposing to you a scheme for representation of the colonies in Parliament. Perhaps I might be inclined to entertain some such thought, but a great flood stops me in my course. *Opposuit natura.* I cannot remove the eternal barriers of the creation. The thing in that mode I do not know to be possible. As I meddle with no theory, I do not absolutely assert the impracticability of such a representation; but I do not see my

way to it; and those who have been more confident have not
been more successful. However, the arm of public benevolence
is not shortened, and there are often several means to the same
end. What nature has disjoined in one way wisdom may unite
in another. When we cannot give the benefit as we would wish,
let us not refuse it altogether. If we cannot give the principal,
let us find a substitute. But how? Where? What substitute?

Fortunately I am not obliged for the ways and means of
this substitute to tax my own unproductive invention. I am not
even obliged to go to the rich treasury of the fertile framers of
imaginary commonwealths; not to the Republic of Plato, not
to the Utopia of More, not to the Oceana of Harrington. It
is before me. It is at my feet.

> " And the dull swain
> Treads daily on it with his clouted shoon."

I only wish you to recognize, for the theory, the ancient constitutional policy of this kingdom with regard to representation, as
that policy has been declared in acts of Parliament; and, as to
the practice, to return to that mode which a uniform experience
has marked out to you as best, and in which you walked with
security, advantage, and honor, until the year 1763.

My resolutions, therefore, mean to establish the equity and
justice of a taxation of America, by grant and not by imposition.
To mark the legal competency of the colony assemblies for the
support of their government in peace, and for public aids in time
of war. To acknowledge that this legal competency had had a
dutiful and beneficial exercise; and that experience has shown
the benefit of their grants, and the futility of parliamentary taxation as a method of supply.

These solid truths compose six fundamental propositions.
There are three more resolutions corollary to these. If you
admit the first set, you can hardly reject the others. But if you
admit the first, I shall be far from solicitous whether you accept
or refuse the last. I think these six massive pillars will be of
strength sufficient to support the temple of British concord.
I have no more doubt than I entertain of my existence, that, if
you admitted these, you would command an immediate peace;
and, with but tolerable future management, a lasting obedience
in America. I am not arrogant in this confident assurance.

The propositions are all mere matters of fact; and if they are such facts as draw irresistible conclusions even in the stating, this is the power of truth, and not any management of mine.

Sir, I shall open the whole plan to you together, with such observations on the motions as may tend to illustrate them where they may want explanation. The first is a resolution:

> " That the colonies and plantations of Great Britain in North America, consisting of fourteen separate governments, and containing two millions and upward of free inhabitants, have not had the liberty and privilege of electing and sending any knights and burgesses or others to represent them in the high court of Parliament."

This is a plain matter of fact, necessary to be laid down, and (excepting the description) it is laid down in the language of the constitution: it is taken nearly *verbatim* from acts of Parliament.

The second is like unto the first:

> " That the said colonies and plantations have been liable to and bounden by several subsidies, payments, rates, and taxes, given and granted by Parliament, though the said colonies and plantations have not their knights and burgesses in the said high court of Parliament, of their own election, to represent the condition of their country; by lack whereof they have been oftentimes touched and grieved by subsidies given, granted, and assented to, in said court, in a manner prejudicial to the commonwealth, quietness, rest, and peace of the subjects inhabiting within the same."

Is this description too hot or too cold, too strong or too weak? Does it arrogate too much to the supreme legislature? Does it lean too much to the claims of the people? If it runs into any of these errors, the fault is not mine. It is the language of your own ancient acts of Parliament.

> " *Non meus hic sermo est sed quæ præcipit Ofellus*
> *Rusticus, abnormis sapiens.*"

It is the genuine produce of the ancient, rustic, manly, home-bred sense of this country. I did not dare to rub off a particle of the venerable rust that rather adorns and preserves, than destroys the metal. It would be a profanation to touch with a tool the stones which construct the sacred altar of peace. I would not violate with modern polish the ingenuous and noble roughness of these truly constitutional materials. Above all things, I was resolved not to be guilty of tampering, the odious vice of restless and unstable minds. I put my foot in the tracks of our forefathers, where I can neither wander nor stumble. Determining to fix articles of peace, I was resolved not to be wise beyond what was written; I was resolved to use nothing else than the form of sound words, to let others abound in their own sense, and carefully to abstain from all expressions of my own. What the law has said, I say. In all things else I am silent. I have no organ but for her words. This, if it be not ingenious, I am sure, is safe.

There are, indeed, words expressive of grievance in this second resolution, which those who are resolved always to be in the right will deny to contain matter of fact, as applied to the present case, although Parliament thought them true with regard to the counties of Chester and Durham. They will deny that the Americans were ever "touched and grieved" with the taxes. If they considered nothing in taxes but their weight as pecuniary impositions, there might be some pretence for this denial. But men may be sorely touched and deeply grieved in their privileges as well as in their purses. Men may lose little in property by the act which takes away all their freedom. When a man is robbed of a trifle on the highway, it is not the twopence lost that constitutes the capital outrage. This is not confined to privileges. Even ancient indulgences withdrawn, without offence on the part of those who enjoy such favors, operate as grievances. But were the Americans then not touched and grieved by the taxes, in some measure merely as taxes? If so, why were they almost all either wholly repealed or exceedingly reduced? Were they not touched and grieved, even by the regulating duties of the sixth of George II? Else why were the duties first reduced to one-third in 1764, and afterward to a third of that third in the year 1766? Were they not touched and grieved by the Stamp Act? I shall say they were, until that tax is revived. Were they not touched and grieved by the duties of 1767, which were likewise repealed, and which Lord Hillsborough tells you, for the ministry, were laid contrary to the true principle of commerce? Is not the assurance given by that noble person to the colonies of a resolution to lay no more taxes on them, an admission that taxes would touch and grieve them? Is not the resolution of the noble lord in the blue ribbon, now standing on your journals, the strongest of all proofs that parliamentary subsidies really touched and grieved them? Else why all these changes, modifications, repeals, assurances, and resolutions?

The next proposition is:

" That, from the distance of the said colonies, and from other circumstances, no method hath hitherto been devised for procuring a representation in Parliament for the said colonies."

This is an assertion of a fact. I go no farther on the paper; though in my private judgment, a useful representation is impossible; I am sure it is not desired by them, nor ought it, perhaps, by us, but I abstain from opinions.

The fourth resolution is:

" That each of the said colonies hath within itself a body chosen in part or in the whole, by the freemen, freeholders, or other free inhabitants thereof, commonly called the General Assembly, or General Court, with powers legally to raise, levy, and assess, according to the several usages of such colonies, duties and taxes towards the defraying all sorts of public services."

This competence in the colony assemblies is certain. It is proved by the whole tenor of their acts of supply in all the assemblies, in which the constant style of granting is, " an aid to His Majesty "; and acts granting to the Crown have regularly for near a century passed the public offices without dispute. Those who have been pleased paradoxically to deny this right, holding that none but the British Parliament can grant to the Crown, are wished to look to what is done, not only in the colonies, but in Ireland, in one uniform, unbroken tenor every session.

Sir, I am surprised that this doctrine should come from some of the law servants of the Crown. I say that if the Crown could be responsible, His Majesty—but certainly the ministers, and even these law officers themselves, through whose hands the acts pass biennially in Ireland, or annually the colonies, are in a habitual course of committing impeachable offences. What habitual offenders have been all presidents of the council, all secretaries of state, all first lords of trade, all attorneys, and all

solicitors-general! However, they are safe, as no one im-
peaches them; and there is no ground of charge against them,
except in their own unfounded theories.

The fifth resolution is also a resolution of fact:

" That the said General Assemblies, General Courts, or other bodies
legally qualified as aforesaid, have at sundry times freely granted several large subsidies and public aids for His Majesty's service, according to their abilities, when required thereto by letter from one of His
Majesty's principal Secretaries of State. And that their right to grant
the same, and their cheerfulness and sufficiency in the said grants, have
been at sundry times acknowledged by Parliament."

To say nothing of their great expenses in the Indian wars;
and not to take their exertion in foreign ones, so high as the
supplies in the year 1695, not to go back to their public contributions in the year 1710, I shall begin to travel only where the
journals give me light; resolving to deal in nothing but fact
authenticated by parliamentary record, and to build myself
wholly on that solid basis.

On April 4, 1748, a committee of this House came to the following resolution:

" Resolved, That it is the opinion of this committee, that it is just
and reasonable that the several provinces and colonies of Massachusetts Bay, New Hampshire, Connecticut, and Rhode Island, be reim-
bursed the expenses they have been at in taking and securing to the
Crown of Great Britain the Island of Cape Breton and its dependencies."

These expenses were immense for such colonies. They were
above £200,000 sterling; money first raised and advanced on
their public credit.

On January 28, 1756, a message from the King came to us to
this effect:

" His Majesty being sensible of the zeal and vigor with which his
faithful subjects of certain colonies in North America have exerted
themselves in defence of His Majesty's just rights and possessions,
recommends it to this House to take the same into their consideration, and to enable His Majesty to give them such assistance as may
be a proper reward and encouragement."

On February 3, 1756, the House came to a suitable resolution, expressed in words nearly the same as those of the mes-

sage; but with the farther addition, that the money then voted
was an encouragement to the colonies to exert themselves
with vigor. It will not be necessary to go through all the
testimonies which your own records have given to the truth of
my resolutions. I will only refer you to the places in the journals: Vol. xxvii., sixteenth and nineteenth May, 1757; vol.
xxviii., June 1, 1758—April 26 and 30, 1759—March 26 and
31, and April 28, 1760—January 9 and 20, 1761; vol. xxix.,
January 22 and 26, 1762—March 14 and 17, 1763.

Sir, here is the repeated acknowledgment of Parliament that
the colonies not only gave, but gave to satiety. This nation
has formally acknowledged two things: first, that the colonies
had gone beyond their abilities, Parliament having thought it
necessary to reimburse them; secondly, that they had acted
legally and laudably in their grants of money, and their maintenance of troops, since the compensation is expressly given
as reward and encouragement. Reward is not bestowed for
acts that are unlawful; and encouragement is not held out
to things that deserve reprehension. My resolution, therefore, does nothing more than collect into one proposition what
is scattered through your journals. I give you nothing but
your own, and you cannot refuse in the gross what you have
so often acknowledged in detail. The admission of this, which
will be so honorable to them and to you, will, indeed, be mortal to all the miserable stories by which the passions of the
misguided people have been engaged in an unhappy system.
The people heard, indeed, from the beginning of these disputes, one thing continually dinned in their ears, that reason
and justice demanded that the Americans, who paid no taxes,
should be compelled to contribute. How did that fact of their
paying nothing stand when the taxing system began? When
Mr. Grenville began to form his system of American revenue,
he stated in this House that the colonies were then in debt
two million six hundred thousand pounds sterling money, and
was of opinion they would discharge that debt in four years.
On this state, those untaxed people were actually subject to
the payment of taxes to the amount of six hundred and fifty
thousand a year. In fact, however, Mr. Grenville was mistaken. The funds given for sinking the debt did not prove
quite so ample as both the colonies and he expected. The

calculation was too sanguine: the reduction was not completed till some years after, and at different times in different colonies. However, the taxes after the war continued too great to bear any addition, with prudence or propriety; and when the burdens imposed in consequence of former requisitions were discharged, our tone became too high to resort again to requisition. No colony, since that time, ever has had any requisition whatsoever made to it.

We see the sense of the Crown, and the sense of Parliament, on the productive nature of a revenue by grant. Now search the same journals for the produce of the revenue by imposition. Where is it? Let us know the volume and the page. What is the gross, what is the net produce? To what service is it applied? How have you appropriated its surplus? What, can none of the many skilful index-makers that we are now employing, find any trace of it? Well, let them and that rest together. But, are the journals, which say nothing of the revenue, as silent on the discontent? Oh, no! a child may find it. It is the melancholy burden and blot of every page.

I think, then, I am, from those journals, justified in the sixth and last resolution, which is:

" That it hath been found by experience that the manner of granting the said supplies and aids, by the said general assemblies, hath been more agreeable to the said colonies, and more beneficial and conducive to the public service, than the mode of giving and granting aids in Parliament, to be raised and paid in the said colonies."

This makes the whole of the fundamental part of the plan. The conclusion is irresistible. You cannot say that you were driven by any necessity to an exercise of the utmost rights of legislature. You cannot assert that you took on yourselves the task of imposing colony taxes, from the want of another legal body, that is competent to the purpose of supplying the exigencies of the State without wounding the prejudices of the people. Neither is it true that the body so qualified, and having that competence, had neglected the duty.

The question now on all this accumulated matter, is—whether you will choose to abide by a profitable experience, or a mischievous theory; whether you choose to build on imagination or fact; whether you prefer enjoyment or hope; satisfaction in your subjects or discontent?

If these propositions are accepted, everything which has been made to enforce a contrary system must, I take it for granted, fall along with it. On that ground I have drawn the following resolution, which, when it comes to be moved, will naturally be divided in a proper manner:

" That it may be proper to repeal an act, made in the seventh year of the reign of his present Majesty, entitled An Act for granting certain duties in the British colonies and plantations in America; for allowing a drawback of the duties of customs upon the exportation from this kingdom of coffee and cocoa-nuts of the produce of the said colonies or plantations; for discontinuing the drawbacks payable on China earthenware exported to America, and for more effectually preventing the clandestine running of goods in the said colonies and plantations; and that it may be proper to repeal an act, made in the fourteenth year of the reign of his present Majesty, entitled, An Act to discontinue, in such manner, and for such time as are therein mentioned, the landing and discharging, lading, or shipping, of goods, wares, and merchandise, at the town and within the harbor of Boston, in the province of Massachusetts Bay, in North America; and that it may be proper to repeal an act, made in the fourteenth year of the reign of his present Majesty, entitled, An Act for the impartial administration of justice in the cases of persons questioned for any acts done by them in the execution of the law, or for the suppression of riots and tumults in the province of Massachusetts Bay, in New England; and that it may be proper to repeal an act, made in the fourteenth year of the reign of his present Majesty, entitled, An Act for the better regulating the government of the province of Massachusetts Bay, in New England; and also, that it may be proper to explain and amend an act, made in the thirty-fifth year of the reign of King Henry VIII, entitled, An Act for the trial of treasons committed out of the King's dominions."

I wish, sir, to repeal the Boston Port Bill, because (independently of the dangerous precedent of suspending the rights of the subject during the King's pleasure) it was passed, as I apprehend, with less regularity, and on more partial principles, than it ought. The corporation of Boston was not heard before it was condemned. Other towns, full as guilty as she was, have not had their ports blocked up. Even the restraining bill of the present session does not go to the length of the Boston Port Act. The same ideas of prudence which induced you not to extend equal punishment to equal guilt, even when you were punishing, induce me, who mean not to chastise, but to reconcile, to be satisfied with the punishment already partially inflicted.

Ideas of prudence, and accommodation to circumstances, prevent you from taking away the charters of Connecticut and Rhode Island, as you have taken away that of Massachusetts Colony, though the Crown has far less power in the two former provinces than it enjoyed in the latter; and though the abuses have been full as great and as flagrant in the exempted as in the punished. The same reasons of prudence and accommodation have weight with me in restoring the charter of Massachusetts Bay. Besides, sir, the act which changes the charter of Massachusetts is in many particulars so exceptionable, that if I did not wish absolutely to repeal, I would by all means desire to alter it, as several of its provisions tend to the subversion of all public and private justice. Such, among others, is the power in the Governor to change the sheriff at his pleasure, and to make a new returning officer for every special cause. It is shameful to behold such a regulation standing among English laws.

The act for bringing persons accused of committing murder under the orders of government to England for trial, is but temporary. That act has calculated the probable duration of our quarrel with the colonies, and is accommodated to that supposed duration. I would hasten the happy moment of reconciliation, and therefore must, on my principle, get rid of that most justly obnoxious act.

The act of Henry VIII, for the trial of treasons, I do not mean to take away, but to confine it to its proper bounds and original intention; to make it expressly for trial of treasons (and the greatest treasons may be committed) in places where the jurisdiction of the Crown does not extend.

Having guarded the privileges of local legislature, I would next secure to the colonies a fair and unbiassed judicature; for which purpose, sir, I propose the following resolution:

" That, from the time when the General Assembly or General Court of any colony or plantation in North America, shall have appointed by act of assembly, duly confirmed, a settled salary to the offices of the Chief Justice and other judges of the Superior Court, it may be proper that the said Chief Justice and other judges of the Superior Court of such colony, shall hold his and their office and offices during their good behavior, and shall not be removed therefrom, but when the said removal shall be adjudged by His Majesty in council, upon a hearing on complaint from the General Asembly, or on a complaint from the Governor, or Council, or the House of Representatives severally, of the colony in which the said Chief Justice and other judges have exercised the said offices."

The next resolution relates to the courts of Admiralty. It is this:

" That it may be proper to regulate the courts of Admiralty, or Vice-Admiralty, authorized by the fifteenth chapter of the 4th of George III, in such a manner as to make the same more commodious to those who sue, or are sued, in the said courts, and to provide for the more decent maintenance of the judges in the same."

These courts I do not wish to take away. They are in themselves proper establishments. This court is one of the capital securities of the Act of Navigation. The extent of its jurisdiction, indeed, has been increased; but this is altogether as proper, and is, indeed, on many accounts, more eligible, where new powers were wanted, than a court absolutely new. But courts incommodiously situated, in effect, deny justice; and a court, partaking in the fruits of its own condemnation, is a robber. The Congress complain, and complain justly, of this grievance.

These are the three consequential propositions. I have thought of two or three more, but they come rather too near detail, and to the province of executive government, which I wish Parliament always to superintend, never to assume. If the first six are granted congruity will carry the latter three. If not, the things that remain unrepealed will be, I hope, rather unseemly encumbrances on the building, than very materially detrimental to its strength and stability.

Here, sir, I should close, but that I plainly perceive some objections remain, which I ought, if possible, to remove. The first will be, that, in resorting to the doctrine of our ancestors, as contained in the preamble to the Chester act, I prove too much; that the grievance from a want of representation stated in that preamble, goes to the whole of legislation as well as to taxation. And that the colonies, grounding themselves upon that doctrine, will apply it to all parts of legislative authority.

To this objection, with all possible deference and humility, and wishing as little as any man living to impair the smallest particle of our supreme authority, I answer, that the words are the words of Parliament, and not mine; and that all false and inconclusive inferences drawn from them are not mine, for I heartily disclaim any such inference. I have chosen the words of an act of Parliament, which Mr. Grenville, surely a tolerably zealous and very judicious advocate for the sovereignty of Parliament, formerly moved to have read at your table, in confirmation of his tenets. It is true that Lord Chatham considered these preambles as declaring strongly in favor of his opinions. He was a no less powerful advocate for the privileges of the Americans. Ought I not from hence to presume that these preambles are as favorable as possible to both, when properly understood; favorable both to the rights of Parliament, and to the privilege of the dependencies of this crown? But, sir, the object of grievance in my resolution I have not taken from the Chester, but from the Durham act, which confines the hardship of want of representation to the case of subsidies, and which, therefore, falls in exactly with the case of the colonies. But whether the unrepresented counties were *de jure* or *de facto* bound, the preambles do not accurately distinguish; nor indeed was it necessary; for, whether *de jure* or *de facto*, the legislature thought the exercise of the power of taxing, as of right, or as of fact without right, equally a grievance, and equally oppressive.

I do not know that the colonies have, in any general way or in any cool hour, gone much beyond the demand of immunity in relation to taxes. It is not fair to judge of the temper or dispositions of any man, or any set of men, when they are composed and at rest, from their conduct or their expressions in a state of disturbance and irritation. It is, besides, a very great mistake to imagine that mankind follow up practically any speculative principle, either of government or freedom, as far as it will go in argument and logical illation. We Englishmen stop very short of the principles upon which we support any given part of our constitution, or even the whole of it together. I could easily, if I had not already tired you, give you very striking and convincing instances of it. This is nothing but what is natural and proper. All government, indeed every human benefit and enjoyment, every virtue and every prudent act, is founded on compromise and barter. We balance inconveniences; we give and take; we remit some rights that we may enjoy others; and we choose rather to be happy citizens than subtle disputants. As we must give away some natural liberty to enjoy civil advantages, so we must sacrifice some civil liberties for the advantages to be derived from the communion and fellowship of a great empire. But, in all fair dealings, the thing bought must bear some proportion to the purchase paid. None will barter away " the immediate jewel of his soul." Though a great house is apt to make slaves haughty, yet it is purchasing a part of the artificial importance of a great empire too dear to pay for it all essential rights and all the intrinsic dignity of human nature. None of us who would not risk his life rather than fall under a government purely arbitrary. But, although there are some among us who think our constitution wants many improvements to make it a complete system of liberty, perhaps none who are of that opinion would think it right to aim at such improvement by disturbing his country, and risking everything that is dear to him. In every arduous enterprise we consider what we are to lose as well as what we are to gain; and the more and better stake of liberty every people possess, the less they will hazard in a vain attempt to make it more. These are *the cords of man.* Man acts from adequate motive relative to his interest, and not on metaphysical speculations. Aristotle, the great master of reasoning, cautions us, and with great weight and propriety, against this species of delusive geometrical accuracy in moral arguments as the most fallacious of all sophistry.

The Americans will have no interest contrary to the grandeur and glory of England, when they are not oppressed by the weight of it; and they will rather be inclined to respect the acts of a superintending legislature, when they see them the acts of that power which is itself the security, not the rival, of their secondary importance. In this assurance my mind most perfectly acquiesces, and I confess I feel not the least alarm from the discontents which are to arise from putting people at their ease; nor do I apprehend the destruction of this empire from giving, by an act of free grace and indulgence, to two millions of my fellow-citizens, some share

of those rights upon which I have always been taught to
value myself.

It is said, indeed, that this power of granting, vested in
American assemblies, would dissolve the unity of the empire,
which was preserved entire, although Wales, and Chester, and
Durham were added to it. Truly, Mr. Speaker, I do not know
what this unity means, nor has it ever been heard of, that I
know, in the constitutional policy of this country. The very
idea of subordination of parts excludes this notion of simple
and undivided unity. England is the head, but she is not the
head and the members too. Ireland has ever had from the beginning a separate, but not an independent legislature, which,
far from distracting, promoted the union of the whole. Everything was sweetly and harmoniously disposed through both
islands for the conservation of English dominion and the communication of English liberties. I do not see that the same
principles might not be carried into twenty islands, and with
the same good effect. This is my model with regard to America, as far as the internal circumstances of the two countries
are the same. I know no other unity of this empire that I
can draw from its example during these periods, when it
seemed to my poor understanding more united than it is now,
or than it is likely to be by the present methods.

But since I speak of these methods, I recollect, Mr. Speaker,
almost too late, that I promised, before I finished, to say something of the proposition of the noble lord [Lord North] on
the floor, which has been so lately received, and stands on
your journals. I must be deeply concerned whenever it is my
misfortune to continue a difference with the majority of this
House. But as the reasons for that difference are my apology
for thus troubling you, suffer me to state them in a very few
words. I shall compress them into as small a body as I possibly can, having already debated that matter at large when
the question was before the committee.

First, then I cannot admit that proposition of a ransom by
auction, because it is a mere project. It is a thing new; unheard of; supported by no experience; justified by no anal-
ogy; without example of our ancestors, or root in the constitution. It is neither regular parliamentary taxation nor
colony grant. "*Experimentum in corpore vili*" is a good rule,

which will ever make me adverse to any trial of experiments on what is certainly the most valuable of all subjects, the peace of this empire.

Secondly, it is an experiment which must be fatal, in the end, to our constitution. For what is it but a scheme for taxing the colonies in the ante-chamber of the noble lord and his successors? To settle the quotas and proportions in this House is clearly impossible. You, sir, may flatter yourself you shall sit a state auctioneer with your hammer in your hand, and knock down to each colony as it bids. But to settle (on the plan laid down by the noble lord) the true proportional payment for four or five-and-twenty governments according to the absolute and the relative wealth of each, and according to the British proportion of wealth and burden, is a wild and chimerical notion. This new taxation must therefore come in by the back door of the constitution. Each quota must be brought to this House ready formed; you can neither add nor alter. You must register it. You can do nothing farther. For on what grounds can you deliberate, either before or after the proposition? You cannot hear the counsel for all these provinces, quarrelling each on its own quantity of payment, and its proportion to others. If you should attempt it, the committee of provincial ways and means, or by whatever other name it will delight to be called, must swallow up all the time of Parliament.

Thirdly, it does not give satisfaction to the complaint of the colonies. They complain that they are taxed without their consent; you answer, that you will fix the sum at which they shall be taxed. That is, you give them the very grievance for the remedy. You tell them indeed, that you will leave the mode to themselves. I really beg pardon. It gives me pain to mention it; but you must be sensible that you will not perform this part of the contract. For, suppose the colonies were to lay the duties which furnished their contingent upon the importation of your manufactures? you know you would never suffer such a tax to be laid. You know, too, that you would not suffer many other modes of taxation; so that when you come to explain yourself, it will be found that you will neither leave to themselves the *quantum* nor the mode, nor, indeed, anything. The whole is delusion from one end to the other.

Fourthly, this method of ransom by auction, unless it be universally accepted, will plunge you into great and inextricable difficulties. In what year of our Lord are the proportions of payments to be settled, to say nothing of the impossibility, that colony agents should have general powers of taxing the colonies at their discretion? Consider, I implore you, that the communication by special messages, and orders between these agents and their constituents on each variation of the case, when the parties come to contend together, and to dispute on their relative proportions, will be a matter of delay, perplexity, and confusion that never can have an end.

If all the colonies do not appear at the outcry, what is the condition of those assemblies, who offer, by themselves or their agents, to tax themselves up to your ideas of their proportion? The refractory colonies who refuse all composition will remain taxed only to your old impositions, which, however grievous in principle, are trifling as to production. The obedient colonies in this scheme are heavily taxed; the refractory remain unburdened. What will you do? Will you lay new and heavier taxes by Parliament on the disobedient? Pray consider in what way you can do it. You are perfectly convinced that in the way of taxing you can do nothing but at the ports. Now suppose it is Virginia that refuses to appear at your auction, while Maryland and North Carolina bid handsomely for their ransom, and are taxed to your quota. How will you put these colonies on a par? Will you tax the tobacco of Virginia? If you do, you give its death wound to your English revenue at home, and to one of the very greatest articles of your own foreign trade. If you tax the import of that rebellious colony, what do you tax but your own manufactures, or the goods of some other obedient and already well-taxed colony? Who has said one word on this labyrinth of detail, which bewilders you more and more as you enter into it? Who has presented, who can present you with a clue to lead you out of it? I think, sir, it is impossible that you should not recollect that the colony bounds are so implicated in one another (you know it by your own experiments in the bill for prohibiting the New England fishery) that you can lay no possible restraints on almost any of them which may not be presently eluded, if you do not confound the innocent with the guilty, and burden those whom, upon every principle, you ought to exonerate. He must be grossly ignorant of America who thinks that, without falling into this confusion of all rules of equity and policy, you can restrain any single colony, especially Virginia and Maryland, the central and most important of them all.

Let it also be considered, that either in the present confusion you settle a permanent contingent which will and must be trifling, and then you have no effectual revenue; or, you change the quota at every exigency, and then on every new repartition you will have a new quarrel.

Reflect, besides, that when you have fixed a quota for every colony, you have not provided for prompt and punctual payment. Suppose one, two, five, ten years' arrears. You cannot issue a Treasury Extent against the failing colony. You must make new Boston Port bills, new restraining laws, new acts for dragging men to England for trial. You must send out new fleets, new armies. All is to begin again. From this day forward the empire is never to know an hour's tranquillity. An intestine fire will be kept alive in the bowels of the colonies, which one time or another must consume this whole empire. I allow, indeed, that the empire of Germany raises her revenue and her troops by quotas and contingents; but the revenue of the empire, and the army of the empire, is the worst revenue and the worst army in the world.

Instead of a standing revenue, you will therefore have a perpetual quarrel. Indeed, the noble lord who proposed this project of a ransom by auction, seemed himself to be of that opinion. His project was rather designed for breaking the union of the colonies than for establishing a revenue. He confessed that he apprehended that his proposal would not be to their taste. I say this scheme of disunion seems to be at the bottom of the project; for I will not suspect that the noble lord meant nothing but merely to delude the nation by an airy phantom which he never intended to realize. But, whatever his views may be, as I propose the peace and union of the colonies as the very foundation of my plan, it cannot accord with one whose foundation is perpetual discord.

Compare the two. This I offer to give you is plain and simple. The other, full of perplexed and intricate mazes. This

is mild; that, harsh. This is found by experience effectual
for its purposes; the other is a new project. This is universal;
the other, calculated for certain colonies only. This is immediate in its conciliatory operation; the other, remote, contingent, full of hazard. Mine is what becomes the dignity of
a ruling people; gratuitous, unconditional, and not held out
as a matter of bargain and sale. I have done my duty in proposing it to you. I have indeed tired you by a long discourse;
but this is the misfortune of those to whose influence nothing
will be conceded, and who must win every inch of their ground
by argument. You have heard me with goodness. May you
decide with wisdom! For my part, I feel my mind greatly
disburdened by what I have done to-day. I have been the
less fearful of trying your patience, because on this subject I
mean to spare it altogether in future. I have this comfort,
that in every stage of the American affairs I have steadily opposed the measures that have produced the confusion, and may
bring on the destruction of this empire. I now go so far as
to risk a proposal of my own. If I cannot give peace to my
country, I give it to my conscience.

But what, says the financier, is peace to us without money?
Your plan gives us no revenue. No! But it does—for it secures to the subject the power of *refusal*—the first of all revenues. Experience is a cheat, and fact a liar, if this power in
the subject of proportioning his grant, or of not granting at
all, has not been found the richest mine of revenue ever discovered by the skill or by the fortune of man. It does not
indeed vote you £152,750 11s. 2¾d., nor any other paltry limited sum, but it gives the strong box itself, the fund, the bank,
from whence only revenues can arise among a people sensible
of freedom: *Posita luditur arca.*

Cannot you in England; cannot you at this time of day;
cannot you—a House of Commons—trust to the principle which
has raised so mighty a revenue, and accumulated a debt of near
one hundred and forty millions in this country? Is this principle
to be true in England and false everywhere else? Is it not true
in Ireland? Has it not hitherto been true in the colonies? Why
should you presume, that in any country, a body duly constituted for any functions will neglect to perform its duty, and
abdicate its trust? Such a presumption would go against all

government in all modes. But, in truth, this dread of penury of supply, from a free assembly, has no foundation in nature. For first observe, that, besides the desire, which all men have naturally, of supporting the honor of their own government, that sense of dignity, and that security of property, which ever attends freedom, has a tendency to increase the stock of the free community. Most may be taken where most is accumulated. And what is the soil or climate where experience has not uniformly proved that the voluntary flow of heaped-up plenty, bursting from the weight of its own rich luxuriance, has ever run with a more copious stream of revenue, than could be squeezed from the dry husks of oppressed indigence, by the straining of all the politic machinery in the world?

Next, we know that parties must ever exist in a free country. We know, too, that the emulations of such parties, their contradictions, their reciprocal necessities, their hopes and their fears, must send them all in their turns to him that holds the balance of the state. The parties are the gamesters, but Government keeps the table, and is sure to be the winner in the end. When this game is played I really think it is more to be feared that the people will be exhausted, than that Government will not be supplied; whereas, whatever is got by acts of absolute power, ill obeyed because odious, or by contracts ill kept because constrained, will be narrow, feeble, uncertain, and precarious.

> " Ease would retract
> Vows made in pain, as violent and void."

I, for one, protest against compounding our demands. I declare against compounding, for a poor limited sum, the immense ever-growing, eternal debt which is due to generous government from protected freedom. And so may I speed in the great object I propose to you, as I think it would not only be an act of injustice, but would be the worst economy in the world, to compel the colonies to a sum certain, either in the way of ransom or in the way of compulsory compact.

But to clear up my ideas on this subject; a revenue from America transmitted hither—do not delude yourselves—you never can receive it—no, not a shilling. We have experienced that from remote countries it is not to be expected. If, when you attempted to extract revenue from Bengal, you were obliged to return in loan what you had taken in imposition, what can you expect from North America? for certainly, if ever there was a country qualified to produce wealth, it is India; or an institution fit for the transmission, it is the East India Company. America has none of these aptitudes. If America gives you taxable objects on which you lay your duties here, and gives you, at the same time, a surplus by a foreign sale of her commodities to pay the duties on these objects which you tax at home, she has performed her part to the British revenue. But with regard to her own internal establishments, she may, I doubt not she will, contribute in moderation; I say in moderation, for she ought not to be permitted to exhaust herself. She ought to be reserved to a war, the weight of which, with the enemies that we are most likely to have, must be considerable in her quarter of the globe. There she may serve you, and serve you essentially.

For that service, for all service, whether of revenue, trade, or empire, my trust is in her interest in the British constitution. My hold of the colonies is in the close affection which grows from common names, from kindred blood, from similar privileges, and equal protection. These are ties which, though light as air, are as strong as links of iron. Let the colonies always keep the idea of their civil rights associated with your government; they will cling and grapple to you, and no force under heaven will be of power to tear them from their allegiance. But let it be once understood that your government may be one thing, and their privileges another; that these two things may exist without any mutual relation; the cement is gone; the cohesion is loosened; and everything hastens to decay and dissolution. As long as you have the wisdom to keep the sovereign authority of this country as the sanctuary of liberty, the sacred temple consecrated to our common faith, wherever the chosen race and sons of England worship Freedom, they will turn their faces towards you. The more they multiply, the more friends you will have. The more ardently they love liberty, the more perfect will be their obedience. Slavery they can have anywhere. It is a weed that grows in every soil. They may have it from Spain; they may have it from Prussia; but, until you become lost to all feeling of your true interest and your natural dignity, freedom they can have from none but you. This is the commodity of price, of which you have the monopoly. This is the true Act of Navigation, which binds to you the commerce of the colonies, and through them secures to you the wealth of the world. Deny them this participation of freedom, and you break that sole bond which originally made, and must still preserve, the unity of the empire. Do not entertain so weak an imagination as that your registers and your bonds, your affidavits and your sufferances, your cockets and your clearances, are what form the great securities of your commerce. Do not dream that your letters of office, and your instructions, and your suspending clauses, are the things that hold together the great contexture of this mysterious whole. These things do not make your government. Dead instruments, passive tools as they are, it is the spirit of the English communion that gives all their life and efficacy to them. It is the spirit of the English constitution, which, infused through the mighty mass, pervades, feeds, unites, invigorates, vivifies every part of the empire, even down to the minutest member.

Is it not the same virtue which does everything for us here in England?

Do you imagine then, that it is the land tax which raises your revenue? that it is the annual vote in the committee of supply which gives you your army? or that it is the mutiny bill, which inspires it with bravery and discipline? No! surely no! It is the love of the people; it is their attachment to their government, from the sense of the deep stake they have in such a glorious institution, which gives you your army and your navy, and infuses into both that liberal obedience, without which your army would be a base rabble, and your navy nothing but rotten timber.

All this, I know well enough, will sound wild and chimerical to the profane herd of those vulgar and mechanical politicians who have no place among us; a sort of people who think that nothing exists but what is gross and material, and who, therefore, far from being qualified to be directors of the great movement of empire, are not fit to turn a wheel in the machine. But to men truly initiated and rightly taught, these ruling and master principles, which, in the opinion of such men as I have mentioned, have no substantial existence, are in truth everything and all in all. Magnanimity in politics is not seldom the truest wisdom; and a great empire and little minds go ill together. If we are conscious of our situation, and glow with zeal to fill our place as becomes our station and ourselves, we ought to auspicate all our public proceeding on America with the old warning of the church, *sursum corda!* We ought to elevate our minds to the greatness of that trust to which the order of Providence has called us. By adverting to the dignity of this high calling our ancestors have turned a savage wilderness into a glorious empire, and have made the most extensive and the only honorable conquests, not by destroying but by promoting, the wealth, the number, the happiness of the human race. Let us get an American revenue as we have got an American empire. English privileges have made it all that it is; English privileges alone will make it all it can be.

In full confidence of this unalterable truth, I now, *quod felix faustumque sit,* lay the first stone in the temple of peace; and I move you,

That the colonies and plantations of Great Britain in North America, consisting of fourteen separate governments, and containing two millions and upward of free inhabitants, have not had the liberty and privilege of electing and sending any knights and burgesses, or others, to represent them in the high court of Parliament.

ON REJECTION OF BONAPARTE'S OVERTURES OF PEACE

—

BY

CHARLES JAMES FOX

CHARLES JAMES FOX

1749—1806

A man who enters Parliament at nineteen, after incurring debts by gambling and other dissipation to the amount of half a million of dollars in two years; who begins political life, at that boyish age, as a Tory, but adopts the principles of the Whigs, and becomes a leader of the party before he is thirty; who was born an aristocrat, with royal blood in his veins on the maternal side, and on that of his father, Lord Holland, inheriting a vast fortune; but who, owing to the soundness of his heart and the clearness of his brain, became a champion of popular rights, and the enemy and terror of his quondam friends; and who died at the age of fifty-seven with a world-wide reputation as a statesman, patriot, and friend of humanity; such a man as this would be sufficient, one might think, to be the adornment of an age. And yet Charles James Fox was but one of the incomparable galaxy of genius which blazed in the firmament of the latter part of the eighteenth century, and made the reign of one of the most stupid and narrow-minded kings that ever sat upon the throne of England the most brilliant epoch, with the exception of that of Elizabeth, that modern history records.

He was born in London in 1749; his mother being Lady Caroline Georgina, daughter of the second Duke of Richmond, who was a grandson of Charles II. He was schooled at Eton, and went to Oxford; but left without taking his degree. His home influences were unfavorable to the right development of his genius and character; and there is little doubt that he might have been a far greater and more useful man than he actually became, had he enjoyed the advantage of wise and strict training where he had the best right to expect it. But his father was a dissolute and cynical man of the world, who encouraged his son to embrace the vices, and surfeit himself with the pleasures of the town; giving him all the money he asked for, and enabling him to get credit for much more. The naturally pure and noble instincts of the boy at first revolted against the coarse and unprincipled self-indulgence which Lord Holland surrounded him with; but though his heart was good, it was hot, and his nature was but too prone to the pleasures of the senses and the excitements of a life of dissipation. On the other hand, we can hardly doubt that Fox gained by the circumstances of his birth, placing him as that did among the highest nobles of the land as their equal or superior. Had he been of plebeian origin, with his own way to make, some of the loftier and more generous traits of his character would have suffered; something of the headlong courage, the matchless audacity, with which he attacked his opponents, and denounced even the King himself—for what was a Guelph to a scion of the Stuarts?—in the cause of the people. Moreover, had he been humble by birth, he would naturally have aimed to lift himself to the nobility; but possessing at the outset every advantage that wealth and lineage could bestow, he had nothing further to see or care for in that direction, and gave himself the more unreservedly to those sympathies which his feelings and intelligence prompted.

After being dismissed by North (at the instance of the King) in 1775, he affiliated himself with the Whig leaders, and when Rockingham formed his ministry in 1782 Fox received the post of Foreign Secretary. But the next year, Rockingham being dead, and Fox having an antipathy to Shelburne, he formed a coalition with Lord North; which resulted in bringing in the Duke of Portland as Prime Minister, with North and Fox as Home and Foreign Secretaries. This rather unnatural combination of clay and iron did not long hold together. Fox's India bill was the arena in which it suffered defeat the same year, and through the direct and unconstitutional interference of the King, who would shrink from no baseness to gain his selfish ends. From this time until the year of his death Fox was forcibly kept from office by the King; but when, in 1806, Lord Grenville bluntly told George III that he would not form a ministry unless Fox were in it, the royal curmudgeon had to yield; but Fox died in September of the year he accepted the post of Foreign Secretary.

Fox made his reputation as an orator in defending the American colonists against the injustice and greed of the King's party in England. The tyranny of England roused his ire as much as if it had been directed against himself; his sympathetic imagination enabled him to enter into the feelings of the colonists; and he supplied himself by research with the facts needed for his argument. His education had in some respects furnished him with the weapons of an orator; but he was deficient in statistics, and in scientific acquaintance with the principles of political economy. These gaps in his training he was obliged to make up by prodigious efforts, or by drawing attention from them by brilliance in other directions. He better loved debate than set oratory; it suited his temperament, and the splendid readiness and resources of his mind. He did not depend upon figurative flights, or appeals to emotion; but he himself felt emotion, and communicated it to others by contagion from himself. He was strong and cogent in argument, and instant in its application; piercing the weak point of his opponent's armor the instant that it was uncovered. His force was tremendous, and his courage astounding; he would thunder out in the House what other men hardly dared to think in the privacy of their chambers. Withal he was one of the kindest and most lovable of men, with a heart as big as his body, and sound enough to balance his brain. His wide reading and knowledge of life furnished him with an inexhaustible supply of allusion and illustrative anecdote. Almost any one of his principal speeches would fairly give the measure of the man; but it is generally conceded that that " On the Rejection of Napoleon's Overtures " is on the whole the best.

ON REJECTION OF BONAPARTE'S OVERTURES OF PEACE

M R. SPEAKER: At so late an hour of the night, I am sure you will do me the justice to believe that I do not mean to go at length into the discussion of this great question. Exhausted as the attention of the House must be, and unaccustomed as I have been of late to attend in my place, nothing but a deep sense of my duty could have induced me to trouble you at all, and particularly to request your indulgence at such an hour.

Sir, my honorable and learned friend [Mr. Erskine] has truly said that the present is a new era in the war, and the right honorable gentleman opposite to me [Mr. Pitt] feels the justice of the remark; for, by travelling back to the commencement of the war, and referring again to all the topics and arguments which he has so often and so successfully urged upon the House, and by which he has drawn them on to the support of his measures, he is forced to acknowledge that, at the end of a seven years' conflict, we are come but to a new era in the war, at which he thinks it necessary only to press all his former arguments to induce us to persevere. All the topics which have so often misled us—all the reasoning which has so invariably failed—all the lofty predictions which have so constantly been falsified by events—all the hopes which have amused the sanguine, and all the assurances of the distress and weakness of the enemy which have satisfied the unthinking, are again enumerated and advanced as arguments for our continuing the war. What! at the end of seven years of the most burdensome and the most calamitous struggle in which this country ever was engaged, are we again to be amused with notions of finance, and calculations of the exhausted resources of the enemy, as a ground of confidence and of hope? Gra-

cious God! were we not told five years ago that France was
not only on the brink and in the jaws of ruin, but that she was
actually sunk into the gulf of bankruptcy? Were we not told,
as an unanswerable argument against treating, " that she
could not hold out another campaign—that nothing but peace
could save her—that she wanted only time to recruit her exhausted finances—that to grant her repose was to grant her the
means of again molesting this country, and that we had nothing to do but persevere for a short time, in order to save ourselves forever from the consequences of her ambition and her
Jacobinism?" What! after having gone on from year to year
upon assurances like these, and after having seen the repeated
refutations of every prediction, are we again to be gravely and
seriously assured, that we have the same prospect of success
on the same identical grounds? And, without any other argument or security are we invited, at this new era of the war, to
conduct it upon principles which, if adopted and acted upon,
may make it eternal? If the right honorable gentleman shall
succeed in prevailing on Parliament and the country to adopt
the principles which he has advanced this night, I see no possible termination to the contest. No man can see an end to it;
and upon the assurances and predictions which have so uniformly failed, we are called upon not merely to refuse all negotiations, but to countenance principles and views as distant
from wisdom and justice, as they are in their nature wild and
impracticable.

I must lament, sir, in common with every genuine friend of
peace, the harsh and unconciliating language which ministers
have held to the French, and which they have even made use
of in their answer to a respectful offer of a negotiation. Such
language has ever been considered as extremely unwise, and has
ever been reprobated by diplomatic men. I remember with
pleasure the terms in which Lord Malmesbury, at Paris, in the
year 1796, replied to expressions of this sort, used by M. de la
Croix. He justly said, " that offensive and injurious insinuations were only calculated to throw new obstacles in the way of
accommodation, and that it was not by revolting reproaches nor
by reciprocal invective that a sincere wish to accomplish the
great work of pacification could be evinced." Nothing could
be more proper nor more wise than this language; and such

ought ever to be the tone and conduct of men intrusted with the very important task of treating with a hostile nation. Being a sincere friend to peace, I must say with Lord Malmesbury, that it is not by reproaches and by invective that we can hope for a reconciliation; and I am convinced, in my own mind, that I speak the sense of this House, and, if not of this House, certainly of a majority of the people of this country, when I lament that any unprovoked and unnecessary recriminations should be flung out, by which obstacles are put in the way of pacification. I believe it is the prevailing sentiment of the people, that we ought to abstain from harsh and insulting language; and in common with them, I must lament that both in the papers of Lord Grenville, and this night, such license has been given to invective and reproach.

For the same reason, I must lament that the right honorable gentleman [Mr. Pitt] has thought proper to go at such length, and with such severity of minute investigation, into all the early circumstances of the war, which (whatever they were) are nothing to the present purpose, and ought not to influence the present feelings of the House. I certainly shall not follow him through the whole of this tedious detail, though I do not agree with him in many of his assertions. I do not know what impression his narrative may make on other gentlemen; but I will tell him fairly and candidly, he has not convinced me. I continue to think, and until I see better grounds for changing my opinion than any that the right honorable gentleman has this night produced, I shall continue to think, and to say, plainly and explicitly, "that this country was the aggressor in the war." But with regard to Austria and Prussia—is there a man who, for one moment, can dispute that they were the aggressors? It will be vain for the right honorable gentleman to enter into long and plausible reasoning against the evidence of documents so clear, so decisive—so frequently, so thoroughly investigated   The unfortunate monarch, Louis XVI, himself, as well as those who were in his confidence, has borne decisive testimony of the fact, that between him and the Emperor [Leopold of Austria] there was an intimate correspondence and a perfect understanding. Do I mean by this that a positive treaty was entered into for the dismemberment of France? Certainly not. But no man can read the declarations which

were made at Mantua as well as at Pilnitz, as they are given
by M. Bertrand de Molville, without acknowledging that this
was not merely an intention, but a declaration of an intention,
on the part of the great powers of Germany, to interfere in the
internal affairs of France, for the purpose of regulating the
government against the opinion of the people. This, though
not a plan for the partition of France, was, in the eye of reason
and common-sense, an aggression against France. The right
honorable gentleman denies that there was such a thing as a
treaty of Pilnitz. Granted. But was there not a declaration
which amounted to an act of hostile aggression? The two
powers, the Emperor of Germany and the King of Prussia,
made a public declaration that they were determined to employ their forces, in conjunction with those of the other sovereigns of Europe, " to put the King of France in a situation to
establish, in perfect liberty, the foundations of a monarchical
government equally agreeable to the rights of sovereigns and
the welfare of the French." Whenever the other princes should
agree to co-operate with them, " then, and in that case, their
majesties were determined to act promptly and by mutual consent, with the forces necessary to obtain the end proposed by
all of them. In the mean time, they declared, that they would
give orders for their troops to be ready for actual service."
Now, I would ask gentlemen to lay their hands upon their hearts,
and say with candor what the true and fair construction of this
declaration was—whether it was not a menace and an insult
to France, since, in direct terms, it declared, that whenever the
other powers should concur, they would attack France, then at
peace with them, and then employed only in domestic and in
internal regulations? Let us suppose the case to be that of
Great Britain. Will any gentleman say that if two of the
great powers should make a public declaration that they were
determined to make an attack on this kingdom as soon as circumstances should favor their intention; that they only waited
for this occasion, and that in the mean time they would keep
their forces ready for the purpose, it would not be considered
by the Parliament and people of this country as a hostile aggression? And is there any Englishman in existence who is
such a friend to peace as to say that the nation could retain
its honor and dignity if it should sit down under such a men-

ace? I know too well what is due to the national character of England to believe that there would be two opinions on the case, if thus put home to our own feelings and understandings. We must, then, respect in others the indignation which such an act would excite in ourselves; and when we see it established on the most indisputable testimony, that both at Pilnitz and at Mantua declarations were made to this effect, it is idle to say that, as far as the Emperor and the King of Prussia were concerned, they were not the aggressors in the war.

"Oh! but the decree of the nineteenth of November, 1792." That, at least, the right honorable gentlemen says, you must allow to be an act of aggression, not only against England, but against all the sovereigns of Europe. I am not one of those, sir, who attach much interest to the general and indiscriminate provocations thrown out at random, like this resolution of the nineteenth of November, 1792. I do not think it necessary to the dignity of any people to notice and to apply to themselves menaces without particular allusion, which are always unwise in the power which uses them, and which it is still more unwise to treat with seriousness. But if any such idle and general provocation to nations is given, either in insolence or in folly, by any government, it is a clear first principle that an explanation is the thing which a magnanimous nation, feeling itself aggrieved, ought to demand; and if an explanation be given which is not satisfactory, it ought clearly and distinctly to say so. There should be no ambiguity, no reserve, on the occasion. Now, we all know, from documents on our table, that M. Chauvelin [the French minister] did give an explanation of this silly decree. He declared, "in the name of his government, that it was never meant that the French Government should favor insurrections; that the decree was applicable only to those people who, after having acquired their liberty by conquest, should demand the assistance of the Republic; but that France would respect not only the independence of England, but also that of her allies with whom she was not at war." This was the explanation of the offensive decree. "But this explanation was not satisfactory." Did you say so to M. Chauvelin? Did you tell him that you were not content with this explanation, and when you dismissed him afterward, on the death of the King [of France], did you say that this explanation was unsatisfactory? No. You did no such thing; and I contend that unless you demanded further explanations, and they were refused, you have no right to urge the decree of the nineteenth of November as an act of aggresssion. In all your conferences and correspondence with M. Chauvelin did you hold out to him what terms would satisfy you? Did you give the French the power or the means of settling the misunderstanding which that decree, or any other of the points at issue, had created? I maintain that when a nation refuses to state to another the thing which would satisfy her, she shows that she is not actuated by a desire to preserve peace between them; and I aver that this was the case here. The Scheldt, for instance. You now say that the navigation of the Scheldt was one of your causes of complaint. Did you explain yourself on that subject? Did you make it one of the grounds for the dismissal of M. Chauvelin? Sir, I repeat it, that a nation, to justify itself in appealing to the last solemn resort, ought to prove that it has taken every possible means, consistent with dignity, to demand the reparation and redress which would be satisfactory; and if she refuses to explain what would be satisfactory, she does not do her duty, nor exonerate herself from the charge of being the aggressor.

But " France," it seems, " then declared war against us; and she was the aggressor, because the declaration came from her." Let us look at the circumstances of this transaction on both sides. Undoubtedly the declaration was made by them; but is a declaration the only thing which constitutes the commencement of a war? Do gentlemen recollect that, in consequence of a dispute about the commencement of war, respecting the capture of a number of ships, an article was inserted in our treaty with France, by which it was positively stipulated that in future, to prevent all disputes, the act of the dismissal of a minister from either of the two courts should be held and considered as tantamount to a declaration of war? I mention this, sir, because when we are idly employed in this retrospect of the origin of a war which has lasted so many years, instead of turning our eyes only to the contemplation of the means of putting an end to it, we seem disposed to overlook everything on our own parts, and to search only for grounds of imputation on the enemy. I almost think it an insult on the House to detain them with this sort of examination. Why, sir, if France was the aggressor, as the right honorable gentleman says she was throughout, did not Prussia call upon us for the stipulated number of troops, according to the article of the definitive treaty of alliance subsisting between us, by which, in case that either of the contracting parties was attacked, they had a right to demand the stipulated aid? and the same thing again may be asked when we were attacked. The right honorable gentleman might here accuse himself, indeed, of reserve; but it unfortunately happened, that at the time the point was too clear on which side the aggression lay. Prussia was too sensible that the war could not entitle her to make the demand, and that it was not a case within the scope of the defensive treaty. This is evidence worth a volume of subsequent reasoning; for if, at the time when all the facts were present to their minds, they could not take advantage of existing treaties, and that too when the courts were on the most friendly terms with one another, it will be manifest to every thinking man that they were sensible they were not authorized to make the demand.

I really, sir, cannot think it necessary to follow the right honorable gentleman into all the minute details which he has thought proper to give us respecting the first aggression; but that Austria and Prussia were the aggressors, not a man in any country, who has ever given himself the trouble to think at all on the subject, can doubt. Nothing could be more hostile than their whole proceedings. Did they not declare to France that it was her internal concerns, not her external proceedings, which provoked them to confederate against her? Look back to the proclamations with which they set out. Read the declarations which they made themselves to justify their appeal to arms. They did not pretend to fear her ambition—her conquests—her troubling her neighbors; but they accused her of new-modelling her own government. They said nothing of her aggressions abroad. They spoke only of her clubs and societies at Paris.

Sir, in all this, I am not justifying the French; I am not trying to absolve them from blame, either in their internal or external policy. I think, on the contrary, that their successive rulers have been as bad and as execrable, in various instances, as any of the most despotic and unprincipled governments that the world ever saw. I think it impossible, sir, that it should have been otherwise. It was not to be expected that the French, when once engaged in foreign wars, should not endeavor to spread destruction around them, and to form plans of aggrandizement and plunder on every side. Men bred in the school of the house of Bourbon could not be expected to act otherwise. They could not have lived so long under their ancient masters without imbibing the restless ambition, the perfidy, and the insatiable spirit of the race. They have imitated the practice of their great prototype, and, through their whole career of mischiefs and of crimes, have done no more than servilely trace the steps of their own Louis XIV. If they have overrun countries and ravaged them, they have done it upon Bourbon principles; if they have ruined and dethroned sovereigns, it is entirely after the Bourbon manner; if they have even fraternized with the people of foreign countries, and pretended to make their cause their own, they have only faithfully followed the Bourbon example. They have constantly had Louis, the Grand Monarque, in their eye. But it may be said, that this example was long ago, and that we ought not to refer to a period so distant. True, it is a remote period applied to the man, but not so of the principle. The principle was never extinct; nor has its operation been suspended in France, except, perhaps, for a short interval, during the administration of Cardinal Fleury; and my complaint against the republic of France is, not that she has generated new crimes—not that she has promulgated new mischief—but that she has adopted and acted upon the principles which have been so fatal to Europe under the practice of the House of Bourbon. It is said, that wherever the French have gone they have introduced revolution— they have sought for the means of disturbing neighboring states, and have not been content with mere conquest. What is this but adopting the ingenious scheme of Louis XIV? He was not content with merely overrunning a state. Whenever he came into a new territory, he established what he called his chamber of claims, a most convenient device, by which he inquired whether the conquered country or province had any dormant or disputed claims—any cause of complaint—any unsettled demand upon any other state or province—upon which he might wage war upon such state, thereby discover again

ground for new devastation, and gratify his ambition by new
acquisitions. What have the republicans done more atrocious,
more Jacobinical than this? Louis went to war with Holland.
His pretext was that Holland had not treated him with sufficient respect. A very just and proper cause for war indeed!

This, sir, leads me to an example which I think seasonable,
and worthy the attention of His Majesty's ministers. When
our Charles II, as a short exception to the policy of his reign,
made the triple alliance for the protection of Europe, and particularly of Holland, against the ambition of Louis XIV, what
was the conduct of that great, virtuous, and most able statesman, M. de Witt, when the confederates came to deliberate
upon the terms upon which they should treat with the French
monarch? When it was said that he had made unprincipled
conquests, and that he ought to be forced to surrender them
all, what was the language of that great and wise man? " No,"
said he; " I think we ought not to look back to the origin of
the war so much as the means of putting an end to it. If you
had united in time to prevent these conquests, well; but now
that he has made them, he stands upon the ground of conquest, and we must agree to treat with him, not with reference
to the origin of the conquest, but with regard to his present
posture. He has those places, and some of them we must be
content to give up as the means of peace; for conquest will
always successfully set up its claims to indemnification." Such
was the language of this minister, who was the ornament of
his time; and such, in my mind, ought to be the language of
statesmen, with regard to the French, at this day; and the
same ought to have been said at the formation of the confederacy. It was true that the French had overrun Savoy; but
they had overrun it upon Bourbon principles; and, having
gained this and other conquests before the confederacy was
formed, they ought to have treated with her rather for future
security than for past correction. States in possession, whether
monarchical or republican, will claim indemnity in proportion
to their success; and it will never so much be inquired by what
right they gained possession as by what means they can be prevented from enlarging their depredations. Such is the safe
practice of the world; and such ought to have been the conduct of the powers when the reduction of Savoy made them

coalesce. The right honorable gentleman may know more of the secret particulars of their overrunning Savoy than I do; but certainly, as they have come to my knowledge, it was a most Bourbon-like act. A great and justly celebrated historian, I mean Mr. Hume, a writer certainly estimable in many particulars, but who is a childish lover of princes, talks of Louis XIV in very magnificent terms. But he says of him, that, though he managed his enterprises with great skill and bravery, he was unfortunate in this, that he never got a good and fair pretence for war. This he reckons among his misfortunes. Can we say more of the republican French? In seizing on Savoy I think they made use of the words " *convénances morales et physiques.*" These were her reasons. A most Bourbon-like phrase. And I therefore contend that as we never scrupled to treat with the princes of the House of Bourbon on account of their rapacity, their thirst of conquest, their violation of treaties, their perfidy, and their restless spirit, so, I contend, we ought not to refuse to treat with their republican imitators.

Ministers could not pretend ignorance of the unprincipled manner in which the French had seized on Savoy. The Sardinian minister complained of the aggression, and yet no stir was made about it. The courts of Europe stood by and saw the outrage; and our ministers saw it. The right honorable gentleman will in vain, therefore, exert his power to persuade me of the interest he takes in the preservation of the rights of nations, since, at the moment when an interference might have been made with effect, no step was taken, no remonstrance made, no mediation negotiated, to stop the career of conquest. All the pretended and hypocritical sensibility " for the rights of nations, and for social order," with which we have since been stunned, cannot impose upon those who will take the trouble to look back to the period when this sensibility ought to have roused us into seasonable exertion. At that time, however, the right honorable gentleman makes it his boast that he was prevented, by a sense of neutrality, from taking any measures of precaution on the subject. I do not give the right honorable gentleman much credit for his spirit of neutrality on the occasion. It flowed from the sense of the country at the time, the great majority of which was clearly and decidedly against all interruptions being given to the French in their desire of regulating their own internal government.

But this neutrality, which respected only the internal rights of the French, and from which the people of England would never have departed but for the impolitic and hypocritical cant which was set up to arouse their jealousy and alarm their fears, was very different from the great principle of political prudence which ought to have actuated the councils of the nation, on seeing the first steps of France towards a career of external conquest. My opinion is, that when the unfortunate King of France offered to us, in the letter delivered by M. Chauvelin and M. Talleyrand, and even entreated us to mediate between him and the allied powers of Austria and Prussia, they [ministers] ought to have accepted of the offer, and exerted their influence to save Europe from the consequence of a system which was then beginning to manifest itself. It was, at least, a question of prudence; and as we had never refused to treat and to mediate with the old princes on account of their ambition or their perfidy, we ought to have been equally ready now, when the same principles were acted upon by other men. I must doubt the sensibility which could be so cold and so indifferent at the proper moment for its activity. I fear that there were at that moment the germs of ambition rising in the mind of the right honorable gentleman, and that he was beginning, like others, to entertain hopes that something might be obtained out of the coming confusion. What but such a sentiment could have prevented him from overlooking the fair occasion that was offered for preventing the calamities with which Europe was threatened? What but some such interested principle could have made him forego the truly honorable task, by which his administration would have displayed its magnanimity and its power? But for some such feeling, would not this country, both in wisdom and in dignity, have interfered, and, in conjunction with the other powers, have said to France: " You ask for a mediation. We will mediate with candor and sincerity, but we will at the same time declare to you our apprehensions. We do not trust to your assertion of a determination to avoid all foreign conquest, and that you are desirous only of settling your own constitution, because your language is contradicted by experience and the evidence of facts. You are Frenchmen, and you cannot so soon have forgotten and thrown off the Bourbon principles in which you

were educated. You have already imitated the bad practice
of your princes. You have seized on Savoy without a color
of right. But here we take our stand. Thus far you have
gone, and we cannot help it; but you must go no farther. We
will tell you distinctly what we shall consider as an attack on
the balance and the security of Europe; and, as the condition
of our interference, we will tell you also the securities that
we think essential to the general repose." This ought to have
been the language of His Majesty's ministers when their mediation was solicited; and something of this kind they evidently
thought of when they sent the instructions to Petersburgh
which they have mentioned this night, but upon which they
never acted. Having not done so, I say they have no right to
talk now about the violated rights of Europe, about the aggression of the French, and about the origin of the war in
which this country was so suddenly afterwards plunged. Instead of this, what did they do? They hung back; they avoided
explanations; they gave the French no means of satisfying
them; and I repeat my proposition—when there is a question
of peace and war between two nations, that government finds
itself in the wrong which refuses to state with clearness and
precision what she should consider as a satisfaction and a pledge
of peace.

Sir, if I understand the true precepts of the Christian religion, as set forth in the New Testament, I must be permitted
to say, that there is no such thing as a rule or doctrine by which
we are directed, or can be justified, in waging a war for religion.
The idea is subversive of the very foundations upon which it
stands, which are those of peace and good-will among men.
Religion never was and never can be a justifiable cause of war;
but it has been too often grossly used as the pretext and the
apology for the most unprincipled wars.

I have already said, and I repeat it, that the conduct of the
French to foreign nations cannot be justified. They have given
great cause of offence, but certainly not to all countries alike.
The right honorable gentlemen opposite to me have made an
indiscriminate catalogue of all the countries which the French
have offended, and, in their eagerness to throw odium on the
nation, have taken no pains to investigate the sources of their
several quarrels. I will not detain you, sir, by entering into

the long detail which has been given of their aggressions and their violences; but let me mention Sardinia as one instance which has been strongly insisted upon. Did the French attack Sardinia when at peace with them? No such thing. The King of Sardinia had accepted of a subsidy from Great Britain; and Sardinia was, to all intents and purposes, a belligerent power. Several other instances might be mentioned; but though, perhaps, in the majority of instances, the French may be unjustifiable, is this the moment for us to dwell upon these enormities—to waste our time and inflame our passions by criminating and recriminating upon each other? There is no end of such a war. I have somewhere read, I think in Sir Walter Raleigh's "History of the World," of a most bloody and fatal battle which was fought by two opposite armies, in which almost all the combatants on both sides were killed, "because," says the historian, "though they had offensive weapons on both sides, they had none for defence." So, in this war of words, if we are to use only offensive weapons—if we are to indulge only in invective and abuse, the contest must be eternal.

If this war of reproach and invective is to be countenanced, may not the French with equal reason complain of the outrages and horrors committed by the powers opposed to them? If we must not treat with the French on account of the iniquity of their former transactions, ought we not to be as scrupulous of connecting ourselves with other powers equally criminal? Surely, sir, if we must be thus rigid in scrutinizing the conduct of an enemy, we ought to be equally careful in not committing ourselves, our honor, and our safety, with an ally who has manifested the same want of respect for the rights of other nations. Surely, if it is material to know the character of a power with whom you are about only to treat for peace, it is more material to know the character of allies with whom you are about to enter into the closest connection of friendship, and for whose exertions you are about to pay. Now, sir, what was the conduct of your own allies to Poland? Is there a single atrocity of the French, in Italy, in Switzerland, in Egypt, if you please, more unprincipled and inhuman than that of Russia, Austria, and Prussia, in Poland? What has there been in the conduct of the French to foreign powers; what in the violation of solemn treaties; what in the plunder, devastation, and dis-

memberment of unoffending countries; what in the horrors
and murders perpetrated upon the subdued victims of their
rage in any district which they have overrun, worse than the
conduct of those three great powers in the miserable, devoted,
and trampled-on kingdom of Poland, and who have been, or
are, our allies in this war for religion and social order, and
the rights of nations? "Oh! but you regretted the partition
of Poland!" Yes, regretted! you regretted the violence, and
that is all you did. You united yourselves with the actors;
you, in fact, by your acquiescence, confirmed the atrocity. But
they are your allies; and though they overran and divided Poland, there was nothing, perhaps, in the manner of doing it
which stamped it with peculiar infamy and disgrace. The hero
of Poland [Suwarrow], perhaps, was merciful and mild! He
was "as much superior to Bonaparte in bravery, and in the
discipline which he maintained, as he was superior in virtue
and humanity!" He was animated by the purest principles of
Christianity, and was restrained in his career by the benevolent
precepts which it inculcates. Was he? Let unfortunate Warsaw, and the miserable inhabitants of the suburb of Praga in
particular, tell! What do we understand to have been the conduct of this magnanimous hero, with whom, it seems, Bonaparte is not to be compared? He entered the suburb of Praga,
the most populous suburb of Warsaw; and there he let his
soldiery loose on the miserable, unarmed, and unresisting people. Men, women, and children, nay, infants at the breast,
were doomed to one indiscriminate massacre! Thousands
of them were inhumanly, wantonly butchered! And for what?
Because they had dared to join in a wish to meliorate their own
condition as a people, and to improve their constitution, which
had been confessed by their own sovereign to be in want of
amendment. And such is the hero upon whom the cause of
religion and social order is to repose! And such is the man
whom we praise for his discipline and his virtue, and whom we
hold out as our boast and our dependence; while the conduct of Bonaparte unfits him to be even treated with as an
enemy?

But the behavior of the French towards Switzerland raises all
the indignation of the right honorable gentleman, and inflames
his eloquence. I admire the indignation which he expresses,

and I think he felt it, in speaking of this country, so dear and so congenial to every man who loves the sacred name of liberty. "He who loves liberty," says the right honorable gentleman, "thought himself at home on the favored and happy mountains of Switzerland, where she seemed to have taken up her abode under a sort of implied compact, among all other states, that she should not be disturbed in this her chosen asylum." I admire the eloquence of the right honorable gentleman in speaking of this country of liberty and peace, to which every man would desire, once in his life at least, to make a pilgrimage! But who, let me ask him, first proposed to the Swiss people to depart from the neutrality, which was their chief protection, and to join the confederacy against the French? I aver that a noble relation of mine [Lord Robert Fitzgerald], then the minister of England to the Swiss Cantons, was instructed, in direct terms, to propose to the Swiss, by an official note, to break from the safe line they had laid down for themselves, and to tell them, "in such a contest neutrality was criminal." I know that noble lord too well, though I have not been in habits of intercourse with him of late, from the employments in which he has been engaged, to suspect that he would have presented such a paper without the express instructions of his Court, or that he would have gone beyond those instructions.

But was it only to Switzerland that this sort of language was held? What was our language also to Tuscany and Genoa? An honorable gentleman [Mr. Canning] has denied the authenticity of a pretended letter which has been circulated, and ascribed to Lord Harvey. He says, it is all a fable and a forgery. Be it so; but is it also a fable that Lord Harvey did speak in terms to the Grand Duke, which he considered as offensive and insulting? I cannot tell, for I was not present; but was it not, and is it not, believed? Is it a fable that Lord Harvey went into the closet of the Grand Duke, laid his watch on the table and demanded, in a peremptory manner, that he should, within a certain number of minutes (I think I have heard within a quarter of an hour), determine, aye or no, to dismiss the French minister, and order him out of his dominions, with the menace, that if he did not, the English fleet should bombard Leghorn? Will the honorable gentleman deny this also? I certainly do not know it from my own knowledge; but I know that persons of the first credit, then at Florence, have stated these facts, and that they have never been contradicted. It is true that, upon the Grand Duke's complaint of this indignity, Lord Harvey was recalled; but was the principle recalled? was the mission recalled? Did not ministers persist in the demand which Lord Harvey had made, perhaps ungraciously? and was not the Grand Duke forced, in consequence, to dismiss the French minister? and did they not drive him to enter into an unwilling war with the republic? It is true that he afterwards made his peace, and that, having done so, he was treated severely and unjustly by the French; but what do I conclude from all this, but that we have no right to be scrupulous, we who have violated the respect due to peaceable powers ourselves, in this war, which, more than any other that ever afflicted human nature, has been distinguished by the greatest number of disgusting and outrageous insults by the great to the smaller powers? And I infer from this, also, that the instances not being confined to the French, but having been perpetrated by every one of the allies, and by England as much as by others, we have no right, either in personal character, or from our own deportment, to refuse to treat with the French on this ground. Need I speak of your conduct to Genoa also? Perhaps the note delivered by Mr. Drake was also a forgery. Perhaps the blockade of the port never took place. It is impossible to deny the facts, which were so glaring at the time. It is a painful thing to me, sir, to be obliged to go back to these unfortunate periods of the history of this war, and of the conduct of this country; but I am forced to the task by the use which has been made of the atrocities of the French as an argument against negotiation. I think I have said enough to prove, that if the French have been guilty, we have not been innocent. Nothing but determined incredulity can make us deaf and blind to our own acts, when we are so ready to yield an assent to all the reproaches which are thrown out on the enemy, and upon which reproaches we are gravely told to continue the war.

"But the French," it seems, "have behaved ill everywhere. They seized on Venice, which had preserved the most exact neutrality, or rather," as it is hinted, "had manifested symptoms of friendship to them." I agree with the right honorable gentleman, it was an abominable act. I am not the apologist, much less the advocate, of their iniquities; neither will I countenance them in their pretences for the injustice. I do not think that much regard is to be paid to the charges which a triumphant soldiery bring on the conduct of a people whom they have overrun. Pretences for outrage will never be wanting to the strong, when they wish to trample on the weak; but when we accuse the French of having seized on Venice, after stipulating for its neutrality, and guaranteeing its independence, we should also remember the excuse that they made for the violence, namely, that their troops had been attacked and murdered. I say I am always incredulous about such excuses; but I think it fair to hear whatever can be alleged on the other side. We cannot take one side of a story only. Candor demands that we should examine the whole before we make up our minds on the guilt. I cannot think it quite fair to state the view of the subject of one party as indisputable fact, without even mentioning what the other party has to say for itself. But, sir, is this all? Though the perfidy of the French to the Venetians be clear and palpable, was it worse in morals, in principle, and in example, than the conduct of Austria? My honorable friend [Mr. Whitbread] properly asked: " Is not the receiver as bad as the thief? " If the French seized on the territory of Venice, did not the Austrians agree to receive it? " But this," it seems, " is not the same thing." It is quite in the nature and within the rule of diplomatic morality, for Austria to receive the country which was thus seized upon unjustly. " The Emperor took it as a compensation. It was his by barter. He was not answerable for the guilt by which it was obtained." What is this, sir, but the false and abominable reasoning with which we have been so often disgusted on the subject of the slave-trade? Just in the same manner have I heard a notorious wholesale dealer in this inhuman traffic justify his abominable trade. " I am not guilty of the horrible crime of tearing that mother from her infants; that husband from his wife; of depopulating that village; of depriving that family of their sons, the support of their aged parents! No, thank Heaven! I am not guilty of this horror. I only bought them in the fair way of trade. They were brought to the market; they had been guilty of crimes, or they had been made prisoners of war; they were accused of witchcraft, of obi, or of some other sort of sorcery; and they were brought to me for sale. I gave a valuable consideration for them. But God forbid that I should have stained my soul with the guilt of dragging them from their friends and families!" Such has been the precious defence of the slave-trade, and such is the argument set up for Austria in this instance of Venice. "I did not commit the crime of trampling on the independence of Venice; I did not seize on the city; I gave a *quid pro quo*. It was a matter of barter and indemnity; I gave half a million of human beings to be put under the yoke of France in another district, and I had these people turned over to me in return! This, sir, is the defence of Austria, and under such detestable sophistry is the infernal traffic in human flesh, whether in white or black, to be continued, and even justified! At no time has that diabolical traffic been carried to a greater length than during the present war, and that by England herself, as well as Austria and Russia.

"But France," it seems, "has roused all the nations of Europe against her;" and the long catalogue has been read to you, to prove that she must have been atrocious to provoke them all. Is it true, sir, that she has roused them all? It does not say much for the address of His Majesty's ministers, if this be the case. What, sir! have all your negotiations, all your declamation, all your money, been squandered in vain? Have you not succeeded in stirring the indignation, and engaging the assistance, of a single power? But you do yourselves injustice. Between the crimes of France and your money the rage has been excited, and full as much is due to your seductions as to her atrocities. My honorable and learned friend [Mr. Erskine] was correct, therefore, in his argument; for you cannot take both sides of the case; you cannot accuse France of having provoked all Europe, and at the same time claim the merit of having roused all Europe to join you.

You talk, sir, of your allies. I wish to know who your allies are? Russia is one of them, I suppose. Did France attack Russia? Has the magnanimous Paul taken the field for social order and religion, or on account of personal aggression? The Emperor of Russia has declared himself Grand Master of Malta, though his religion is as opposite to that of the Knights as ours is; and he is as much considered a heretic by the Church of Rome as we are. The King of Great Britain might, with as much reason and propriety, declare himself the head of the order of the Chartreuse monks. Not content with taking to himself the commandery of this institution of Malta, Paul has even created a married man a knight, contrary to all the most sacred rules and regulations of the order; and yet this ally of ours is fighting for religion! So much for his religion. Let us see his regard to social order! How does he show his abhorrence of the principles of the French, in their violation of the rights of other nations? What has been his conduct to Denmark? He says to her: " You have seditious clubs at Copenhagen; no Danish vessel shall therefore enter the ports of Russia! " He holds a still more despotic language to Hamburg. He threatens to lay an embargo on her trade; and he forces her to surrender up men who are claimed by the French as their citizens, whether truly or not, I do not inquire. He threatens her with his own vengeance if she refuse, and subjects her to that of the French if she comply. And what has been his conduct to Spain? He first sends away the Spanish minister from Petersburgh, and then complains, as a great insult, that his minister was dismissed from Madrid! This is one of our allies; and he has declared that the object for which he has taken up arms is to replace the ancient race of the House of Bourbon on the throne of France, and that he does this for the cause of religion and social order! Such is the respect for religion and social order which he himself displays, and such are the examples of it with which we coalesce.

No man regrets, sir, more than I do, the enormities that France has committed; but how do they bear upon the question as it at present stands? Are we forever to deprive ourselves of the benefits of peace because France has perpetrated acts of injustice? Sir, we cannot acquit ourselves upon such ground. We have negotiated. With the knowledge of these acts of injustice and disorder, we have treated with them twice; yet the right honorable gentleman cannot enter into negotiation with them again; and it is worth while to attend to the reasons that he gives for refusing their offer. The Revolution itself is no more an objection now than it was in the year 1796, when he did negotiate. For the government of France at that time was surely as unstable as it is at present.

The crimes of the French, the instability of their government, did not then prevent him; and why are they to prevent him now? He negotiated with a government as unstable, and, baffled in that negotiation, he did not scruple to open another at Lisle in the year 1797. We have heard a very curious account of these negotiations this day, and, as the right honorable gentleman has emphatically told us, an honest account of them. He says he has no scruple in avowing that he apprehended danger from the success of his own efforts to procure a pacification, and that he was not displeased at its failure. He was sincere in his endeavors to treat, but he was not disappointed when they failed. I wish accurately to understand the right honorable gentleman. His declaration on the subject, then, I take to be, that though sincere in his endeavors to procure peace in 1797, yet he apprehended greater danger from accomplishing his object, than from the continuance of war; and that he felt this apprehension from the comparative views of the probable state of peace and war at that time. I hope I state the right honorable gentleman correctly. I have no hesitation in allowing the fact that a state of peace, immediately after a war of such violence, must, in some respects, be a state of insecurity; but does this not belong, in a certain degree, to all wars? and are we never to have peace, because that peace may be insecure? But there was something, it seems, so peculiar in this war, and in the character and principles of the enemy, that the right honorable gentleman thought a peace in 1797 would be comparatively more dangerous than war. Why, then, did he treat? I beg the attention of the House to this point. He treated " because the unequivocal sense of the people of England was declared to be in favor of a negotiation." The right honorable gentleman, therefore, confesses the truth, that in 1797 the people were for peace. I thought so at the time, but you all recollect that, when I stated it in my place, it was denied. " True," ministers said, " you have procured petitions, but we have petitions also. We all know in what strange ways petitions may be procured, and how little they deserve to be considered as the sense of the people." This was their language at the time; but now we find these petitions did speak the sense of the people, and that it was on this side of the House only the sense of the people was spoken. The majority spoke a contrary language! It hence follows that the unequivocal sense of the people of England may be spoken by the minority of this House, and that it is not always by the test of numbers that an honest decision is to be ascertained. This House decided against what the right honorable gentleman knew to be the sense of the country; but he himself acted upon that sense against the vote of Parliament.

The negotiations in 1796 went off, as my honorable and learned friend [Mr. Erskine] has said, upon the question of Belgium; or, as the right honorable gentleman asserts, upon a question of principle. He negotiated to please the people, but it was defeated on account of a " monstrous principle advanced by France, incompatible with all negotiation." This is now said. Did the right honorable gentleman say so at the time? Did he fairly and candidly inform the people of England that they broke off the negotiation because the French had urged a basis that it was totally impossible for England at any time to grant? No such thing. On the contrary, when the negotiation broke off, they [the ministry] published a manifesto, " renewing, in the face of Europe, the solemn declaration, that whenever the enemy should be disposed to enter on the work of a general pacification in a spirit of conciliation and equity, nothing should be wanting on their part to contribute to the accomplishment of that great object." And, accordingly, in the year 1797, notwithstanding this " incompatible principle," and with all the enormities of the French on their heads, they opened a new negotiation at Lisle. They did not wait for any retraction of this incompatible principle; they did not wait even till overtures were made to them; but they solicited and renewed a negotiation themselves. I do not blame them for this, sir; I say only that it is an argument against the assertion of an " incompatible principle." It is a proof that they did not then think as the right honorable gentleman now says they thought, but that they yielded to the sentiments of the nation, who were generally inclined to peace, against their own judgment; and, from a motive which I shall come to presently, they had no hesitation, on account of the first rupture, to renew the negotiation. It was renewed at Lisle; and this the French broke off after the Revolution at Paris on September 4, 1797. What was the conduct of ministers upon this occasion? One would have

thought, that with the fresh insult at Lisle in their minds, with
the recollection of their failure the year before at Paris, if it
had been true that they found an incompatible principle, they
would have talked a warlike language, and would have an-
nounced to their country and to all Europe that peace was not
to be obtained; that they must throw away the scabbard, and
think only of the means of continuing the contest. No such
thing. They put forth a declaration, in which they said that
they should look with anxious expectation for the moment
when the Government of France should show a disposition and
spirit corresponding with their own; and renewing before all
Europe the solemn declaration, that at the very moment when
the brilliant victory of Lord Duncan might have justified them
to demand more extravagant terms, they were willing, if the
calamities of war could be closed, to conclude peace on the
same moderate and equitable principles and terms which they
had before proposed. Such was their declaration upon that
occasion; and in the discussions which we had upon it in this
House, ministers were explicit. They said that, by that negotiation, there had been given to the world what might be regarded as an unequivocal test of the sincerity and disposition of
a government towards peace or against it. For those who refuse
discussion show that they are disinclined to pacification; and
it is therefore, they said, always to be considered as a test, that
the party who refuses to negotiate is the party who is disinclined
to peace. This they themselves set up as the criterion. Try
them now, sir, by it. An offer is made them. They rashly, and
I think rudely, refuse it. Have they, or have they not, broken
their own test?

But they say "they have not refused all discussion." They
have put a case. They have expressed a wish for the restoration of the House of Bourbon, and have declared that to be an
event which would immediately remove every obstacle to negotiation. Sir, as to the restoration of the House of Bourbon,
if it shall be the wish of the people of France, I, for one, will be
perfectly content to acquiesce. I think the people of France,
as well as every other people, ought to have the government
which they like best, and the form of that government, or the
persons who hold it in their hands, should never be an obstacle
with me to treat with the nation for peace, or to live with them

in amity. But as an Englishman, sir, and actuated by English feelings, I surely cannot wish for the restoration of the House of Bourbon to the throne of France. I hope that I am not a man to bear heavily upon any unfortunate family. I feel for their situation; I respect their distresses; but as a friend of England I cannot wish for their restoration to the power which they abused. I cannot forget that the whole history of the last century is little more than an account of the wars and the calamities arising from the restless ambition, the intrigues, and the perfidy of the House of Bourbon.

I cannot discover, in any part of the labored defence which has been set up for not accepting the offer now made by France, any argument to satisfy my mind that ministers have not forfeited the test which they held out as infallible in 1797. An honorable gentleman [Mr. Canning] thinks that Parliament should be eager only to approach the throne with declarations of their readiness and resolution to support His Majesty in the further prosecution of the war without inquiry; and he is delighted with an address, which he has found upon the journals, to King William, in which they pledged themselves to support him in his efforts to resist the ambition of Louis XIV. He thinks it quite astonishing how much it is in point, and how perfectly it applies to the present occasion. One would have thought, sir, that in order to prove the application he would have shown that an offer had been respectfully made by the Grand Monarque to King William, to treat, which he had peremptorily and in very irritating terms, refused; and that, upon this, the House of Commons had come forward, and with one voice declared their determination to stand by him, with their lives and fortunes, in prosecuting the just and necessary war. Not a word like this; and yet the honorable gentleman finds it exactly a parallel case, and a model for the House on this day to imitate. I really think, sir, he might as well have taken any other address upon the journals, upon any other topic, as this address to King William. It would have been equally in point, and would have equally served to show the honorable gentleman's talent for reasoning.

Sir, I cannot here overlook another instance of this honorable gentleman's candid style of debating, and of his respect for Parliament. He has found out, it seems, that in former periods of our history, and even in periods which have been denominated good times, intercepted letters have been published; and he reads from the gazette instances of such publication. Really, sir, if the honorable gentleman had pursued the profession to which he turned his thoughts when younger he would have learned that it was necessary to find cases a little more apposite. And yet, full of his triumph on this notable discovery, he has chosen to indulge himself in speaking of a most respectable and a most honorable person as any that his country knows, and who is possessed of as sound an understanding as any man that I have the good-fortune to be acquainted with, in terms the most offensive and disgusting, on account of words which he may be supposed to have said in another place. He has spoken of that noble person, and of his intellect, in terms, which, were I disposed to retort, I might say, show himself to be possessed of an intellect which would justify me in passing over in silence anything that comes from him. Sir, the noble person did not speak of the mere act of publishing the intercepted correspondence; and the honorable gentleman's reference to the gazettes of former periods is, therefore, not in point. The noble duke complained of the manner in which these intercepted letters had been published, not of the fact itself of their publication; for, in the introduction and notes to those letters, the ribaldry is such that they are not screened from the execration of every honorable mind even by their extreme stupidity. The honorable gentleman [Mr. Canning] says that he must treat with indifference the intellect of a man who can ascribe the present scarcity of corn to the war. Sir, I think there is nothing either absurd or unjust in such an opinion. Does not the war necessarily, by its magazines, and still more by its expeditions, increase consumption? But when we learn that corn is at this very moment sold in France for less than half the price which it bears here, is it not fair to suppose that, but for the war and its prohibitions, a part of that grain would be brought to this country, on account of the high price which it would command, and that, consequently, our scarcity would be relieved from their abundance? I speak, of course, only upon report; but I see that the prices quoted in the French markets are less, by one half, than the prices in England. There was nothing, therefore, very absurd in what fell from the noble person; and I would really advise the honorable gentleman, when he speaks of persons distinguished for every virtue, to be a little more guarded in his language. I see no reason why he and his friends should not leave to persons in another place, holding the same opinions as themselves, the task of answering what may be thrown out there. Is not the phalanx sufficient? It is no great compliment to their talents, considering their number, that they cannot be left to the task of answering the few to whom they are opposed; but perhaps the honorable gentleman has too little to do in this House, and is to be sent there himself. In truth, I see no reason why even he might not be sent, as well as some others who have been raised to the peerage. But while he continues with us, I really think that the honorable gentleman will find full employment for all his talents in answering the arguments which are urged in this House, without employing them in disparaging one of the finest understandings in this kingdom.

And now, sir, to return to the subject of the negotiation in 1797. It is, in my mind, extremely material to attend to the account which the minister gives of his memorable negotiation of 1797, and of his motives for entering into it. In all questions of peace and war, he says, many circumstances must necessarily enter into the consideration; and that they are not to be decided upon by the extremes. The determination must be made upon a balance and a comparison of the evils or the advantages upon the one side and the other and that one of the greatest considerations is that of finance. In 1797, the right honorable gentleman confesses he found himself peculiarly embarrassed as to the resources for the war, if they were to be found in the old and usual way of the funding system. Now, though he thought, upon his balance and comparison of considerations, that the evils of war would be fewer than those of peace, yet they would only be so, provided that he could establish " a new and solid system of finance " in the place of the old and exhausted funding system; and to accomplish this scheme, it was necessary to have the unanimous assent and approbation of the people. To procure unanimity, he pretended to be a friend to negotiation, though he did not wish for the success of that negotiation, but hoped only through that means he should bring the people to agree to his new and solid system of finance. I trust I state the right honorable gentleman fairly. I am sure that I mean to do so. With these views, then, what does he do? Knowing that, contrary to his declarations in this House, the opinion of the people of England was generally for peace, he enters into a negotiation, in which, as the world believed at the time, and even until this day, he completely failed. No such thing, sir. He completely succeeded! For his object was not to gain peace. It was to gain over the people of this country to a " new and solid system of finance "—that is, to the raising a great part of the supplies within the year, to the triple assessment, and to the tax upon income! And how did he gain them over? By pretending to be a friend of peace, which he was not; and by opening a negotiation which he secretly wished might not succeed! The right honorable gentleman says that in all this he was honest and sincere. He negotiated fairly, and would have obtained the peace, if the French had shown a disposition correspondent to his own; but he rejoiced that their conduct was such as to convince the people of England of the necessity of concurring with him in the views which he had, and in granting him the supplies which he thought essential to their posture at the time. Sir, I will not say that in all this he was not honest to his own purpose, and that he has not been honest in his declarations and confessions this night; but I cannot agree that he was honest to this House, or honest to the people of this country. To this House it was not honest to make them counteract the sense of the people, as he knew it to be expressed in the petitions upon the table, nor was it honest to the country to act in a disguise, and to pursue a secret purpose unknown to them, while affecting to take the road which they pointed out. I know not whether this may not be honesty in the political ethics of the right honorable gentleman; but I know that it would be called a very different name in the common transactions of society, and in the rules of morality established in private life. I know of nothing in the history of this country that it resembles, except, perhaps, one of the most profligate periods —the reign of Charles II, when the sale of Dunkirk might probably have been justified by the same pretence. That monarch also declared war against France, and did it to cover a negotiation by which, in his difficulties, he was to gain a " solid system of finance."

But, sir, I meet the right honorable gentleman on his own ground. I say that you ought to treat on the same principle on which you treated in 1797, in order to gain the cordial co-operation of the people. We want " experience and the evidence of facts." Can there be any evidence of facts equal to that of a frank, open, and candid negotiation. Let us see whether Bonaparte will display the same temper as his predecessors. If he shall do so, then you will confirm the people of England in their opinion of the necessity of continuing the war, and you will revive all the vigor which you roused in 1797. Or will you not do this until you have a reverse of fortune? Will you never treat but when you are in a situation of distress, and when you have occasion to impose on the people?

But you say you have not refused to treat. You have stated a case in which you will be ready immediately to enter into a negotiation, viz., the restoration of the House of Bourbon. But you deny that this is a *sine qua non;* and in your nonsensical language, which I do not understand, you talk of " limited possibilities," which may induce you to treat without the restoration of the House of Bourbon. But do you state what they are? Now, sir, I say, that if you put one case upon which you declare that you are willing to treat immediately, and say that there are other possible cases which may induce you to treat hereafter, without mentioning what these possible cases are, you do state a *sine qua non* of immediate treaty. Suppose I have an estate to sell, and I say my demand is £1,000 for it. For that sum I will sell the estate immediately. To be sure, there may be other terms upon which I may be willing to part with it; but I mention nothing of them. The £1,000 is the only condition that I state at the time. Will any gentleman assert that I do not make the £1,000 the *sine qua non* of the immediate sale? Thus you say the restoration of the Bourbons is not the only possible ground; but you give no other. This is your project. Do you demand a counter-project? Do you follow your own rule? Do you not do the thing of which you complained in the enemy? You seemed to be afraid of receiving another proposition; and, by confining yourselves to this one point, you make it in fact, though not in terms, your *sine qua non.*

But the right honorable gentleman, in his speech, does what

the official note avoids. He finds there the convenient words,
" experience and the evidence of facts." Upon these he goes
into detail; and in order to convince the House that new evidence is required, he reverts to all the earliest acts and crimes
of the Revolution; to all the atrocities of all the governments
that have passed away; and he contends that he must have
experience that these foul crimes are repented of, and that a
purer and a better system is adopted in France, by which he
may be sure that they will be capable of maintaining the relations of peace and amity. Sir, these are not conciliatory words;
nor is this a practicable ground to gain experience. Does he
think it possible that evidence of a peaceable demeanor can
be obtained in war? What does he mean to say to the French
consul? "Until you shall, in war, behave yourself in a peaceable manner, I will not treat with you!" Is there not in this
something extremely ridiculous? In duels, indeed, we have
often heard of such language. Two gentlemen go out and
fight, when, having discharged their pistols at one another, it
is not unusual for one of them to say to the other: "Now I
am satisfied. I see that you are a man of honor, and we are
friends again." There is something, by the by, ridiculous, even
here. But between nations it is more than ridiculous. It is
criminal. It is a ground which no principle can justify, and
which is as impracticable as it is impious. That two nations
should be set on to beat one another into friendship, is too
abominable even for the fiction of romance; but for a statesman seriously and gravely to lay it down as a system upon
which he means to act, is monstrous. What can we say of
such a test as he means to put the French Government to, but
that it is hopeless? It is in the nature of war to inflame animosity; to exasperate, not to soothe; to widen, not to approximate. So long as this is to be acted upon, I say it is in vain to
hope that we can have the evidence which we require.

The right honorable gentleman, however, thinks otherwise;
and he points out four distinct possible cases, besides the re-
establishment of the Bourbon family, in which he would agree
to treat with the French.

1. "If Bonaparte shall conduct himself so as to convince
him that he has abandoned the principles which were objection-
able in his predecessors, and that he will be actuated by a more

moderate system." I ask you, sir, if this is likely to be ascertained in war? It is the nature of war not to allay, but to inflame the passions; and it is not by the invective and abuse which have been thrown upon him and his government, nor by the continued irritations which war is sure to give, that the virtues of moderation and forbearance are to be nourished.

2. " If, contrary to the expectations of ministers, the people of France shall show a disposition to acquiesce in the government of Bonaparte." Does the right honorable gentleman mean to say that because it is a usurpation on the part of the present chief, therefore the people are not likely to acquiesce in it? I have not time, sir, to discuss the question of this usurpation, or whether it is likely to be permanent; but I certainly have not so good an opinion of the French, nor of any people, as to believe that it will be short-lived, merely because it was a usurpation, and because it is a system of military despotism. Cromwell was a usurper; and in many points there may be found a resemblance between him and the present Chief Consul of France. There is no doubt but that, on several occasions of his life, Cromwell's sincerity may be questioned, particularly in his self-denying ordinance, in his affected piety, and other things; but would it not have been insanity in France and Spain to refuse to treat with him because he was a usurper or wanted candor? No, sir, these are not the maxims by which governments are actuated. They do not inquire so much into the means by which power may have been acquired, as into the fact of where the power resides. The people did acquiesce in the government of Cromwell. But it may be said that the splendor of his talents, the vigor of his administration, the high tone with which he spoke to foreign nations, the success of his arms, and the character which he gave to the English name, induced the nation to acquiesce in his usurpation; and that we must not try Bonaparte by his example. Will it be said that Bonaparte is not a man of great abilities? Will it be said that he has not, by his victories, thrown a splendor over even the violence of the Revolution, and that he does not conciliate the French people by the high and lofty tone in which he speaks to foreign nations? Are not the French, then, as likely as the English in the case of Cromwell, to acquiesce in his government? If they should do so, the right honorable gentle-

man may find that this possible predicament may fail him. He may find that though one power may make war, it requires two to make peace. He may find that Bonaparte was as insincere as himself in the proposition which he made; and in his turn he may come forward and say: " I have no occasion now for concealment. It is true that, in the beginning of the year 1800, I offered to treat, not because I wished for peace, but because the people of France wished for it; and besides, my old resources being exhausted, and there being no means of carrying on the war without ' a new and solid system of finance,' I pretended to treat, because I wished to procure the unanimous assent of the French people to this ' new and solid system of finance.' Did you think I was in earnest? You were deceived. I now throw off the mask. I have gained my point, and I reject your offers with scorn." Is it not a very possible case that he may use this language? Is it not within the right honorable gentleman's knowledge of human nature? But even if this should not be the case, will not the very test which you require, the acquiescence of the people of France in his government, give him an advantage-ground in the negotiation which he does not now possess? Is it quite sure, that when he finds himself safe in his seat, he will treat on the same terms as at present, and that you will get a better peace some time hence than you might reasonably hope to obtain at this moment? Will he not have one interest less to do it? and do you not overlook a favorable occasion for a chance which is exceedingly doubtful? These are the considerations which I would urge to His Majesty's ministers against the dangerous experiment of waiting for the acquiescence of the people of France.

3. " If the allies of this country shall be less successful than they have every reason to expect they will be in stirring up the people of France against Bonaparte, and in the further prosecution of the war." And,

4. " If the pressure of the war should be heavier upon us than it would be convenient for us to continue to bear." These are the other two possible emergencies in which the right honorable gentleman would treat even with Bonaparte. Sir, I have often blamed the right honorable gentleman for being disingenuous and insincere. On the present occasion I certainly cannot charge him with any such thing. He has made

to-night a most honest confession. He is open and candid. He tells Bonaparte fairly what he has to expect. " I mean," says he, " to do everything in my power to raise up the people of France against you; I have engaged a number of allies, and our combined efforts shall be used to excite insurrection and civil war in France. I will strive to murder you, or to get you sent away. If I succeed, well; but if I fail, then I will treat with you. My resources being exhausted; even my ' solid system of finance ' having failed to supply me with the means of keeping together my allies, and of feeding the discontents I have excited in France, then you may expect to see me renounce by high tone, my attachment to the House of Bourbon, my abhorrence of your crimes, my alarm at your principles; for then I shall be ready to own that, on the balance and comparison of circumstances, there will be less danger in concluding a peace than in the continuance of war! " Is this political language for one State to hold to another? And what sort of peace does the right honorable gentleman expect to receive in that case? Does he think that Bonaparte would grant to baffled insolence, to humiliated pride, to disappointment, and to imbecility the same terms which he would be ready to give now? The right honorable gentleman cannot have forgotten what he said on another occasion:

" *Potuit quæ plurima virtus*
Esse, fuit. Toto certatum est corpore regni."

He would then have to repeat his words, but with a different application. He would have to say: " All our efforts are vain. We have exhausted our strength. Our designs are impracticable, and we must sue to you for peace."

Sir, what is the question to-night? We are called upon to support ministers in refusing a frank, candid, and respectful offer of negotiation, and to countenance them in continuing the war. Now I would put the question in another way. Suppose that ministers had been inclined to adopt the line of conduct which they pursued in 1796 and 1797, and that to-night, instead of a question on a war address, it had been an address to His Majesty to thank him for accepting the overture, and for opening a negotiation to treat for peace, I ask the gentlemen opposite—I appeal to the whole five hundred and fifty-

eight representatives of the people—to lay their hands upon
their hearts and to say whether they would not have cordially
voted for such an address. Would they, or would they not?
Yes, sir, if the address had breathed a spirit of peace, your
benches would have resounded with rejoicings, and with
praises of a measure that was likely to bring back the blessings
of tranquillity. On the present occasion, then, I ask for the vote
of no gentlemen but of those who, in the secret confession of
their consciences, admit, at this instant, while they hear me,
that they would have cheerfully and heartily voted with the
minister for an address directly the reverse of the one proposed. If every such gentleman were to vote with me, I
should be this night in the greatest majority that ever I had
the honor to vote with in this House. I do not know that the
right honorable gentleman would find, even on the benches
around him, a single individual who would not vote with me.
I am sure he would not find many. I do not know that in this
House I could single out the individual who would think himself bound by consistency to vote against the right honorable
gentleman on an address for negotiation. There may be some,
but they are very few. I do know, indeed, one most honorable
man in another place, whose purity and integrity I respect,
though I lament the opinion he has formed on this subject,
who would think himself bound, from the uniform consistency
of his life, to vote against an address for negotiation. Earl
Fitzwilliam would, I verily believe, do so. He would feel himself bound, from the previous votes he has given, to declare
his objection to all treaty. But I own I do not know more
in either House of Parliament. There may be others, but I
do not know them. What, then, is the House of Commons
come to, when, notwithstanding their support given to the
right honorable gentleman in 1796 and 1797 on his entering
into negotiation; notwithstanding their inward conviction that
they would vote with him this moment for the same measure;
who, after supporting the minister in his negotiation for a solid
system of finance, can now bring themselves to countenance
his abandonment of the ground he took, and to support him
in refusing all negotiation! What will be said of gentlemen
who shall vote in this way, and yet feel, in their consciences, that
they would have, with infinitely more readiness, voted the
other?

Sir, we have heard to-night a great many most acrimonious invectives against Bonaparte, against all the course of his conduct, and against the unprincipled manner in which he seized upon the reins of government. I will not make his defence. I think all this sort of invective, which is used only to inflame the passions of this House and of the country, exceedingly ill-timed, and very impolitic. But I say I will not make his defence. I am not sufficiently in possession of materials upon which to form an opinion on the character and conduct of this extraordinary man. On his arrival in France, he found the government in a very unsettled state, and the whole affairs of the Republic deranged, crippled, and involved. He thought it necessary to reform the government; and he did reform it just in the way in which a military man may be expected to carry on a reform. He seized on the whole authority for himself. It will not be expected from me that I should either approve or apologize for such an act. I am certainly not for reforming governments by such expedients; but how this House can be so violently indignant at the idea of military despotism, is, I own, a little singular, when I see the composure with which they can observe it nearer home; nay, when I see them regard it as a frame of government most peculiarly suited to the exercise of free opinion, on a subject the most important of any that can engage the attention of a people. Was it not the system which was so happily and so advantageously established of late, all over Ireland, and which even now the government may, at its pleasure, proclaim over the whole of that kingdom? Are not the persons and property of the people left, in many districts, at this moment, to the entire will of military commanders? and is not this held out as peculiarly proper and advantageous, at a time when the people of Ireland are freely, and with unbiassed judgments, to discuss the most interesting question of a legislative union? Notwithstanding the existence of martial law, so far do we think Ireland from being enslaved, that we presume it precisely the period and the circumstances under which she may best declare her free opinion. Now, really, sir, I cannot think that gentlemen who talk in this way about Ireland, can, with a good grace, rail at military despotism in France.

But, it seems, " Bonaparte has broken his oaths. He has

violated his oath of fidelity to the constitution of the third year." Sir, I am not one of those who hold that any such oaths ought ever to be exacted. They are seldom or never of any effect; and I am not for sporting with a thing so sacred as an oath. I think it would be good to lay aside all such oaths. Who ever heard that, in revolutions, the oath of fidelity to the former government was ever regarded, or even that, when violated, it was imputed to the persons as a crime? In times of revolution men who take up arms are called rebels. If they fail, they are adjudged to be traitors; but who before ever heard of their being perjured? On the restoration of King Charles II, those who had taken up arms for the Commonwealth were stigmatized as rebels and traitors, but not as men forsworn. Was the Earl of Devonshire charged with being perjured, on account of the allegiance he had sworn to the House of Stuart, and the part he took in those struggles which preceded and brought about the Revolution? The violation of oaths of allegiance was never imputed to the people of England, and will never be imputed to any people. But who brings up the question of oaths? He who strives to make twenty-four millions of persons violate the oaths they have taken to their present constitution, and who desires to reëstablish the House of Bourbon by such violation of their vows. I put it so, sir, because, if the question of oaths be of the least consequence, it is equal on both sides! He who desires the whole people of France to perjure themselves, and who hopes for success in his project only upon their doing so, surely cannot make it a charge against Bonaparte that he has done the same!

"Ah! but Bonaparte has declared it as his opinion that the two governments of Great Britain and of France cannot exist together. After the treaty of Campo Formio he sent two confidential persons, Berthier and Monge, to the Directory, to say so in his name." Well, and what is there in this absurd and puerile assertion, if it were ever made? Has not the right honorable gentleman, in this House, said the same thing? In this at least they resemble one another! They have both made use of this assertion; and I believe that these two illustrious persons are the only two on earth who think it! But let us turn the tables. We ought to put ourselves at times in the place of the enemy, if we are desirous of really examining

with candor and fairness the dispute between us. How may
they not interpret the speeches of ministers and their friends,
in both Houses of the British Parliament? If we are to be
told of the idle speech of Berthier and Monge, may they not
also bring up speeches, in which it has not been merely hinted,
but broadly asserted, that " the two constitutions of England
and France could not exist together "? May not these offences
and charges be reciprocated without end? Are we ever to go on
in this miserable squabble about words? Are we still, as we
happen to be successful on the one side or the other, to bring
up these impotent accusations, insults, and provocations against
each other; and only when we are beaten and unfortunate, to
think of treating? Oh! pity the condition of man, gracious
God, and save us from such a system of malevolence, in which
all our old and venerated prejudices are to be done away, and
by which we are to be taught to consider war as the natural state
of man, and peace but as a dangerous and difficult extremity!

Sir, this temper must be corrected. It is a diabolical spirit,
and would lead to an interminable war. Our history is full of
instances that, where we have overlooked a proffered occasion
to treat, we have uniformly suffered by delay. At what
time did we ever profit by obstinately persevering in war?
We accepted at Ryswick the terms we refused five years before, and the same peace which was concluded at Utrecht
might have been obtained at Gertruydenberg; and as to security from the future machinations or ambition of the French,
I ask you what security you ever had or could have? Did the
different treaties made with Louis XIV serve to tie up his
hands, to restrain his ambition, or to stifle his restless spirit?
At what time, in old or in recent periods, could you safely repose on the honor, forbearance, and moderation of the French
Government? Was there ever an idea of refusing to treat, because the peace might be afterwards insecure? The peace of
1763 was not accompanied with securities; and it was no sooner
made them the French court began, as usual, its intrigues. And
what security did the right honorable gentleman exact at the
peace of 1783, in which he was engaged? Were we rendered
secure by that peace? The right honorable gentleman knows
well that, soon after that peace, the French formed a plan, in
conjunction with the Dutch, of attacking our India possessions,

of raising up the native powers against us, and of driving us
out of India; as they were more recently desirous of doing,
only with this difference, that the cabinet of France formerly
entered into this project in a moment of profound peace, and
when they conceived us to be lulled into a perfect security.
After making the peace of 1783, the right honorable gentleman and his friends went out, and I, among others, came into
office. Suppose, sir, that we had taken up the jealousy upon
which the right honorable gentleman now acts, and had refused
to ratify the peace which he had made. Suppose that we had
said—No! France is acting a perfidious part; we see no security for England in this treaty; they want only a respite in
order to attack us again in an important part of our dominions,
and we ought not to confirm the treaty. I ask you would the
right honorable gentleman have supported us in this refusal?
I say, that upon his present reasoning he ought. But I put it
fairly to him, would he have supported us in refusing to ratify
the treaty upon such a pretence? He certainly ought not, and
I am sure he would not; but the course of reasoning which he
now assumes would have justified his taking such a ground.
On the contrary, I am persuaded that he would have said:
" This security is a refinement upon jealousy. You have security, the only security that you can ever expect to get. It
is the present interest of France to make peace. She will keep
it, if it be her interest. She will break it, if it be her interest.
Such is the state of nations; and you have nothing but your
own vigilance for your security."

    " It is not the interest of Bonaparte," it seems, " sincerely
to enter into a negotiation, or, if he should even make peace,
sincerely to keep it." But how are we to decide upon his sincerity? By refusing to treat with him? Surely, if we mean
to discover his sincerity, we ought to hear the propositions
which he desires to make. " But peace would be unfriendly
to his system of military despotism." Sir, I hear a great deal
about the short-lived nature of military despotism. I wish the
history of the world would bear gentlemen out in this description of it. Was not the government erected by Augustus Cæsar
a military despotism? and yet it endured for six or seven hundred years. Military despotism, unfortunately, is too likely
in its nature to be permanent, and it is not true that it depends

on the life of the first usurper. Though half of the Roman emperors were murdered, yet the military despotism went on; and so it would be, I fear, in France. If Bonaparte should disappear from the scene, to make room, perhaps, for Berthier, or any other general, what difference would that make in the quality of French despotism, or in our relation to the country? We may as safely treat with a Bonaparte, or with any of his successors, be they whom they may, as we could with a Louis XVI, a Louis XVII, or a Louis XVIII. There is no difference but in the name. Where the power essentially resides, thither we ought to go for peace.

But, sir, if we are to reason on the fact, I should think that it is the interest of Bonaparte to make peace. A lover of military glory, as that general must necessarily be, may he not think that his measure of glory is full; that it may be tarnished by a reverse of fortune, and can hardly be increased by any new laurels? He must feel that, in the situation to which he is now raised, he can no longer depend on his own fortune, his own genius, and his own talents, for a continuance of his success. He must be under the necessity of employing other generals, whose misconduct or incapacity might endanger his power, or whose triumphs even might affect the interest which he holds in the opinion of the French. Peace, then, would secure to him what he has achieved, and fix the inconstancy of fortune. But this will not be his only motive. He must see that France also requires a respite—a breathing interval, to recruit her wasted strength. To procure her this respite, would be, perhaps, the attainment of more solid glory, as well as the means of acquiring more solid power, than anything which he can hope to gain from arms, and from the proudest triumphs. May he not, then, be zealous to secure this fame, the only species of fame, perhaps, that is worth acquiring? Nay, granting that his soul may still burn with the thirst of military exploits, is it not likely that he is disposed to yield to the feelings of the French people, and to consolidate his power by consulting their interests? I have a right to argue in this way when suppositions of his insincerity are reasoned upon on the other side. Sir, these aspersions are, in truth, always idle, and even mischievous. I have been too long accustomed to hear imputations and calumnies thrown out upon great and honorable characters,

to be much influenced by them. My honorable and learned
friend [Mr. Erskine] has paid this night a most just, deserved,
and eloquent tribute of applause to the memory of that great
and unparalleled character, who is so recently lost to the world.
I must, like him, beg leave to dwell a moment on the venerable
George Washington, though I know that it is impossible for
me to bestow anything like adequate praise on a character
which gave us, more than any other human being, the example
of a perfect man; yet, good, great, and unexampled as General
Washington was, I can remember the time when he was not
better spoken of in this House than Bonaparte is at present.
The right honorable gentleman who opened this debate [Mr.
Dundas] may remember in what terms of disdain, or virulence,
even of contempt, General Washington was spoken of by gentlemen on that side of the House. Does he not recollect with
what marks of indignation any member was stigmatized as
an enemy to his country who mentioned with common respect
the name of General Washington? If a negotiation had then
been proposed to be opened with that great man, what would
have been said? Would you treat with a rebel, a traitor!
What an example would you not give by such an act! I do
not know whether the right honorable gentleman may not yet
possess some of his old prejudices on the subject. I hope not:
I hope by this time we are all convinced that a republican government, like that of America, may exist without danger or
injury to social order, or to established monarchies. They have
happily shown that they can maintain the relations of peace
and amity with other states. They have shown, too, that they
are alive to the feelings of honor; but they do not lose sight
of plain good sense and discretion. They have not refused to
negotiate with the French, and they have accordingly the hopes
of a speedy termination of every difference. We cry up their
conduct, but we do not imitate it. At the beginning of the
struggle we were told that the French were setting up a set
of wild and impracticable theories, and that we ought not to be
misled by them; that they were phantoms with which we could
not grapple. Now we are told that we must not treat, because, out of the lottery, Bonaparte has drawn such a prize as
military despotism. Is military despotism a theory? One
would think that that is one of the practical things which min-

isters might understand, and to which they would have no particular objection. But what is our present conduct founded on but a theory, and that a most wild and ridiculous theory? For what are we fighting? Not for a principle; not for security; not for conquest; but merely for an experiment and a speculation, to discover whether a gentleman at Paris may not turn out a better man than we now take him to be.

My honorable friend [Mr. Erskine] has been censured for an opinion which he gave, and I think justly, that the change of property in France since the Revolution must form an almost insurmountable barrier to the return of the ancient proprietors. " No such thing," says the right honorable gentleman, " nothing can be more easy. Property is depreciated to such a rate, that the purchasers would easily be brought to restore the estates." I think differently. It is the character of every such convulsion as that which has ravaged France, that an infinite and undescribable load of misery is inflicted upon private families. The heart sickens at the recital of the sorrows which it engenders. The Revolution did not imply, though it may have occasioned, a total change of property; the restoration of the Bourbons does imply it; and such is the difference. There is no doubt but that if the noble families had foreseen the duration and the extent of the evils which were to fall upon their heads, they would have taken a very different line of conduct; but they unfortunately flew from their country. The King and his advisers sought foreign aid, and a confederacy was formed to restore them by military force. As a means of resisting this combination, the estates of the fugitives were confiscated and sold. However compassion may deplore their case, it cannot be said that the thing is unprecedented. The people have always resorted to such means of defence. Now the question is, how this property is to be got out of their hands. If it be true, as I have heard it said, that the purchasers of national and forfeited estates amount to one million and a half of persons, I see no hopes of their being forced to deliver up their property; nor do I even know that they ought. I doubt whether it would be the means of restoring tranquillity and order to a country, to attempt to divest a body of one million and a half of inhabitants, in order to reinstate a much smaller body. I question the policy, even if the thing were practicable; but I assert, that such a body of new proprietors forms an insurmountable barrier to the restoration of the ancient order of things.   Never was a revolution consolidated by a pledge so strong.

But, as if this were not of itself sufficient, Louis XVIII, from his retirement at Mittau, puts forth a manifesto, in which he assures the friends of his house that he is about to come back with all the powers that formerly belonged to his family.   He does not promise to the people a constitution which might tend to conciliate their hearts; but, stating that he is to come with all the old *régime*, they would naturally attach to it its proper appendages of bastiles, *lettres de cachet, gabelle,* etc.; and the *noblesse,* for whom this proclamation was peculiarly conceived, would also naturally feel that, if the monarch was to be restored to all his privileges, they surely were to be reinstated in their estates without a compensation to the purchasers.   Is this likely to make the people wish for the restoration of royalty? I have no doubt but there may be a number of Chouans in France, though I am persuaded that little dependence is to be placed on their efforts.   There may be a number of people dispersed over France, and particularly in certain provinces, who may retain a degree of attachment to royalty; how the Government will contrive to compromise with that spirit I know not.   I suspect, however, that Bonaparte will try.   His efforts have been already turned to that object; and, if we may believe report, he has succeeded to a considerable degree.   He will naturally call to his recollection the precedent which the history of France itself will furnish.   The once formidable insurrection of the Huguenots was completely stifled, and the party conciliated, by the policy of Henry IV, who gave them such privileges and raised them so high in the Government, as to make some persons apprehend danger therefrom to the unity of the empire.   Nor will the French be likely to forget the revocation of the edict; one of the memorable acts of the house of Bourbon, which was never surpassed in atrocity, injustice, and impolicy, by anything that has disgraced jacobinism.   If Bonaparte shall attempt with the Chouans some similar arrangement to that of Henry IV, who will say that he is likely to fail?   He will meet with no great obstacle to success from the influence which our ministers have established with the chiefs, or in the attachment and dependence which they have on our protection.   For what has the right honorable gentleman told them, in stating the contingencies in which he will treat with Bonaparte?   He will excite a rebellion in France. He will give support to the Chouans, if they can stand their ground; but he will not make common cause with them; for, unless they can depose Bonaparte, send him into banishment, or execute him, he will abandon the Chouans, and treat with this very man, whom, at the same time, he describes as holding the reins and wielding the powers of France for purposes of unexampled barbarity.

Sir, I wish the atrocities, of which we hear so much, and which I abhor as much as any man, were, indeed, unexampled. I fear that they do not belong exclusively to the French.   When the right honorable gentleman speaks of the extraordinary successes of the last campaign, he does not mention the horrors by which some of these successes were accompanied.   Naples, for instance, has been, among others, what is called delivered; and yet, if I am rightly informed, it has been stained and polluted by murders so ferocious, and by cruelties of every kind so abhorrent, that the heart shudders at the recital.   It has been said, not only that the miserable victims of the rage and brutality of the fanatics were savagely murdered, but that, in many instances, their flesh was eaten and devoured by the cannibals, who are the advocates and the instruments of social order!   Nay, England is not totally exempt from reproach, if the rumors which are circulated be true.   I will mention a fact, to give ministers the opportunity, if it be false, to wipe away the stain that it must otherwise affix on the British name.   It is said, that a party of the republican inhabitants of Naples took shelter in the fortress of the Castel de Uovo.   They were besieged by a detachment from the royal army, to whom they refused to surrender; but demanded that a British officer should be brought forward, and to him they capitulated.   They made terms with him under the sanction of the British name. It was agreed that their persons and property should be safe, and that they should be conveyed to Toulon.   They were accordingly put on board a vessel; but, before they sailed, their property was confiscated, numbers of them taken out, thrown into dungeons, and some of them, I understand, notwithstanding the British guaranty, actually executed!

Where, then, sir, is this war, which on every side is pregnant with such horrors, to be carried? Where is it to stop? Not till we establish the House of Bourbon! And this you cherish the hope of doing, because you have had a successful campaign. Why, sir, before this you have had a successful campaign.

The situation of the allies, with all they have gained, is surely not to be compared now to what it was when you had taken Valenciennes, Quesnoy, Condé, etc., which induced some gentlemen in this House to prepare themselves for a march to Paris. With all that you have gained, you surely will not say that the prospect is brighter now than it was then. What have you gained but the recovery of a part of what you before lost? One campaign is successful to you; another to them; and in this way, animated by the vindictive passions of revenge, hatred, and rancor, which are infinitely more flagitious, even, than those of ambition and the thirst of power, you may go on forever; as, with such black incentives, I see no end to human misery.

And all this without an intelligible motive. All this because you may gain a better peace a year or two hence! So that we are called upon to go on merely as a speculation. We must keep Bonaparte for some time longer at war, as a state of probation. Gracious God, sir! is war a state of probation? Is peace a rash system? Is it dangerous for nations to live in amity with each other? Are your vigilance, your policy, your common powers of observation, to be extinguished by putting an end to the horrors of war? Cannot this state of probation be as well undergone without adding to the catalogue of human sufferings? "But we must pause!" What! must the bowels of Great Britain be torn out—her best blood be spilled —her treasure wasted—that you may make an experiment? Put yourselves, oh! that you would put yourselves in the field of battle, and learn to judge of the sort of horrors that you excite! In former wars a man might, at least, have some feeling, some interest, that served to balance in his mind the impressions which a scene of carnage and of death must inflict. If a man had been present at the battle of Blenheim, for instance, and had inquired the motive of the battle, there was not a soldier engaged who could not have satisfied his curiosity, and even, perhaps, allayed his feelings. They were fighting, they knew, to repress the uncontrolled ambition of the Grand Monarch. But if a man were present now at a field of slaughter, and were to inquire for what they were fighting—" Fighting!" would be the answer; " they are not fighting; they are paus- ing." " Why is that man expiring? Why is that other writh- ing with agony? What means this implacable fury?" The answer must be: " You are quite wrong, sir; you deceive yourself—they are not fighting—do not disturb them—they are merely pausing! This man is not expiring with agony— that man is not dead—he is only pausing! Lord help you, sir! they are not angry with one another; they have now no cause of quarrel; but their country thinks that there should be a pause. All that you see, sir, is nothing like fighting—there is no harm, nor cruelty, nor bloodshed in it whatever; it is nothing more than a political pause! It is merely to try an experiment—to see whether Bonaparte will not behave him- self better than heretofore; and in the mean time we have agreed to a pause, in pure friendship!" And is this the way, sir, that you are to show yourselves the advocates of order? You take up a system calculated to uncivilize the world—to destroy order—to trample on religion—to stifle in the heart, not merely the generosity of noble sentiment, but the affec- tions of social nature; and in the prosecution of this system, you spread terror and devastation all around you.

Sir, I have done. I have told you my opinion. I think you ought to have given a civil, clear, and explicit answer to the overture which was fairly and handsomely made you. If you were desirous that the negotiation should have included all your allies, as the means of bringing about a general peace, you should have told Bonaparte so. But I believe you were afraid of his agreeing to the proposal. You took that method before. Ay, but you say the people were anxious for peace in 1797. I say they are friends to peace now; and I am confident that you will one day acknowledge it. Believe me, they are friends to peace; although by the laws which you have made, restrain- ing the expression of the sense of the people, public opinion can- not now be heard as loudly and unequivocally as heretofore. But I will not go into the internal state of this country. It is too afflicting to the heart to see the strides which have been made by means of, and under the miserable pretext of, this war, against liberty of every kind, both of power of speech and of writing, and to observe in another kingdom the rapid approaches to that military despotism which we affect to make an argument against peace. I know, sir, that public opinion, if it could be collected, would be for peace, as much now as in 1797; and that it is only by public opinion, and not by a sense of their duty, or by the inclination of their minds, that ministers will be brought, if ever, to give us peace.

I conclude, sir, with repeating what I said before: I ask for no gentleman's vote who would have reprobated the compliance of ministers with the proposition of the French Government. I ask for no gentleman's support to-night who would have voted against ministers, if they had come down and proposed to enter into a negotiation with the French. But I have a right to ask, and in honor, in consistency, in conscience, I have a right to expect, the vote of every honorable gentleman who would have voted with ministers in an address to His Majesty, diametrically opposite to the motion of this night.

ON THE LIBERTY OF THE PRESS

—

BY

JOHN PHILPOT CURRAN

JOHN PHILPOT CURRAN

1750—1817

John Philpot Curran was a self-made man, though he obtained a university education. But he was born (at Newmarket, near Cork) of humble parents; and his person was mean and diminutive. Despite his physical disadvantages he manifested prodigious eloquence and intrepid courage in espousing the cause of political outlaws. He was able to touch the deepest springs of feeling, and to display sentiments of the purest and loftiest humanity. He possessed the charm and fascination often found in his race; he was a winning companion, and his conversation had irresistible magnetism.

He took his degree at Trinity College, Dublin, studied law at the Middle Temple, London, and was admitted to the Bar in 1775, at the age of five-and-twenty. In 1783 he entered the Irish Parliament, where he joined the opposition, of which Grattan was the leader. He was an orator first of all, and by profession; his forensic triumphs constitute his hold on fame; and the accidents of the epoch gave him abundant material for practice.

The insurrectionists of 1798 in Ireland were persecuted by the English government with relentless cruelty, and it fell to Curran to defend many of them, which he did with a courage and ability which gave him an immense reputation. There is hardly anything finer in forensic oratory than many of these speeches; it stirs the blood even of a later generation to read them; the denunciation of injustice and oppression has never been more forcibly and daringly worded, or the wrongs of the victims more feelingly portrayed. It is easy to believe that a man who could speak thus would be accounted " the most popular advocate of his age and country." His speech on " The Liberty of the Press " was delivered in the trial of a newspaper proprietor who had offended the British government.

Nor can one marvel, after reading his attacks upon the prosecutors, that his chief opponent in the courts, Mr. Fitzgibbons, afterwards Lord Clare, should have passed from a professional to a personal animosity against the great Irishman; a challenge passed between them, and a meeting ensued; but this duel followed the modern French fashion in being bloodless. Nobody was hurt, and both gentlemen preserved their honor.

During the vice-royalty of the Duke of Bedford, in 1806, Curran's patriotism was recognized by his appointment as Master of the Rolls, which he retained till 1814. He then resigned and retired with a pension of three thousand pounds a year. He took up his residence near London, and died at Brompton in 1817, in the sixty-seventh year of his life. " His talents," says a contemporary critic, " were of the highest order; his wit, his drollery, his eloquence, his pathos, were irresistible, and the style of his oratory was striking and splendid."

ON THE LIBERTY OF THE PRESS

A ND now, gentlemen, let us come to the immediate subject of the trial,[1] as it is brought before you by the charge in the indictment, to which it ought to have been confined; and also, as it is presented to you by the statement of the learned counsel who has taken a much wider range than the mere limits of the accusation, and has endeavored to force upon your consideration extraneous and irrelevant facts, for reasons which it is my duty to explain. The indictment states simply that Mr. Finnerty has published a false and scandalous libel upon the Lord Lieutenant of Ireland, tending to bring his government into disrepute, and to alienate the affections of the people; and one would have expected that, without stating any other matter, the counsel for the Crown would have gone directly to the proof of this allegation. But he has not done so; he has gone to a most extraordinary length, indeed, of preliminary observation, and an allusion to facts, and sometimes an assertion of facts, at which, I own, I was astonished, until I saw the drift of these allusions and assertions. Whether you have been fairly dealt with by him, or are now honestly dealt with by me, you must be judges. He has been pleased to say that this prosecution is brought against this letter signed *Marcus,* merely

[1] [This speech was delivered before the Commission court, on December 22, 1797, in behalf of Peter Finnerty, the publisher of the Dublin " Press." Finnerty had been indicted for publishing a severe letter, signed *Marcus,* addressed to the Lord Lieutenant of Ireland, in reference to the execution of William Orr. Orr had been tried and executed for administering the oath to a United Irishman. His trial and execution were peculiarly atrocious, because, it was developed soon after the trial, many of the witnesses were perjured, the chief informer was a man of the blackest character, and the jury was openly intimidated, several of them being made drunk while sitting on the case. These facts were communicated to the Lord Lieutenant, and Orr was reprieved three times, but, after a year's delay, was finally executed. A wave of popular indignation swept over Ireland. Medals were struck bearing the words " Remember Orr," and his name became a watch-word of resistance to tyranny. During this period Finnerty's paper published the *Marcus* letter, and he was immediately indicted for libel. Curran, as his counsel, made in his behalf the speech here given. His eloquent plea was unavailing. Finnerty was found guilty, and sentenced to spend one hour in the stocks, and to be imprisoned for two years—a sentence which was carried out. Curran's speech is remarkable in that it was delivered impromptu. He had had no time for preparation, and had seen the briefs in the case only a few minutes before speaking—EDITOR.]

as a part of what he calls a system of attack upon government by the paper called the " Press." As to this I will only ask you whether you are fairly dealt with? Whether it is fair treatment to men upon their oaths, to insinuate to them, that the general character of a newspaper (and that general character founded merely upon the assertion of the prosecutor) is to have any influence upon their minds when they are to judge of a particular publication? I will only ask you what men you must be supposed to be when it is thought that even in a court of justice, and with the eyes of the nation upon you, you can be the dupes of that trite and exploded expedient, so scandalous of late in this country, of raising a vulgar and mercenary cry against whatever man or whatever principle it is thought necessary to put down; and I shall therefore merely leave it to your own pride to suggest upon what foundation it could be hoped that a senseless clamor of that kind could be echoed back by the yell of a jury upon their oaths. I trust you see that this has nothing to do with the question.

Gentlemen of the jury, other matters have been mentioned, which I must repeat for the same purpose—that of showing you that they have nothing to do with the question. The learned counsel has been pleased to say, that he comes forward in this prosecution as the real advocate for the liberty of the press, and to protect a mild and merciful government from its licentiousness; and he has been pleased to add, that the constitution can never be lost while its freedom remains, and that its licentiousness alone can destroy that freedom. As to that, gentlemen, he might as well have said that there is only one mortal disease of which a man can die. I can die the death inflicted by tyranny; and when he comes forward to extinguish this paper in the ruin of the printer by a state prosecution, in order to prevent its dying of licentiousness, you must judge how candidly he is treating you, both in the fact and in the reasoning. Is it in Ireland, gentlemen, that we are told licentiousness is the only disease that can be mortal to the press? Has he heard of nothing else that has been fatal to the freedom of publication? I know not whether the printer of the " Northern Star " may have heard of such things in his captivity, but I know that his wife and children are well apprised that a press may be destroyed in the open day, not by its own licentiousness, but by the licentiousness of a military force.[2] As to the sincerity of the declaration that the State has prosecuted in order to assert the freedom of the press, it starts a train of thought, of melancholy retrospect and direful prospect, to which I did not think the learned counsel would have wished to commit your minds. It leads you naturally to reflect at what times, from what motives, and with what consequences the government has displayed its patriotism by prosecutions of this sort. As to the motives, does history give you a single instance in which the state has been provoked to these conflicts, except by the fear of truth, and by the love of vengeance? Have you ever seen the rulers of any country bring forward a prosecution from motives of filial piety, for libels upon their departed ancestors? Do you read that Elizabeth directed any of those state prosecutions against the libels which the divines of her time had written against her Catholic sister; or against the other libels which the same gentlemen had written against her Protestant father? No, gentlemen, we read of no such thing; but we know she did bring forward a prosecution from motives of personal resentment, and we know that a jury was found time-serving and mean enough to give a verdict which she was ashamed to carry into effect!

I said the learned counsel drew you back to the times that have been marked by these miserable conflicts. I see you turn your thoughts to the reign of the second James. I see you turn your eyes to those pages of governmental abandonment, of popular degradation, of expiring liberty, of merciless and sanguinary persecution; to that miserable period, in which the fallen and abject state of man might have been almost an argument in the mouth of the atheist and blasphemer against the existence of an all-just and an all-wise First Cause; if the glorious era of the Revolution that followed it had not refuted the impious inference, by showing that if man descends, it is not in his own proper motion; that it is with labor and with pain, and that he can continue to sink only until, by the force and pressure of the descent, the spring of his immortal faculties acquires that recuperative energy and effort that hurry him as many miles aloft. He sinks but to rise again. It is at that period that the state seeks for shelter in the destruction of the press; it is in a

[2] The "Northern Star" was a paper published in Belfast, which was broken down and destroyed by the government in the way here referred to.

period like that that the tyrant prepares for the attack upon the people, by destroying the liberty of the press; by taking away that shield of wisdom and of virtue, behind which the people are invulnerable, in whose pure and polished convex, ere the lifted blow has fallen, he beholds his own image, and is turned into stone.[3] It is at those periods that the honest man dares not speak, because truth is too dreadful to be told; it is then humanity has no ears, because humanity has no tongue. It is then the proud man scorns to speak, but like a physician baffled by the wayward excesses of a dying patient, retires indignantly from the bed of an unhappy wretch, whose ear is too fastidious to bear the sound of wholesome advice, whose palate is too debauched to bear the salutary bitter of the medicine that might redeem him; and therefore leaves him to the felonious piety of the slaves that talk to him of life, and strip him before he is cold.

I do not care, gentlemen, to exhaust too much of your attention by following this subject through the last century with much minuteness; but the facts are too recent in your minds not to show you that the liberty of the press and the liberty of the people sink and rise together, and that the liberty of speaking and the liberty of acting have shared exactly the same fate. You must have observed in England that their fate has been the same in the successive vicissitudes of their late depression; and sorry I am to add that this country has exhibited a melancholy proof of their inseparable destiny, through the various and further stages of deterioration down to the period of their final extinction; when the constitution has given place to the sword, and the only printer in Ireland who dares to speak for the people is now in the dock.

Gentlemen, the learned counsel has made the real subject of this prosecution so small a part of his statement, and has led you into so wide a range, certainly as necessary to the object, as inapplicable to the subject of this prosecution, that I trust you will think me excusable in somewhat following his example. Glad am I to find that I have the authority of the same example for coming at last to the subject of this trial. I agree with the learned counsel that the charge made against the Lord Lieuten-

[3] The allusion here is to the shield of Minerva having the head of Medusa in its centre, which turned the beholder into stone.

ant of Ireland is that of having grossly and inhumanly abused the royal prerogative of mercy, of which the King is only the trustee for the benefit of the people. The facts are not controverted. It has been asserted that their truth or falsehood is indifferent, and they are shortly these, as they appear in this publication:

William Orr was indicted for having administered the oath of a United Irishman. Every man now knows what that oath is; that it is simply an engagement, first, to promote a brotherhood of affection among men of all religious distinctions; secondly, to labor for the attainment of a parliamentary reform; and, thirdly, an obligation of secrecy, which was added to it when the convention law made it criminal and punishable to meet by any public delegation for that purpose. After remaining upwards of a year in jail Mr. Orr was brought to his trial; was prosecuted by the State; was sworn against by a common informer by the name of Wheatley, who himself had taken the obligation, and was convicted under the Insurrection Act, which makes the administering such an obligation felony of death. The jury recommended Mr. Orr to mercy. The judge, with a humanity becoming his character, transmitted the recommendation to the noble prosecutor in this case [the Lord Lieutenant]. Three of the jurors made solemn affidavit in court that liquor had been conveyed into their box; that they were brutally threatened by some of their fellow-jurors with capital prosecution if they did not find the prisoner guilty; and that, under the impression of those threats, and worn down by watching and intoxication, they had given a verdict of guilty against him, though they believed him, in their conscience, to be innocent. That further inquiries were made, which ended in a discovery of the infamous life and character of the informer; that a respite was therefore sent once, and twice, and thrice, to give time, as Mr. Attorney-General has stated, for his Excellency to consider whether mercy could be extended to him or not; and that, with a knowledge of all these circumstances, his Excellency did finally determine that mercy should not be extended to him, and that he was accordingly executed upon that verdict.

Of this publication, which the indictment charges to be false and seditious, Mr. Attorney-General is pleased to say that the design of it is to bring the courts of justice into contempt. As to this point of fact, gentlemen, I beg to set you right. To the administration of justice, so far as it relates to the judges, this publication has not even an allusion in any part mentioned in this indictment. It relates to a department of justice that cannot begin until the duty of the judge is closed. Sorry should I be that, with respect to this unfortunate man, any censure should be flung on those judges who presided at his trial, with the mildness and temper that became them, upon so awful an occasion as the trial of life and death. Sure am I, that if they had been charged with inhumanity or injustice, and if they had condescended at all to prosecute the reviler, they would not have come forward in the face of the public to say, as has been said this day, that it was immaterial whether the charge was true or not. Sure I am, their first object would have been to show that it was false; and ready, should I have been an eye-witness of the fact, to have discharged the debt of ancient friendship, of private respect, and of public duty, and upon my oath, to have repelled the falsehood of such an imputation. Upon this subject, gentlemen, the presence of those venerable judges restrains what I might otherwise have said, nor should I have named them at all if I had not been forced to do so, and merely to undeceive you, if you have been made to believe their characters to have any community of cause whatever with the Lord Lieutenant of Ireland. To him alone it is confined, and against him the charge is made, as strongly, I suppose, as the writer could find words to express it, " that the Viceroy of Ireland has cruelly abused the prerogative of royal mercy, in suffering a man under such circumstances to perish like a common malefactor." For this Mr. Attorney-General calls for your conviction as a false and scandalous libel, and after stating himself every fact that I have repeated to you, either from his statement or from the evidence, he tells you that you ought to find it false, though he almost in words admits that it is not false, and has resisted the admission of the evidence by which we offered to prove every word of it to be true.

And here, gentlemen, give me leave to remind you of the parties before you. The traverser⁴ is a printer, who follows that profession for bread, and who at a time of great public misery and terror, when the people are restrained by law from

⁴ The name of traverser is usually given to the defendant in the Irish courts.

debating under any delegated form; when the few constituents
that we have are prevented by force from meeting in their own
persons to deliberate or to petition; when every other newspaper in Ireland is put down by force, or purchased by the
administration (though here, gentlemen, perhaps I ought to beg
your pardon for stating without authority, I recollect, when we
attempted to examine as to the number of newspapers in the pay
of the Castle, that the evidence was objected to), at a season like
this, Mr. Finnerty has had the courage, perhaps the folly, to
print the publication in question, from no motive under heaven
of malice or vengeance, but in the mere duty which he owes to
his family and to the public. His prosecutor is the King's minister in Ireland. In that character does the learned gentleman
mean to say that his conduct is not a fair subject of public observation? Where does he find his authority for that in the law
or practice of the sister country? Have the virtues, or the
exalted station, or the general love of his people preserved the
sacred person even of the royal master of the prosecutor from
the asperity and the intemperance of public censure, unfounded
as it ever must be, with any personal respect to His Majesty, justice, or truth? Have the gigantic abilities of Mr. Pitt, have the
more gigantic talents of his great antagonist, Mr. Fox, protected either of them from the insolent familiarity, and, for aught
I know, the injustice with which writers have treated them?
What latitude of invective has the King's minister escaped upon
the subject of the present war? Is there an epithet of contumely
or of reproach, that hatred or that fancy could suggest, that are
not publicly lavished upon him? Do you not find the words,
" advocate of despotism—robber of the public treasure—murderer of the King's subjects—debaucher of the public morality
—degrader of the constitution—tarnisher of the British Empire," by frequency of use lose all meaning whatsoever, and
dwindling into terms, not of any peculiar reproach, but of
ordinary appellation? And why, gentlemen, is this permitted in
that country? I will tell you why. Because in that country
they are yet wise enough to see that the measures of the state
are the proper subjects for the freedom of the press; that the
principles relating to personal slander do not apply to rulers or
to ministers; that to publish an attack upon a public minister,
without any regard to truth, but merely because of its tendency

to a breach of the peace, would be ridiculous in the extreme.
What breach of the peace, gentlemen, I pray you, is it in such a
case? Is it the tendency of such publications to provoke Mr.
Pitt, or Mr. Dundas, to break the head of the writer, if they
should happen to meet him? No, gentlemen. In that country
this freedom is exercised, because the people feel it to be their
right, and it is wisely suffered to pass by the state, from a consciousness that it would be vain to oppose it; a consciousness
confirmed by the event of every incautious experiment. It is
suffered to pass from a conviction that, in a court of justice at
least, the bulwarks of the constitution will not be surrendered
to the State, and that the intended victim, whether clothed in
the humble guise of honest industry, or decked in the honors
of genius, and virtue, and philosophy; whether a Hardy or a
Tooke, will find certain protection in the honesty and spirit of
an English jury.

But, gentlemen, I suppose Mr. Attorney will scarcely wish
to carry his doctrine altogether so far. Indeed, I remember,
he declared himself a most zealous adocate for the liberty of the
press. I may, therefore, even according to him, presume to
make some observations on the conduct of the existing government. I should wish to know how far he supposes it to extend.
Is it to the composition of lampoons and madrigals, to be sung
down the grates by ragged ballad-mongers, to kitchen maids and
footmen? I will not suppose that he means to confine it to those
ebullitions of billingsgate, to those cataracts of ribaldry and
scurrility that are daily spouting upon the miseries of our
wretched fellow-sufferers, and the unavailing efforts of those
who have vainly labored in their cause. I will not suppose that
he confines it to the poetic license of a birth-day ode. The laureate would not use such language! in which case I do entirely
agree with him, that the truth or the falsehood is as perfectly
immaterial to the law as it is to the laureate, as perfectly unre-
strained by the law of the land as it is by any law of decency,
or shame, or modesty, or decorum. But as to the privilege of
censure or blame, I am sorry that the learned gentleman has
not favored you with his notion of the liberty of the press. Suppose an Irish viceroy acts " a very little absurdly." May the
press venture to be " respectfully comical upon that absurdity "?
The learned counsel does not, at least in terms, give a negative

to that. But let me treat you honestly, and go further, to a more material point. Suppose an Irish viceroy does an act that brings scandal upon his master; that fills the mind of a reasonable man with the fear of approaching despotism; that leaves no hope to the people of preserving themselves and their children from chains, but in common confederacy for common safety. What is an honest man in that case to do? I am sorry the right honorable advocate for the liberty of the press has not told you his opinion, at least in any express words. I will, therefore, venture to give you my humbler thoughts upon the subject.

I think an honest man ought to tell the people frankly and boldly of their peril, and, I must say, I can imagine no villany greater than that of his holding a traitorous silence at such a crisis, except the villany and baseness of prosecuting him, or of finding him guilty for such an honest discharge of his public duty. And I found myself on the known principle of the Revolution of England, namely, that the Crown itself may be abdicated by certain abuses of the trust reposed, and that there are possible excesses of arbitrary power, which it is not only the right, but the bounden duty of every honest man to resist at the risk of his fortune and his life. Now, gentlemen, if this reasoning be admitted, and it cannot be denied, if there be any possible event in which the people are obliged to look only to themselves, and are justified in doing so, can you be so absurd as to say that it is lawful to the people to act upon it when it unfortunately does arrive; but that it is criminal in any man to tell them that the miserable event has actually arrived, or is imminently approaching? Far am I, gentlemen, from insinuating that (extreme as it is) our misery has been matured into any deplorable crisis of this kind, from which I pray that the Almighty God may forever preserve us. But I am putting my principle upon the strongest ground, and most favorable to my opponents; namely, that it never can be criminal to say anything of the government but what is false; and I put this in the extreme, in order to demonstrate to you *a fortiori*, that the privilege of speaking truth to the people, which holds in the last extremity, must also obtain in every stage of inferior importance; and that however a court may have decided before the late act [the Libel Act of Mr. Fox] that the truth was immaterial in case of libel, that since that act no honest jury can be governed by such a principle.

Be pleased now, gentlemen, to consider the grounds upon which this publication is called a libel, and criminal. Mr. Attorney tells you it tends to excite sedition and insurrection. Let me again remind you that the truth of this charge is not denied by the noble prosecutor. What is it, then, that tends to excite sedition and insurrection? " The act that is charged upon the prosecutor, and is not attempted to be denied." And, gracious God! gentlemen of the jury, is the public statement of the King's representative this? " I have done a deed that must fill the mind of every feeling or thinking man with horror and indignation, that must alienate every man that knows it, from the King's government, and endanger the separation of this distracted empire; the traverser has had the guilt of publishing this fact, which I myself acknowledge, and I pray you to find him guilty." Is this the case which the Lord Lieutenant of Ireland brings forward? Is this the principle for which he ventures, at a dreadful crisis like the present, to contend in a court of justice? Is this the picture which he wishes to hold out of himself, to the justice and humanity of his own countrymen? Is this the history which he wishes to be read by the poor Irishman of the south and of the north, by the sister nation, and the common enemy?

With the profoundest respect, permit me humbly to defend his Excellency, even against his own opinion. The guilt of this publication, he is pleased to think, consists in this, that it tends to insurrection. Upon what can such a fear be supported? After the multitudes which have perished in this unhappy nation within the last three years, and which has been borne with a patience unparalleled in the story of nations, can any man suppose that the fate of a single individual could lead to resistance or insurrection? But suppose that it might, what ought to be the conduct of an honest man? Should it not be to apprise the government and the country of the approaching danger? Should it not be to say to the viceroy, " You will drive the people to madness if you persevere in such bloody counsels; you will alienate the Irish nation; you will distract the common force; and you will invite the common enemy." Should not an honest man say to the people, " the measure of your affliction is great, but you need not resort for remedy to any desperate expedients. If the King's minister is defective in humanity or wisdom, his royal master and your beloved sovereign is abounding in both." At such a moment, can you be so senseless as not to feel that any one of you ought to hold such language, or is it possible you could be so infatuated as to punish the man who was honest enough to hold it? Or is it possible that you could bring yourselves to say to your country, that at such a season the press ought to sleep upon its post, or to act like the perfidious watchman on his round that sees the villain wrenching the door, or the flames bursting from the windows, while the inhabitant is wrapped in sleep, and cries out, " Past five o'clock; the morning is fair, and all well ! "

On this part of the case I shall only put one question to you. I do not affect to say that it is similar in all its points; I do not affect to compare the humble fortunes of Orr with the sainted names of Russell or of Sydney; still less am I willing to find any likeness between the present period and the year 1683. But I will put a question to you completely parallel in principle. When that unhappy and misguided monarch had shed the sacred blood which their noble hearts had matured into a fit cement of revolution, if any honest Englishman had been brought to trial for daring to proclaim to the world his abhorrence of such a deed, what would you have thought of the English jury that could have said, " We know in our hearts that what he said was true and honest; but we will say, upon our oaths, that it was false and criminal; and we will, by that base subserviency, add another item to the catalogue of public wrongs, and another argument for the necessity of an appeal to Heaven for redress."

Gentlemen, I am perfectly aware that what I say may be easily misconstrued; but if you listen to me with the same fairness that I address you, I cannot be misunderstood. When I show you the full extent of your political rights and remedies; when I answer those slanderers of British liberty who degrade the monarch into a despot, who degrade the steadfastness of law into the waywardness of will; when I show you the inestimable stores of political wealth so dearly acquired by our ancestors, and so solemnly bequeathed; and when I show you how much of that precious inheritance has yet survived all the prodigality of their posterity, I am far from saying that I stand in need of it all upon the present occasion. No, gentlemen, far, indeed, am I from such a sentiment. No man more deeply than myself deplores the present melancholy state of our unhappy country. Neither does any man more fervently wish for the return of peace and tranquillity through the natural channels of mercy and of justice. I have seen too much of force and of violence, to hope much good from the continuance of them on one side, or retaliation from another. I have seen too much of late of political rebuilding, not to have observed that to demolish is not the shortest way to repair. It is with pain and anguish that I should search for the miserable right of breaking ancient ties, or going in quest of new relations or untried adventures. No, gentlemen, the case of my client rests not upon these sad privileges of despair. I trust that as to the fact, namely, the intention of exciting insurrection, you must see it cannot be found in this publication; that it is the mere idle, unsupported imputation of malice, or panic, or falsehood. And that as to the law, so far has he been from transgressing the limits of the constitution, that whole regions lie between him and those limits which he has not trod; and which I pray to Heaven it may never be necessary for any of us to tread.

Gentlemen, Mr. Attorney-General has been pleased to open another battery upon this publication, which I do trust I shall silence, unless I flatter myself too much in supposing that hitherto my resistance has not been utterly unsuccessful. He abuses it for the foul and insolent familiarity of its address. I do clearly understand his idea; he considers the freedom of the press to be the license of offering that paltry adulation which no man ought to stoop to utter or to hear; he supposes the freedom of the press ought to be like the freedom of a king's jester, who, instead of reproving the faults of which majesty ought to be ashamed, is base and cunning enough, under the mask of servile and adulatory censure, to stroke down and pamper those vices of which it is foolish enough to be vain. He would not have the press presume to tell the Viceroy that the prerogative of mercy is a trust for the benefit of the subject, and not a gaudy feather stuck in the diadem to shake in the wind, and by the waving of the gaudy plumage to amuse the vanity of the wearer. He would not have it say to him that the discretion of the Crown, as to mercy, is like the discretion of a court of justice as to law, and that in the one case as well as the other, wherever the propriety of the exercise of it appears, it is equally a matter of right. He would have the press all fierceness to the people, and all sycophancy to power; he would have it consider the mad and phrenetic depopulations of authority like the awful and inscrutable dispensations of Providence, and say to the unfeeling and despotic spoiler, in the blasphemed and insulted language of religious resignation, " the Lord hath given, and the Lord hath taken away, blessed be the name of the Lord ! "

But let me condense the generality of the learned gentleman's invective into questions that you can conceive. Does he mean that the air of this publication is rustic and uncourtly? Does he mean that when *Marcus* presumed to ascend the steps of the castle, and to address the Viceroy, he did not turn out his toes as he ought to have done? But, gentlemen, you are not a jury of dancing-masters. Or does the learned gentleman mean that the language is coarse and vulgar? If this be his complaint, my client has but a poor advocate. I do not pretend to be a mighty grammarian, or a formidable critic; but I would beg leave to suggest to you in serious humility, that a *free press* can be supported only by the ardor of men who feel the prompting sting of real or supposed capacity; who write from the enthusiasm of virtue or the ambition of praise, and over whom, if you exercise the rigor of grammatical censorship, you will inspire them with as mean an opinion of your integrity as your wisdom, and inevitably drive them from their post; and if you do, rely upon it, you will reduce the spirit of publication, and with it the press of this country, to what it for a long interval has been, the register of births, and fairs, and funerals, and the general abuse of the people and their friends.

But, gentlemen, in order to bring this charge of insolence and vulgarity to the test, let me ask you whether you know of any language which could have adequately described the idea of mercy denied where it ought to have been granted, or of any phrase vigorous enough to convey the indignation which an honest man would have felt upon such a subject? Let me beg of you for a moment to suppose that any one of you had been the writer of this very severe expostulation with the Viceroy, and that you had been the witness of the whole progress of this never-to-be-forgotten catastrophe. Let me suppose that you had known the charge upon which Mr. Orr was apprehended, the charge of abjuring the bigotry which had torn and disgraced his country; of pledging himself to restore the people of his country to their place in the constitution; and of binding himself never to be the betrayer of his fellow-laborers in that enterprise—that you had seen him upon that charge removed from his industry, and confined in a jail—that through the slow and lingering progress of twelve tedious months you had seen him confined in a dungeon, shut out from the common use of air and of his own limbs—that day after day you had marked the unhappy captive, cheered by no sound but the cries of his family, or the clanking of his chains; that you had seen him at last brought to his trial—that you had seen the vile and perjured informer deposing against his life—that you had seen the drunken, and worn-out, and terrified jury give in a verdict of death—that you had seen the same jury, when their returning sobriety had brought back their consciences, prostrate themselves before the humanity of the bench, and pray that the mercy of the Crown might save their characters from the reproach of an involuntary crime, their consciences from the torture of eternal self-condemnation, and their souls from the indelible stain of innocent blood.

Let me suppose that you had seen the respite given, and that contrite and honest recommendation transmitted to that seat where mercy was presumed to dwell—that new and before unheard-of crimes are discovered against the informer—that the royal mercy seems to relent, and that a new respite is sent to the prisoner—that time is taken, as the learned counsel for the Crown has expressed it, to see whether mercy could be extended or not!—that after that period of lingering deliberation passed, a third respite is transmitted—that the unhappy captive himself feels the cheering hope of being restored to a family that he had adored, to a character that he had never stained, and to a country that he had ever loved—that you had seen his wife and children upon their knees, giving those tears to gratitude which their locked and frozen hearts could not give to anguish and despair, and imploring the blessings of eternal Providence upon his head, who had graciously spared the father, and restored him to his children—that you had seen the olive branch sent into his little ark, but no sign that the waters had subsided.

" Alas!
Nor wife, nor children more shall he behold,
Nor friends, nor sacred home ! "

No seraph mercy unbars his dungeon, and leads him forth to light and life, but the minister of death hurries him to the scene of suffering and of shame, where, unmoved by the hostile array of artillery and armed men, collected together to secure, or to insult, or to disturb him, he dies with a solemn declaration of his innocence, and utters his last breath in a prayer for the liberty of his country! Let me now ask you, if any of you had addressed the public ear upon so foul and monstrous a subject, in what language would you have conveyed the feelings of horror and indignation? Would you have stooped to the meanness of qualified complaint? would you have been mean enough? but I entreat your forgiveness, I do not think meanly of you. Had I thought so meanly of you, I could not suffer my mind to commune with you as it has done. Had I thought you that base and vile instrument, attuned by hope and by fear, into discord and falsehood, from whose vulgar string no groan of suffering could vibrate, no voice of integrity or honor could speak—let me honestly tell you, I should have scorned to fling my hand across it; I should have left it to a fitter minstrel. If I do not, therefore, grossly err in my opinion of you, I could use no language upon such a subject as this that must not lag behind the rapidity of your feelings, and that would not disgrace those feelings if it attempted to describe them.

Gentlemen, I am not unconscious that the learned counsel for the Crown seemed to address you with a confidence of a very different kind; he seemed to expect a kind and respectful sympathy from you with the feelings of the Castle, and the griefs of chided authority. Perhaps, gentlemen, he may know you better than I do. If he does, he has spoken to you as he ought. He has been right in telling you that if the reprobation of this writer is weak, it is because his genius could not make is stronger; he has been right in telling you that his language has not been braided and festooned as elegantly as it might; that he has not pinched the miserable plaits of his phraseology, nor placed his patches and feathers with that correctness of millinery which became so exalted a person. If you agree with him, gentlemen of the jury, if you think that the man who ventures at the hazard of his own life, to rescue from the deep, " the drowned honor of his country," must not presume upon the guilty familiarity of plucking it up by the locks, I have no more to say. Do a courteous thing. Upright and honest jurors, find a civil and obliging verdict against the printer! And when you have done so, march through the ranks of your fellow-citizens to your own homes, and bear their looks as ye pass along. Retire to the bosom of your families and your children, and when you are presiding over the morality of the parental board, tell those infants, who are to be the future men of Ireland, the history of this day. Form their young minds by your precepts, and confirm those precepts by your own example; teach them how discreetly allegiance may be perjured on the table, or loyalty be forsworn in the jury box. And when you have done so, tell them the story of Orr. Tell them of his captivity, of his children, of his hopes, of his disappointments, of his courage, and of his death; and when you find your little hearers hanging upon your lips, when you see their eyes overflow with sympathy and sorrow, and their young hearts bursting with the pangs of anticipated orphanage, tell them that you had the boldness and the injustice to stigmatize the man who had dared to publish the transaction!

Gentlemen, I believe I told you before that the conduct of the Viceroy was a small part, indeed, of the subject of this trial. If the vindication of his mere personal character had been, as it ought to have been, the sole object of this prosecution, I should have felt the most respectful regret at seeing a person of his high consideration come forward in a court of public justice in one and the same breath to admit the truth, and to demand the punishment of a publication like the present; to prevent the chance he might have had of such an accusation being disbelieved, and by a prosecution like this, to give to the passing stricture of a newspaper, that life, and body, and action, and reality, that proves it to all mankind, and makes the record of it indelible. Even as it is, I do own I feel the utmost concern that his name should have been soiled by being mixed in a question of which it is the mere pretext and scape-goat. Mr. Attorney was too wise to state to you the real question, or the object which he wished to be answered by your verdict. Do you remember that he was pleased to say that this publication was a base and foul misrepresentation of the virtue and wisdom of the government, and a false and audacious statement to the world, that the King's government in Ireland was base enough to pay informers for taking away the lives of the people? When I heard this statement to-day, I doubted whether you were aware of its tendency or not. It is now necessary that I should explain it to you more at large.

You cannot be ignorant of the great conflict between prerogative and privilege which hath convulsed the country for the last fifteen years. When I say privilege, you cannot suppose that I mean the privileges of the House of Commons; I mean the privileges of the people. You are no strangers to the various modes by which the people labored to approach their object. Delegations, conventions, remonstrances, resolutions, petitions to the Parliament, petitions to the throne. It might not be decorous in this place to state to you with any sharpness the various modes of resistance that were employed on the other side. But you all of you seem old enough to remember the variety of acts of Parliament that have been made, by which the people were deprived, session after session, of what they had supposed to be the known and established fundamentals of the constitution; the right of public debate, the right of public petition, the right of bail, the right of trial, the right of arms for self-defence; until at last even the relics of popular privilege became superseded by military force; the press extinguished; and the state found its last intrenchment in the grave of the constitution. As little can you be strangers to the tremendous confederations of hundreds of thousands of our countrymen, of the nature and the objects of which such a variety of opinions have been propagated and entertained.

The writer of this letter has presumed to censure the recall of Lord Fitzwilliam as well as the measures of the present Viceroy. Into this subject I do not enter; but you cannot yourselves forget that the conciliatory measures of the former noble lord had produced an almost miraculous unanimity in this country; and much do I regret, and sure I am that it is not without pain you can reflect how unfortunately the conduct of his successor has terminated. His intentions might have been the best. I neither know them nor condemn them; but their terrible effects you cannot be blind to. Every new act of coercion has been followed by some new symptom of discontent, and every new attack provoked some new paroxysm of resentment or some new combination of resistance. In this deplorable state of affairs, convulsed and distracted within, and menaced by a most formidable enemy from without, it was thought that public safety might be found in union and conciliation, and repeated applications were made to the Parliament of this kingdom for a calm inquiry into the complaints of the people. These applications were made in vain. Impressed by the same motives, Mr. Fox brought the same subject before the Commons of England, and ventured to ascribe the perilous state of Ireland to the severity of its government. Even his stupendous abilities, excited by the liveliest sympathy with our sufferings, and animated by the most ardent zeal to restore the strength with the union of the empire, were repeatedly exerted without success. The fact of discontent was denied; the fact of coercion was denied; and the consequence was, the coercion became more implacable, and the discontent more threatening and irreconcilable. A similar application was made, in the beginning of this session, in the Peers of Great Britain, by our illustrious countryman, Lord Moira, of whom I do not wonder that my learned friend should have observed how much virtue can fling pedigree into the shade, or how much the transient honor of a body inherited from man is obscured by the lustre of an intellect derived from God. He, after being an eye-witness of this country, presented the miserable picture of what he had seen; and, to the astonishment of every man in Ireland, the existence of those facts was ventured to be denied. The conduct of the present Viceroy was justified and applauded; and the necessity of continuing that conduct was insisted upon as the only means of preserving the constitution, the peace, and the prosperity of Ireland. The moment the learned counsel had talked of this publication as a false statement of the conduct of the government and the condition of the people, no man could be at a loss to see that that awful question which had been dismissed from the Commons of Ireland, and from the Lords and Commons of Great Britain, is now brought forward to be tried by a side wind, and in a collateral way, by a criminal prosecution.

I tell you, therefore, gentlemen of the jury, it is not with respect to Mr. Orr that your verdict is now sought. You are called upon, on your oaths, to say that the government is wise and merciful; that the people are prosperous and happy; that military law ought to be continued; that the British constitution could not, with safety, be restored to this country; and that the statements of a contrary import by your advocates in either country were libellous and false. I tell you these are the questions; and I ask you, can you have the front to give the expected answer in the face of a community who know the country as well as you do? Let me ask you how you could reconcile with such a verdict the jails, the tenders, the gibbets, the conflagrations, the murders, the proclamations that we hear of every day in the streets, and see every day in the country. What are the processions of the learned counsel himself, circuit after circuit? Merciful God, what is the state of Ireland, and where shall you find the wretched inhabitant of this land! You may find him, perhaps, in a jail, the only place of security, I had almost said of ordinary habitation; you may see him flying, by the conflagration of his own dwelling; or you may find his bones bleaching on the green fields of his country; or he may be found tossing upon the surface of the ocean, and mingling his groans with those tempests, less savage than his persecutors, that drift him to a returnless distance from his family and his home. And yet, with these facts ringing in the ears, and staring in the face of the prosecutor, you are called upon to say, on your oaths, that these facts do not exist. You are called upon, in defiance of shame, of truth, of honor, to deny the sufferings under which you groan, and to flatter the persecution that tramples you under foot.

But the learned gentleman is further pleased to say that the traverser has charged the government with the encouragement of informers. This, gentlemen, is another small fact that you are to deny at the hazard of your souls, and upon the solemnity of your oaths. You are upon your oaths to say to the sister country, that the government of Ireland uses no such abominable instruments of destruction as informers. Let me ask you honestly, what do you feel, when in my hearing, when in the face of this audience, you are called upon to give a verdict that every man of us, and every man of you, knows by the testimony of his own eyes to be utterly and absolutely false? I speak not now of the public proclamation of informers, with a promise of secrecy and of extravagant reward. I speak not of the fate of those horrid wretches who have been so often transferred from the table to the dock, and from the dock to the pillory; [5] I speak of what your own eyes have seen day after day, during the course of this commission, from the box where you are now sitting—the number of horrid miscreants who avowed upon their oaths that they had come from the very seat of government, from the Castle, where they had been worked upon by the fear of death and the hopes of compensation to give evidence against their fellows—[I speak of the well-known fact] that the mild and wholesome counsels of this government are holden over these catacombs of living death, where the wretch that is buried a man lies till his heart has time to fester and dissolve, and is then dug up a witness.

Is this fancy, or is it fact? Have you not seen him after his resurrection from that tomb, after having been dug out of the region of death and corruption, make his appearance upon the table, the living image of life and of death, and the supreme arbiter of both? Have you not marked, when he entered, how the stormy wave of the multitude retired at his approach? Have you not marked how the human heart bowed to the supremacy of his power in the undissembled homage of deferential horror? How his glance, like the lightning of heaven, seemed to rive the body of the accused and mark it for the grave, while his voice warned the devoted wretch of woe and death—a death which no innocence can escape, no art elude, no force resist, no antidote prevent. There was an antidote—a juror's oath—but even that adamantine chain, which bound the integrity of man to the throne of eternal justice, is solved and melted in the breath that issues from the informer's mouth. Conscience swings from her mooring, and the appalled and affrighted juror consults his own safety in the surrender of the victim:

> "————*Et quæ sibi quisque timebat,*
> *Unius in miseri exitium conversa tulere.*"

Gentlemen, I feel I must have tired your patience, but I have been forced into this length by the prosecutor, who has thought fit to introduce those extraordinary topics, and to bring a ques-

[5] There were many government witnesses at this time, who so obviously perjured themselves in their testimony, that they were taken immediately to the criminal's box (the dock), and thence, on conviction, to the pillory, where they were sentenced to stand for their perjuries.

tion of mere politics to trial, under the form of a criminal prosecution. I cannot say I am surprised that this has been done, or that you should be solicited by the same inducements and from the same motives, as if your verdict was a vote of approbation. I do not wonder that the government of Ireland should stand appalled at the state to which we are reduced. I wonder not that they should start at the public voice, and labor to stifle or to contradict it. I wonder not that at this arduous crisis, when the very existence of the empire is at stake, when its strongest and most precious limb is not girt with the sword for battle, but pressed by the tourniquet for amputation; when they find the coldness of death already begun in those extremities where it never ends, that they are terrified at what they have done, and wish to say to the surviving parties of that empire, " they cannot say that we did it." I wonder not that they should consider their conduct as no immaterial question for a court of criminal jurisdiction, and wish anxiously, as on an inquest of blood, for the kind acquittal of a friendly jury. I wonder not that they should wish to close the chasm they have opened by flinging you into the abyss. But trust me, my countrymen, you might perish in it, but you could not close it. Trust me, if it is yet possible to close it, it can be done only by truth and honor. Trust me, that such an effect could no more be wrought by the sacrifice of a jury than by the sacrifice of Orr. As a state measure, the one would be as unwise and unavailing as the other. But while you are yet upon the brink, while you are yet visible, let me, before we part, remind you once more of your awful situation. The law upon this subject gives you supreme dominion. Hope not for much assistance from his lordship. On such occasions, perhaps, the duty of the court is to be cold and neutral. I cannot but admire the dignity he has supported during this trial; I am grateful for his patience. But let me tell you it is not his province to fan the sacred flame of patriotism in the jury box. As he has borne with the little extravagances of the law, do you bear with the little failings of the press. Let me, therefore, remind you, that though the day may soon come when our ashes shall be scattered before the winds of heaven, the memory of what you do cannot die. It will carry down to your posterity your honor or your shame. In the presence, and in the name of that ever-living God, I do therefore conjure you to reflect that you have your characters, your consciences, that you have also the character, perhaps the ultimate destiny, of your country in your hands. In that awful name I do conjure you to have mercy upon your country and upon yourselves, and so to judge now as you will hereafter be judged; and I do now submit the fate of my client, and of that country which we yet have in common to your disposal.

THE RIGHTS OF THE IRISH PEOPLE

—

BY

HENRY GRATTAN

HENRY GRATTAN

1746—1820

Grattan was a sturdy and tireless soldier in the cause of Ireland against England in the Irish and English legislatures; and the earnestness of his purpose, and the loftiness of his patriotism, combined with the native skill and felicity of the Celt to make him one of the notable orators of his day. He could not be named in the same category with his mighty countrymen, Burke, Sheridan, or even O'Connell; but he did effective and lasting work, and Ireland had no more faithful son.

He was born in 1746, in Dublin, and lived into his seventy-fifth year, dying in London in 1820. His career was divided between the Irish and the English Parliaments; but the work he did in both was devoted to the same general ends. After taking his degree at Trinity College, Dublin, he studied law in the Middle Temple at London, and was admitted to the Irish bar in 1772; but three years later he joined the opposition in the Irish Parliament. This body was not at that time independent, owing to the effect of the Statute of Drogheda, also known as Poynings's Law, passed in 1494. This provided that all English laws should have force in Ireland; that no Irish Parliament should sit without permission of the English King; and that any laws it might enact should not go into effect until they had been approved by England. By the exertions and eloquence of Grattan, this law was repealed, and the Irish Parliament became independent for the first time in nearly three centuries. After more than twenty years' service, he retired; but reappeared once more in 1800 in order to throw his influence against the proposed union of the Irish with the English legislature. His impassioned appeals were again successful.

He might now reasonably look forward to passing the rest of his days in retirement; but his countrymen could not spare him, and he was elected to the imperial Parliament in 1806, when he was sixty years of age. He retained his seat there until his death. The chief work to which he addressed himself during these years was the advocacy of the emancipation of the Roman Catholics, who were at that period laboring under severe disabilities. The Bill of Toleration, passed for their relief in 1778, had led to the Gordon Riots in 1780; and the dread of the papal influence had become a sort of bogey in England. Grattan's speeches on this theme are full of fire and cogency; nothing that he did reflects upon the whole more credit upon his character and his abilities. Learning, philosophy, argument, and passion, are fused together in these addresses, and even the reading of them stirs the sympathies and rouses indignation against persecution and prejudice. It was a noble theme, worthily handled by a master of his art. The speech entitled " The Rights of the Irish People," was delivered during the discussion of Poynings's Law.

THE RIGHTS OF THE IRISH PEOPLE

Delivered, April 19, 1780, in the Irish House of Commons in moving a Declaration of Irish Rights [1]

I HAVE entreated an attendance on this day, that you might, in the most public manner, deny the claim of the British Parliament to make law for Ireland, and with one voice life up your hands against it.

If I had lived when the ninth of William took away the woollen manufacture, or when the sixth of George I took away your constitution, I should have made a covenant with my own conscience, to seize the first reasonable moment of rescuing my country from the ignominy of such acts of power; or, if I had a son, I should have administered to him an oath that he would consider himself as a person separate and set apart for the discharge of so important a duty.

Upon the same principle am I now come to move a Declaration of Right, the first moment occurring in my time in which such a declaration could be made with any chance of success, and without an aggravation of oppression.

Sir, it must appear to every person that, notwithstanding the import of sugar, and export of woollens, the people of this country are not satisfied; something remains—the greater work is behind—the public heart is not well at ease. To promulgate our satisfaction, to stop the throats of millions with the votes of

[1] [Ireland had been treated by the English, for three centuries, like a conquered nation. A Parliament had indeed been granted her, but by a well-known statute, called Poynings's Act, the English government had power to prevent the Irish Parliament from ever assembling, except for purposes which the King saw reason to approve. Under such an administration, the commercial and manufacturing interests of Ireland were wholly sacrificed to those of the English; the exportation of woollen goods, and of most other articles of English manufacture, and also the direct import of foreign articles, being denied the Irish. These restrictions had been removed in part, on the ground of " expediency," by an act of the British Parliament, passed December 13, 1779, under the terror of the Irish Volunteers, and Mr. Grattan, with the same instrument of compulsion in his hands, now moved the Irish Parliament to a Declaration of Right, which should deny the authority of England to make laws for Ireland—an authority asserted by an act of the British Parliament, passed in the sixth year of George I.—EDITOR.]

Parliament, to preach homilies to the Volunteers, to utter invectives against the people under the pretence of affectionate advice, is an attempt, weak, suspicious, and inflammatory.

You cannot dictate to those whose sense you are instructed to represent.

Your ancestors, who sat within these walls, lost to Ireland trade and liberty. You, by the assistance of the people, have recovered trade. You owe the kingdom a constitution; she calls upon you to restore it.

The ground of public discontent seems to be, " We have gotten commerce, but not freedom." The same power which took away the export of woollen and the export of glass, may take them away again. The repeal is partial, and the ground of repeal is a principle of expediency.

Sir, expedient is a word of appropriated and tyrannical import—expedient is a word selected to express the reservation of authority, while the exercise is mitigated—expedient is the ill-omened expression in the repeal of the American Stamp Act. England thought it " expedient " to repeal that law. Happy had it been for mankind if, when she withdrew the exercise, she had not reserved the right. To that reservation she owes the loss of her American empire, at the expense of millions; and America the seeking of liberty through a scene of bloodshed. The repeal of the Woollen Act, similarly circumstanced, pointed against the principle of our liberty, may be a subject for illuminations to a populace, or a pretence for apostacy to a courtier, but cannot be a subject of settled satisfaction to a free-born, an intelligent, and an injured community.

It is, therefore, they [the people of Ireland] consider the free trade as a trade *de facto,* not *de jure*—a license to trade under the Parliament of England, not a free trade under the charter of Ireland—a tribute to her strength, to maintain which she must continue in a state of armed preparation, dreading the approach of a general peace, and attributing all she holds dear to the calamitous condition of the British interest in every quarter of the globe. This dissatisfaction, founded upon a consideration of the liberty we have lost, is increased when they consider the opportunity they are losing; for, if this nation, after the death-wound given to her freedom, had fallen on her knees in anguish, and besought the Almighty to frame an occasion in which a weak and injured people might recover their rights, prayer could not have asked, nor God have formed, a moment more opportune for the restoration of liberty, than this in which I have the honor to address you.

England now smarts under the lesson of the American war. The doctrine of imperial legislature she feels to be pernicious— the revenues and monopolies annexed to it she found to be untenable. Her enemies are a host pouring upon her from all quarters of the earth—her armies are dispersed—the sea is not hers—she has no minister, no ally, no admiral, none in whom she long confides, and no general whom she has not disgraced. The balance of her fate is in the hands of Ireland. You are not only her last connection—you are the only nation in Europe that is not her enemy. Besides, there does, of late, a certain damp and supineness overcast her arms and councils, miraculous as that vigor which has lately inspirited yours. With you everything is the reverse. Never was there a Parliament in Ireland so possessed of the confidence of the people. You are now the greatest political assembly in the world. You are at the head of an immense army; nor do we only possess an unconquerable force, but a certain unquenchable fire, which has touched all ranks of men like a visitation. Turn to the growth and spring of your country, and behold and admire it!

Where do you find a nation who, upon whatever concerns the rights of mankind, expresses herself with more truth or force, perspicuity or justice—not in the set phrases of the scholiast; not the tame unreality of the courtier; not the vulgar raving of the rabble; but the genuine speech of liberty, and the unsophisticated oratory of a free nation. See her military ardor, expressed not in forty thousand men conducted by instinct, as they were raised by inspiration, but manifested in the zeal and promptitude of every young member of the growing community. Let corruption tremble! Let the enemy, foreign or domestic, tremble! but let the friends of liberty rejoice at these means of safety and this hour of redemption—an enlightened sense of public right, a young appetite for freedom, a solid strength, and a rapid fire, which not only put a Declaration of Right within your power, but put it out of your power to decline one! Eighteen counties are at your bar. There they stand, with the compact of Henry, with the charter of John, and with all the passions of the people! "Our lives are at your service; but our liberties—we received them from God, we will not resign them to man!" Speaking to you thus, if you repulse these petitioners, you abdicate the office of Parliament, you forfeit the rights of the kingdom, you repudiate the instructions of your constituent, you belie the sense of your country, you palsy the enthusiasm of the people, and you reject that good which not a minister—not a Lord North—not a Lord Buckinghamshire—not a Lord Hillsborough, but a certain providential conjuncture, or, rather, the hand of God, seems to extend to you.

I read Lord North's propositions, and I wish to be satisfied, but I am controlled by a paper (for I will not call it a law); it is the sixth of George I. [Here the clerk, at Mr. Grattan's request, read from the act of the sixth of George I, "that the kingdom of Ireland hath been, is, and of right ought to be, subordinate to and dependent upon the Imperial Crown of Great Britain, as being inseparably united to and annexed thereunto; and that the King's Majesty, by and with the consent of the lords spiritual and temporal, and the Commons of Great Britain in Parliament assembled, hath, and of right ought to have, full power and .uthority to make laws and statutes of sufficient force and validity to bind the kingdom and the people of Ireland."]

I will ask the gentlemen of the long robe, is this the law? I ask them whether it is not the practice? I appeal to the judges of the land, whether they are not in a course of declaring that the Parliament of England naming Ireland, binds her? I appeal to the magistrates of Ireland whether they do not, from time to time, execute certain acts of the British Parliament? I appeal to the officers of the army, whether they do not confine and execute their fellow-subjects by virtue of the Mutiny Act of England? And I appeal to this House whether a country so circumstanced is free? Where is the freedom of trade? Where is the security of property? Where the liberty of the people? I here, in this Declaratory Act, see my country proclaimed a slave! I see every man in this House enrolled a bondsman! I see the judges of the realm, the oracles of the law, borne down by an unauthorized power! I see the magistrates prostrate; and I see Parliament witness to these infringements, and silent! I therefore say, with the voice of three millions of people, that, notwithstanding the import of sugar, and export of woollen and kerseys, beetle-wood and prunellas, nothing is safe, satisfactory, or honorable; nothing, except a Declaration of Right! What! Are you, with three millions of men at your back, with charters in one hand and arms in the other, afraid to say, We are a free people? Are you—the greatest House of Commons that ever sat in Ireland, that want but this one act to equal that English House of Commons which passed the Petition of Right, or that other, which passed the Declaration—are you, are you afraid to tell the British Parliament that you are a free people? Are the cities and the instructing counties, who have breathed a spirit that would have done honor to old Rome, when Rome did honor to mankind—are they to be free by connivance? Are the military associations—those bodies whose origin, progress, and deportment have transcended, equalled, at least, anything in modern or ancient story, in the vast line of Northern array—are they to be free by connivance? What man will settle among you? Who will leave a land of liberty and a settled government for a kingdom controlled by the Parliament of another country; whose liberty is a thing by stealth; whose trade a thing by permission; whose judges deny her charters; whose Parliament leaves everything at random; where the hope of freedom depends on the chance that the jury shall despise the judge stating a British act, or a rabble stop the magistrate in the execution of it, rescue your abdicated privileges by anarchy and confusion, and save the constitution by trampling on the government?

But I shall be told that these are groundless jealousies, and that the principal cities, and more than one-half the counties of the kingdom, are misguided men, raising those groundless jealousies. Sir, they may say so, and they may hope to dazzle with illuminations, and they may sicken with addresses, but the public imagination will never rest, nor will her heart be well at ease; never, so long as the Parliament of England claims or exercises legislation over this country. So long as this shall be the case that very free trade (otherwise a perpetual attachment) will be the cause of new discontent. It will create a pride and wealth, to make you feel your indignities; it will furnish you with strength to bite your chain; the liberty withheld poisons the good communicated. The British minister mistakes the Irish character. Had he intended to make Ireland a slave, he should have kept her a beggar. There is no middle policy. Win her heart by a restoration of her right, or cut off the nation's right hand; greatly emancipate, or fundamentally destroy! We may talk plausibly to England; but so long as she exercises a power to bind this country, so long are the nations in a state of war. The claims of the one go against the liberty of the other, and the sentiments of the latter go to oppose those claims to the last drop of her blood.

The English Opposition, therefore, are right; mere trade will not satisfy Ireland. They judge of us by other great nations; by the English nation, whose whole political life has been a struggle for liberty. They judge of us with a true knowledge and just deference for our character, that a country enlightened as Ireland, armed as Ireland, and injured as Ireland, will be satisfied with nothing less than liberty. I admire that public-spirited merchant who spread consternation at the custom-house, and, despising the example which great men afforded, tendered for entry prohibited manufactures, and sought, at his private risk, the liberty of his country. With him, I am convinced it is necessary to agitate the question of right. In vain will you endeavor to keep it back; the passion is too natural, the sentiment too irresistible; the question comes on of its own vitality. You must reinstate the laws.

There is no objection to this resolution except fears. I have examined your fears; I pronounce them to be frivolous. If England is a tyrant, it is you have made her so. It is the slave that makes the tyrant, and then murmurs at the master whom he himself has constituted. I do allow, on the subject of commerce, England was jealous in the extreme; and I do say, it was commercial jealousy; it was the spirit of monopoly. The woollen trade and the Act of Navigation had made her tenacious of a comprehensive legislative authority, and, having now ceded that monopoly, there is nothing in the way of our liberty except our own corruption and pusillanimity. Nothing can prevent your being free, except yourselves; it is not in the disposition of England, it is not in the interest of England, it is not in her force. What! can eight millions of Englishmen, opposed to twenty millions of French, seven millions of Spanish, to three millions of Americans, reject the alliance of three millions in Ireland? Can eight millions of British men, thus outnumbered by foes, take upon their shoulders the expense of an expedition to enslave Ireland? Will Great Britain, a wise and magnanimous country, thus tutored by experience and wasted by war, the French navy riding her channel, send an army to Ireland to levy no tax, to enforce no law, to answer no end whatever, except to spoliate the charters of Ireland, and enforce a barren oppression?

What! has England lost thirteen provinces? has she reconciled herself to this loss, and will she not be reconciled to the liberty of Ireland? Take notice, that the very constitution which I move you to declare, Great Britain herself offered to America: it is a very instructive proceeding in the British history. In 1778 a commission went out with powers to cede to the thirteen provinces of America totally and radically the legislative authority claimed over her by the British Parliament; and the commissioners, pursuant to their powers, did offer to all, or any of the American States, the total surrender of the legislative authority of the British Parliament. I will read you their letter to the Congress. [Here the letter was read, surrendering the power, as aforesaid.] What! has England offered this to the resistance of America, and will she refuse this to the loyalty of Ireland? But, though you do not hazard disturbance by agreeing to this resolution, you do most exceedingly hazard tranquillity by rejecting it. Do not imagine that the question will be over when this motion shall be negatived. No! it will recur in a vast variety of shapes and diversity of places. Your constituents have instructed you, in great numbers, with a powerful uniformity of sentiment, and in a style not the less awful because full of respect. They will find resources in their own virtue, if they have found none in yours. Public pride and conscious liberty, wounded by repulse, will find ways and means of vindication. You are in that situation in which every man, every hour of the day, may shake the pillars of the state. Every court may swarm with questions of right, every quay and wharf with prohibited goods. What shall the judges, what the commissioners, do upon such occasion? Shall they comply with the laws of Ireland against the claims of England, and stand firm where you have trembled? Shall they, on the other hand, not comply; and shall they persist to act against the law? Will you punish them, will you proceed against them, for not showing a spirit superior to your own? On the other hand, will you

not punish them? Will you leave your liberties to be trampled
on by those men? Will you bring them and yourselves, all constituted orders, executive power, judicial power, parliamentary
authority, into a state of odium, impotence, and contempt;
transferring the task of defending public right into the hands
of the populace, and leaving it to the judges to break the laws,
and to the people to assert them? Such would be the consequence of false moderation, of irritating timidity, of inflammatory palliations, of the weak and corrupt hope of compro-
mising with the court before you have emancipated the country.

I have answered the only semblance of a solid reason against
the motion. I will now try to remove some lesser pretences,
some minor impediments; for instance: first, that we have a
resolution of the same kind already in our journals. But how
often was the Great Charter confirmed? Not more frequently
than your rights have been violated. Is one solitary resolution,
declaratory of your rights, sufficient for a country, whose history, from the beginning unto the end, has been a course of violation?

The fact is, every new breach is a reason for a new repair;
every new infringement should be a new declaration, lest charters should be overwhelmed by precedents, and a nation's rights
lost in oblivion, and the people themselves lose the memory of
their own freedom.

I shall hear of ingratitude, and name the argument to despise
it. I know the men who use it are not grateful. They are
insatiate; they are public extortioners, who would stop the tide
of public prosperity, and turn it to the channel of their own
wretched emolument. I know of no species of gratitude which
should prevent my country from being free; no gratitude which
should oblige Ireland to be the slave of England. In cases of
robbery or usurpation, nothing is an object of gratitude, except
the thing stolen, the charter spoliated. A nation's liberty cannot,
like her money, be rated and parcelled out in gratitude. No
man can be grateful or liberal of his conscience, nor woman of
her honor, nor nation of her liberty. There are certain inim-
partable, inherent, invaluable properties not to be alienated
from the person, whether body politic or body natural. With the
same contempt do I treat that charge which says that Ireland is
insatiable; seeing that Ireland asks nothing but that which

Great Britain has robbed her of—her rights and privileges. To say that Ireland is not to be satisfied with liberty, because she is not satisfied with slavery, is folly.

I laugh at that man who supposes that Ireland will not be content with a free trade and a free constitution; and would any man advise her to be content with less?

I shall be told that we hazard the modification of the law of Poynings, and the Judges Bill, and the Habeas Corpus Bill, and the Nullum Tempus Bill; but I ask, have you been for years begging for these little things, and have you not yet been able to obtain them? And have you been contending against a little body of eighty men, in Privy Council assembled, convocating themselves into the image of a Parliament, and ministering your high office; and have you been contending against one man, an humble individual, to you a leviathan—the English Attorney-General, exercising Irish legislation in his own person, and making your parliamentary deliberations a blank, by altering your bills or suppressing them; have you not been able to quell this little monster? Do you wish to know the reason? I will tell you; because you have not been a Parliament, nor your country a people. Do you wish to know the remedy? Be a Parliament, become a nation, and those things will follow in the train of your consequence.

I shall be told that titles are shaken, being vested by force of English acts. But in answer to that, I observe, time may be a title, but an English Act of Parliament certainly cannot. It is an authority which, if a judge would charge, no jury would find, and which all the electors of Ireland have already disclaimed—disclaimed unequivocally, cordially, and universally.

Sir, this is a good argument for an act of title, but no argument against a Declaration of Right. My friend, who sits above me, has a bill of confirmation.[2] We do not come unprepared to Parliament. I am not come to shake property, but to confirm property, and to restore freedom. The nation begins to form—we are mouldering into a people; freedom asserted, property secured, and the army, a mercenary band, likely to be dependent on your Parliament, restrained by law. Never was such a revolution accomplished in so short a time, and with such

[2] A bill to be immediately introduced on passing the Declaration, by which all laws of the English Parliament affecting property were to be confirmed by the Irish Parliament.

public tranquillity. In what situation would those men, who call themselves friends of constitution and of government, have left you? They would have left you without a title (as they stole it) to your estates, without an assertion of your constitution, or a law for your army; and this state of private and public insecurity, this anarchy, raging in the kingdom for eighteen months, these mock-moderators would have had the presumption to call peace.

The King has no other title to his crown than that which you have to your liberty. Both are founded, the throne and your freedom, upon the right vested in the subject to resist by arms, notwithstanding their oaths of allegiance, any authority attempting to impose acts of power as laws; whether that authority be one man or a host, the second James or the British Parliament, every argument for the House of Hanover is equally an argument for the liberties of Ireland. The Act of Settlement is an act of rebellion, or the sixth of George I an act of usurpation. I do not refer to doubtful history, but to living record, to common charters, to the interpretation England has put on those charters (an interpretation made, not by words only, but crowned by arms), to the revolution she has formed upon them, to the King she has established, and, above all, to the oath of allegiance solemnly plighted to the House of Stuart, and afterward set aside in the instance of a grave and moral people, absolved by virtue of those very charters; and as anything less than liberty is inadequate to Ireland, so is it dangerous to Great Britain. We are too near the British nation; we are too conversant with her history; we are too much fired by her example to be anything less than equals; anything less, we should be her bitterest enemies. An enemy to that power which smote us with her mace, and to that constitution from whose blessings we were excluded, to be ground, as we have been, by the British nation, bound by her Parliament, plundered by her Crown, threatened by her enemies, and insulted with her protection, while we returned thanks for her condescension, is a system of meanness and misery which has expired in our determination and in her magnanimity.

That there are precedents against us, I allow; acts of power I would call them, not precedents; and I answer the English pleading such precedents, as they answered their kings when they urged precedents against the liberty of England. Such things are the tyranny of one side, the weakness of the other, and the law of neither. We will not be bound by them; or rather, in the words of the Declaration of Right, no doing, judgment, or proceeding to the contrary shall be brought into precedent or example. Do not, then, tolerate a power, the power of the British government, over this land, which has no foundation in necessity, or utility, or empire, or the laws of England, or the laws of Ireland, or the laws of nature, or the laws of God. Do not suffer that power, which banished your manufactures, dishonored your peerage, and stopped the growth of your people. Do not, I say, be bribed by an export of woollen, or an import of sugar, and suffer that power, which has thus withered the land, to have existence in your pusillanimity. Do not send the people to their own resolves for liberty, passing by the tribunals of justice, and the high court of Parliament; neither imagine that, by any formation of apology, you can palliate such a commission to your hearts, still less to your children, who will sting you in your grave for interposing between them and their Maker, and robbing them of an immense occasion, and losing an opportunity which you did not create and can never restore.

Hereafter, when these things shall be history, your age of thraldom, your sudden resurrection, commercial redress, and miraculous armament, shall the historian stop at liberty, and observe, that here the principal men among us were found wanting, were awed by a weak ministry, bribed by an empty treasury; and when liberty was within their grasp, and her temple opened its folding doors, fell down, and were prostituted at the threshold?

I might, as a constituent, come to your bar and demand my liberty. I do call upon you by the laws of the land, and their violation; by the instruction of eighteen counties; by the arms, inspiration, and providence of the present moment—tell us the rule by which we shall go; assert the law of Ireland; declare the liberty of the land! I will not be answered by a public lie, in the shape of an amendment; nor, speaking for the subjects' freedom, am I to hear of faction. I wish for nothing but to breathe in this our island, in common with my fellow-subjects, the air of liberty. I have no ambition, unless it be to break your chain and contemplate your glory. I never will be satisfied so long as the meanest cottager in Ireland has a link of the British chain clanking to his rags. He may be naked, he shall not be in irons. And I do see the time at hand; the spirit is gone forth; the Declaration of Right is planted; and though great men should fall off, yet the cause shall live; and though he who utters this should die, yet the immortal fire shall outlast the humble organ who conveys it, and the breath of liberty, like the word of the holy man, will not die with the prophet, but survive him.

THE
LIMITATIONS OF FREE SPEECH

—

BY

LORD THOMAS ERSKINE

LORD THOMAS ERSKINE

1750—1823

The third son of a rather impecunious Scotch peer, Thomas Erskine was obliged to look to himself for a living; and after attending school at Edinburgh, and getting some further instruction at St. Andrews University, he was embarked at Leith as a midshipman in the navy. The year of his birth was 1750; and after this early departure from Scotland, he never saw it again until his life was drawing to its close. After serving four years in the navy, he quitted it for the army, in 1768. Two years later he married, and went with his regiment to Minorca for three years. Altogether, his army service lasted six years; but no opportunity for military distinction offered itself, and he was noted chiefly for a remarkable conversational talent; which seems to have led his friends, and chief among them his mother, a woman of talent and discernment—to urge upon him the career of the bar. He took the advice; entered Trinity College, Cambridge, for the degree to which his being the son of a nobleman entitled him; became a student at Lincoln's Inn and was called to the bar in 1778. By an accident, he was almost immediately called upon to plead against a motion of the Attorney-General in the case of Baillie against Lord Sunderland; and his spirit and eloquence were so marked in this maiden effort, that as he left the court he received no less than thirty retainers from attorneys who had heard him. Again, a few months later, he was called on to plead at the bar of the House of Commons in behalf of the publisher Carnan, against the university monopoly in almanacs; his argument was successful, and the reputation he thus gained assured his fortune; and he was engaged in every important case for the ensuing twenty-five years.

In 1783 he was elected member of Parliament for Portsmouth, and retained his seat for that constituency till his elevation to the peerage in 1806. But his speeches in the House were not his chief title to fame as an orator; it was in his forensic efforts that he excelled. His defence of Stockdale from libel in 1789 was one of his most admired achievements; and in 1792 he defended Thomas Paine, when prosecuted for his " Rights of Man." This cost him his place at Attorney-General. Another famous instance of his ability was in the trial of Tooke and others for high treason. In 1802 he was restored to the office of Attorney-General, and on the death of Pitt, he was made a peer and raised to the dignity of Lord High Chancellor. His latter years were somewhat embittered, owing to loss of fortune through unfortunate land investments. He performed a good deal of literary labor in his leisure times, but his ability in this direction was not of the first order. He died in 1823.

THE LIMITATIONS OF FREE SPEECH

Delivered in 1797 at the trial of Williams for the publication of Paine's " Age of Reason "

GENTLEMEN OF THE JURY: The charge of blasphemy, which is put upon the record against the publisher of this publication, is not an accusation of the servants of the Crown, but comes before you sanctioned by the oaths of a grand jury of the country. It stood for trial upon a former day; but it happening, as it frequently does, without any imputation upon the gentlemen named in the panel, that a sufficient number did not appear to constitute a full special jury, I thought it my duty to withdraw the cause from trial, till I could have the opportunity of addressing myself to you who were originally appointed to try it.

I pursued this course from no jealousy of the common juries appointed by the laws for the ordinary service of the court, since my whole life has been one continued experience of their virtues; but because I thought it of great importance that those who were to decide upon a cause so very momentous to the public, should have the highest possible qualifications for the decision; that they should not only be men capable from their educations of forming an enlightened judgment, but that their situations should be such as to bring them within the full view of their country, to which, in character and in estimation, they were in their own turns to be responsible.

Not having the honor, gentlemen, to be sworn for the King as one of his counsel, it has fallen much oftener to my lot to defend indictments for libels than to assist in the prosecution of them; but I feel no embarrassment from that recollection. I shall not be bound to-day to express a sentiment or to utter an expression inconsistent with those invaluable principles for which I have uniformly contended in the defence of others.

375

Nothing that I have ever said, either professionally or person-ally, for the liberty of the press, do I mean to-day to contradict or counteract. On the contrary, I desire to preface the very short discourse I have to make to you with reminding you that it is your most solemn duty to take care that it suffers no injury in your hands. A free and unlicensed press, in the just and legal sense of the expression, has led to all the blessings, both of religion and government, which Great Britain or any part of the world at this moment enjoys, and it is calculated to advance mankind to still higher degrees of civilization and happiness. But this freedom, like every other, must be limited to be enjoyed, and, like every human advantage, may be defeated by its abuse.

Gentlemen, the defendant stands indicted for having pub-lished this book, which I have only read from the obligations of professional duty, and which I rose from the reading of with astonishment and disgust. Standing here with all the privileges belonging to the highest counsel for the Crown, I shall be en-titled to reply to any defence that shall be made for the pub-lication. I shall wait with patience till I hear it.

Indeed, if I were to anticipate the defence which I hear and read of, it would be defaming by anticipation the learned coun-sel who is to make it; since, if I am to collect it from a formal notice given to the prosecutors in the course of the proceedings, I have to expect that, instead of a defence conducted according to the rules and principles of English law, the foundation of all our laws, and the sanctions of all justice, are to be struck at and insulted. What gives the court its jurisdiction? What but the oath which his lordship, as well as yourselves, has sworn upon the gospel to fulfil? Yet in the King's Court, where His Majesty is himself also sworn to administer the justice of Eng-land—in the King's Court—who receives his high authority under a solemn oath to maintain the Christian religion, as it is promulgated by God in the Holy Scriptures, I am nevertheless called upon as counsel for the prosecution to "produce a cer-tain book described in the indictment to be the Holy Bible." No man deserves to be upon the rolls who has dared as an attorney to put his name to such a notice. It is an insult to the authority and dignity of the court of which he is an officer; since it calls in question the very foundations of its jurisdiction. If this is to be the spirit and temper of the defence; if, as I collect from that array of books which are spread upon the benches behind me, this publication is to be vindicated by an attack of all the truths which the Christian religion promulgates to mankind, let it be remembered that such an argument was neither suggested nor justified by anything said by me on the part of the prosecution.

In this stage of the proceedings I shall call for reverence to the sacred Scriptures, not from their merits, unbounded as they are, but from their authority in a Christian country; not from the obligations of conscience, but from the rules of law. For my own part, gentlemen, I have been ever deeply devoted to the truths of Christianity; and my firm belief in the Holy Gospel is by no means owing to the prejudices of education, though I was religiously educated by the best of parents, but has arisen from the fullest and most continued reflections of my riper years and understanding. It forms at this moment the great consolation of a life, which, as a shadow passeth away; and without it, I should consider my long course of health and prosperity, too long perhaps and too uninterrupted to be good for any man, only as the dust which the wind scatters, and rather as a snare than as a blessing.

Much, however, as I wish to support the authority of Scripture from a reasonable consideration of it, I shall repress that subject for the present. But if the defence, as I have suspected, shall bring them at all into argument or question, I must then fulfil a duty which I owe not only to the court, as counsel for the prosecution, but to the public, and to the world, to state what I feel and know concerning the evidences of that religion, which is denied without being examined, and reviled without being understood.

I am well aware that by the communications of a free press, all the errors of mankind, from age to age, have been dissipated and dispelled; and I recollect that the world, under the banners of reformed Christianity, has struggled through persecution to the noble eminence on which it stands at this moment, shedding the blessings of humanity and science upon the nations of the earth.

It may be asked, then, by what means the Reformation would have been effected if the books of the reformers had been suppressed, and the errors of now exploded superstitions had been supported by the terrors of an unreformed state? or how, upon such principles, any reformation, civil or religious, can in future be effected? The solution is easy: let us examine what are the genuine principles of the liberty of the press, as they regard writings upon general subjects, unconnected with the personal reputations of private men, which are wholly foreign to the present inquiry. They are full of simplicity, and are brought as near perfection, by the law of England, as perhaps is attainable by any of the frail institutions of mankind.

Although every community must establish supreme authorities, founded upon fixed principles, and must give high powers to magistrates to administer laws for the preservation of government, and for the security of those who are to be protected by it; yet as infallibility and perfection belong neither to human individuals nor to human establishments, it ought to be the policy of all free nations, as it is most peculiarly the principle of our own, to permit the most unbounded freedom of discussion, even to the detection of errors in the constitution of the very government itself; so as that common decorum is observed, which every state must exact from its subjects and which imposes no restraint upon any intellectual composition, fairly, honestly, and decently addressed to the consciences and understandings of men. Upon this principle I have an unquestionable right, a right which the best subjects have exercised, to examine the principles and structure of the constitution, and by fair, manly reasoning, to question the practice of its administrators. I have a right to consider and to point out errors in the one or in the other; and not merely to reason upon their existence, but to consider the means of their reformation.

By such free, well-intentioned, modest, and dignified communication of sentiments and opinions, all nations have been gradually improved, and milder laws and purer religions have been established. The same principles which vindicate civil controversies, honestly directed, extend their protection to the sharpest contentions on the subject of religious faiths. This rational and legal course of improvement was recognized and ratified by Lord Kenyon as the law of England, in the late trial at Guildhall, where he looked back with gratitude to the labors of the reformers, as the fountains of our religious emancipation, and of the civil blessings that followed in their train. The English constitution, indeed, does not stop short in the toleration of religious opinions, but liberally extends it to practice. It permits every man, even publicly, to worship God according to his own conscience, though in marked dissent from the national establishment, so as he professes the general faith, which is the sanction of all our moral duties, and the only pledge of our submission to the system which constitutes the state.

Is not this freedom of controversy and freedom of worship sufficient for all the purposes of human happiness and improvement? Can it be necessary for either, that the law should hold out indemnity to those who wholly abjure and revile the government of their country, or the religion on which it rests for its foundation? I expect to hear in answer to what I am now saying, much that will offend me. My learned friend, from the difficulties of his situation, which I know from experience how to feel for very sincerely, may be driven to advance propositions which it may be my duty with much freedom to reply to; and the law will sanction that freedom. But will not the ends of justice be completely answered by my exercise of that right, in terms that are decent, and calculated to expose its defects? Or will my argument suffer, or will public justice be impeded, because neither private honor and justice nor public decorum would endure my telling my very learned friend, because I differ from him in opinion, that he is a fool, a liar, and a scoundrel, in the face of the court? This is just the distinction between a book of free legal controversy, and the book which I am arraigning before you. Every man has a right to investigate, with decency, controversial points of the Christian religion; but no man consistently with a law which only exists under its sanctions has a right to deny its very existence, and to pour forth such shocking and insulting invectives as the lowest establishments in the gradation of civil authority ought not to be subjected to, and which soon would be borne down by insolence and disobedience, if they were.

The same principle pervades the whole system of the law, not merely in its abstract theory, but in its daily and most applauded practice. The intercourse between the sexes, which, properly regulated, not only continues, but humanizes and adorns our natures, is the foundation of all the thousand romances, plays, and novels, which are in the hands of everybody. Some of them lead to the confirmation of every virtuous principle; others, though with the same profession, address the imagination in a manner to lead the passions into dangerous excesses; but though the law does not nicely discriminate the various shades which distinguish such works from one another, so as to suffer many to pass, through its liberal spirit, that upon principle ought to be suppressed, would it or does it tolerate, or does any decent man contend that it ought to pass by unpunished, libels of the most shameless obscenity, manifestly pointed to debauch innocence and to blast and poison the morals of the rising generation? This is only another illustration to demonstrate the obvious distinction between the work of an author who fairly exercises the powers of his mind in investigating the religion or government of any country, and him who attacks the rational existence of every religion or government, and brands with absurdity and folly the state which sanctions, and the obedient tools who cherish, the delusion. But this publication appears to me to be as cruel and mischievous in its effects, as it is manifestly illegal in its principles; because it strikes at the best—sometimes, alas!—the only refuge and consolation amidst the distresses and afflictions of the world. The poor and humble, whom it affects to pity, may be stabbed to the heart by it. They have more occasion for firm hopes beyond the grave than the rich and prosperous who have other comforts to render life delightful. I can conceive a distressed but virtuous man, surrounded by his children looking up to him for bread when he has none to give them; sinking under the last day's labor, and unequal to the next, yet still, supported by confidence in the hour when all tears shall be wiped from the eyes of affliction, bearing the burden laid upon him by a mysterious Providence which he adores, and anticipating with exultation the revealed promises of his Creator, when he shall be greater than the greatest, and happier than the happiest of mankind. What a change in such a mind might be wrought by such a merciless publication? Gentlemen, whether these remarks are the overcharged declamations of an accusing counsel, or the just reflections of a man anxious for the public happiness, which is best secured by the morals of a nation, will be soon settled by an appeal to the passages in the work, that are selected by the indictment for your consideration and judgment. You are at liberty to conᵤect them with every context and sequel, and to bestow upon them the mildest interpretations. [Here Mr. Erskine read several of the selected passages, and then proceeded as follows:]

Gentlemen, it would be useless and disgusting to enumerate the other passages within the scope of the indictment. How any man can rationally vindicate the publication of such a book, in a country where the Christian religion is the very foundation of the law of the land, I am totally at a loss to conceive, and have no ideas for the discussion of. How is a tribunal whose whole jurisdiction is founded upon the solemn belief and practice of what is here denied as falsehood, and reprobated as impiety, to deal with such an anomalous defence? Upon what principle is it even offered to the court, whose authority is contemned and mocked at? If the religion proposed to be called in question, is not previously adopted in belief and solemnly acted upon, what authority has the court to pass any judgment at all of acquittal or condemnation? Why am I now or upon any other occasion to submit to his lordship's authority? Why am I now or at any time to address twelve of my equals, as I am now addressing you, with reverence and submission? Under what sanction are the witnesses to give their evidence, without which there can be no trial? Under what obligations can I call upon you, the jury representing your country, to administer justice? Surely upon no other than that you are sworn to administer it, under the oaths you have taken. The whole judicial fabric, from the King's sovereign authority to the lowest office of magistracy, has no other foundation. The whole is built, both in form and substance, upon the same oath of every one of its ministers to do justice, as God shall help them hereafter. What God? And what hereafter? That God, undoubtedly, who has commanded kings to rule, and judges to decree justice; who has said to witnesses, not only by the voice of nature but in revealed commandments, " Thou shalt not bear false testimony against thy neighbor "; and who has enforced obedience to them by the revelation of the unutterable blessings which shall attend their observance, and the awful punishments which shall await upon their transgression.

But it seems this is an age of reason, and the time and the person are at last arrived that are to dissipate the errors which have overspread the past generations of ignorance. The be-

lievers in Christianity are many, but it belongs to the few that
are wise to correct their credulity. Belief is an act of reason,
and superior reason may, therefore, dictate to the weak. In
running the mind over the long list of sincere and devout Christians, I cannot help lamenting that Newton had not lived to this
day, to have had his shallowness filled up with this new flood
of light. But the subject is too awful for irony, I will speak
plainly and directly. Newton was a Christian; Newton, whose
mind burst forth from the fetters fastened by nature upon our
finite conceptions; Newton, whose science was truth, and the
foundations of whose knowledge of it was philosophy; not
those visionary and arrogant presumptions which too often
usurp its name, but philosophy resting upon the basis of mathe-
matics, which, like figures, cannot lie; Newton, who carried the
line and rule to the uttermost barriers of creation, and explored
the principles by which all created matter exists and is held together. But this extraordinary man, in the mighty reach of his
mind, overlooked, perhaps, the errors which a minuter investigation of the created things on this earth might have taught
him. What shall then be said of Mr. Boyle, who looked into the
organic structure of all matter, even to the inanimate substances
which the foot treads upon? Such a man may be supposed to
have been equally qualified with Mr. Paine to look up through
nature to nature's God; yet the result of all his contemplations
was the most confirmed and devout belief in all which the other
holds in contempt, as despicable and drivelling superstition.
But this error might, perhaps, arise from a want of due attention to the foundations of human judgment and the structure
of that understanding which God has given us for the investigation of truth. Let that question be answered by Mr. Locke,
who to the highest pitch of devotion and adoration was a
Christian; Mr. Locke, whose office was to detect the errors
of thinking, by going up to the very fountains of thought,
and to direct into the proper track of reasoning the devious
mind of man, by showing him its whole process, from the first
perceptions of sense to the last conclusions of ratiocination;
putting a rein upon false opinion, by practical rules for the conduct of human judgment.

But these men, it may be said, were only deep thinkers, and
lived in their closets, unaccustomed to the traffic of the world,

and to the laws which practically regulate mankind. Gentlemen, in the place where we now sit to administer the justice of
this great country, the never-to-be-forgotten Sir Matthew Hale
presided; whose faith in Christianity is an exalted commentary
upon its truth and reason, and whose life was a glorious example
of its fruits; whose justice, drawn, from the pure fountain of
the Christian dispensation, will be, in all ages, a subject of the
highest reverence and admiration. But it is said by the author,
that the Christian fable is but the tale of the more ancient superstitions of the world, and may be easily detected by a proper understanding of the mythologies of the heathens. Did Milton
understand those mythologies? Was he less versed than Mr.
Paine in the superstitions of the world? No; they were the
subject of his immortal song; and, though shut out from all
recurrence to them, he poured them forth from the stores of a
memory rich with all that man ever knew, and laid them in their
order as the illustration of real and exalted faith, the unquestionable source of that fervid genius which has cast a kind of
shade upon most of the other works of man:

> " He pass'd the flaming bounds of place and time:
>   The living throne, the sapphire blaze,
>   Where angels tremble while they gaze,
>   He saw, but blasted with excess of light,
>   Closed his eyes in endless night."

But it was the light of the body only that was extinguished:
" The celestial light shone inward, and enabled him to justify the
ways of God to man." The result of his thinking was, nevertheless, not quite the same as the author's before us. The mysterious incarnation of our blessed Saviour, which this work
blasphemes in words so wholly unfit for the mouth of a Christian, or for the ear of a court of justice, that I dare not, and will
not, give them utterance, Milton made the grand conclusion
of his " Paradise Lost," the rest from his finished labors, and
the ultimate hope, expectation, and glory of the world.

> " A virgin is his mother, but his sire,
>   The power of the Most High; he shall ascend
>   The throne hereditary, and bound his reign
>   With earth's wide bounds, his glory with the heavens."

The immortal poet having thus put into the mouth of the angel the prophecy of man's redemption, follows it with that solemn and beautiful admonition, addressed in the poem to our great first parent, but intended as an address to his posterity through all generations:

> " This having learn'd, thou hast attain'd the sum
> Of wisdom; hope no higher, though all the stars
> Thou knew'st by name, and all th' ethereal powers,
> All secrets of the deep, all nature's works,
> Or works of God in heaven, air, earth, or sea,
> And all the riches of this world enjoy'dst,
> And all the rule, one empire; only add
> Deeds to thy knowledge answerable, add faith,
> And virtue, patience, temperance, add love,
> By name to some call'd charity, the soul
> Of all the rest; then wilt thou not be loth
> To leave this paradise, but shalt possess
> A paradise within thee, happier far."

Thus, you find all that is great, or wise, or splendid, or illustrious, amongst created things; all the minds gifted beyond ordinary nature, if not inspired by its universal Author for the advancement and dignity of the world, though divided by distant ages, and by clashing opinions, yet joining as it were in one sublime chorus, to celebrate the truths of Christianity; laying upon its holy altars the never-fading offerings of their immortal wisdom.

Against all this concurring testimony, we find suddenly, from the author of this book, that the Bible teaches nothing but " lies, obscenity, cruelty, and injustice." Had he ever read our Saviour's Sermon on the Mount, in which the great principles of our faith and duty are summed up? Let us all but read and practise it, and lies, obscenity, cruelty, and injustice, and all human wickedness, will be banished from the world!

Gentlemen, there is but one consideration more, which I cannot possibly omit, because I confess it affects me very deeply. The author of this book has written largely on public liberty and government; and this last performance, which I am now prosecuting, has, on that account, been more widely circulated, and principally among those who attached themselves from principle to his former works. This circumstance renders a public attack upon all revealed religion from such a writer infinitely more dangerous. The religious and moral sense of the people of Great Britain is the great anchor which alone can hold the vessel of the state amidst the storms which agitate the world; and if the mass of the people were debauched from the principles of religion, the true basis of that humanity, charity, and benevolence, which have been so long the national characteristic, instead of mixing myself, as I sometimes have done, in political reformations, I would retire to the uttermost corners of the earth, to avoid their agitation; and would bear, not only the imperfections and abuses complained of in our own wise establishment, but even the worst government that ever existed in the world, rather than go to the work of reformation with a multitude set free from all the charities of Christianity, who had no other sense of God's existence, than was to be collected from Mr. Paine's observations of nature, which the mass of mankind have no leisure to contemplate, which promises no future rewards to animate the good in the glorious pursuit of human happiness, nor punishments to deter the wicked from destroying it even in its birth. The people of England are a religious people, and, with the blessing of God, so far as it is in my power, I will lend my aid to keep them so.

I have no objections to the most extended and free discussions upon doctrinal points of the Christian religion; and though the law of England does not permit it, I do not dread the reasonings of deists against the existence of Christianity itself, because, as was said by its divine author, if it be of God, it will stand. An intellectual book, however erroneous, addressed to the intellectual world upon so profound and complicated a subject, can never work the mischief which this indictment is calculated to repress. Such works will only incite the minds of men enlightened by study, to a closer investigation of a subject well worthy of their deepest and continued contemplation. The powers of the mind are given for human improvement in the progress of human existence. The changes produced by such reciprocations of lights and intelligences are certain in their progression, and make their way imperceptibly, by the final and irresistible power of truth. If Christianity be founded in falsehood, let us become deists in this manner, and I am contented. But this book has no such object, and no such capacity; it presents no arguments to the wise and enlightened; on the contrary, it treats the faith and opinions of the wisest with the most shocking contempt, and stirs up men, without the advantages of learning, or sober thinking, to a total disbelief of everything hitherto held sacred; and consequently to a rejection of all the laws and ordinances of the State, which stand only upon the assumption of their truth.

Gentlemen, I cannot conclude without expressing the deepest regret at all attacks upon the Christian religion by authors who profess to promote the civil liberties of the world. For under what other auspices than Christianity have the lost and subverted liberties of mankind in former ages been reasserted? By what zeal, but the warm zeal of devout Christians, have English liberties been redeemed and consecrated? Under what other sanctions, even in our own days, have liberty and happiness been spreading to the uttermost corners of the earth? What work of civilization, what Commonwealth of greatness, has this bald religion of nature ever established? We see, on the contrary, the nations that have no other light than that of nature to direct them, sunk in barbarism, or slaves to arbitrary governments; whilst under the Christian dispensation, the great career of the world has been slowly but clearly advancing, lighter at every step from the encouraging prophecies of the gospel, and leading, I trust, in the end to universal and eternal happiness. Each generation of mankind can see but a few revolving links of this mighty and mysterious chain; but by doing our several duties in our allotted stations, we are sure that we are fulfilling the purposes of our existence. You, I trust, will fulfil yours this day.

SPEECH AT THE TRIAL OF WARREN HASTINGS

—

BY

RICHARD BRINSLEY SHERIDAN

RICHARD BRINSLEY SHERIDAN

1751—1816

The marvellous breadth of human nature could hardly be better illustrated than by the fact that two such man as Burke and Sheridan were contemporaries. Both were Irishmen, born in Dublin, both orators and members of the Whig party, associated in Parliament; and both were orators of the very highest calibre and genius; and yet no two men could well have been more different in all that goes to make character. Sheridan was more the typical Celt than Burke; he overflowed with the purest wit and humor, and was gifted with the wider variety of talent. But he had, what not all Irishmen possess, extraordinary powers of application and sustained diligence, and the faculty not merely of imagining great things, but of doing them. He had already lived one life and achieved a national reputation, before he entered politics; yet a political career had always been his prime ambition; and after he had conquered the stage and made a fortune from it, he turned to Parliament as the consummation of his hopes. For a time, fortune seemed disposed to deny him the high place he coveted here; the very renown which he gathered elsewhere stood in his way; but he was not the man to be defeated by a first rebuff; he only applied himself more persistently to his task, and presently his hour of triumph came, and it was as complete as he could have desired.

Richard Brinsley Butler Sheridan was born in 1751, got his education at Harrow School, married a pretty singer, and settled in London in 1773. Within seven years he had written all his incomparable plays, making him the first dramatist of the age. Among them are "The Rivals," "The Critic," and the "School for Scandal." In 1780 he entered Parliament as Whig member for Stafford; four years later he had been Under-Secretary for Foreign Affairs and Secretary of the Treasury; and in 1787, at the trial of Warren Hastings, he had put the cap-stone to the edifice of his renown by delivering that speech, of which Burke declared that it was the most astonishing effort of eloquence of which there is any record or tradition. Sheridan was then thirty-six years old, and had been in London fourteen years.

In fact he was a man who could not fail. His literary training had given that appreciation of the force and value of words—that discrimination and felicity in their employment, and that wealth and readiness of resource which formed the most available foundation for the superstructure of eloquence. For the latter he prepared himself studiously; but he was vitally helped by a natural gift of insight into character; by his abounding humor; by his wit; and by a natural shrewdness and manly good sense, which recommended him to the solid intelligence of Englishmen.

It is obvious that such a man as Sheridan, with his eye, his voice, his manner, his vivacity and dramatic power, must depend for much of the wonderful effects he produced upon his actual appearance and movements before his audience. By allowing our imagination to come to the aid of our intelligence, however, we may form an approximate notion, from the published report of the speech delivered at Warren Hastings's trial, of what the reality must have been; we can see the noble hall, the vast audience, composed of the foremost men of England, the accused, himself a man of matchless ability; and above all, the brilliant, graceful figure of the marvellous Irishman, filling the eye and ear, master of laughter and of tears, making the heart leap in the bosom, and compelling the pride of intellect to acknowledge him its lord.

SPEECH AT THE TRIAL OF WARREN HASTINGS

M Y LORDS: I shall not waste your lordships' time nor my own by any preliminary observations on the importance of the subject before you, or on the propriety of our bringing it in this solemn manner to a final decision.[1] My honorable friend [Mr. Burke], the principal mover of the impeachment, has already executed the task in a way the most masterly and impressive. He, whose indignant and enterprising genius, roused by the calls of public justice, has, with unprecedented labor, perseverance, and eloquence, excited one branch of the legislature to the vindication of our national character, and through whose means the House of Commons now makes this embodied stand in favor of man against man's iniquity, need hardly be followed on the general grounds of the prosecution.

Confiding in the dignity, the liberality, and intelligence of the tribunal before which I now have the honor to appear in my delegated capacity of a manager, I do not, indeed, conceive it necessary to engage your lordships' attention for a single moment with any introductory animadversions. But there is one point which here presents itself that it becomes me not to overlook. Insinuations have been thrown out that my honorable colleagues and myself are actuated by motives of malignity against the unfortunate prisoner at the bar. An imputation of so serious a nature cannot be permitted to pass altogether without comment; though it comes in so loose a shape, in such whispers and oblique hints as to prove to a certainty that it was made in the consciousness, and, therefore, with the circumspection of falsehood.

I can, my lords, most confidently aver, that a prosecution more

[1] This speech was delivered before the House of Lords, sitting as a High Court of Parliament, June, 1788.

disinterested in all its motives and ends; more free from personal malice or personal interest; more perfectly public, and more purely animated by the simple and unmixed spirit of justice, never was brought in any country, at any time, by any body of men, against any individual. What possible resentment can we entertain against the unfortunate prisoner? What possible interest can we have in his conviction? What possible object of a personal nature can we accomplish by his ruin? For myself, my lords, I make this solemn asseveration, that I discharge my breast of all malice, hatred, and ill-will against the prisoner, if at any time indignation at his crimes has planted in it these passions; and I believe, my lords, that I may with equal truth answer for every one of my colleagues.

We are, my lords, anxious, in stating the crimes with which he is charged, to keep out of recollection the person of the unfortunate prisoner. In prosecuting him to conviction, we are impelled only by a sincere abhorrence of his guilt, and a sanguine hope of remedying future delinquency. We can have no private incentive to the part we have taken. We are actuated singly by the zeal we feel for the public welfare, and by an honest solicitude for the honor of our country, and the happiness of those who are under its dominion and protection.

With such views, we really, my lords, lose sight of Mr. Hastings, who, however great in some other respects, is too insignificant to be blended with these important circumstances. The unfortunate prisoner is, at best, to my mind, no mighty object. Amid the series of mischiefs and enormities to my sense seeming to surround him, what is he but a petty nucleus, involved in its laminæ, scarcely seen or heard of?

This prosecution, my lords, was not, as is alleged, " begot in prejudice, and nursed in error." It originated in the clearest conviction of the wrongs which the natives of Hindostan have endured by the maladministration of those in whose hands this country had placed extensive powers; which ought to have been exercised for the benefit of the governed, but which was used by the prisoner for the shameful purpose of oppression. I repeat with emphasis, my lords, that nothing personal or malicious has induced us to institute this prosecution. It is absurd to suppose it. We come to your lordships' bar as the representatives of the Commons of England; and, as acting in this public capacity, it might as truly be said that the Commons, in whose name the impeachment is brought before your lordships, were actuated by enmity to the prisoner, as that we, their deputed organs, have any private spleen to gratify in discharging the duty imposed upon us by our principals.

Your lordships will also recollect and discriminate between impeachment for capital offences and impeachment for high crimes and misdemeanors. In an impeachment of the former kind, when the life of an individual is to be forfeited on conviction, if malignity be indulged in giving a strong tincture and coloring to facts, the tenderness of man's nature will revolt at it; for, however strongly indignant we may be at the perpetration of offences of a gross quality, there is a feeling that will protect an accused person from the influence of malignity in such a situation; but where no traces of this malice are discoverable, where no thirst for blood is seen, where, seeking for exemplary more than sanguinary justice, an impeachment is brought for high crimes and misdemeanors, malice will not be imputed to the prosecutors if, in illustration of the crimes alleged, they should adduce every possible circumstance in support of their allegations. Why will it not? Because their ends have nothing abhorrent to human tenderness. Because, in such a case as the present, for instance, all that is aimed at in convicting the prisoner is a temporary seclusion from the society of his countrymen, whose name he has tarnished by his crimes, and a deduction from the enormous spoils which he has accumulated by his greedy rapacity.

I. The only matter which I shall, in this stage of my inquiry, lay before your lordships, in order to give you an impression of the influence of the crimes of the prisoner over the country in which they were committed, is to refer to some passages in a letter of the Earl of Cornwallis.

You see, my lords, that the British government, which ought to have been a blessing to the powers in India connected with it, has proved a scourge to the natives, and the cause of desolation to their most flourishing provinces.

Behold, my lords, this frightful picture of the consequences of a government of violence and oppression! Surely the condition of wretchedness to which this once happy and independent prince is reduced by our cruelty, and the ruin which in some way

has been brought upon his country, call loudly upon your lordships to interpose, and to rescue the national honor and reputation from the infamy to which both will be exposed if no
investigation be made into the causes of their calamities, and no
punishment inflicted on the authors of them. By policy as well
as justice you are vehemently urged to vindicate the English
character in the East; for, my lords, it is manifest that the native
powers have so little reliance on our faith, that the preservation
of our possessions in that division of the world can only be
effected by convincing the princes that a religious adherence to
its engagements with them shall hereafter distinguish our India government.

To these letters what answer shall we return? Let it not,
my lords, be by words, which will not find credit with the natives, who have been so often deceived by our professions, but
by deeds which will assure them that we are at length truly in
earnest. It is only by punishing those who have been guilty of
the delinquencies which have ruined the country, and by showing that future criminals will not be encouraged or countenanced
by the ruling powers at home, that we can possibly gain confidence with the people of India. This alone will revive their respect for us, and secure our authority over them. This alone
will restore to us the alienated attachment of the much-injured
nabob, silence his clamors, heal his grievances, and remove his
distrust. This alone will make him feel that he may cherish his
people, cultivate his lands, and extend the mild hand of parental
care over a fertile and industrious kingdom, without dreading
that prosperity will entail upon him new rapine and extortion.
This alone will inspire the nabob with confidence in the English
government, and the subjects of Oude with confidence in the
nabob. This alone will give to the soil of that delightful country the advantages which it derived from a beneficent Providence, and make it again what it was when invaded by an English spoiler, the garden of India.

It is in the hope, my lords, of accomplishing these salutary
ends, of restoring character to England and happiness to India,
that we have come to the bar of this exalted tribunal.

In looking round for an object fit to be held out to an oppressed people, and to the world as an example of national justice, we are forced to fix our eyes on Mr. Hastings. It is he, my

lords, who has degraded our fame, and blasted our fortunes in the East. It is he who has tyrannized with relentless severity over the devoted natives of those regions. It is he who must atone, as a victim, for the multiplied calamities he has produced!

But though, my lords, I designate the prisoner as a proper subject of exemplary punishment, let it not be presumed that I wish to turn the sword of justice against him merely because some example is required. Such a wish is as remote from my heart as it is from equity and law. Were I not persuaded that it is impossible I should fail to render the evidence of his crimes as conclusive as the effects of his conduct are confessedly afflicting, I should blush at having selected him as an object of retributive justice. If I invoke this heavy penalty on Mr. Hastings, it is because I honestly believe him to be a flagitious delinquent, and by far the most so of all those who have contributed to ruin the natives of India and disgrace the inhabitants of Britain. But while I call for justice upon the prisoner, I sincerely desire to render him justice. It would indeed distress me, could I imagine that the weight and consequence of the House of Commons, who are a party in this prosecution, could operate in the slightest degree to his prejudice; but I entertain no such solicitude or apprehension. It is the glory of the constitution under which we live, that no man can be punished without guilt, and this guilt must be publicly demonstrated by a series of clear, legal, manifest evidence, so that nothing dark, nothing oblique, nothing authoritative, nothing insidious, shall work to the detriment of the subject. It is not the peering suspicion of apprehended guilt. It it not any popular abhorrence of its widespread consequences. It is not the secret consciousness in the bosom of the judge which can excite the vengeance of the law, and authorize its infliction! No! In this good land, as high as it is happy, because as just as it is free, all is definite, equitable, and exact. The laws must be satisfied before they are incurred; and ere a hair of the head can be plucked to the ground, legal guilt must be established by legal proof.

But this cautious, circumspect, and guarded principle of English jurisprudence, which we all so much value and revere, I feel at present in some degree inconvenient, as it may prove an impedient to public justice; for the managers of this impeachment labor under difficulties with regard to evidence that can scarcely occur in any other prosecution. What! my lords, it may perhaps be asked, have none of the considerable persons who are sufferers by his crimes arrived to offer at your lordships' bar their testimony, mixed with their execrations against the prisoner? No—there are none. These sufferers are persons whose manners and prejudices keep them separate from all the world, and whose religion will not admit them to appear before your lordships. But are there no witnesses, unprejudiced spectators of these enormities, ready to come forward, from the simple love of justice, and to give a faithful narrative of the transactions that passed under their eyes? No—there are none. The witnesses whom we have been compelled to summon are, for the most part, the emissaries and agents employed, and involved in these transactions; the wily accomplices of the prisoner's guilt, and the supple instruments of his oppressions. But are there collected no written documents or authentic papers, containing a true and perfect account of his crimes? No—there are none. The only papers we have procured are written by the party himself, or the participators in his proceedings, who studied, as it was their interest, though contrary to their duty, to conceal the criminality of their conduct, and, consequently, to disguise the truth.

But though, my lords, I dwell on the difficulties which the managers have to encounter with respect to the evidence in this impeachment, I do not solicit indulgence, or even mean to hint that what we have adduced is in any material degree defective. Weak no doubt it is in some parts, and deplorable, as undistinguished by any compunctious visitings of repenting accomplices. But there is enough, and enough in sure validity, notwithstanding every disadvantage and impediment, to abash the front of guilt no longer hid, and to flash those convictions on the minds of your lordships, which should be produced.

II. I now proceed, my lords, to review the evidence.

1. The first article which I shall notice must, I think, be considered pretty strong. It is the defence, or rather the defences, of the prisoner before the House of Commons; for he has already made four: three of which he has since abandoned and endeavored to discredit. I believe it is a novelty in the history of criminal jurisprudence that a person accused should first set up a defence, and afterwards strive to invalidate it. But this,

certainly, has been the course adopted by the prisoner; and I am the more surprised at it, as he has had the full benefit of the ablest counsel. Rescued from his own devious guidance, I could hardly have imagined that he would have acted so unwisely or indecently as to evince his contempt of one House of Parliament by confessing the impositions which he had practised on the other. But by this extraordinary proceeding he has given, unwarily, to your lordships a pledge of his past truth, in the acknowledged falsehood of his present conduct.

In every court of law in England the confession of a criminal, when not obtained by any promise of favor or lenity, or by violent threats, is always admitted as conclusive evidence against himself. And if such confession were made before a grave and respectable assembly of persons competent to take cognizance of crimes, there is no doubt but that it would have due weight, because it is fair to presume that it must be voluntary, and not procured by any undue or improper means. The prisoner has, in his defence, admitted many facts; and it is the intention of the managers, accordingly, to urge in support of the charges his admission of them. For, when he did it, he was speaking the language not of inconsiderate rashness and haste, but of deliberate consideration and reflection, as will appear to your lordships by a passage which I shall cite from the introduction to the defence read by Mr. Hastings himself at the bar of the House of Commons. He employs the following words: " Of the discouragement to which I allude I shall mention but two points, and these it is incumbent upon me to mention, because they relate to effects which the justice of this honorable House may, and I trust will, avert. The first is an obligation to my being at all committed in my defence; since, in so wide a field for discussion, it would be impossible not to admit some things of which an advantage might be taken to turn them into evidence against myself, whereas another might as well use as I could, or better, the same materials of my defence, without involving me in the same consequences. But I am sure the honorable House will yield me its protection against the cavils of unwarranted inference, and if truth can tend to convict me, I am content to be myself the channel to convey it. The other objection lies in my own breast. It was not till Monday last that I formed the resolution, and I knew not then whether I might not, in consequence, be laid under the obligation of preparing and completing in five days (and in effect so it proved) the refutation of charges which it has been the labor of my accuser, armed with all the powers of Parliament, to compile during as many years of almost undisturbed leisure."

Here, then, my lords, the prisoner has, upon deliberation, committed his defence to paper; and after having five days to consider whether he should present it or not, he actually delivers it himself to the House of Commons as one founded in truth, and triumphantly remarks, that " if truth could tend to convict him, he was willing to be himself the channel to convey it."

But what is his language now that he has the advice of counsel? Why, that there is not a word of truth in what he delivered to the House of Commons as truth! He did not, it seems, himself prepare the defence which he read as his own before that body. He employed others to draw it up. Major Scott comes to your bar, and represents Mr. Hastings, as it were, contracting for a character, to be made ready to his hands. Knowing, no doubt, that the accusation of the Commons had been drawn up by a committee, he thought it necessary, as a point of punctilio, to answer it by a committee also. For himself, he had no knowledge of the facts! no recollection of the circumstances! He commits his defence wholly to his friends! He puts his memory in trust, and duly nominates and appoints commissioners to take charge of it! One furnishes the raw material of fact, the second spins the argument, and the third twines up the conclusion; while Mr. Hastings, with a master's eye, is cheering them on, and overlooking the loom. To Major Scott he says, " You have my good faith in your hands—take care of my consistency—manage my veracity to the best advantage!" " Mr. Middleton, you have my memory in commission!" " Mr. Shore, make me out a good financier!" " Remember, Mr. Impey, you have my humanity in your hands!" When this product of their skill was done, he brings it to the House of Commons, and says, " I was equal to the task. I knew the difficulties, but I scorned them: here is the truth, and if the truth tends to convict me, I am content myself to be the channel of it." His friends hold up their heads and say, " What noble magnanimity! This must be the effect of real innocence!"

But this journeyman's work, after all, is found to be defective. It is good enough for the House of Commons, but not for your lordships. The prisoner now presents himself at your bar, and his only apprehension seems to arise from what had been thus done for him. He exclaims, " I am careless of what the managers say or do. Some of them have high passions, and others have bitter words, but these I heed not. Save me from the peril of my own panegyric; snatch me from my own friends. Do not believe a syllable of what I said before! I cannot submit now to be tried, as I imprudently challenged, by the account which I have myself given of my own transactions!" Such is the language of the prisoner, by which it appears that truth is not natural to him, but that falsehood comes at his beck. Truth, indeed, it is said, lies deep, and requires time and labor to gain; but falsehood swims on the surface, and is always at hand.

It is in this way, my lords, that the prisoner shows you how he sports with the dignity and feelings of the House by asserting that to be false and not entitled to credit this day, which, on a former, he had averred to be truth itself. Indeed, from this avowal and disavowal of defences, and from the present defence differing from all the former which have been delivered to your lordships, it does seem that Mr. Hastings thinks he may pursue this course just as far as best suits his convenience or advantage. It is not at all improbable, if he should deem it expedient, that he will hereafter abandon the one now submitted to you, and excuse himself by saying, " It was not made by me, but by my counsel, and I hope, therefore, your lordships will give no credit to it." But if he will abide by this, his last revised and amended defence, I will join issue with him upon it, and prove it to be in numerous places void of truth, and almost every part of it unfounded in argument as well as fact.

2. I am now to advert more particularly to the evidence in support of the allegations of the charge on which the prisoner is arraigned. We have already shown, most satisfactorily, that the begums of Oude were of high birth and distinguished rank; the elder, or grandmother of the reigning prince, being the daughter of a person of ancient and illustrious lineage, and the younger, or prince's mother, of descent scarcely less noble. We have also shown, with equal clearness, by the testimony of several witnesses, how sacred is the residence of women in India. To menace, therefore, the dwelling of these princesses with vio-

lation, as the prisoner did, was a species of torture, the cruelty
of which can only be conceived by those who are conversant
with the peculiar customs and notions of the inhabitants of
Hindostan.

We have nothing in Europe, my lords, which can give us an
idea of the manners of the East. Your lordships cannot even
learn the right nature of the people's feelings and prejudices
from any history of other Mohammedan countries—not even
from that of the Turks, for they are a mean and degraded race
in comparison with many of these great families, who, inheriting
from their Persian ancestors, preserve a purer style of prejudice
and a loftier superstition. Women there are not as in Turkey—
they neither go to the mosque nor to the bath. It is not the thin
veil alone that hides them, but, in the inmost recesses of their
zenana, they are kept from public view by those reverenced and
protected walls, which, as Mr. Hastings and Sir Elijah Impey
admit, are held sacred even by the ruffian hand of warfare, or
the more uncourteous hand of the law. But, in this situation,
they are not confined from a mean and selfish policy of man, or
from a coarse and sensual jealousy. Enshrined, rather than im-
mured, their habitation and retreat is a sanctuary, not a prison—
their jealousy is their own—a jealousy of their own honor, that
leads them to regard liberty as a degradation, and the gaze of
even admiring eyes as inexpiable pollution to the purity of their
fame and the sanctity of their honor.

Such being the general opinion (or prejudices, let them be
called) of this country, your lordships will find that whatever
treasures were given or lodged in a zenana of this description
must, upon the evidence of the thing itself, be placed beyond
the reach of resumption. To dispute with the counsel about the
original right to those treasures—to talk of a title to them by
the Mohammedan law! Their title to them is the title of a saint
to the relics upon an altar, placed there by piety, guarded by holy
superstition, and to be snatched from thence only by sacrilege.

What, now, my lords, do you think of the tyranny and savage
apathy of a man who could act in open defiance of those prejudices which are so interwoven with the very existence of the
females of the East, that they can be removed only by death?
What do your lordships think of the atrocity of a man who
could threaten to profane and violate the sanctuary of the Prin-

cesses of Oude, by declaring that he would storm it with his troops, and expel the inhabitants from it by force? There is, my lords, displayed in the whole of this black transaction a wantonness of cruelty and ruffian-like ferocity that, happily, are not often incident even to the most depraved and obdurate of our species.

Had there been in the composition of the prisoner's heart one generous propensity, or lenient disposition even slumbering and torpid, it must have been awakened and animated into kindness and mercy towards these singularly interesting females. Their character, and situation at the time, presented every circumstance to disarm hostility, and to kindle the glow of manly sympathy; but no tender impression could be made on his soul, which is as hard as adamant, and as black as sin. Stable as the everlasting hills in its schemes and purposes of villany, it has never once been shaken by the cries of affliction, the claims of charity, or the complaints of injustice. With steady and undeviating step he marches on to the consummation of the abominable projects of wickedness which are engendered and contrived in its gloomy recesses. What his soul prepares, his hands are ever ready to execute.

It is true, my lords, that the prisoner is conspicuously gifted with the energy of vice, and the firmness of indurated sensibility. These are the qualities which he assiduously cultivates, and of which his friends vauntingly exult. They have, indeed, procured him his triumphs and his glories. Truly, my lords, they have spread his fame, and erected the sombre pyramids of his renown.

That the treasures, my lords, of the zenana, the object of the prisoner's rapacity, and the incentive to his sacrilegious violation of this hallowed abode of the Princesses of Oude, were their private property, justly acquired and legally secured, and not the money of the state, as is alleged, has been clearly and incontestably demonstrated. It must be recollected how conclusive was the testimony, both positive and circumstantial, which we brought to support this point. Believing that it must have pressed itself upon your memories, I shall avoid here the tediousness of a detailed recapitulation. Permit me, however, to call your attention to a very brief summary of it.

It is in complete evidence before you that Sujah ul Dowlah,

the husband of the elder [younger] begum, entertained the warmest affection for his wife, and the liveliest solicitude for her happiness. Endeared to him by the double ties of conjugal attachment, and the grateful remembrance of her exemplary conduct towards him in the season of his severest misfortunes and accumulated distress, he seems, indeed, to have viewed her with an extravagance of fondness bordering on enthusiasm. You know, my lords, that when the nabob [Sujah Dowlah] was reduced, by the disastrous defeat which he sustained at Buxar, to the utmost extremity of adverse fortune, she, regardless of the danger and difficulties of the enterprise, fled to him, for the purpose of administering to his misery the solace of tenderness; and, prompted by the noblest sentiment, took along with her, for his relief, the jewels with which he had enriched her in his happier and more prosperous days. By the sale of these he raised a large sum of money, and retrieved his fortunes. After this generous and truly exemplary conduct on her part, the devotion of the husband to the wife knew no bounds. Can any further proof be required of it than the appointment of his son, by her [Asoph Dowlah, the reigning nabob], as the successor to his throne? With these dispositions, then, towards his wife, and from the manifest ascendancy which she had acquired over him, is it, my lords, I ask, an unwarrantable presumption that he did devise to her the treasures which she claimed? On the question of the legal right which the nabob had to make such a bequest I shall not now dwell; it having been already shown, beyond disputation, by the learned manager [Mr. Adam] who opened the charge, that, according to the theory as well as the practice of the Mohammedan law, the reigning prince may alienate and dispose of either real or personal property. And it further appears, my lords, from the testimony which has been laid before you, that the younger begum, or the nabob's [Asoph Dowlah] mother, lent money to her son, amounting to twenty-six lacs of rupees, for which she received, as a pledge, his bonds. Here is the *evidentia rei* that the money so lent was acknowledged to be hers; for no one borrows his own money and binds himself to repay it!

But, my lords, let us look into the origin of this pretended claim to the begum's treasures. We hear nothing of it till the nabob [Asoph] became embarrassed by the enormous expense of maintaining the military establishments to which he was compelled by the prisoner. Then, as a *dernier ressort,* the title to the treasures was set up, as the property of the Crown, which could not be willed away. This, truly, was the dawn of the claim. Not long afterwards we detect the open interference of Mr. Hastings in this fraudulent transaction. It was, indeed, hardly to be expected that he would permit so favorable an occasion to escape of indulging his greedy rapacity. We find, accordingly, that Mr. Bristow, the resident at the Court of Lucknow [the capital of Oude], duly received instructions to support, with all possible dexterity and intrigue, the pretensions of the nabob. The result of the negotiation which in consequence took place, was, that the mother, as well to relieve the distresses of her son as to secure a portion of her property, agreed finally to cancel his bond for the twenty-six lacs of rupees already lent, and to pay him thirty additional lacs, or £300,000, making in the whole £560,000 sterling. Part of this sum it was stipulated should be paid in goods contained in the zenana, which, as they consisted of arms and other implements of war, the nabob alleged to be the property of the state, and refused to receive in payment. The point, however, being referred to the Board at Calcutta, Mr. Hastings then, it is important to remark, vindicated the right of the begums to all the goods of the zenana, and brought over a majority of the council to his opinion. The matter in dispute being thus adjusted, a treaty between the mother and son was formally entered into, and to which the English became parties, guaranteeing its faithful execution. In consideration of the money paid to him by the mother, the son agreed to release all claim to the landed and remaining parts of the personal estate left by his father, Sujah ul Dowlah, to the princess his widow. Whatever, therefore, might have been her title to this property before, her right, under this treaty and the guarantee, became as legal, as strong, and obligatory, as the laws of India, and the laws of nations, could possibly make it.

But, my lords, notwithstanding the opinion which Mr. Hastings so strenuously supported in the council at Calcutta of the absolute right of the princes to all the property in the zenana, yet when it became convenient to his nefarious purposes to disown it, he, with an effrontery which has no example, declared that this recorded decision belonged not to him, but to the majority of the council! That, in short, being reduced to an inefficient minority in the council, he did not consider himself as responsible for any of their acts, either of those he opposed or those he approved. My lords, you are well acquainted with the nature of majorities and minorities; but how shall I instance this new doctrine? It is as if Mr. Burke, the great leader of this prosecution, should, some ten years hence, revile the managers, and commend Mr. Hastings! "What, sir!" might one of us exclaim to him, " do you, who instigated the inquiry, who brought the charge against him, who impeached him, who convinced me, by your arguments, of his guilt, speak of Mr. Hastings in this plausive style?" "Oh! but sir," replies Mr. Burke, "this was done in the House of Commons, where, at the time, I was one of an inefficient minority, and, consequently, I am not responsible for any measure, either those I opposed or approved."

If, my lords, at any future period, my honorable friend should become so lost to truth, to honor, and consistency, as to speak in this manner, what must be the public estimation of his character? Just such was the conduct of the prisoner in avowing that he did not consider himself responsible for the measures which he approved while controlled in the council by General Clavering, Colonel Monson, and Mr. Francis, the only halcyon season that India saw during his administration.

But, my lords, let it be observed that the claims of the nabob to the treasures of the begums were, at this time, the only plea alleged for the seizure. These were founded on a passage of the Koran, which is perpetually quoted, but never proved. Not a word was then mentioned of the strange rebellion which was afterwards conjured up, and of which the existence and the notoriety were equally a secret! a disaffection which was at its height at the very moment when the begums were dispensing their liberality to the nabob, and exercising the greatest generosity to the English in distress! a disturbance without its parallel in history, which was raised by two women, carried on by eunuchs, and finally suppressed by an affidavit!

No one, my lords, can contemplate the seizure of this treasure, with the attendant circumstances of aggravation, without being struck with horror at the complicated wickedness of the transaction. We have already seen the noblest heroism and magnanimity displayed by the mother begum. It was she, my lords,

you will recollect, who extricated, by the most generous interposition, her husband, Sujah Dowlah, from the rigors of his
fortune after the fatal battle of Buxar. She even saved her son,
the reigning nabob, from death, at the imminent hazard of her
own life. She also, as you know, gave to her son his throne. A
son so preserved, and so befriended, Mr. Hastings did arm
against his benefactress, and his mother. He invaded the rights
of that prince, that he might compel him to violate the laws of
nature and the obligations of gratitude, by plundering his
parent. Yes, my lords, it was the prisoner who cruelly instigated
the son against the mother. That mother, who had twice given
life to her son, who had added to it a throne, was (incredible as
it may appear), by the compulsion of that man at your bar, to
whose guardianship she was bequeathed by a dying husband—
by that man, who is wholly insensible to every obligation which
sets bounds to his rapacity and his oppression, was she pillaged
and undone! But the son was not without his excuse. In the
moment of anguish, when bewailing his hapless condition, he ex-
claimed that it was the English who had driven him to the perpetration of such enormities. " It is they who have reduced
me. They have converted me to their use. They have made
me a slave, to compel me to become a monster."

Let us now, my lords, turn to the negotiations of Mr. Middleton with the begums in 1778, when the " discontents of the superior begum would have induced her to leave the country, unless her authority was sanctioned and her property secured by
the guarantee of the Company." This guarantee the counsel of
Mr. Hastings have thought it necessary to deny; knowing that
if the agreements with the elder begum were proved, it would
affix to their client the guilt of all the sufferings of the women of
the *khord mahal* [dwelling of the female relatives of the nabob],
the revenues for whose support were secured by the same engagement. In treating this part of the subject, the principal difficulty arises from the uncertain evidence of Mr. Middleton,
who, though concerned in the negotiation of four treaties, could
not recollect affixing his signature to three out of that number!
It can, however, be shown, even by his evidence, that a treaty
was signed in October, 1778, wherein the rights of the elder
begum were fully recognized; a provision secured for thè
women and children of the late vizier in the *khord mahal;* and

that these engagements received the fullest sanction of Mr. Hastings. These facts are, moreover, confirmed by the evidence of Mr. Purling, a gentleman who delivered himself fairly, and as having no foul secrets to conceal. Mr. Purling swears he transmitted copies of these engagements, in 1780, to Mr. Hastings at Calcutta; the answer returned was " that, in arranging the taxes of the other districts, he should pass over the *jaghires* of the begums." No notice was then taken of any impropriety in the transactions in 1778, nor any notice given of an intended revocation of those engagements.

In June, 1781, however, when General Clavering and Colonel Monson were no more, and Mr. Francis had returned to Europe, all the hoard and arrear of collected evil burst out without restraint, and Mr. Hastings determined on his journey to the upper provinces. It was then that, without adverting to intermediate transactions, he met with the Nabob Asoph Dowlah at Chunar, and received from him the mysterious present of £100,000. To form a proper idea of this transaction, it is only necessary to consider the respective situations of him who gave and of him who received this present. It was not given by the nabob from the superflux of his wealth, nor in the abundance of his esteem for the man to whom it was presented. It was, on the contrary, a prodigal bounty, drawn from a country depopulated by the natural progress of British rapacity. It was after the country had felt still other calamities—it was after the angry dispensations of Providence had, with a progressive severity of chastisement, visited the land with a famine one year, and with a Colonel Hannay the next—it was after he, this Hanney, had returned to retrace the steps of his former ravages—it was after he and his voracious crew had come to plunder ruins which himself had made, and to glean from desolation the little that famine had spared, or rapine overlooked; then it was that this miserable bankrupt prince, marching through his country, besieged by the clamors of his starving subjects, who cried to him for protection through their cages—meeting the curses of some of his subjects, and the prayers of others—with famine at his heels, and reproach following him—then it was that this prince is represented as exercising this act of prodigal bounty to the very man whom he here reproaches—to the very man whose policy had extinguished his power, and whose creatures had desolated his country. To talk of a free-will gift! It is audacious and ridiculous to name the supposition. It was not a free-will gift. What was it, then? Was it a bribe? Or was it extortion? I shall prove it was both—it was an act of gross bribery and of rank extortion. The secrecy which marked this transaction is not the smallest proof of its criminality. When Benarum Pundit had, a short time before, made a present to the Company of a lac of rupees, Mr. Hastings, in his own language, deemed it "worthy the praise of being recorded." But in this instance, when ten times that sum was given, neither Mr. Middleton nor the council were acquainted with the transaction, until Mr. Hastings, four months afterwards, felt himself compelled to write an account of it to England; and the intelligence returned thus circuitously to his friends in India! It is peculiarly observable in this transaction, how much the distresses of the different parties were at variance. The first thing Mr. Hastings does is to leave Calcutta in order to go to the relief of the distressed nabob. The second thing is to take £100,000 from that distressed nabob, on account of the distressed Company. The third thing is, to ask of the distressed Company this very same £100,000 on account of the distresses of Mr. Hastings! There never were three distresses that seemed so little reconcilable with one another. This money, the prisoner alleges, was appropriated to the payment of the army. But here he is unguardedly contradicted by the testimony of his friend, Major Scott, who shows it was employed for no such purpose. My lords, through all these windings of mysterious hypocrisy, and of artificial concealment, is it not easy to discern the sense of hidden guilt?

III. Driven from every other hold, the prisoner is obliged to resort, as a justification of his enormities, to the stale pretext of state necessity! Of this last disguise it is my duty to strip him. I will venture to say, my lords, that no one instance of real necessity can be adduced. The necessity which the prisoner alleges listens to whispers for the purpose of crimination, and deals in rumor to prove its own existence. His a state necessity! No, my lords, that imperial tyrant, state necessity, is yet a generous despot—bold in his demeanor, rapid in his decisions, though terrible in his grasp. What he does, my lords, he dares avow; and avowing, scorns any other justification than the high motives that placed the iron sceptre in his hand. Even where its rigors are suffered, its apology is also known; and men learn to consider it in its true light, as a power which turns occasionally aside from just government, when its exercise is calculated to prevent greater evils than it occasions. But a quibbling, prevaricating necessity, which tries to steal a pitiful justification from whispered accusations and fabricated rumors—no, my lords, that is no state necessity! Tear off the mask, and you see coarse, vulgar avarice lurking under the disguise. The state necessity of Mr. Hastings is a juggle. It is a being that prowls in the dark. It is to be traced in the ravages which it commits, but never in benefits conferred or evils prevented. I can conceive justifiable occasions for the exercise even of outrage, where high public interests demand the sacrifice of private right. If any great man, in bearing the arms of his country—if any admiral, carrying the vengeance and the glory of Britain to distant coasts, should be driven to some rash acts of violence, in order, perhaps, to give food to those who are shedding their blood for their country—there is a state necessity in such a case, grand, magnanimous, and all-commanding, which goes hand in hand with honor, if not with use! If any great general, defending some fortress, barren, perhaps, itself, but a pledge of the pride and power of Britain—if such a man, fixed like an imperial eagle on the summit of his rock, should strip its sides of the verdure and foliage with which it might be clothed, while covered on the top with that cloud from which he was pouring down his thunders on the foe—would he be brought by the House of Commons to your bar? No, my lords, never would his grateful and admiring countrymen think of questioning actions which, though accompanied by private wrong, yet were warranted by real necessity. But is the state necessity which is pleaded by the prisoner, in defence of his conduct, of this description? I challenge him to produce a single instance in which any of his private acts were productive of public advantage, or averted impending evil.

IV. We come now to the treaty of Chunar, which preceded the acceptance of the bribe to which we have already alluded. This transaction, my lords, had its beginning in corruption, its continuance in fraud, and its end in violence. The first proposition of the nabob was, that our army should be removed and all the English be recalled from his dominions. He declared, to use his own language, that " the English are the bane and ruin of my affairs. Leave my country to myself, and all will yet be recovered." He was aware, my lords, that though their predecessors had exhausted his revenue; though they had shaken the tree till nothing remained upon its leafless branches, yet that a new flight was upon the wing to watch the first buddings of its prosperity, and to nip every promise of future luxuriance. To the demands of the nabob, Mr. Hastings finally acceded. The bribe was the price of his acquiescence. But with the usual perfidy of the prisoner, this condition of the treaty never was performed. You will recollect, my lords, that Mr. Middleton was asked whether the orders which were pretended to be given for the removal of the English were, in any instance, carried into effect? To this question he refused at first to answer, as tending to criminate himself. But when his objection was overruled, and it was decided that he should answer, so much was he agitated, that he lost all memory. It turned out, however, by an amended recollection, that he never received any direct order from Mr. Hastings. But, my lords, who can believe that a direct order is necessary when Mr. Hastings wants the services of Mr. Middleton? Rely upon it, a hint is sufficient to this servile dependant and obsequious parasite. Mr. Hastings has only to turn his eye towards him—that eye at whose scowl princes turn pale—and his wishes are obeyed.

But, my lords, this is not the only instance in which the nabob was duped by the bad faith of the prisoner. In the agreement relative to the resumption of the *jaghires,* the prince had demanded and obtained leave to resume those of certain individuals; but Mr. Hastings, knowing that there were some favorites of the nabob whom he could not be brought to dispossess, defeated the permission, without the least regard to the existing stipulations to the contrary, by making the order general.

Such, my lords, is the conduct of which Mr. Hastings is capable, not in the moment of cold or crafty policy, but in the hour of confidence, and during the effervescence of his gratitude for a favor received! Thus did he betray the man to whose liberality he stood indebted. Even the gratitude, my lords, of the prisoner, seems perilous; for we behold here the danger which actually awaited the return he made to an effusion of generosity!

The fact is, my lords, as appears from the clearest evidence, that when Mr. Hastings left Calcutta he had two resources in view, Benares and Oude. The first having failed him, in consequence of the unexpected insurrection which terminated, unhappily for him, in the capture of Bedjigar, he turned his attention to Oude, previously, however, desolating the former province, which he was unable to pillage, destroying, and cutting off the very sources of life. Thus frustrated in his original design, the genius of the prisoner, ever fertile in expedients, fixed itself on the treasures of the begums, and now devised, as an apology for the signal act of cruelty and rapacity which he was meditating, the memorable rebellion; and, to substantiate the participation of these unfortunate princesses in it, he despatched the Chief Justice of India to collect materials.

The conduct of Sir Elijah Impey in this business, with all deference to the protest which he has entered against being spoken of in a place where he cannot have the privilege of replying, I do not think ought to be passed over without animadversion. Not that I mean to say anything harsh of this elevated character, who was selected to bear forth and to administer to India the blessings of English jurisprudence. I will not question either his feebleness of memory, or dispute in any respect the convenient doctrine which he has set up in his vindication, "that what he ought to have done it is likely he actually did perform." I have always thought, my lords, that the appointment of the chief justice to so low and nefarious an office as that in which he was employed is one of the strongest aggravations of Mr. Hastings's guilt. That an officer, the purity and lustre of whose character should be maintained even in the most domestic retirement; that he, who, if consulting the dignity of British justice, ought to have continued as stationary as his court at Calcutta; that such an exalted character, I repeat, as the Chief Justice of India, should have been forced on a circuit of five hundred miles for the purpose of transacting such a business, was a degradation without example, and a deviation from propriety which has no apology. But, my lords, this is, in some degree, a question which is to be abstracted for the consideration of those who adorn and illumine the seats of justice in Britain, and the rectitude of whose deportment precludes the necessity of any further observation on so opposite a conduct.

The manner, my lords, in which Sir Elijah Impey delivered his evidence deserves, also, your attention. He admitted, you will recollect, that, in giving it, he never answered without looking equally to the probability and the fact in question. Sometimes he allowed circumstances of which he said he had no recollection beyond the mere " probability " that they had taken place. By consulting in this manner what was " probable " and the contrary, he may certainly have corrected his memory at times. I am, at all events, content to accept of this mode of giving his testimony, provided that the converse of the proposition has also a place: and that where a circumstance is improbable, a similar degree of credit may be subtracted from the testimony of the witness. Five times in the House of Commons, and twice in this court, for instance, has Sir Elijah Impey borne testimony that a rebellion was raging at Fyzabad [the abode of the begums], at the period of his journey to Lucknow [the residence of the nabob]. Yet, on the eighth examination, he contradicted all the former, and declared that what he meant was, that the rebellion had been raging, and the country was then in some degree restored to quiet. The reasons he assigned for the former errors were, that he had forgotten a letter received from Mr. Hastings, informing him that the rebellion was quelled, and that he had also forgotten his own proposition of travelling through Fyzabad to Lucknow! With respect to the letter, nothing can be said, as it is not in evidence; but the other observation can scarcely be admitted when it is recollected that, in the House of Commons, Sir Elijah Impey declared that it was his proposal to travel through Fyzabad, which had originally brought forth the intelligence that the way was obstructed by the rebellion, and that in consequence of it he altered his route and went by the way of Illahabad. But what is yet more singular is, that on his return he again would have come by the way of Fyzabad, if he had not been once more informed of the danger; so that, had it not been for these friendly informations, the chief justice would have run plump into the very focus of the rebellion!

These, my lords, are the pretexts by which the fiction of a rebellion was endeavored to be forced on the public credulity;

but the trick is now discovered, and the contriver and the executor are alike exposed to the scorn and derision of the world.

There are two circumstances here which are worthy of remark. The first is, that Sir Elijah Impey, when charged with so dangerous a commission as that of procuring evidence to prove that the begums had meditated the expulsion of the nabob from the throne, and the English from Bengal, twice intended to pass through the city of their residence. But, my lords, this giddy chief justice disregards business. He wants to see the country! Like some innocent schoolboy, he takes the primrose path, and amuses himself as he goes! He thinks not that his errand is in danger and death, and that his party of pleasure ends in loading others with irons. When at Lucknow, he never mentions the affidavits to the nabob. No! He is too polite. Nor, from the same courtesy, to Mr. Hastings. He is, indeed, a master of ceremonies in justice!

When examined, the witness sarcastically remarked " that there must have been a sworn interpreter, from the looks of the manager." How I looked, Heaven knows! but such a physiognomist there is no escaping. He sees a sworn interpreter in my looks! He sees the manner of taking an oath in my looks! He sees the basin of the Ganges in my looks! As for himself, he looks only at the tops and bottoms of affidavits! In seven years he takes care never to look at these swearings; but when he does examine them, he knows less than before.

The other circumstance, my lords, to which I have alluded, is, that it is fair to presume that Sir Elijah Impey was dissuaded by Mr. Hastings and Middleton from passing by the way of Fyzabad, as they well knew that if he approached the begums he would be convinced by their reception of him as the friend of the Governor-General, that nothing could be more foreign from the truth than their suspected disaffection. Neither should it escape your notice, my lords, that while he was taking evidence at Lucknow in the face of day, in support of the charge of rebellion against the princesses, the chief justice heard not a word either from the nabob or his minister, though he frequently conversed with both, of any treasonable machinations or plottings! Equally unaccountable does it appear that Sir Elijah Impey, who advised the taking of these affidavits for the safety of the prisoner at your bar, did not read them at the time to see whether or not they were adequate to this purpose!

At length, it seems, he did read the affidavits, but not till after having declared on oath that he thought it unnecessary. To this he acknowledged he was induced " by having been misled by one of the managers on the part of the Commons, who, by looking at a book which he held in his hand, had entrapped him to own that a sworn interpreter was present when he received these affidavits, and that he was perfectly satisfied with his conduct on the occasion."

Now, my lords, how I, by merely looking into a book, could intimate the presence of an interpreter, and could also look the satisfaction conceived by the chief justice on the occasion, when it clearly appears by the evidence that there was no interpreter present, are points which I believe he alone can explain!

I will concede to the witness, as he seems desirous it should be done, that he did not strictly attend to form when taking these affidavits. I will admit that he merely directed the Bible to be offered to the whites, and the Koran to the blacks, and packed up their depositions in his wallet without any examination. Or, I will admit that he glanced them over in India, having previously cut off all communication between his eye and his mind, so that nothing was transferred from the one to the other. Extraordinary as these circumstances certainly are, I will, nevertheless, admit them all; or if it be preferred by the prisoner, I will admit that the affidavits were legally and properly taken; for, in whatever light they may be received, I will prove that they are not sufficient to sustain a single allegation of criminality against those they were designed to inculpate.

But it is to these documents, my lords, such as they are, that the defence of the prisoner is principally confided; and on the degree of respect which may be given to them by your lordships does the event of this trial materially depend.

Considered, therefore, in this view, I shall presently solicit your lordships' attention, while I examine them at some length, and with some care. But before I enter into the analysis of the testimony, permit me to remind the court that the charge against the Princesses of Oude, to substantiate which these affidavits were taken, consisted originally of two allegations. They were accused of a uniform spirit of hostility to the British government, as well as the overt act of rebellion. But, my lords, the first part of the charge the counsel for the prisoner has been compelled to abandon, not being able to get one fact out of the whole farrago of these depositions to support it.

When the half of an accusation is thus deserted for the want of proof, is it not natural for us to suspect the whole? I do not say that it absolutely shows the falsity of it, nor do I mean to employ such an argument; but I maintain that it should influence the mind so far as to make it curious and severely inquisitive into the other branch of the charge, and to render it distrustful of its truth.

But in this particular case the court have an additional motive for jealousy and suspicion. It will not escape the recollection of your lordships, in weighing the validity of the allegation which now remains to be considered, namely, " that the begums influenced the *jaghiredars*,[2] and excited the discontents in Oude," what were the circumstances in which it arose, and by whom it was preferred. You will bear in mind, my lords, that it appears in evidence that Mr. Hastings left Calcutta in the year 1781, for the avowed purpose of collecting a large sum of money, and that he had only two resources. Failing in Benares, as we have already seen, he next lays his rapacious hand on the treasures of the begums. Here, then, we have in the person of the prisoner both the accuser and the judge. With much caution, therefore, should this judge be heard, who has, apparently at least, a profit in the conviction, and an interest in the condemnation of the party to be tried. I say nothing of the gross turpitude of such a double character, nor of the frontless disregard of all those feelings which revolt at mixing offices so distinct and incompatible.

The next point which I wish to press on your lordships' consideration, previously to my taking up the affidavits, is the infinite improbability of the attempt which is alleged to have been made by the begums to dethrone the nabob and exterminate the English. Estimating the power of the princesses at the highest standard, it manifestly was not in their reach to accomplish any overthrow, decisive or even momentary, of their sovereign, much less of the English. I am not so weak, however, as to argue that, because the success of an enterprise seems impossible, and

---

2 Persons holding jaghires. The jaghire is a fief or lordship granted to an individual for life, generally for military purposes.

no adequate reason can be assigned for undertaking it, it will therefore never be attempted; or that, because the begums had no interest in exciting a rebellion, or sufficient prospect of succeeding in it, they are innocent of the charge. I cannot look at the prisoner without knowing, and being compelled to confess that there are persons of such a turn of mind as to prosecute mischief without interest; and that there are passions of the human soul which lead, without a motive, to the perpetration of crimes.

I do not, therefore, my lords, wish it to be understood that I am contending that the charge is rendered, by the matter I have stated, absolutely false. All I mean is, that an accusation, made under such circumstances, should be received with much doubt and circumspection; and that your lordships, remembering how it is preferred, will accompany me through the discussion of the affidavits, free and uninfluenced by any bias derived from the positive manner in which the guilt of the begums has been pronounced.

We now come to the examination of this mass of evidence which Mr. Hastings conceives of so much consequence to his acquittal on the present charge. In the defence which has been submitted to your lordships the prisoner complains most bitterly that the chief mover of the prosecution treated these affidavits in his peculiar manner. What the peculiar manner of my honorable friend [Mr. Burke], here alluded to, was, I cannot tell. But I will say, that if he treated them in any other way than as the most rash, irregular, and irrelevant testimony which was ever brought before a judicial tribunal, he did not do as they deserved. The prisoner has had, moreover, the hardihood to assert that they were taken for the purpose of procuring the best possible information of the state of the country, and of the circumstances of the insurrection; and being, therefore, merely accessory evidence in the present case, were entitled to more weight. This I declare, without hesitation, to be a falsehood. They were taken, I aver, for the sole and exclusive purpose of vindicating the plunder of the begums. They were taken to justify what was afterwards to be done. Disappointed at Benares, he turned to the remaining resource, the treasures of the princesses; and prepared, as a pretext for his meditated robbery, these documents.

I shall proceed to examine the affidavits severally, as far as they relate to the charge against the begums. They really contain, my lords, nothing except vague rumor and improbable surmise. It is stated, for example, by one of those deponents, a black officer in a regiment of sepoys, that having a considerable number of persons as hostages in a fort where he commanded, who were sent thither by Colonel Hannay, the country people surrounded the fort and demanded their release; but instead of complying with their demand, he put twenty of these hostages to death; and on a subsequent day the heads of eighteen more were struck off, including the head of a great rajah. In consequence of this last execution, the populace became exceedingly exasperated, and among the crowd several persons were heard to say that the begums had offered a reward of a thousand rupees for the head of every European, one hundred for the head of every sepoy officer, and ten for the head of a common sepoy. Now, my lords, it appears pretty clearly that no such reward was ever offered; for, when this garrison evacuated the fort, the people told Captain Gordon, who then commanded it, that if he would deliver up his arms and baggage, they would permit him and his men to continue their march unmolested. So little did the people, indeed, think of enriching themselves by this process of decapitation, that, when the detachment of British forces was reduced to ten men, and when of course the slaughter of them would have been a work of no danger or difficulty, they were still permitted to proceed on their route without any interruption.

Captain Gordon himself supposes that the begums encouraged the country people to rise, because, when he arrived at the bank of the river Saunda Nutta, at the opposite side of which stands the town of Nutta, the *fowzdar,* or governor, who commanded there for the bow [younger] begum, in whose *jaghire* the town lay, did not instantly send boats to carry him and his men over the river; and because the *fowzdar* [governor] pointed two or three guns across the river. Even admitting this statement to be true, I cannot see how it is to affect the begums. Where is the symptom of hostility? Surely it was the duty of the commanding officer of the fort not to let any troops pass until he ascertained who they were, and for what purpose they came. To have done otherwise would have been unmilitary, and a violation of the most sacred duties of his station. But, my lords, after a while Captain Gordon crosses the river, and finds himself in a place of safety as soon as he enters a town which was under the authority of the begums, where he was treated with kindness, and afterwards sent with a protecting guard to Colonel Hannay. This last circumstance, which is mentioned in the first affidavit of Captain Gordon, is suppressed in the second, for what purpose it is obvious. But let us attend to the testimony of Hyder Beg Cawn, who, as the minister of the nabob, was the person, certainly, of all others, the best acquainted with the transactions then passing in the country. Though with every source of intelligence open to him, and swearing both to rumor and to fact, he does not mention a syllable in proof of the pretended rebellion which was to dethrone his sovereign, nor even hint at anything of the kind.

Neither, my lords, is the evidence of the English officers more conclusive. That of Mr. Middleton, which has been so much relied upon, contains but a single passage which is at all pertinent, and this is not legal evidence. He says, " There was a general report that the begums had given much encouragement and some aid to the *jaghiredars* in resisting the resumption, and that he had heard there had been a good disposition in them towards the Rajah Cheyte Sing." His evidence is mere hearsay. He knows nothing of himself. He saw no insurrection. He met with no unfriendly dispositions. But on the mere rumors which he had stated did this conscientious servant of Mr. Hastings with promptitude execute the scheme of plunder which his master had devised.

The testimony of Colonel Hannay is of the same description. He simply states that " three *zemindars* told him that they were credibly informed that the begums had a hostile design against the nabob." When asked who these *zemindars* were, he replied that he was not at liberty to disclose their names. They had made the communication to him under an express injunction of secrecy which he could not violate.

There is also the deposition of a Frenchman, which is drawn up quite in the style of magnificence and glitter which belongs to his nation. He talks of having penetrated immeasurable wilds; of having seen tigers and other prowling monsters of the forest; of having surveyed mountains, and navigated streams; of having been entertained in palaces and menaced with dungeons; of having heard a number of rumors, but that he never saw any rebellious or hostile appearances.

Such, my lords, are the contents of these memorable depositions, on which the prisoner relies as a vindication of an act of the most transcendent rapacity and injustice of which there is any record or tradition.

I know, my lords, that if I were in a court of law, sitting merely to try the question of the validity of this testimony, to rise in order to comment upon it, I should be prevented from proceeding. By the bench I should be asked, "What do you mean to do? There is nothing in these affidavits upon which we can permit you for a minute to occupy the time of the court. There is not, from the beginning to the end, one particle of legal, substantial, or even defensible proof. There is nothing except hearsay and rumor." But though, my lords, I am persuaded that such would be the admonition which I should receive from the court, yet, being exceedingly anxious to meet everything at your lordships' bar on which the prisoner can build the smallest degree of dependence, I must pray your indulgence while I examine separately the points which are attempted to be set up by these affidavits.

They are three in number:

1. That the begums gave assistance to Cheyte Sing, Rajah of Benares.

2. That they encouraged and assisted the *jaghiredars* to resist the resumption of the *jaghires*. And,

3. That they were the principal movers of all the commotions in Oude.

These, my lords, are the three allegations that the affidavits are to sustain, and which are accompanied with the general charge that the begums were in rebellion.

1. Of the rebellion here pretended, I cannot, my lords, find a trace. With the care and indefatigable industry of an antiquary, hunting for some precious vestige which is to decide the truth of his speculations, have I searched for the evidence of it. Though we have heard it spoken of with as much certainty as the one which happened in Scotland in the year 1745, not the slightest appearance of it can I discover. I am unable to ascertain either the time when, or the place where it raged. No army has been seen to collect; no battle to be fought; no blood to

be spilt. It was a rebellion which had for its object the destruction of no human creature but those who planned it—it was a
rebellion which, according to Mr. Middleton's expression, no
man, either horse or foot, ever marched to quell! The chief justice was the only one who took the field against it. The force
against which it was raised instantly withdrew to give it elbow-
room; and even then, it was a rebellion which perversely showed
itself in acts of hospitality to the nabob whom it was to dethrone,
and to the English whom it was to extirpate! Beginning in
nothing, it continued without raging, and ended as it originated!

If, my lords, rebellions of this mysterious nature can happen,
it is time to look about us. Who can say that one does not now
exist which menaces our safety? Perhaps at the very moment
I am speaking one ravages our city! Perhaps it may be by lying
perdue in a neighboring village! Perhaps, like the ostentatious
encampment which has given celebrity to Brentford and Eal-
ing, it may have fixed its quarters at Hammersmith or Islington,
ready to pour down its violence at the approach of night!

But, my lords, let us endeavor to fix the time when this horrid
rebellion occurred. To August 1, 1781, it is clear there was
none. At this date letters were received from Colonel Morgan,
the commanding officer of Oude, who is silent on the subject.
On September 27th, he gives an account of some insurrections
at Lucknow, the seat of the Court, but of none at Fyzabad,
where the begums resided. Nearly of the same date there is a
letter from Major Hannay, then at the rajah's Court, in which
the state of his affairs is described, but no suspicion expressed
of his being assisted by the begums.

At this time, therefore, there was certainly no rebellion or
disaffection displayed. Nay, we find, on the contrary, the nabob
going to visit his mother, the very princess who is charged with
revolting against his authority. But, my lords, it is alleged that
he was attended by two thousand horse, and the inference is
drawn by the counsel of the prisoner that he took this military
force to quell the insurrection; to confirm which they appealed
to Mr. Middleton, who, being asked whether these troops were
well appointed, caught in an instant a gleam of martial memory,
and answered in the affirmative. Unfortunately, however, for
the martial memory of Mr. Middleton, it is stated by Captain
Edwards, who was with the nabob as his aide-de-camp, that

there were not more than five or six hundred horse, and these so bad and miserably equipped that they were unable to keep up with him, so that very few were near his person or within the reach of his command. That of these few, the most were mutinous from being ill paid, and were rather disposed to promote than put down any insurrection. But, my lords, I will concede to the prisoner the full amount of military force for which he anxiously contends. I will allow the whole two thousand cavalry to enter in a gallop into the very city of Fyzabad. For, has not Captain Edwards proved that they were only the usual guard of the nabob? Has not, moreover, Mr. Middleton himself declared, rather indiscreetly, I confess, " that it is the constant custom of the princes of India to travel with a great equipage, and that it would be considered an unpardonable disrespect to the person visited were they to come unescorted." This, my lords, is really the truth. The Indian princes never perform a journey without a splendid retinue. The habits of the East require ostentation and parade. They do not, as the princes of Europe—who, sometimes from one motive and sometimes from another, at times from political views and at times from curiosity, travel, some to France to learn manners, and others to England to learn liberty—choose to be relieved from the pomps of state and the drudgery of equipage. But, my lords, perhaps, in this instance, the nabob, wishing to adapt himself to the service on which he was going, did dispense with his usual style. Hearing of a rebellion without an army, he may have thought that it could only, with propriety, be attacked by a prince without a guard!

It has also been contended, my lords, in proof of this rebellion, that one thousand nudgies were raised at Fyzabad, and sent to the assistance of Cheyte Sing.

It is deemed a matter of no consequence that the officer second in command to the rajah [Cheyte Sing], has positively sworn that these troops came from Lucknow, and not from Fyzabad. This the prisoner wishes to have considered as only the trifling mistake of the name of one capital for another. But he has found it more difficult to get over the fact which has been attested by the same witness, that the troops were of a different description from those in the service of the begums, being matchlock, and not swords men. It is, therefore, manifest that the troops were not furnished by the princesses, and it seems highly probable that they did come from Lucknow; not that they were sent by the nabob, but by some of the powerful *jaghiredars* who have uniformly avowed an aversion to the English.

It has been more than once mentioned by some of the witnesses, my lords, that Sabid Ally, the younger son of the bow [younger] begum, was deeply and criminally concerned in these transactions. Why was he, therefore, permitted to escape with impunity? To this question Sir Elijah Impey gave a very satisfactory answer when he informed us that the young man was miserably poor, and a bankrupt. Here is a complete solution of the enigma. There never enters into the mind of Mr. Hastings a suspicion of treason where there is no treasure! Sabid Ally found, therefore, protection in his poverty, and safety in his insolvency. My lords, the political sagacity of Mr. Hastings exhibits the converse of the doctrine which the experience of history has established. Hitherto it has generally been deemed that the possession of property attaches a person to the country which contains it, and makes him cautious how he hazards any enterprise which might be productive of innovation, or draw upon him the suspicion or displeasure of government; and that, on the contrary, the needy, having no permanent stake, are always desperate, and easily seduced into commotions which promise any change; but, my lords, the prisoner, inverting this doctrine, has, in the true spirit of rapacity and speculation which belongs to him, never failed to recognize loyalty in want, and to discern treason in wealth!

Allow me now, my lords, to lay before you some of those proofs which we have collected of the steady friendship and good dispositions of the begums to the English interests. I have in my hands a letter **from** one of them, which I will read, complaining of the cruel and unjust suspicions that were entertained of her fidelity. Your lordships must perceive the extraordinary energy which the plain and simple language of truth gives to her representations. Her complaints are eloquence; her supplications, persuasion; her remonstrances, conviction.

I call, moreover, the attention of the court to the interference of the bow [younger] begum in behalf of Captain Gordon, by which his life was saved, at a moment when, if the princesses

wished to strike a blow against the English, they might have
done it with success. This man, whose life was thus preserved,
and who, in the first burst of the natural feelings of his heart,
poured forth his grateful acknowledgments of the obligation,
afterwards became the instrument of the destruction of his pro-
tectress. I will produce the letter wherein he thanks her for her
interference, and confesses that he owes his life to her bounty.

It has been asked, with an air of some triumph, why Captain Gordon was not called to the bar? Why call him to the
bar? Would he not, as he has done in his affidavit, suppress
the portion of testimony we require? I trust that he may
never be brought to swear in this case till he becomes sensible
of his guilt, and feels an ardent, contrite zeal to do justice
to his benefactress, and to render her the most ample atonement
for the injuries which she has sustained by his ingratitude and
wickedness. The conduct of Captain Gordon, in this instance,
is so astonishingly depraved, that I confess I am in some degree
disposed to incredulity. I can scarcely believe it possible that,
after having repeatedly acknowledged that he owed his life
and liberty to her beneficent hand, he could so far forget these
obligations, as spontaneously, and of his own free-will, to come
forward, and expend a part of that breath which she had preserved, in an affidavit by which her ruin was to be effected! My
knowledge of the human heart will hardly permit me to think
that any rational being could deliberately commit an act of
such wanton atrocity. I must imagine that there has been some
scandalous deception; that, led on by Mr. Middleton, he made
his deposition, ignorant to what purpose it would be applied.
Every feeling of humanity recoils at the transaction viewed in
any other light. It is incredible that any intelligent person could
be capable of standing up in the presence of God, and of exclaiming, "To you, my benevolent friend, the breath I now
draw, next to Heaven, I owe to you. My existence is an emanation from your bounty. I am indebted to you beyond all possibility of return, and therefore my gratitude shall be your destruction!"

If, my lords—if I am right in my conjecture, that Captain
Gordon was thus seduced into the overthrow of his benefactress,
I hope he will present himself at your bar, and, by stating the
imposition which was practised upon him, vindicate his own

character, and that of human nature, from this foul imputation.

The original letters which passed on this occasion between Captain Gordon and the begum were transmitted by her to Mr. Middleton, for the purpose of being shown to the Governor-General. These letters Mr. Middleton endeavored to conceal. His letter-book, into which they were transcribed, is despoiled of those leaves which contained them. When questioned about them, he said that he had deposited Persian copies of the letters in the office at Lucknow, and that he did not bring translations of them with him to Calcutta, because he left the former city the very next day after receiving the originals; but, my lords, I will boldly assert that this pretext is a black and barefaced perjury. It can be proved that Middleton received the letters at least a month before he departed from Lucknow. He left that city on the seventeenth of October, and he received them on the twentieth of the preceding month. Well aware that by these documents the purity of the begums' intentions would be made manifest, that while accused of disaffection, their attachment was fully displayed, he, as their punishment was predetermined, found it necessary to suppress the testimonials of their innocence; but, my lords, these letters, covered as they were by every artifice which the vilest ingenuity could devise to hide them, have been discovered, and are now bared to view by the aid of that Power to whom all creation must bend—to whom nothing, in the whole system of thought or action, is impossible; who can invigorate the arm of infancy with a giant's nerve; who can bring light out of darkness, and good out of evil; can view the confines of hidden mischief, and drag forth each minister of guilt from amid his deeds of darkness and disaster, reluctant, alas! and unrepenting, to exemplify, at least, if not atone, and to qualify any casual sufferings of innocence by the final doom of its opposite; to prove there are the never-failing corrections of God, to make straight the obliquity of man!

My lords, the prisoner, in his defence, has ascribed the benevolent interposition of the begum in favor of Captain Gordon to her knowledge of the successes of the English. This is an imputation as ungenerous as it is false. The only success which the British troops met with at this time was that of Colonel Blair, on the third of September; but he himself acknowledged, that another victory gained at such a loss would be equal to a defeat. The reports that were circulated throughout the country, so far from being calculated to strike the princesses with awe of the English, were entirely the reverse. These were, that Mr. Hastings had been slain at Benares, and that the English had sustained the most disastrous defeats.

But, my lords, to remove every doubt from your minds, I will recur to what never fails me—the evidence of the prisoner against himself. In a letter to the council, which is on record, he confesses that, from the twenty-second of August to the twenty-second of September, he was confined in a situation of the utmost hazard; that his safety during this period was exceedingly precarious, and that the affairs of the English were generally thought to be unfavorable in the extreme. In his defence, however, Mr. Hastings has forgotten entirely these admissions. It certainly appears that the princesses demonstrated the firmness of their attachment to the British; not in the season of prosperity or triumph; not from the impulse of fear, nor the prospect of future protection; but that they, with a magnanimity almost unexampled, came forward at a moment when the hoard of collected vengeance was about to burst over our heads; when the measure of European guilt in India was completely filled by the oppressions which had just been exercised on the unfortunate Cheyte Sing; and when offended Heaven seemed, at last, to interfere to change the meek dispositions of the natives, to awaken their resentment, and to inspirit their revenge.

2. On the second allegation, my lords, namely, " That the begums encouraged and aided the *jaghiredars*," I do not think it necessary to say much. It is evident, from the letters of Mr. Middleton, that no such aid was required to awaken resentments, which must, indeed, unavoidably have arisen from the nature of an affair in which so many powerful interests were involved. The *jaghires* depending were of an immense amount, and as their owners, by the resumption of them, would be at once reduced to poverty and distress, they wanted surely no new instigation to resistance. It is ridiculous to attempt to impute to the begums, without a shadow of proof, the inspiring of sentiments which must inevitably have been excited in the breast of every *jaghiredar* by the contemplation of the injury and injustice which were intended to be done him. Reluctant to

waste the time of the court, I will dismiss the discussion of this charge by appealing to your lordships individually to determine, whether, on a proposal being made to confiscate your several estates (and the cases are precisely analogous), the incitements of any two ladies of this kingdom would be at all required to kindle your resentments and to rouse you to opposition?

3. The commotions, my lords, which prevailed in Oude have also been attributed to the begums, and constitute the third and remaining allegation against them. But these disorders, I confidently aver, were, on the contrary, the work of the English, which I will show by the most incontestable evidence.

They were produced by their rapacity and violence, and not by the " perfidious artifices " of these old women. To drain the province of its money, every species of cruelty, of extortion, of rapine, of stealth, was employed by the emissaries of Mr. Hastings. The nabob perceived the growing discontents among the people, and, alarmed at the consequences, endeavored, by the strongest representations, to rid his devoted country of the oppressions of its invaders, and particularly from the vulture grasp of Colonel Hannay; swearing by Mohammed that if " this tyrant were not removed he would quit the province," as a residence in it was no longer to be endured. Thus this mild people suffered for a while in barren anguish and ineffectual bewailings. At length, however, in their meek bosoms, where injury never before begot resentment, nor despair aroused to courage, increased oppression had its effect. They determined on resistance. They collected round their implacable foe [Colonel Hannay], and had nearly sacrificed him. So deeply were they impressed with the sense of their wrongs, that they would not even accept of life from their oppressors. They threw themselves upon the swords of the soldiery, and sought death as the only termination of their sorrows and persecutions. Of a people thus injured and thus feeling, it is an audacious fallacy to attribute their conduct to any external impulse. My lords, the true cause of it is to be traced to the first-born principles of man. It grows with his growth; it strengthens with his strength. It teaches him to understand; it enables him to feel. For where there is human fate, can there be a penury of human feeling? Where there is injury, will there not be resentment? Is not despair to be followed by courage? The God of battles pervades and penetrates the inmost spirit of man, and, rousing him to shake off the burden that is grievous, and the yoke that is galling, reveals the law written on his heart, and the duties and privileges of his nature.

If, my lords, a stranger had at this time entered the province of Oude, ignorant of what had happened since the death of Sujah Dowlah—that prince who with a savage heart had still great lines of character, and who, with all his ferocity in war, had, with a cultivating hand, preserved to his country the wealth which it derived from benignant skies and a prolific soil—if, observing the wide and general devastation of fields unclothed and brown; of vegetation burned up and extinguished; of villages depopulated and in ruin; of temples unroofed and perishing; of reservoirs broken down and dry, this stranger should ask, " What has thus laid waste this beautiful and opulent land; what monstrous madness has ravaged with widespread war; what desolating foreign foe; what civil discords; what disputed succession; what religious zeal; what fabled monster has stalked abroad, and, with malice and mortal enmity to man, withered by the grasp of death every growth of nature and humanity, all means of delight, and each original, simple principle of bare existence?" the answer would have been, " Not one of these causes! No wars have ravaged these lands and depopulated these villages! No desolating foreign foe! No domestic broils! No disputed succession! No religious, super-serviceable zeal! No poisonous monster! No affliction of Providence, which, while it scourged us, cut off the sources of resuscitation! No! This damp of death is the mere effusion of British amity! We sink under the pressure of their support! We writhe under their perfidious gripe! They have embraced us with their protecting arms, and lo! these are the fruits of their alliance? "

What then, my lords! shall we bear to be told that, under such circumstances, the exasperated feelings of a whole people, thus spurred on to clamor and resistance, were excited by the poor and feeble influence of the begums? After hearing the description given by an eye-witness [Colonel Naylor, successor of Hannay] of the paroxysm of fever and delirium into which despair threw the natives when on the banks of the polluted Ganges, panting for breath, they tore more widely open the lips of their gaping wounds, to accelerate their dissolution; and while their blood was issuing, presented their ghastly eyes to heaven, breathing their last and fervent prayer that the dry earth might not be suffered to drink their blood, but that it might rise up to the throne of God, and rouse the eternal Providence to avenge the wrongs of their country—will it be said that all this was brought about by the incantations of these begums in their secluded zenana; or that they could inspire this enthusiasm and this despair into the breasts of a people who felt no grievance, and had suffered no torture? What motive, then, could have such influence in their bosom? What motive! That which nature, the common parent, plants in the bosom of man; and which, though it may be less active in the Indian than in the Englishman, is still congenial with, and makes a part of his being. That feeling which tells him that man was never made to be the property of man; but that, when in the pride and insolence of power, one human creature dares to tyrannize over another, it is a power usurped, and resistance is a duty. That principle which tells him that resistance to power usurped is not merely a duty which he owes to himself and to his neighbor, but a duty which he owes to his God, in asserting and maintaining the rank which He gave him in his creation. That principle which neither the rudeness of ignorance can stifle, nor the enervation of refinement extinguish! That principle which makes it base for a man to suffer when he ought to act; which, tending to preserve to the species the original designations of Providence, spurns at the arrogant distinctions of man, and indicates the independent quality of his race.

I trust now that your lordships can feel no hesitation in acquitting the unfortunate princesses of this allegation. But though the innocence of the begums may be confessed, it does not necessarily follow, I am ready to allow, that the prisoner must be guilty. There is a possibility that he might have been deluded by others, and incautiously led into a false conclusion. If this be proved, my lords, I will cheerfully abandon the present charge. But if, on the other hand, it shall appear, as I am confident it will, that in his subsequent conduct there was a mysterious concealment denoting conscious guilt; if all his narrations of the business be found marked with inconsistency and contradiction, there can be, I think, a doubt no longer entertained of his criminality.

It will be easy, my lords, to prove that such concealment was actually practised. From the month of September, in which the seizure of the treasures took place, till the succeeding January, no intimation whatever was given of it by Mr. Hastings to the council at Calcutta. But, my lords, look at the mode in which this concealment is attempted to be evaded. The first pretext is, the want of leisure! Contemptible falsehood! He could amuse his fancy at this juncture with the composition of Eastern tales, but to give an account of a rebellion which convulsed an empire, or of his acquiring so large an amount of treasure, he had no time!

The second pretext is, that all communication between Calcutta and Fyzabad was cut off. This is no less untrue. By comparing dates, it will be seen that letters, now in our possession, passed at this period between Mr. Middleton and the prisoner. Even Sir Elijah Impey has unguardedly declared that the road leading from the one city to the other was as clear from interruption as that between London and any of the neighboring villages. So satisfied am I, indeed, on this point, that I am willing to lay aside every other topic of criminality against the prisoner, and to rest this prosecution alone on the question of the validity of the reasons assigned for the concealment we have alleged. Let those, my lords, who still retain any doubts on the subject, turn to the prisoner's narrative of his journey to Benares. They will there detect, amid a motley mixture of cant and mystery, of rhapsody and enigma, the most studious concealment.

It may, perhaps, be asked, why did Mr. Hastings use all these efforts to veil this business? Though it is not strictly incumbent on me to give an answer to the question, yet I will say that he had obviously a reason for it. Looking to the natural effect of deep injuries on the human mind, he thought that oppression must beget resistance. The attempt which the begums might be driven to make in their own defence, though really the effect, he was determined to represent as the cause of his proceedings. He was here only repeating the experiment which he so successfully performed in the case of Cheyte Sing. Even when disappointed in those views by the natural meekness and submission of the princesses, he could not relinquish the scheme; and hence, in his letter to the Court of Directors, January 5, 1782, he

represents the subsequent disturbances in Oude as the cause of
the violent measures he had adoptd two months previous to the
existence of these disturbances! He there congratulates his
masters on the seizure of the treasures which he declares, by the
law of Mohammed, were the property of Asoph ul Dowlah.

My lords, the prisoner more than once assured the House of
Commons that the inhabitants of Asia believed him to be a
preternatural being, gifted with good fortune or the peculiar
favorite of Heaven; and that Providence never failed to take up
and carry, by wise but hidden means, every project of his to its
destined end. Thus, in his blasphemous and vulgar puritanical
jargon, did Mr. Hastings libel the course of Providence. Thus,
according to him, when his corruptions and briberies were on
the eve of exposure, Providence inspired the heart of Nuncomar
to commit a low, base crime, in order to save him from ruin.[3]
Thus, also, in his attempts on Cheyte Sing, and his plunder of
the begums, Providence stepped forth, and inspired the one with
resistance and the other with rebellion, to forward his purposes!
Thus, my lords, did he arrogantly represent himself as a man
not only the favorite of Providence, but as one for whose sake
Providence departed from the eternal course of its own wise
dispensations, to assist his administration by the elaboration of
all that is deleterious and ill; heaven-born forgeries—inspired treasons—providential rebellions! arraigning that Providence—

"Whose works are goodness, and whose ways are right."

It does undoubtedly, my lords, bear a strange appearance,
that a man of reputed ability, like the prisoner, even when acting
wrongly, should have recourse to so many bungling artifices,
and spread so thin a veil over his deceptions. But those who
are really surprised at this circumstance must have attended
very little to the demeanor of Mr. Hastings. Through the whole
of his defence upon this charge, sensible that truth would undo
him, he rests his hopes on falsehood. Observing this rule, he
has drawn together a set of falsehoods without consistency, and
without connection; not knowing, or not remembering, that

[3] Nuncomar, a Hindoo of high rank, who at one time accused Hastings of receiving bribes. He was at the same time accused by Hastings of forging a bond, when he was arraigned before the Supreme Court of Bengal and condemned to death.

there is nothing which requires so much care in the fabrication, as a system of lies. The series must be regular and unbroken; but his falsehoods are eternally at variance, and demolish one another. Indeed, in all his conduct, he seems to be actuated but by one principle, to do things contrary to the established form. This architect militates against the first principles of the art. He begins with the frieze and the capital, and lays the base of the column at the top. Thus turning his edifice upside down, he plumes himself upon the novelty of his idea, till it comes tumbling about his ears. Rising from these ruins, he is soon found rearing a similar structure. He delights in difficulties, and disdains a plain and secure foundation. He loves, on the contrary, to build on a precipice, and to encamp on a mine. Inured to falls, he fears not danger. Frequent defeats have given him a hardihood, without impressing a sense of disgrace.

It was once, my lords, a maxim, as much admitted in the practice of common life as in the schools of philosophy, that where Heaven is inclined to destroy, it begins with frenzying the intellect. *"Quem Deus vult perdere prius dementat."* This doctrine the right honorable manager (Mr. Burke), who opened generally to your lordships the articles of impeachment, still further extended. He declared that the coexistence of vice and prudence was incompatible; that the vicious man, being deprived of his best energies, and curtailed in his proportion of understanding, was left with such a short-sighted penetration as could lay no claim to prudence. This is the sentiment of my noble and exalted friend, whose name I can never mention but with respect and admiration due to his virtue and talents; whose proud disdain of vice can only be equalled by the ability with which he exposes and controls it; to whom I look up with homage; whose genius is commensurate with philanthropy; whose memory will stretch itself beyond the fleeting objects of any little partial shuffling—through the whole wide range of human knowledge and honorable aspiration after good—as large as the system which forms life—as lasting as those objects which adorn it; but in this sentiment, so honorable to my friend, I cannot implicitly agree. If the true definition of prudence be the successful management and conduct of a purpose to its end, I can at once bring instances into view where this species of prudence belonged to minds distinguished by the atrocity of their actions.

When I survey the history of a Philip of Macedon, of a Cæsar, of a Cromwell, I perceive great guilt successfully conducted, if not by legitimate discretion, at least by a consummate craft, or by an all-commanding sagacity, productive of precisely the same effects. These, however, I confess, were isolated characters, who left the vice they dared to follow either in the state of dependent vassalage, or involved it in destruction. Such is the perpetual law of nature, that virtue, whether placed in a circle, more contracted or enlarged, moves with sweet concert. There is no dissonance to jar; no asperity to divide; and that harmony which makes its felicity at the same time constitutes its protection. Of vice, on the contrary, the parts are disunited, and each in barbarous language clamors for its pre-eminence. It is a scene where, though one domineering passion may have sway, the others still press forward with their dissonant claims; and, in the moral world, effects waiting on their causes, the discord which results, of course, insures defeat.

In this way, my lords, I believe the failure of Mr. Hastings is to be explained, and such, I trust, will be the fate of all who shall emulate his character or his conduct. The doctrine of my friend, from what I have said, can, therefore, hold only in those minds which cannot be satisfied with the indulgence of a single crime; where, instead of one base master passion having the complete sway, to which all the faculties are subject, and on which alone the mind is bent, there is a combustion and rivalry among a number of passions yet baser, when pride, vanity, avarice, lust of power, cruelty, all at once actuate the human soul and distract its functions; all of them at once filling their several spaces, some in their larger, some in their more contracted orbits; all of them struggling for pre-eminence, and each counteracting the other. In such a mind, undoubtedly, great crimes can never be accompanied by prudence. There is a fortunate disability, occasioned by the contention, that rescues the human species from the villany of the intention. Such is the original denunciation of nature. Not so with the nobler passions. In the breast where they reside, the harmony is never interrupted by the number. A perfect and substantial agreement gives an accession of vigor to each, and, spreading their influence in every direction, like the divine intelligence and benignity from which they flow, they ascertain it to the individual by which they are possessed, and communicate it to the society of which he is a member.

My lords, I shall now revert again to the claims made on the Princesses of Oude. The counsel for the prisoner have labored to impress on the court the idea that the nabob was a prince sovereignly independent, and in no degree subject to the control of Mr. Hastings; but, after the numberless proofs we have adduced of his being, on the contrary, a mere cipher in the hands of the Governor-General, your lordships will require of them, to create such a conviction on your minds, much more conclusive evidence than any which they have hitherto presented. I believe, both as regards the resumption of the *jaghires,* and especially the seizure of the treasures, they will find it very difficult to show the independence of the prince.

It has, my lords, been strenuously contended on our parts that the measure of seizing the treasures originated with the prisoner, and in maintenance of the position we have brought forward a chain of testimony clear, and, we think, satisfactory; but the counsel for the prisoner, on the other hand, assert with equal earnestness, that the proposition for seizing the treasures came originally from the nabob. It is therefore incumbent on them to support their assertion by proof, as we have done. Certainly the best evidence of the fact would be the exhibition of the letter of the nabob to Mr. Hastings, in which they allege the proposition was made. Why, then, is not this document, which must at once settle all disputation on the subject, produced? The truth is, there is no such letter. I peremptorily deny it, and challenge the prisoner and his counsel to produce a letter or paper containing any proposition of the kind coming immediately from the prince.

My lords, the seizure of the treasures and the *jaghires* was the effect of a dark conspiracy, in which six persons were concerned. Three of the conspirators were of a higher order. These were Mr. Hastings, who may be considered as the principal and leader in this black affair; Mr. Middleton, the English resident at Lucknow; and Sir Elijah Impey. The three inferior or subordinate conspirators were Hyder Beg Cawn, the nominal minister of the nabob, but in reality the creature of Mr. Hastings, Colonel Hannay, and Ali Ibrahim Khan.

Sir Elijah Impey was intrusted by Mr. Hastings to carry his

orders to Mr. Middleton, and to concert with him the means of carrying them into execution. The chief justice, my lords, being a principal actor in the whole of this iniquitous business, it will be necessary to take notice of some parts of the evidence which he has delivered upon oath at your lordships' bar.

When asked what became of the Persian affidavits sworn before him, after he had delivered them to Mr. Hastings, he replied that he really did not know! He was also asked if he had them translated, or knew of their having been translated, or had any conversation with Mr. Hastings on the subject of the affidavits. He replied, " that he knew nothing at all of their having been translated, and that he had no conversation whatever with Mr. Hastings on the subject of the affidavits after he had delivered them to him." He was next asked whether he did not think it a little singular that he should not have held any conversation with the Governor-General on a subject of so much moment as that of the affidavits which he had taken. His answer was that he did not think it singular, because he left Chunar the very day after he delivered the affidavits to Mr. Hastings. By this answer the witness certainly meant it should be understood that when he quitted Chunar he left the Governor-General behind him; but it appears, from letters written by the witness himself, and which we have already laid before the court, that he arrived at Chunar on December 1, 1781; that he then began to take the affidavits, and, when completed, he and Mr. Hastings left Chunar in company, and set out on the road to Benares; and that, after being together from the first to the sixth of the month, the former took leave of the latter, and proceeded on his journey to Calcutta. Here, then, my lords, we detect a subterfuge artfully contrived to draw you into a false conclusion! There is also another part of the witness's evidence which is entitled to as little credit. He has sworn that he knew nothing of the Persian affidavits having been translated. Now, my lords, we formerly produced a letter from Major William Davy, the confidential secretary and Persian translator to the Governor-General, in which he states that he made an affidavit before Sir Elijah Impey at Buxar on the twelfth of December, just six days after Sir Elijah parted from Mr. Hastings, swearing that the papers annexed to the affidavits were faithful translations of the Persian affidavits! What shall we say, my lords, of such testimony? I will make only one remark upon it, which I shall borrow from an illustrious man: " That no one could tell where to look for truth, if it could not be found on the judgment seat, or know what to credit, if the affirmation of a judge was not to be trusted."

I have, my lords, before observed, that the chief justice was intrusted by the prisoner to concert with Mr. Middleton the means of carrying into execution the order of which he was the bearer from the Governor-General to the resident. These orders do not appear anywhere in writing, but your lordships are acquainted with their purport. The court must recollect that Mr. Middleton was instructed by them to persuade the nabob to propose, as from himself, to Mr. Hastings, the seizure of the begums' treasures. That this was really so appears undeniably as well from the tenor of Mr. Middleton's letter on the subject, as from the prisoner's account of the business in his defence. Evidently, Mr. Hastings was on this occasion hobbled by difficulties which put all his ingenuity into requisition. He was aware that it must seem extraordinary that at the very moment he was confiscating the property of the begums, on the plea of their treasonable machinations, he should stipulate that an annual allowance equal almost to the produce of that property should be secured to them. Though he had accused the princesses of rebellion, by which, of course, their treasures were forfeited to the state, yet he was reluctant to appear as the principal in seizing them.

Do not, my lords, these embarrassments prove that the prisoner was sensible of the injustice of his proceedings? If the princesses were in rebellion, there could be no ground for his demurring to seize their property. The consciousness of their innocence could alone, therefore, make him timid and irresolute. To get rid at once of his difficulties, he resorts to the expedient which I have before stated, namely, of giving directions to Sir Elijah Impey that Mr. Middleton should urge the nabob to propose, as from himself, the seizure of the treasures. My lords, the unhappy prince, without a will of his own, consented to make the proposal, as an alternative for the resumption of the *jaghires;* a measure to which he had the most unconquerable reluctance. Mr. Hastings, as it were to indulge the nabob, agreed to the proposal; rejoicing, at the same time, that his

scheme had proved so far successful; for he thought this proposal, coming from the nabob, would free him from the odium
of so unpopular a plundering. But the artifice was too shallow;
and your lordships are now able to trace the measure to its
source. The court will see from the evidence that Mr. Hastings
suggested it to Sir Elijah Impey, that Sir Elijah Impey might
suggest it to Middleton, that Middleton might suggest it to the
nabob, that his Highness might suggest it to Mr. Hastings; and
thus the suggestion returned to the place from which it had
originally set out!

One single passage of a letter, written by Middleton to Mr.
Hastings on December 2, 1781, will make this point as clear as
day. He informs the Governor-General that " the nabob, wishing to evade the measure of resuming the *jaghires,* had sent him
a message to the following purport: that if the measure proposed was intended to procure the payment of the balance due to
the Company, he could better and more expeditiously effect
that object by taking from his mother the treasures of his father,
which he asserted to be in her hands, and to which he claimed
a right, founded on the laws of the Koran; and that it would be
sufficient that he [Mr. Hastings] would hint his opinion upon
it, without giving a formal sanction to the measure proposed."
Mr. Middleton added, " the resumption of the *jaghires* it is
necessary to suspend till I have your answer to this letter."

In the first place, it is clear from this letter that, though the
nabob consented to make the desired proposal for seizing the
treasures, it was only as an alternative; for it never entered into
his head both to seize the treasures and resume the *jaghires.*
The former measure he wished to substitute in the room of the
latter, and by no means to couple them together. But Mr.
Hastings was too nice a reasoner for the prince. He insisted
that one measure should be carried into execution, because the
nabob had proposed it; and the other, because he himself determined upon it.

It also appears that the nabob was taught to plead his right
to the treasures, as founded upon the laws of the Koran. Not
a word was said about the guarantee and treaty which had
barred that right, whatever it might have been! But, my lords,
if all Mr. Hastings would have the world believe is true, he
[the nabob] had still a much better title—one against which

the treaty and guarantee could not be raised, and this was the treason of the begums, by which they forfeited all their property to the state, and every claim upon English protection. On this right by forfeiture, the nabob, however, was silent. Being a stranger to the rebellion, and to the treason of his parents, he was reduced to the necessity of reviving a right under the laws of the Koran, which the treaty and guarantee had forever extinguished.

This letter, moreover, contains this remarkable expression, namely, " that it would be sufficient to hint his [Mr. Hastings'] opinion upon it, without giving a formal sanction to the measure proposed." Why this caution? If the begums were guilty of treason why should he be fearful of declaring to the world that it was not the practice of the English to protect rebellious subjects, and prevent their injured sovereigns from proceeding against them according to law?—that he considered the treaty and guarantee, by which the begums held their property, as no longer binding upon the English Government, who consequently could have no further right to interfere between the nabob and his rebellious parents, but must leave him at liberty to punish or forgive them as he should think fit? But, my lords, instead of holding this language, which manliness and conscious integrity would have dictated, had he been convinced of the guilt of the begums, Mr. Hastings wished to derive all possible advantage from active measures against them, and at the same time so far to save appearances, as that he might be thought to be passive in the affair.

My lords, in another part of the same letter, Mr. Middleton informs the Governor-General " that he sent him, at the same time, a letter from the nabob on the subject of seizing the treasures." This letter has been suppressed. I challenge the counsel for the prisoner to produce it, or to account satisfactorily to your lordships for its not having been entered upon the Company's records. Nor is this, my lords, the only suppression of which we have reason to complain. The affidavit of Goulass Roy, who lived at Fyzabad, the residence of the begums, and who was known to be their enemy, is also suppressed. No person could be so well informed of their guilt, if they had been guilty, as Goulass Roy, who resided upon the spot where levies were said to have been made for Cheyte Sing by their order. If, therefore, his testimony had not destroyed the charge of a rebllion on the part of the begums there is no doubt but it would have been carefully preserved. The information of Mr. Scott has, moreover, been withheld from us. This gentleman lived unmolested at Taunda, where Sumshire Khan commanded for the begums, and where he carried on an extensive manufacture without the least hinderance from this supposed disaffected Governor. Mr. Scott was at Taunda, too, when it was said that the Governor pointed the guns of the fort upon Captain Gordon's party. If this circumstance, my lords, did really happen, Mr. Scott must have heard of it, as he was himself at the time under the protection of those very guns. Why, then, is not the examination of this gentleman produced? I believe your lordships are satisfied that, if it had supported the allegations against Sumshire Khan, it would not have been cancelled.

It is not clear to me, my lords, that, as servile a tool as Mr. Middleton was, the prisoner entrusted him with every part of his intentions throughout the business of the begums. He certainly mistrusted, or pretended to mistrust him, in his proceedings relative to the resumption of the *jaghires*. When it began to be rumored abroad that terms so favorable to the nabob as he obtained in the treaty of Chunar—by which Mr. Hastings consented to withdraw the temporary brigade, and to remove the English gentlemen from Oude—would never have been granted, if the nabob had not bribed the parties concerned in the negotiation to betray the interests of the Company, Mr. Hastings confirmed the report by actually charging Mr. Middleton and his assistant resident, Mr. Johnson, with having accepted bribes. They both joined in the most solemn assurances of their innocence, and called God to witness the truth of their declarations. Mr. Hastings, after this, appeared satisfied; possibly the consciousness that he had in his own pocket the only bribe which was given on the occasion, the £100,000, might have made him the less earnest in prosecuting any further inquiry into the business.

A passage in a letter from Mr. Hastings shows that he did not think proper to commit to writing all the orders which he wished Mr. Middleton to execute; for there Mr. Hastings expresses his doubts of the resident's " firmness and activity; and, above all, of his recollection of his instructions and their importance; and said, that if he, Mr. Middleton, could not rely on his own power, and the means he possessed for performing those services, he would free him from the charge, and proceed to Lucknow and undertake it himself." My lords, you must presume that the instructions here alluded to were verbal; for had they been written there could be no danger of their being forgot. I call upon the counsel to state the nature of those instructions, which were deemed of so much importance that the Governor was so greatly afraid Mr. Middleton would not recollect them, and which, nevertheless, he did not dare to commit to writing.

To make your lordships understand some other expressions in the above passage, I must recall to your memory, that it has appeared in evidence that Mr. Middleton had a strong objection to the resumption of the *jaghires;* which he thought a service of so much danger that he removed Mrs. Middleton and his family when he was about to enter upon it; for he expected resistance not only from the begums, but from the nabob's own *aumeels* [agents] ; who, knowing that the prince was a reluctant instrument in the hands of the English, thought they would please him by opposing a measure to which he had given his authority against his will. Middleton undoubtedly expected the whole country would unanimously rise against him; and therefore it was, my lords, that he suspended the execution of the order of resumption, until he should find whether the seizure of the treasures, proposed as an alternative, would be accepted as such. The prisoner pressed him to execute the order for resuming the *jaghires*, and offered to go himself upon that service if he should decline it. Middleton at last, having received a thundering letter from Mr. Hastings, by which he left him to act under "a dreadful responsibility," set out for Fyzabad.

My lords, for all the cruelties and barbarities that were executed there, the Governor-General in his narrative says he does not hold himself answerable, because he commanded Middleton to be personally present during the whole of the transaction, until he should complete the seizing of the treasures and resuming the *jaghires*. But for what purpose did he order Middleton to be present? I will show, by quoting the orders verbatim:

" You yourself must be personally present; you must not allow any negotiation or forbearance, but must prosecute both services, until the begums are at the entire mercy of the nabob." These peremptory orders, given under " a dreadful responsibility," were not issued, my lords, as you see, for purposes of humanity; not that the presence of the resident might restrain the violence of the soldier; but that he might be a watch upon the nabob; to steel his heart against the feelings of returning nature in his breast, and prevent the possibility of his relenting, or granting any terms to his mother and grandmother. This truly was the abominable motive which induced the prisoner to command the personal attendance of Middleton, and yet, my lords, he dares to say that he is not responsible for the horrid scene which ensued.

[Here Mr. Sheridan was taken ill, and retired for a while to try if in the fresh air he could recover, so as that he might conclude all he had to say upon the evidence on the second charge. Some time after, Mr. Fox informed their lordships that Mr. Sheridan was much better, but that he felt he was not sufficiently so to be able to do justice to the subject he had in hand. The managers therefore hoped their lordships would be pleased to appoint a future day, on which Mr. Sheridan would finish his observations on the evidence. Upon this, their lordships returned to their own House, and adjourned the court.]

My lords, permit me to remind you that when I had last the honor of addressing you I concluded with submitting to the court the whole of the correspondence, as far as it could be obtained, between the principal and agents in the nefarious plot carried on against the nabob vizier and the begums of Oude. These letters demand of the court the most grave and deliberate attention, as containing not only a narrative of that foul and unmanly conspiracy, but also a detail of the motives and ends for which it was formed, and an exposition of the trick and quibble, the prevarication and the untruth, with which it was then acted, and is now attempted to be defended. It will here be naturally inquired, with some degree of surprise, how the private correspondence which thus establishes the guilt of its authors came to light? This was owing to a mutual resentment which broke out about the middle of December, 1782, between the parties. Mr. Middleton, on the one hand, became jealous of the abatement of Mr. Hastings' confidence; and the Governor-General was incensed at the tardiness with which the resident proceeded.

From this moment, shyness and suspicion between the principal and the agent took place. Middleton hesitated about the expediency of resuming the *jaghires*, and began to doubt whether the advantage would be equal to the risk. Mr. Hastings, whether he apprehended that Middleton was retarded by any return of humanity or sentiments of justice, by any secret combination with the begum and her son, or a wish to take the lion's share of the plunder to himself, was exasperated at the delay. Middleton represented the unwillingness of the nabob to execute the measure—the low state of his finances—that his troops were mutinous for want of pay—that his life had been in danger from an insurrection among them—and that in this moment of distress he had offered £100,000, in addition to a like sum paid before, as an equivalent for the resumption which was demanded of him. Of this offer, however, it now appears, the nabob knew nothing! In conferring an obligation, my lords, it is sometimes contrived, from motives of delicacy, that the name of the donor shall be concealed from the person obliged; but here it was reserved for Middleton to refine this sentiment of delicacy, so as to leave the person giving utterly ignorant of the favor he bestowed!

But notwithstanding these little differences and suspicions Mr. Hastings and Mr. Middleton, on the return of the latter to Calcutta in October, 1782, lived in the same style of friendly collusion and fraudulent familiarity as formerly. After, however, an intimacy of about six months, the Governor-General very unexpectedly arraigns his friend before the Board at Calcutta. It was on this occasion that the prisoner, rashly for himself, but happily for the purposes of justice, produced these letters. Whatever, my lords, was the meaning of this proceeding—whether it was a juggle to elude inquiry, or whether it was intended to make an impression at Fyzabad—whether Mr. Hastings drew up the charge, and instructed Mr. Middleton how to prepare the defence; or whether the accused composed the charge, and the accuser the defence, there is discernible in the transaction the same habitual collusion in which the parties lived, and the prosecution ended, as we have seen, in a rhapsody, a repartee, and a poetical quotation by the prosecutor!

The private letters, my lords, are the only part of the correspondence thus providentially disclosed which is deserving of attention. They were written in the confidence of private communication, without any motives to palliate and color facts, or to mislead. The counsel for the prisoner have, however, chosen to rely on the public correspondence, prepared, as appears on the very face of it, for the concealment of fraud and the purpose of deception. They, for example, dwelt on a letter from Mr. Middleton, dated December, 1781, which intimates some supposed contumacy of the begums; and this they thought countenanced the proceedings which afterwards took place, and particularly the resumption of the *jaghires;* but, my lords, you cannot have forgotten that both Sir Elijah Impey and Mr. Middleton declared, in their examination at your bar, that the letter was totally false. Another letter, which mentions "the determination of the nabob to resume the *jaghires*," was also dwelt upon with great emphasis; but it is in evidence that the nabob, on the contrary, could not, by any means, be induced to sanction the measure; that it was not indeed, till Mr. Middleton had actually issued his own *perwannas* [warrants] for the collection of the rents that the prince, to avoid a state of the lowest degradation, consented to give it the appearance of his act.

In the same letter, the resistance of the begums to the seizure of their treasures is noticed as an instance of female levity, as if their defence of the property assigned for their subsistence was a matter of censure, or that they merited a reproof for feminine lightness because they urged an objection to being starved!

The opposition, in short, my lords, which was expected from the princesses, was looked to as a justification of the proceedings which afterwards happened. There is not, in the private letters, the slightest intimation of the anterior rebellion, which by prudent afterthought was so greatly magnified. There is not a syllable of those dangerous machinations which were to dethrone the nabob, nor of those sanguinary artifices by which the English were to be extirpated. It is indeed sad, that if such measures were rigorously pursued, as had been set on foot, the people might be driven from murmurs to resistance, and rise up in arms against their oppressors.

Where then, my lords, is the proof of this mighty rebellion?
It is contained alone, where it is natural to expect it, in the
fabricated correspondence between Middleton and Hastings,
and in the affidavits collected by Sir Elijah Impey!

The gravity of the business on which the chief justice was
employed on this occasion contrasted with the vivacity, the
rapidity, and celerity of his movements, is exceedingly curious.
At one moment he apppeared in Oude, at another in Chunar, at
a third in Benares, procuring testimony, and in every quarter
exclaiming like Hamlet's Ghost, "*Swear!*" To him might also
have been applied the words of Hamlet to the Ghost, " What,
Truepenny! are you there?" But the similitude goes no further. He was never heard to give the injunction:

> " Taint not thy mind, nor let thy soul contrive
> Against thy mother aught ! "

V. It is, my lords, in some degree worthy of your observation, that not one of the private letters of Mr. Hastings has
at any time been disclosed. Even Middleton, when all confidence was broken between them by the production of his private correspondence at Calcutta, either feeling for his own
safety, or sunk under the fascinating influence of his master, did
not dare attempt a retaliation! The letters of Middleton, however, are sufficient to prove the situation of the nabob, when
pressed to the resumption of the *jaghires*. He is there described
as being sometimes lost in sullen melancholy—at others, agitated beyond expression, exhibiting every mark of agonized
sensibility. Even Middleton was moved by his distresses to
interfere for a temporary respite, in which he might become
more reconciled to the measure. " I am fully of opinion," said
he, " that the despair of the nabob must impel him to violence.
I know, also, that the violence must be fatal to himself; but yet
I think, that with his present feelings, he will disregard all consequences."

Mr. Johnson, the assistant resident, also wrote to the same
purpose. The words of his letter are memorable. "He thought
it would require a campaign to execute the orders for the
resumption of the *jaghires!*" A campaign against whom?
Against the nabob, our friend and ally, who had voluntarily
given the order! This measure, then, which we have heard con-

tended was for his good and the good of his country, could truly be only enforced by a campaign! Such is British justice! such is British humanity! Mr. Hastings guarantees to the allies of the Company their prosperity and his protection. The former he secures by sending an army to plunder them of their wealth and to desolate their soil. The latter produces the misery and the ruin of the protected. His is the protection which the vulture gives to the lamb, which covers while it devours its prey; which stretching its baleful pinions and hovering in mid-air, disperses the kites and lesser birds of prey, and saves the innocent and helpless victim from all talons but its own.

It is curious, my lords, to remark, that in the correspondence of these creatures of Mr. Hastings, and in their earnest endeavors to dissuade him from the resumption of the *jaghires*, not a word is mentioned of the measure being contrary to honor—to faith; derogatory to national character; unmanly or unprincipled. Knowing the man to whom they were writing, their only arguments were that it was contrary to policy and to expediency. Not one word do they mention of the just claims which the nabob had to the gratitude and friendship of the English. Not one syllable of the treaty by which we were bound to protect him. Not one syllable of the relation which subsisted between him and the princesses they were about to plunder. Not one syllable is hinted of justice or mercy. All which they addressed to him was the apprehension that the money to be procured would not be worth the danger and labor with which it must be attended. There is nothing, my lords, to be found in the history of human turpitude; nothing in the nervous delineations and penetrating brevity of Tacitus; nothing in the luminous and luxuriant pages of Gibbon, or of any other historian, dead or living, who, searching into measures and characters with the rigor of truth, presents to our abhorrence depravity in its blackest shapes, which can equal, in the grossness of the guilt, or in the hardness of heart with which it was conducted, or in low and grovelling motives, the acts and character of the prisoner. It was he who, in the base desire of stripping two helpless women, could stir the son to rise up in vengeance against them; who, when that son had certain touches of nature in his breast, certain feelings of awakened conscience, could accuse him of entertaining peevish objections to the plunder and sacrifice of his mother; who, having finally divested him of all thought, all reflection, all memory, all conscience, all tenderness and duty as a son, all dignity as a monarch; having destroyed his character and depopulated his country, at length brought him to violate the dearest ties of nature, in countenancing the destruction of his parents. This crime, I say, has no parallel or prototype in the Old World or the New, from the day of original sin to the present hour. The victims of his oppression were confessedly destitute of all power to resist their oppressors. But their debility, which from other bosoms would have claimed some compassion, at least with respect to the mode of suffering, with him only excited the ingenuity of torture. Even when every feeling of the nabob was subdued; when, as we have seen, my lords, nature made a last, lingering, feeble stand within his breast; even then, that cold spirit of malignity, with which his doom was fixed, returned with double rigor and sharper acrimony to its purpose, and compelled the child to inflict on the parent that destruction of which he was himself reserved to be the final victim.

Great as this climax, in which, my lords, I thought the pinnacle of guilt was attained, there is yet something still more transcendently flagitious. I particularly allude to his [Hastings'] infamous letter, falsely dated February 15, 1782, in which, at the very moment that he had given the order for the entire destruction of the begums, and for the resumption of the *jaghires*, he expresses to the nabob the warm and lively interest which he took in his welfare; the sincerity and ardor of his friendship; and that, though his presence was eminently wanted at Calcutta, he could not refrain from coming to his assistance, and that in the mean time he had sent four regiments to his aid; so deliberate and cool, so hypocritical and insinuating, is the villany of this man! What heart is not exasperated by the malignity of a treachery so barefaced and dispassionate? At length, however, the nabob was on his guard. He could not be deceived by this mask. The offer of the four regiments developed to him the object of Mr. Hastings. He perceived the dagger bunglingly concealed in the hand, which was treacherously extended as if to his assistance. From this moment the last faint ray of hope expired in his bosom. We accordingly find no further confidence of the nabob in the prisoner. Mr.

Middleton now swayed his iron sceptre without control. The *jaghires* were seized. Every measure was carried. The nabob, mortified, humbled, and degraded, sunk into insignificance and contempt. This letter was sent at the very time when the troops surrounded the walls of Fyzabad; and then began a scene of horrors, which, if I wished to inflame your lordships' feelings, I should only have occasion minutely to describe—to state the violence committed on that palace which the piety of the kingdom had raised for the retreat and seclusion of the objects of its pride and veneration! It was in these shades, rendered sacred by superstition, that innocence reposed. Here venerable age and helpless infancy found an asylum! If we look, my lords, into the whole of this most wicked transaction, from the time when this treachery was first conceived, to that when, by a series of artifices the most execrable, it was brought to a completion, the prisoner will be seen standing aloof, indeed, but not inactive. He will be discovered reviewing his agents, rebuking at one time the pale conscience of Middleton, at another relying on the stouter villany of Hyder Beg Cawn. With all the calmness of veteran delinquency, his eye will be seen ranging through the busy prospect, piercing the darkness of subordinate guilt, and disciplining with congenial adroitness the agents of his crimes and the instruments of his cruelty.

The feelings, my lords, of the several parties at the time will be most properly judged of by their respective correspondence. When the bow [younger] begum, despairing of redress from the nabob, addressed herself to Mr. Middleton, and reminded him of the guarantee which he had signed, she was instantly promised that the amount of her *jaghire* should be made good, though he said he could not interfere with the sovereign decision of the nabob respecting the lands. The deluded and unfortunate woman " thanked God that Mr. Middleton was at hand for her relief." At this very instant he was directing every effort to her destruction; for he had actually written the orders which were to take the collection out of the hands of her agents! But let it not be forgotten, my lords, when the begum was undeceived—when she found that British faith was no protection—when she found that she should leave the country, and prayed to the God of nations not to grant His peace to those who remained behind—there was still no charge of rebellion, no re-

crimination made to all her reproaches for the broken faith of
the English; that, when stung to madness, she asked "how long
would be her reign," there was no mention of her disaffection.
The stress is therefore idle, which the counsel for the prisoner
have strove to lay on these expressions of an injured and enraged woman. When, at last, irritated beyond bearing, she
denounced infamy on the heads of her oppressors, who is there
that will not say that she spoke in a prophetic spirit; and that
what she then predicted has not, even to its last letter, been accomplished? But did Mr. Middleton, even to this violence,
retort any particle of accusation? No! he sent a jocose reply,
stating that he had received such a letter under her seal, but
that from its contents he could not suspect it to come from
her; and begged therefore that she would endeavor to detect the
forgery! Thus did he add to foul injuries the vile aggravation
of a brutal jest. Like the tiger he showed the savageness of his
nature by grinning at his prey, and fawning over the last ago-
nies of his unfortunate victim!

The letters, my lords, were then enclosed to the nabob, who,
no more than the rest, made any attempt to justify himself by
imputing any criminality to the begums. He only sighed a
hope that his conduct to his parents had drawn no shame upon
his head; and declared his intention to punish, not any disaffection in the begums, but some officious servants who had dared
to foment the misunderstanding between them and himself.
A letter was finally sent to Mr. Hastings, about six days before
the seizure of the treasures from the begums, declaring their
innocence; and referring the Governor-General, in proof of it,
to Captain Gordon, whose life they had protected, and whose
safety should have been their justification. The inquiry was
never made. It was looked on as unnecessary, because the conviction of their innocence was too deeply impressed already.

The counsel, my lords, in recommending an attention to the
public in reference to the private letters, remarked particularly
that one of the latter should not be taken in evidence, because
it was evidently and abstractedly private, relating the anxieties
of Mr. Middleton on account of the illness of his son. This is
a singular argument indeed. The circumstance, however, undoubtedly merits strict observation, though not in the view in
which it was placed by the counsel. It goes to show that some,
at least, of the persons concerned in these transactions felt the

force of those ties which their efforts were directed to tear asunder; that those who could ridicule the respective attachment of a mother and a son; who could prohibit the reverence of the son to the mother; who could deny to maternal debility the protection which filial tenderness should afford, were yet sensible of the straining of those chords by which they are connected. There is something in the present business, with all that is horrible to create aversion, so vilely loathsome, as to excite disgust. It is, my lords, surely superfluous to dwell on the sacredness of the ties which those aliens to feeling, those apostates to humanity, thus divided. In such an assembly as the one before which I speak, there is not an eye but must look reproof to this conduct, not a heart but must anticipate its condemnation. Filial piety! It is the primal bond of society. It is that instinctive principle which, panting for its proper good, soothes, unbidden, each sense and sensibility of man. It now quivers on every lip. It now beams from every eye. It is that gratitude, which, softening under the sense of recollected good, is eager to own the vast, countless debt it never, alas! can pay, for so many long years of unceasing solicitudes, honorable self-denials, life-preserving cares. It is that part of our practice where duty drops its awe, where reverence refines into love. It asks no aid of memory. It needs not the deductions of reason. Pre-existing, paramount over all, whether moral law or human rule, few arguments can increase, and none can diminish it. It is the sacrament of our nature; not only the duty, but the indulgence of man. It is the first great privilege. It is among his last most endearing delights. It causes the bosom to glow with reverberated love. It requites the visitations of nature, and returns the blessings that have been received. It fires emotion into vital principle. It changes what was instinct into a master passion; sways all the sweetest energies of man; hangs over each vicissitude of all that must pass away; and aids the melancholy virtues in their last sad tasks of life, to cheer the languors of decrepitude and age, and

" Explore the thought, explain the aching eye! " [4]

[4] Really " asking eye " in the original:

" Me, let the tender office long engage
To rock the cradle of reposing age,
With lenient arts extend a mother's breath,
Make languor smile, and smooth the bed of death;
Explore the thought, explain the asking eye,
And keep awhile one parent from the sky! "
—Pope's Epistle to Dr. Arbuthnot.

But, my lords, I am ashamed to consume so much of your lordships' time in attempting to give a cold picture of this sacred impulse, when I behold so many breathing testimonies of its influence around me; when every countenance in this assembly is beaming, and erecting itself into the recognition of this universal principle!

The expressions contained in the letter of Mr. Middleton of tender solicitude for his son have been also mentioned as a proof of the amiableness of his affections. I confess that they do not tend to raise his character in my estimation. Is it not rather an aggravation of his guilt, that he, who thus felt the anxieties of a parent, and who, consequently, must be sensible of the reciprocal feelings of a child, could be brought to tear asunder, and violate in others, all those dear and sacred bonds? Does it not enhance the turpitude of the transaction that it was not the result of idiotic ignorance or brutal indifference? I aver that his guilt is increased and magnified by these considerations. His criminality would have been less had he been insensible to tenderness—less, if he had not been so thoroughly acquainted with the true quality of paternal love and filial duty.

The *jaghires* being seized, my lords, the begums were left without the smallest share of that pecuniary compensation promised by Mr. Middleton as an equivalent for the resumption. And as tyranny and injustice, when they take the field, are always attended by their camp followers, paltry pilfering and petty insult, so in this instance, the goods taken from the princesses were sold at a mock sale at an inferior value. Even gold and jewels, to use the language of the begums, instantly lost their value when it was known that they came from them. Their ministers were imprisoned to extort the deficiency which this fraud occasioned; and every mean art was employed to justify a continuance of cruelty towards them. Yet this was small to the frauds of Mr. Hastings. After extorting upwards of £600,000, he forbade Mr. Middleton to come to a conclusive settlement with the princesses. He knew that the treasons of our allies in India had their origin solely in the wants of the Company. He could not, therefore, say that the begums were entirely innocent until he had consulted the General Record of Crimes, the cash account of Calcutta! His prudence was fully justified by the event! for there was actually found a balance of twenty-six lacs more against the begums, which £260,000 worth of treason had never been dreamed of before. " Talk not to us," said the Governor-General, " of their guilt or innocence, but as it suits the Company's credit! We will not try them by the Code of Justinian, nor the Institutes of Timur. We will not judge them either by British laws or their local customs! No! we will try them by the multiplication table; we will find them guilty by the rule of three; and we will condemn them according to the unerring rules of—Cocker's Arithmetic!"

My lords, the prisoner has said in his defence that the cruelties exercised towards the begums were not of his order. But in another part of it he avows, " that whatever their distresses, and whoever was the agent in the measure, it was, in his opinion, reconcilable to justice, honor, and sound policy." By the testimony of Major Scott, it appears that though the defence of the prisoner was not drawn up by himself, yet that this paragraph he wrote with his own proper hand. Middleton, it seems, had confessed his share in these transactions with some degree of compunction and solicitude as to the consequences. The prisoner observing it, cries out to him: " Give me the pen; I will defend the measure as just and necessary. I will take something upon myself. Whatever part of the load you cannot bear, my unburdened character shall assume! Your conduct I will crown with my irresistible approbation. Do you find memory and I will find character, and thus twin warriors we will go into the field, each in his proper sphere of action, and assault, repulse, and contumely shall all be set at defiance."

If I could not prove, my lords, that those acts of Mr. Middleton were in reality the acts of Mr. Hastings, I should not trouble your lordships by combating them; but as this part of his criminality can be incontestably ascertained, I appeal to the assembled legislators of this realm to say whether these acts were justifiable on the score of policy. I appeal to all the august presidents in the courts of British justice, and to all the learned ornaments of the profession, to decide whether these acts were reconcilable to justice. I appeal to the reverend assemblage of prelates feeling for the general interests of humanity and for the honor of the religion to which they belong, to determine whether these acts of Mr. Hastings and Mr. Middleton were such as a Christian ought to perform, or a man to avow.

My lords, with the ministers of the nabob [Bahar Ally Cawn and Jewar Ally Cawn] was confined in the same prison that arch-rebel Sumshire Khan, against whom so much criminality has been charged by the counsel for the prisoner. We hear, however, of no inquiry having been made concerning his treason, though so many were held respecting the treasures of the others. With all his guilt, he was not so far noticed as to be deprived of his food, to be complimented with fetters, or even to have the satisfaction of being scourged, but was cruelly liberated from a dungeon, and ignominiously let loose on his parole!

[Here Mr. Sheridan read the following order from Mr. Middleton to Lieutenant Rutledge in relation to the begums' ministers, dated January 28, 1782:

" SIR: When this note is delivered to you by Hoolas Roy, I have to desire that you order the two prisoners to be put in irons, keeping them from all food, etc., agreeably to my instructions of yesterday. NATH. MIDDLETON."]

The begums' ministers, on the contrary, to extort from them the disclosure of the place which concealed the treasures, were, according to the evidence of Mr. Holt, after being fettered and imprisoned, led out on a scaffold, and this array of terrors proving unavailing, the meek-tempered Middleton, as a *dernier ressort*, menaced them with a confinement in the fortress of Chunargar. Thus, my lords, was a British garrison made the climax of cruelties! To English arms, to English officers, around whose banners humanity has even entwined her most glorious wreath, how will this sound? It was in this fort, where the British flag was flying, that these helpless prisoners were doomed to deeper dungeons, heavier chains, and severer punishments. Where that flag was displayed which was wont to cheer the depressed, and to dilate the subdued heart of misery, these venerable but unfortunate men were fated to encounter every aggravation of horror and distress. It, moreover, appears that they were both cruelly flogged, though one was above seventy years of age. Being charged with disaffection, they vindicated their innocence: " Tell us where are the remaining treasures," was the reply. " It is only treachery to your immediate sovereigns, and you will then be fit associates for the representatives of British faith and British justice in India!" O Faith! O Justice! I conjure you by your sacred names to depart for a moment from this place, though it be your peculiar residence; nor hear your names profaned by such a sacrilegious combination as that which I am now compelled to repeat—where all the fair forms of nature and art, truth and peace, policy and honor, shrink back aghast from the deleterious shade—where all existences, nefarious and vile, have sway—where, amid the black agents on one side and Middleton with Impey on the other, the great figure of the piece—characteristic in his place, aloof and independent from the puny profligacy in his train, but far from idle and inactive, turning a malignant eye on all michief that awaits him; the multiplied apparatus of temporizing expedients and intimidating instruments, now cringing on his prey, and fawning on his vengeance—now quickening the limping pace of craft, and forcing every stand that retiring nature can make to the heart; the attachments and the decorums of life; each emotion of tenderness and honor; and all the distinctions of national pride; with a long catalogue of crimes and aggravations beyond the reach of thought for human malignity to perpetrate or human vengeance to punish; lower than perdition—blacker than despair!

It might, my lords, have been hoped, for the honor of the human heart, that the begums were themselves exempted from a share in these sufferings, and that they had been wounded only through the sides of their ministers. The reverse of this, however, is the fact. Their palace was surrounded by a guard, which was withdrawn by Major Gilpin to avoid the growing resentments of the people, and replaced by Mr. Middleton, through his fears of that "dreadful responsibility" which was imposed upon him by Mr. Hastings. The women, also, of the *khord mahal*, who were not involved in the begums' supposed crimes; who had raised no sub-rebellion of their own; and who, it had been proved, lived in a distinct dwelling, were causelessly implicated, nevertheless, in the same punishment. Their residence surrounded with guards, they were driven to despair by famine, and when they poured forth in sad procession, were beaten with bludgeons, and forced back by the soldiery to the scene of madness which they had quitted. These are acts, my lords, which, when told, need no comment. I will not offer a single syllable to awaken your lordships' feelings; but leave it to the facts which have been stated to make their own impression.

VI. The inquiry which now only remains, my lords, is whether Mr. Hastings is to be answerable for the crimes committed by his agents? It has been fully proved that Mr. Middleton signed the treaty with the superior begum in October, 1778. He also acknowledged signing some others of a different date, but could not recollect the authority by which he did it! These treaties were recognized by Mr. Hastings, as appears by the evidence of Mr. Purling, in the year 1780. In that of October, 1778, the *jaghire* was secured, which was allotted for the support of the women in the *khord mahal*. But still the prisoner pleads that he is not accountable for the cruelties which were exercised. His is the plea which tyranny, aided by its prime minister, treachery, is always sure to set up. Mr. Middleton has attempted to strengthen this ground by endeavoring to claim the whole infamy in these transactions, and to monopolize the guilt! He dared even to aver that he had been condemned by Mr. Hastings for the ignominious part he had acted. He dared to avow this, because Mr. Hastings was on his trial, and he thought he never would be arraigned; but in the face of this court, and before he left the bar, he was compelled to confess that it was for the lenience and not the severity of his proceedings that he had been reproved by the prisoner.

It will not, I trust, be concluded that because Mr. Hastings has not marked every passing shade of guilt, and because he has only given the bold outline of cruelty, he is therefore to be acquitted. It is laid down by the law of England, that law which is the perfection of reason, that a person ordering an act to be done by his agent is answerable for that act with all its consequences. "*Quod facit per alium, facit per se.*" Middleton was appointed, in 1777, the confidential agent, the second self, of Mr. Hastings. The Governor-General ordered the measure. Even if he never saw nor heard afterwards of its consequences, he was therefore answerable for every pang that was inflicted, and for all the blood that was shed. But he did hear, and that instantly, of the whole. He wrote to accuse Middleton of forbearance and of neglect! He commanded him to work upon the hopes and fears of the princesses, and to leave no means untried, until, to speak his own language, which was better suited to the banditti of a cavern, " he obtained possession of the secret hoards of the old ladies." He would not allow even of a delay of two days to smooth the compelled approaches of a son to his mother, on this occasion! His orders were peremptory. After this, my lords, can it be said that the prisoner was ignorant of the acts, or not culpable for their consequences? It is true he did not direct the guards, the famine, and the bludgeons; he did not weigh the fetters, nor number the lashes to be inflicted on his victims; but yet he is just as guilty as if he had borne an active and personal share in each transaction. It is as if he had commanded that the heart should be torn from the bosom, and enjoined that no blood should follow. He is in the same degree accountable to the law, to his country, to his conscience, and to his God!

The prisoner has endeavored also to get rid of a part of his guilt by observing that he was but one of the supreme council, and that all the rest had sanctioned those transactions with their approbation. Even if it were true that others did participate in the guilt, it cannot tend to diminish his criminality. But the fact is, that the council erred in nothing so much as in a reprehensible credulity given to the declarations of the Governor-General. They knew not a word of those transactions until they were finally concluded. It was not until the January following that they saw the mass of falsehood which had been published under the title of " Mr. Hastings' Narrative." They were, then, unaccountably duped to permit a letter to pass, dated the twenty-ninth of November, intended to seduce the directors into a belief that they had received intelligence at that time, which was not the fact. These observations, my lords, are not meant to cast any obloquy on the council; they undoubtedly were deceived; and the deceit practised on them is a decided proof of his consciousness of guilt. When tired of corporeal infliction Mr. Hastings was gratified by insulting the understanding. The coolness and reflection with which this act was managed and concerted raises its enormity and blackens its turpitude. It proves the prisoner to be that monster in nature, a deliberate and reasoning tyrant! Other tyrants of whom we read, such as a Nero, or a Caligula, were urged to their crimes by the impetuosity of passion. High rank disqualified them from advice, and perhaps equally prevented reflection. But in the prisoner we have a man born in a state of mediocrity; bred to mercantile life; used to system; and accustomed to regularity; who was accountable to his masters, and therefore was compelled to think and to deliberate on every part of his conduct. It is this cool deliberation, I say, which renders his crimes more horrible, and his character more atrocious.

When, my lords, the Board of Directors received the advices which Mr. Hastings thought proper to transmit, though unfurnished with any other materials to form their judgment, they expressed very strongly their doubts, and properly ordered an inquiry into the circumstances of the alleged disaffection of the begums, declaring it, at the same time, to be a debt which was due to the honor and justice of the British nation. This inquiry, however, Mr. Hastings thought it absolutely necessary to elude. He stated to the council, in answer, "that it would revive those animosities that subsisted between the begums and the nabob [Asoph Dowlah], which had then subsided. If the former were inclined to appeal to a foreign jurisdiction, they were the best judges of their own feeling, and should be left to make their own complaint." All this, however, my lords, is nothing to the magnificent paragraph which concludes this communication. "Besides," says he, "I hope it will not be a departure from official language to say that the majesty of justice ought not to be approached without solicitation. She ought not to descend to inflame or provoke, but to withhold her judgment until she is called on to determine." What is still more astonishing is that Sir John Macpherson, who, though a man of sense and honor, is rather Oriental in his imagination, and not learned in the sublime and beautiful from the immortal leader of this prosecution, was caught by this bold, bombastic quibble, and joined in the same words, "That the majesty of justice ought not to be approached without solicitation." But, my lords, do you, the judges of this land, and the expounders of its rightful laws—do you approve of this mockery and call it the character of justice, which takes the form of right to excite wrong? No, my lords, justice is not this halt and miserable object; it is not the ineffective bauble of an Indian pagod; it is not the portentous phantom of despair; it is not like any fabled monster, formed in the eclipse of reason, and found in some un-hallowed grove of superstitious darkness and political dismay! No, my lords. In the happy reverse of all this, I turn from the digusting caricature to the real image! Justice I have now before me august and pure! The abstract idea of all that would be perfect in the spirits and the aspirings of men!—where the mind rises; where the heart expands; where the countenance is ever placid and benign; where her favorite attitude is to stoop to the unfortunate; to hear their cry and to help them; to rescue and relieve, to succor and save; majestic, from its mercy; venerable, from its utility; uplifted, without pride; firm, without obduracy; beneficent in each preference; lovely, though in her frown!

On that justice I rely—deliberate and sure, abstracted from all party purpose and political speculation; not on words, but on facts. You, my lords, will hear me, I conjure, by those rights which it is your best privilege to preserve; by that fame which it is your best pleasure to inherit; by all those feelings which refer to the first term in the series of existence, the original compact of our nature, our controlling rank in the creation. This is the call on all to administer to truth and equity, as they would satisfy the laws and satisfy themselves, with the most exalted bliss possible or conceivable for our nature; the self-approving consciousness of virtue, when the condemnation we look for will be one of the most ample mercies accomplished for mankind since the creation of the world! My lords, I have done.